Stepping Up
to the Creator

By Daniel J. Shepard:

You & I Together: Have a Purpose in Reality
Reality and Existence

In the Image of God:
Free Will and Determinism

Stepping Up to the Creator:
Symbiotic Panentheism

*Special thanks to
Steve and Sarah.*

Stepping Up to the Creator

Symbiotic Panentheism

Daniel J. Shepard

Proctor Publications

© 1998 by Daniel J. Shepard, First Edition

The copyright is a gift from me to you, from one soul to another. The gift: Any part of this trilogy may be reproduced or utilized in any form or by any means. The legal copyright was obtained only to protect the source and the integrity of the work and to guarantee your access and authorization to freely use and reproduce this work. These concepts are not my own. They are the merging and logical conclusion to the blending of ideas created within a society supported and maintained by vast numbers of people, including you and those before you.

Published by Proctor Publications
PO Box 2498
Ann Arbor, MI 48106

Publisher's Cataloging-in-Publication
(Provided by Quality Books, Inc.)

Shepard, Daniel J., 1945–
    Stepping up to the creator : symbiotic panentheism / Daniel J. Shepard. -- 1st ed.
    p. cm.
    Preassigned LCCN: 97–75524
    ISBN: 1–882792–58–0

    1. Panentheism. 2. God--History of doctrines--20th century. 3. Whole and parts (Philosophy) 4. Science--Philosophy. I. Title.

BT98.S44 1998   211'.2
                              QBI98-229

This book is written for all beings of the universe as a Universal Magna Carta.

Table of Contents

Introduction — *1*
    A Model — *3*
    Beginning a Universal Philosophy — *13*
    Matrix Writing — *19*
    The Ten Questions — *23*

Religion — *25*
    #100 - 109. Hinduism — *29*
    #110 - 119. Judaism — *41*
    #120 - 129. Buddhism — *53*
    #130 - 139. Christianity — *65*
    #140 - 149. Islam — *77*
    #150 - 159. Ontology — *89*
    #160 - 169. Modern Science — *101*
    #170 - 179. . . . Atheism — *113*
    #180 - 189. . . . Classical/Traditional Theism — *125*
    #190 - 199. Panentheism — *137*
        Religion – Conclusion — *149*

Science — *153*
    #200 - 209. Entropy — *157*
    #210 - 219. Big Bang Theory — *169*
    #220 - 229. Symmetry — *181*
    #230 - 239. Set Theory — *193*
    #240 - 249. Space — *205*
    #250 - 259. Topology — *217*
    #260 - 269. Ecological Niche — *229*
    #270 - 279. Palaeomagnetism — *241*
    #280 - 289. Homo- — *253*
   #290 - 299. Symbiosis — *265*
        Science – Conclusion — *277*

Philosophy *281*
#300 - 309. Unified View *285*
#310 - 319. Philosophy, Religion, and Science *297*
#320 - 329. Confucianism *309*
#330 - 339. Taoism *321*
#340 - 349. Ancient Philosophy *333*
#350 - 359. Early Christian Philosophy *345*
#360 - 369. Renaissance Philosophy *357*
#370 - 379. Appeal to Reason and Experience *369*
#380 - 389. Appeal to Humanism and Adjustment *381*
#390 - 399. Symbiotic Panentheism *393*
    Philosophy – Conclusion *405*

Prophecy *411*
   0. Mexico *414*
   1. The Great Pyramid *415*
   2. Mayan Calendar *416*
   3. Prophecy Rock *417*
   4. Wheel of Dharma *418*
   5. Revelations *419*
   6. Papal Prophecies *420*
   7. Nostradamus *421*
   8. Edgar Cayce *422*

Conclusion *425*

Symbiotic Panentheism

•

A Perceptual Shift for Humankind

INTRODUCTION

You and I are the basis of this trilogy. This work takes the scientific knowledge we have today and blends it with the religious beliefs that have existed for thousands of years by using the logic of philosophy. In the process, a model is constructed demonstrating the connection between a Causative Force, the universe, and life. With this comes understanding.

A UNIVERSAL MODEL
Why utilize a model?
We are a visual creature.

Why utilize the question format for the work?
First, as a teacher, I am most familiar and comfortable with the question format. Second, it provides a means of maneuvering easily within the text.

How do we build a model of the relationship between a Causative Force, the universe, and life?
We do this by building a model of a universal philosophy and examining it against what we've been told; what we believe; what we see; what we reason; social problems we cannot resolve; social problems we think will not be solvable; and the impact the model would have had, would have or will have on society. We examine the significance of this model against the ideas of beginning/end concepts and against the idea of creation/destruction of the very universe within which we are located.

We do this by starting from where we are and using what we have learned of the universe through science, what we believe through religion, and what we reason through philosophy. We then construct a model which seems to encompass and fuse together all this information without destroying any of it. We have worked long and suffered much to gain this information. We do not want to destroy it. We must respect the effort, the pain, and the blood that was spilled to gain it.

How do we know this model will be the correct model?
As strange as this may sound, we don't.

Then why do it?
In science, we try to understand what is taking place in the world around us. We do so by building models that we think explain what is taking place. This helps develop what is called a reference point. This is a point from which we do further investigation. As we continue to investigate a phenomenon, we either find the new information we gather: supports the model, creates a need to slightly modify the model, creates a need to greatly modify the model or creates a need to scrap the model and start over.

Whatever the case, the original model we created acts as a means of understanding what we had at the moment. The original model is not what is to be protected. What is to be protected is the idea that the original model is only a starting point. Its purpose is to allow growth in understanding as new knowledge is gained. The whole point of the model is to explain what we know presently. We must allow the model to become obsolete as we move into the future and gain a better understanding of what is taking place around us.

What if the model does not grow, does not change?
If the model does not change, then we are not growing; we are stagnating.

Couldn't the model be the correct model and wouldn't that explain why it may not change?
That would only be true if we knew everything. It would be true only if we were omniscient. If we were omniscient, we would be the Causative Force Herself, and few of us would be so bold as to make that declaration.

So now what?
Now, we begin.

A MODEL
What makes humans a unique life form on this planet?

For one thing, we appear to be the only life form on this planet capable of leaving the planet through its own effort. We appear to be the only earthly life form capable of traveling throughout the heavens amongst the stars without assistance from other species.

Why do we appear to be the only life form with this capability?

No other life form seems to have the necessary combination of physical dexterity, intelligence, curiosity, sense of purpose, and determinism to do so. No other earthly life form seems to be obsessed with finding the answer to the question, 'Why do I exist?'

What makes us think our presence will be allowed in space?

It is not a case of our seeking permission to step into the heavens. It is a case of knowing it will happen. It has already happened and as we have stepped into space, we have taken our presence with us.

What does 'taking our presence with us' mean?

We take the sense of who we are with us as we step into the heavens. We have already strewn the very edge of near space with scientific, military, and civilian space equipment. We have left our footprints on the moon and thrown our first space debris beyond the gravitational attraction of our sun. The next stop of this humanly created space object is another solar system potentially occupied by other life forms. With it, we once again inject the sense of what we are and what we believe ourselves to be upon other life forms.

What is it we have sent beyond our own solar system, our home?

We have sent a message on a metal plate: we exist, we look like this, we think like this. With it, we have sent small bacterial and viral particles capable of having immense impact upon other atmospheres and life forms.

What does this show us?

It shows us we are correct when we think we may be the only life form on this planet capable of leaving this earth.

What implications does this have for us as individuals and as a species?

If we are, once again in our history, to encounter new cultures, civilizations, and species, we must put some thought into who it is we believe ourselves to be. Previously, we have had very dramatic experiences when stepping into other cultures, environments, and civilizations. American Indians, Central American Mayans, South American Incas, Africans, rain forests, Chernobyl, and American buffalo are all examples of what can happen when our species blindly explores new opportunities.

Does this mean we should not step into the heavens?

By no means! It is the heavens to which we have always dreamed of going. But, on the other hand, we do not need to step into the heavens blind to what we are, what we have to offer, and likewise what we believe others in the heavens have to offer.

How do we avoid stepping into space 'blindly'?

We must have an understanding of what the universe is and what the purpose of the universe is. We also must have an understanding of what our purpose and the purpose of life is before we start stepping into the regions of space occupied by other life forms.

How do we accomplish such a monumental task?

We recognize the task for what it is. It is a process of building what Steven Hawking calls a 'universal philosophy.' A universal philosophy is a model of what we believe the universe is. It is a model of what we believe.

A model of a universal philosophy could be considered a mission statement for our species. It is a statement we use to guide us as individuals and as a species as we travel through life and space. It is a statement we establish to allow others in space to understand what it is we are trying to do. It is a marker we establish which allows us as individuals, as a species, and others in the heavens to 'judge' just how successful we have been in the past, are being in the present, and will be in the future at accomplishing our defined purpose. Then, as in science, once having built the model, we test it.

INTRODUCTION

Isn't this an impossible task?
If we can go to the moon, clone animals, create artificial intelligence, genetically create new species of plants and animals, place telescopes in space, split the atom, fuse the atom, fly from one city to another, put an encyclopedia on a small disc, mass produce personal computers, connect all homes with a world wide Internet, and operate on the brain, we can build a universal philosophy.

We are unique amongst the earth's life forms. We don't accept the idea of, 'We can't..."

By searching for answers to what we are, what the universe is, and what the purpose of life is, will we have to throw everything away to begin?
No, just the opposite.

How do we begin?
We look at what we have developed as a human species over the last 10,000 years. We look at the most fundamental, the most basic, the broadest, most universally accepted ideas we have developed as a species.

Some of these ideas and concepts have arisen from the shedding of huge quantities of blood and tears. Do we want to develop a universal understanding of who we are based upon such violent acts?
Absolutely! It is this very sacrifice of blood and tears that we must embrace and incorporate into our understanding of what we are and why life exists.

Why must we incorporate the ideas generated by the sacrifice of those that came before us?
This sacrifice, this shedding of blood by those that came before us, represents just how strongly we believe in the importance and purpose of life.

Why do we need to search for the understanding of what our purpose is, what the purpose of life is, what the purpose of the universe is?
We treat each other based upon the value we have of each other. If we think of others as having no value, we treat them as such. If we think of ourselves as having no value, we treat ourselves as such. Just as impor-

tantly, not only do we treat ourselves and others according to the value we place on life, we allow and encourage others to do the same.

Why do we need to search now, at this particular point in our history?

We are on the verge of taking our attitudes and influence into the heavens. We are about to disperse throughout the stars and come into contact with other life forms and their environments, their homes. We must have an understanding of what we are and why it is we exist or we will repeat history – a history not only filled with hope, but with atrocities.

How do we begin this search?

We have many choices. Since we have to begin somewhere, and since we are a visual creature, we may find it useful by beginning with a technique science has used successfully. We can build a basic model that begins just before the 'beginning' of our universe and ends just after the 'end' of our universe.

Once we have built this model, what do we do?

We test it.

How do we test the model?

We apply it to the past to see if it reinforces the ideas for which our ancestors were willing to spill their blood. We apply it to the present to see if it resolves our present day social conflicts. We apply it to the future to check its capability to resolve future dilemmas we could possibly face. We verify it through examining how it stands up to what we have established as being key ideas applicable to our universe. And lastly, we apply it to what visionaries and prophets tell us we must do to avoid future trauma and bloodletting.

What does this process have to do with the uniqueness of our travels?

We are the only life form existing on earth that has accumulated and built upon a wealth of knowledge gained through the spilling of rivers of blood over thousands and thousands of years. Now, we can finally start to put these pieces of the puzzle together which will show us the answer to the question, 'Why?'

INTRODUCTION

Does this make us unique?

Is there any other creature that would attempt to establish a universal philosophy, a 'Magna Carta,' that would not only embrace themselves, but all life forms that exist within the distant boundary of the universe itself? There is no doubt we are truly a unique species. We have earned the right to be proud of our history, as traumatic as it has been. Many have suffered in order to bring us to the point of understanding a universal philosophy.

How can we allow all this bloodletting and suffering to go for naught? It is time to bring closure to our past. It is time to examine our past in order to understand our future. It is time to examine our past in order to change the future.

Once we build the model of a universal philosophy, how do we decide what items and ideas to test it against?

It seems to be almost impossible to decide which items deserve the honor of acting as the first ideas against which a universal philosophy will be tested. The wealth of knowledge located upon the seemingly endless shelves and infinite books within our libraries is overwhelming. Our beliefs, observations, and analyses seem to be unending.

How shall we choose?

We should choose based upon our beliefs (religions), observations (science), and logic (philosophy).

How shall we pick from each in order to test our model?

To be fair to each, to do our best to avoid conflict, we will pick ten items from each category.

How do we decide upon the items?

One of the basic requirements for a universal understanding of what we are and why we exist is the requirement set up by Steven Hawking. Hawking said a universal philosophy of what we are must be understandable by all humans so we can logically discuss it. Therefore, we need to pick a source of information that represents basic ideas from the areas of religion, science, and philosophy.

Once we have picked the reference for each and the ten items from each of these sources, what questions shall we ask in order to test the model?

The questions have to be very broad, yet very specific. The questions have to get to the heart of why we constructed the universal model in the first place.

Won't this take a huge number of questions?

We are limited in terms of space, so we will have no choice but to limit our questions. Since we picked ten items from each area of influence, we may as well choose ten questions to test the model.

What ideas should the ten questions address?

They should address very basic ideas we have worked long and hard to develop over the course of our painful journey through history.

We already have beacons in society that guide our actions. Why do we need a universal philosophy?

The question becomes do we want to reinforce our present beacons or do we feel they are adequate for us as we step into the heavens? Are we okay with the idea of believing we are superior to others? Are we okay with our past history generated by these beacons? Are we okay with repeating the history of pain and suffering we impose upon each other as fellow humans? If we are okay with our present behavior, then this must mean we are okay with the idea of repeating these same actions. This must mean we are okay with bringing superiority, subjugation, domination, and abuse to others throughout the heavens, because that is exactly what will happen if we do not modify our past and present beliefs.

We will also bring our good points with us, but that is not the point. The point is, do we wish to *also* bring with us our negatives?

Couldn't this violence, conflict, suffering, intolerance, subjugation, and domination already exist in space?

It may, but if it doesn't, would we want to be the species that introduces it and spreads it throughout the heavens? If it already exists in space, would we want to be the ones to accelerate it and add to the misery and pain? Or would we prefer to be the ones to bring to the heavens an impenetrable argument against such actions? Would we prefer to step into the heavens as peacemakers, as a new species entering the wonders of the heavens with a voice of hope?

We have a choice. We can build a universal philosophy, a model of the total picture of what we are, what our universe is, and what lies beyond our universe, or we can ignore the idea.

Whatever choice we make, we must understand we cannot avoid being responsible for our actions just because we ignored trying to understand what significance we play in the universe. By choosing not to build the model representing a Causative Force, the universe, and ourselves, we will have made a decision. We will have decided not to change, not to examine what it is we have been struggling to establish throughout our history. Thus, we will continue as we are. We will repeat history by taking our past into the heavens themselves. We will spread our present behaviors to the very ends of the universe.

Is there a lot of abuse, violence, intolerance, and inhumane action taking place in society?
Most people would say, 'Yes.'

Why do people act as they do?
People act according to how they perceive themselves and their reality.

How do people gain a perception of themselves?
People basically form perceptions of themselves through belief, observation, and analysis.

Are you implying that theistic religions are to blame for our abuse, violence, intolerance, and inhumane actions?
We cannot blame an inanimate (nonliving) object or concept. We have to be responsible for our own actions. Nothing will change if we constantly lay blame elsewhere.

How much of the world is based on a religious foundation?
The majority of humanity base their religions upon a foundation of theism:

1. Christianity   1.9 billion believers
2. Islam   1.1 billion
3. Hinduism   0.8 billion
4. nonreligious   0.8 billion
5. Buddhism   0.3 billion
6. atheism   0.3 billion

Total   5.2 billion
World population   5.7 billion

But I believe in theism: one caring, intervening, tolerant, compassionate God; an eternal soul; a God that sent His only son; a God of justice; etc. Do I have to change any of that?
No! Destroying beliefs, faiths, and religions is not a process of addition; it is a process of destruction and that goes against the concept of a universal philosophy.

Do we have to change religions in order to change people's perceptions?
No. We have to add to the foundations upon which religions are built.

A great deal of abuse has come about through technological advances such as atomic weapons, biological research, etc. Should we stop this abuse?
Absolutely, but we cannot stop abusive actions by trying to stop learning. The inquisitive nature of humanity goes to the core of who we are. We have to stop abuse by changing what we think of each other.

Science provides the understanding of the concrete aspect of our reality. Is science to blame?
We cannot blame our behavior upon what we have learned regarding what is, for what exists in reality exists. Nor can we blame our behavior upon the inherent characteristics of our species, the characteristics of curiosity and awe.

Philosophy provides the logic, the analysis explaining our existence. Is philosophy to blame?
Philosophy can only work with what it has available. Logic can and must flow in an orderly, sequential manner.

1. atheism: the Causative Force of the universe has no size
2. pantheism: the Causative Force of the universe and the universe are the same size
3. classical/traditional theism: the Causative Force of the universe is almost all present, for although the Causative Force is bigger than the universe; the universe is outside, not inside, the Causative Force
4. panentheism: the Causative Force of the universe is truly omnipresent; the universe lies inside the Causative Force; the universe is a part of the Causative Force

This, then, is the beginning of the model.

If panentheism states that God is truly all present, omnipresent, what does the universal philosophy model of symbiotic panentheism state?

Symbiotic panentheism states that the Causative Force is truly omnipresent; therefore, the universe is in the Causative Force. In addition, we need the Causative Force and the Causative Force needs us.

What does symbiotic panentheism do for us as individuals and as a species?

Symbiotic panentheism helps us understand where we are. We are inside the Causative Force. If we are inside the Causative Force, it would only seem logical we have some interactive function with the Causative Force. Symbiotic panentheism says the Causative Force needs us just as we need the Causative Force. Symbiotic panentheism says we are inside the Causative Force and in a symbiotic relationship with the Causative Force of the universe. This is a perceptual shift for humankind. With a change in perception of what we are will come a change in behavior.

How will behavior change?

With an elevation of what we believe we are, what we believe others are, will come an elevation of how we behave towards ourselves and towards others. This improved behavioral change will be generated not by destroying what we have but by adding to what we have. This change has to be one of addition in order to elevate behavior. A change of subtraction, destruction, elimination of what we have would diminish behavior. Therefore, the change must not be one of dismantling, but of adding.

What needs to be added?

We need to add a meaningful significance to ourselves as beings existing in a limited, temporary form.

Is this complicated?

It is very simple. It has to be simple or it is not valid. Complexity is a characteristic of a lack of understanding. The ramifications and intertwining intricacies generated by the model may be difficult to follow and untangle, but the core idea, the concept, must be simple.

BEGINNING A UNIVERSAL PHILOSOPHY

What is this simple foundation that we can add to the present theistic foundation of religions, science, and philosophy?

Theism (the foundation of our present perceptions) says souls exist and souls need a Causative Force. Symbiotic panentheism adds two things: souls are within the Causative Force and the Causative Force needs souls. However, just making the statement is not enough. It has to be supported by all three areas representing the primary means by which we perceive what it is we are. The model must be supported by religious, scientific, and philosophical concepts. It must not be supported by just a few ideas from each of these fields; it must be supported by the most prominent aspects of each of these fields.

If this book is intended to provide the initial verification for the concept of symbiotic panentheism, what is the objective of the other two books in the trilogy?

You & I Together explores the scientific logic of a universe being created from nothing, the universe being located within the Causative Force, and the Causative Force needing you as well as you needing the Causative Force. This model is then examined in terms of the impact it would have had on the past, would have on the present, and could have on the future if our society accepts it.

In the Image of God explores ten present social dilemmas and twenty possible futuristic dilemmas which seem unresolvable under our current perceptions. It then examines why these issues would be resolvable with the slightly different perception generated by the model.

Why is symbiotic panentheism such a major perceptual shift?

If panentheism is correct, then we are located within the Causative Force and thus we, each of us, are a part of the Causative Force. If symbiosis is correct, then we have an interdependent relationship with the Causative Force: we need the Causative Force and the Causative Force needs us. The startling implication is that if you abuse yourself, if you let others abuse you, if you abuse others, if you let others abuse others, if you abuse the environment, you are not only allowing abuse to happen to other people, you are allowing the Causative Force Herself to be abused. This is, without a doubt, a new way of looking at yourself, of looking at others, and of looking at the environment.

How do religion, science, and philosophy fit in?

With a universal philosophy, religion, science, and philosophy become fused. The three start working in a cooperative fashion rather than a competitive, antagonistic fashion. As individuals, we benefit, for we gain three allies working together with the intent of uniting and strengthening us to our sense of purpose. Under symbiotic panentheism, the three would work to bolster us as we step into the heavens, rather than divide us.

What are we as individuals and as a human species?

We are what we think we are. If we perceive ourselves to be animals, we act as animals and we kill each other when we don't have to, as in capital punishment. If we perceive ourselves to be 'soldiers of the Causative Force,' we act like soldiers, as in the time of the crusades. If we perceive ourselves to be 'seekers' and 'exorcists' of evil, we act as 'seekers' and 'exorcists' of evil, as in the time of the inquisition. If we perceive ourselves to be the chosen race, we act as the chosen race, as in WWII. If we perceive ourselves to be a 'piece of the Causative Force,' then we will act as we would expect the Causative Force would act.

How are we different from other animals?

Most animals are what they are. Humankind is not what it is but rather what it thinks it is, perceives itself to be. Likewise, the individual is what they think they are, what they perceive themselves to be. We are probably the only species that can decide what we think we are and then strive to become that perception. An ant acts like an ant because it is an ant. A wolf acts like a wolf because it is a wolf. This is not true for humans. If we perceive ourselves to be forgiving, we are forgiving. If we perceive ourselves to need to look out for our own self interests, we use others for our personal gain. Depending on the degree we perceive ourselves to be better than others, we treat others as inferior. We usually act confused as a species because we are confused. We do not have a universally accepted conception of what we are as individuals and why we exist in reality. Thus, our actions take on a number of conflicting, self destructive behavior patterns in relationship to ourselves, others, and our own species.

INTRODUCTION

But if humanity is what it thinks it is, isn't that okay?
It is okay, if we like what we are. If we look at humanity and see child abuse, spousal abuse, violence, poverty, brutality, abuse of authority, war, environmental abuse, and on and on, and if we do not like what we see, then it is not okay. Then we must change it.

What if I like what I am?
That is fine, but that is only part of the picture. You are more than just yourself; you are a part of your species and what your species represents within reality. Therefore, you must ask yourself if you like what you see when you view all actions of humankind.

If I am a Christian, Moslem, Jew, Buddhist, isn't that what I am?
You are not a Christian, Moslem, Jew or Buddhist. That is what you believe; that is your faith.

Why do I have to change?
You don't have to change. No one can make you change, nor should they be able to force you to do so.

If I don't have to change, then why should I put the effort into thinking about changing?
You shouldn't put the effort into changing if you like everything you are, everything your species is, and everything your species is doing to individuals, itself, and to the environment. But if you don't like everything about yourself, your species, or both, then you need to consider changing.

I am only one person. How can I change things?
You can change things through the 'butterfly effect' and the 'broken window' effect. The butterfly effect says every action ripples through society. Some ripples fade away; others add just enough energy to be responsible for the generation of a ripple that culminates into a tidal wave of phenomenal proportions. Regardless of the end result, you are responsible for your actions and the results they generate.

The broken window effect says every action we generate, every action we tolerate, every action we encourage leads to the acceleration of the same actions. As an example, if we are the first to break a window in an abandoned building, others will follow suit, and the process of breaking windows in the building then accelerates until they are all broken. We are responsible for not only our actions, but the ripples our actions generate.

We are trying to change things already. Why do I need to do more?
You don't if you are satisfied with the way things are. All forms of status – racial, occupational, intellectual, economic, physical, geographic, educational, etc. – are based upon our perceptions of who we are and what significance we attach to ourselves and others in terms of our role in reality. The only way to change significantly is to change the perceptions we have of who we are and what role we are responsible for in reality.

What general perceptions do we have as humans that we can change?
We can alter our perceptions of who we are and what our purpose is in life. We can do something we have never done before as a human species. We can build a universal model which uses what we have today to explain our significance in reality and our significance in eternity.

Isn't this forming a new religion?
No, this is philosophy.

Wouldn't this destroy my religious beliefs, my faith in God?
No, it might modify them somewhat, but not destroy them.

Doesn't this philosophy require me to change my faith?
We are not talking about changing your faith. We are talking about changing what it is you think you are. We are talking about a perceptual change in terms of what we perceive human beings to be. You are a member of the human species. We are talking about defining what that means. If you look at the human race, and like everything you see, then there is no need to change anything. But this would imply we do not need to grow in terms of our perceptions of what we are.

The idea of remaining the same, not growing, goes against our basic instincts as a species. We have always reached out to expand our knowledge base, our perceptions of the Causative Force and the limits of our world. To refuse to do so now would go against everything we have been attempting to understand.

What perceptual change would create a perceptual shift in the way we look at ourselves and humankind in general?

We presently look at ourselves as needing a Causative Force. If we add to this the idea that the Causative Force also needs us, we begin to see ourselves as having a purpose. We begin seeing ourselves as having a responsibility to the Causative Force Herself.

In other words, we would see ourselves in a close, interdependent relationship with the Causative Force, a symbiotic relationship. (The degree of symbiosis is debatable.)

Secondly, we, for the most part, acknowledge the Causative Force's omnipresence, but many theisms reject the universe being inside the Causative Force. If we continue accepting the omnipresence of the Causative Force but add the idea of our universe existing within the Causative Force, then you have the basic concept of panentheism.

What does symbiotic panentheism mean?

Symbiotic is defined as, "A close, prolonged association between two or more different organisms of different species that may, but does not necessarily, benefit each member." *Panentheism* means, "all in God." *Pan* is Greek meaning, "all;" *en* means, "in;" *the* comes from *theo* and means, "God," and *ism* means, "action, process, practice."

The basic concept is one which says that the individual, the human species, is important to the Causative Force. Symbiotic panentheism says that the Causative Force created each of us for a reason and we are important to the Causative Force, just as the Causative Force is important to us. We, as individuals, have a function. We are a necessity to what lies beyond our reality, our universe. We contribute something to the Causative Force that the Causative Force cannot accomplish in the state of being omnipotent (all powerful), omnipresent (all present), omniscient (all knowing). Being everywhere, knowing everything, and being all powerful prevents the Causative Force from growing and thus limits the Causative Force to a state of permanent equilibrium, an unnatural state.

Why do we keep science, philosophy, and religion apart?

Most of us have a primary interest in one or the other. Each area of study looks at the other as infringing upon its 'turf' and questioning its authority. The struggle between the academic areas of philosophy, religion, and science is actually nothing other than a power struggle. Each area wants to maintain its influence over what it believes to be its constituents.

We, as observers and participants, cheer for one or the other depending upon our primary interest.

Why is it important to fuse the three?

Fusing the three could give us a complete picture of where we are, what we are, and why we exist.

Why are science, religion, and philosophy so distrusting and confrontational of each other?

None of the three understand they are not entities unto themselves. Science, religion, and philosophy do not understand they are companions of souls. They do not understand they exist for our purposes, not their own. They do not understand they are intended to help us understand our journey through reality, to assist us in accomplishing our purpose. Without us, science, religion, and philosophy would cease to exist in terms of our awareness.

INTRODUCTION

MATRIX WRITING
What is a matrix?

A matrix is a means of navigating throughout a document. This matrix happens to be three dimensional. The concept need not be understood to understand the concepts being discussed.

If I am interested in the matrix, what should I be looking for?

The matrix is built upon numbers and patterns. For example, all religious questions are numbered in the one hundreds, the sciences in the two hundreds, philosophy in the three hundreds.

Ten concepts are then selected from each area. These concepts are listed in the table of contents where they are numbered accordingly. For example, religious ideas include Hinduism, Christianity, theism...; scientific ideas include the Big Bang theory, the prefix 'homo-,' symmetry...; philosophical ideas include Confucianism, Taoism, Appeal to Reason, Appeal to Humanism... Each of the ten ideas in the three sections are then asked to address the same ten questions.

How does the matrix help the reader?

The matrix is mathematical. Anyone interested in religion would go to the questions numbered in the 100's. Science is numbered in the 200's. Philosophy is numbered in the 300's.

The tens digit represents the particular idea of religion, science or philosophy being discussed as outlined in the table of contents. And lastly, the ones digit represents the ten questions asked of all thirty ideas chosen for the purpose of testing the model.

Can you give me an example?

All questions ending in '7' would deal with the thirty ideas humankind has developed and how they in turn would affect extraterrestrial life forms under the model being examined. Thus, anyone interested in extraterrestrial life would refer to all the questions ending in '7'. As an example, take the matrix #137. The one in the hundreds place deals with religion, the three in the tens place deals with Christianity, and the '7' in the ones place deals with the significance Christianity would have to extraterrestrials with the symbiotic panentheism model in place.

I'm confused. Can you give me another example?

Say you were interested in how Buddhism helps us understand what significance life has within the model being tested. You would go to the 100's because the 100's are the religion section. Then you would go to the 20's because as the table of contents shows, Buddhism is addressed in the 20's part of religion. Then, you would go to the 3 in the unit's place because question #3 always asks: 'What does ...(Buddhism in this case) reinforce about the significance of existence, life?' A list of these questions can be found on page 23.

I still don't get it. What should I do?

Skip the concept of the matrix for the time being. Its purpose is only intended to help you search for very specific information and does not affect the concepts in general. As you read the material, the concept of the matrix will most likely make more sense.

What sources were used from which the thirty ideas were chosen?

The sources used are common references available to the general reader, written for the general reader. The source for religion is *Dictionary of Philosophy and Religion: Eastern and Western Thought* by William L. Reese. The source for science is the *Oxford Concise Science Dictionary*. The source for philosophy is the *World Book Encyclopedia*.

Why bother writing this work using general reader references and terminology?

The answer comes from Steven Hawking, who discussed the idea of a universal philosophy in his book *A Brief History of Time*. In it, he provided the basic guideline a universal philosophy must follow:

> "If we do discover a complete [unified] theory [of the universe], it should in time be understandable in broad principle by everyone, not just a few scientists. Then we shall all, philosophers, scientists and just ordinary people, be able to take part in the discussion of the question of why it is that we and the universe exist."

Won't such basic reference books diminish the significance of the model?

No, these books make the concepts of the thirty ideas understandable to the general reader. The idea of a universal philosophy being understandable to the general reader is the whole basis upon which a universal model must be build.

How were the thirty ideas picked?

That was one of the more difficult tasks. They were chosen from a search for ten religious, ten scientific, and ten philosophical ideas which appeared to lie at the very fundamental core of our religious, scientific, and philosophical beliefs. The degree, however, to which these choices represent the foundation of God, the universe, and ourselves is not what is important. What is important is the process of testing the model.

Could other sources be used?

Absolutely. If the model is a strong model, it should hold up to examination using universally accepted reference sources.

Is it possible to build a model that fits every religious, scientific or philosophical piece of information we can find? If not, what's the point of building this universal philosophy?

No model will perfectly fit everything. The point is to obtain the best understanding of the total picture of what our universe is, what we are, why our universe exists, why we exist, and how all this is tied to what lies beyond the boundaries of our universe.

No working model is created with the expectation that it is 'right.' The models are created in the hopes of being able to best explain what it is we perceive around us. It is generally recognized that the model is only a starting point and is intended to change slightly or even be completely taken apart and reassembled as we learn more. As we move through life, we are constantly learning and new knowledge brings us new understanding, which should change our universal philosophical model.

The model's best hope is to be able to explain what we know at any point in time. If this is accomplished, the model acts as a new starting point from which we can advance our knowledge and understanding. No model can be expected to do more than this.

STEPPING UP TO THE CREATOR

Why does the matrix begin with question #100?

This question is the 89th question. Page 23 lists the ten questions to be asked of each religious, scientific, and philosophical concept. This brings the total number of questions to 99. The next logical place to begin is with question #100. In addition, beginning with question #100 allows the matrix to take on the characteristics required of it: order and logic.

THE TEN QUESTIONS
The concept:
#0. What does the particular belief, observation or analysis have to teach us?

Impact on the physical universe:
#1. What does the particular belief, observation or analysis imply about the universe within which we live?

Impact on the model:
#2. How does the particular belief, observation or analysis reinforce the concept of the model?

Impact on life:
#3. What does the particular belief, observation or analysis reinforce about the significance of existence, life?

#4. How does the particular belief, observation or analysis help us understand what life is?

#5. What significance does the particular belief, observation or analysis have to offer us as individuals?

#6. What significance does the particular belief, observation or analysis have to offer us as a species?

#7. What significance does the particular belief, observation or analysis have to offer other life forms in the universe?

Impact on eternity:
#8. What does the particular belief, observation or analysis imply about our significance in eternity?

#9. What does the particular belief, observation or analysis imply about our relationship to the Causative Force?

Roger Bacon:

(1) Four chief causes of error among men are:
  a. authority
  b. custom
  c. the opinion of the unskilled majority
  d. concealment of ignorance under the pretense of wisdom

–Dictionary of Philosophy and Religion,
William L. Reese, p. 63

RELIGION
What We Believe

On earth over the last 3,500 years, religions have evolved in what appears to be a pattern. Hinduism (1500's BC), Judaism (1000's BC), Buddhism (500's BC), Christianity (0's BC), and Islam (500's AD) have emerged and set a tone for societies within which we live. These major religions have accepted the Hindu principles of monotheism and the eternal soul.

Each religion after Hinduism has had a basic concept to present to our world. Judaism, by accepting the basic Hindu concepts, bridged the West with the East by providing a conduit by which these concepts were able to filter through to Western religions. Buddhism identified the irrationality of human suffering and offered a solution to this problem. Christianity introduced the warmth of love to our perception of human interactions toward each other. Islam introduced justice, the means of discouraging interference with the journey of others.

Two points stand out in this process of global religious emergence. First, no rationality had been put forward that explains the reason for the emergence of each of these basic premises. Second, these religions each popped up at surprisingly consistent 500 year intervals.

The emergence of the new major religious contributions to humankind ended with Islam in the 500 AD's. This brings up a major question. Why had the apparent termination of new religious contributions come to an abrupt halt? Maybe it is because we have not developed the answer to the first point concerning why these major religious concepts appeared to be taking on a near global consensus. Or maybe it is because we have, in fact, been developing but in a way we did not associate with religious development. Maybe the development was taking place within other areas that were indirectly supporting religions, but not recognized as doing so.

Why was there an abrupt 1,500 year break in religious development? Perhaps we can gain some insight into this question if we look at other developments that took place during these years. Much of the main progress of our species over these years seems to have been in the areas of philosophy and science – areas that appeared to be religiously antagonistic but may, in fact, have been very much religion-friendly.

Western philosophical development of religion appears to have begun with St. Anselm in 1033 AD, approximately 500 years after the introduction of Islam into the world. St. Anselm was the archbishop of Canterbury and among the first to argue the concept of God from a purely philosophical point of view or what could be called a purely logical point of view. This introduces logic, for the first time, into the discussion concerning a Causative Force. Thus emerged the significance of logic or philosophy in understanding the Causative Force.

Following this 500 year cycle, the emergence of science in its modern form began. Around the 1500's AD, Nicolaus Copernicus' *De Revolution Orbium Celestium* was published. This work is recognized as the onset of modern science and the affirmation of Leonardo da Vinci's perception of the importance of observation and experimentation in the process of gaining understanding. Thus, the cycle appears to be continuing. Five hundred years after the emergence of the philosophical approach to understanding the Causative Force, science emerges and brings with it the importance of observation.

The 500 year cycles appear to be continuing with great consistency. Interestingly enough, we have now ended the last 500 year cycle and are at the beginning of a new cycle, which leads to the question, what next?

There are basically only three means by which we are able to understand ourselves, understand each other, understand our universe, and understand the Causative Force behind our universe. All three are merely means of understanding, gaining insights, and obtaining perceptions of what we are. The three means by which we understand what we are, what our universe is, and what a Causative Force is, are perception through faith or what we call religion; perception through logic or what we call philosophy; and perception through observation or what we call science.

With this in mind, we may find it useful to seek an understanding of where a Causative Force would be, where we are in relation to a Causative Force, and what significance this has for us as individuals and as a species. This step provides the understanding of the religious concept that a Causative Force is truly omnipresent – located everywhere – as panentheism asserts.

INTRODUCTION

Religion is the oldest of the three means by which we can understand ourselves, others, our universe, and our Causative Force. Therefore, it is the first place we should look for verification regarding the potential for a universal philosophy. Support needs to be drawn from what religious concepts imply – not what humans themselves say. Verification must be provided by examining concepts large groups of us believe, hold dear, and consider sacred.

Very few people are experts in all fields of religion, science, and philosophy. Recognizing this to be the case, we must seek a source that is neutral, holds credentials, and is written for the general reader. For this, we will utilize the appropriate *Eastern and Western Thought – Dictionary of Philosophy and Religion* by William L. Reese.

HINDUISM
1500 BC

*What new concept has Hinduism
firmly established within the East?*

1. Monotheism
2. The Identicality of the Causative Force and the Self
3. The Eternal Soul

#0. What does the conceptual framework of Hinduism have to offer us?

1. *Hinduism:*
a. *Implicitly monotheistic, it is the message of the Upanishads that the indwelling, all-pervading Supreme Being, or Brahman, is identical with the individual self, or Atman.*
b. *Hindu six systems of philosophy:*

1–2: nine substances (the four atoms, and space, time, ether, mind, and soul) created the world by fashioning the nine substances into an ordered universe;

3–4: two basic categories...eternal spirits and natural order...periodically dissolving the cosmos and reinitiating the process;

5–6: held the entire world to be an illusion and Brahman to be the sole reality; held the world to be the appearance whose reality is Brahman.
Dictionary of Philosophy and Religion, William L. Reese, p. 302

•

Hinduism is the most ancient of our modern religions. Hinduism gave us the broad based support of the concepts of monotheism – "a" Causative Force; the soul; and individuality existing into eternity.

•

The Hindus give us the knowledge, faith, and belief in one Causative Force, Creator, Initiator, Cosmic Force which leads to a sense of the characteristic of the Causative Force being everywhere, omnipresent. Without this understanding of one Causative Force, omnipresence is not possible. Without omnipresence, we could not have globally progressed to the Judaic (1000's BC), Buddhist (500's BC), Christian (0's BC) or Islamic (500's AD) concepts, for they all evolve around the concept of one Causative Force, the soul, an eternal state of being for the soul, and a place of existence to which the soul can go. In other words, Hinduism established in our modern times the concept of the soul and the soul having a home base from which to operate.

#1. What does the conceptual framework of Hinduism imply about the universe within which we live?

Hinduism implies that the universe is an illusion and the Causative Force is the only true reality. The Causative Force is the guiding force of evolution and She periodically dissolves the universe and reinitiates the creation of a new universe.

•

The first concept – the world is just an illusion – may sound strange upon first glance. It is, however, no different than most of us believe or sense through our various faiths. Most faiths profess that the Causative Force created the heavens and earth. Since our basic faiths acknowledge nothing existed but the Causative Force before the creation of the universe, then the creation of the cosmos, universe, from nothingness is not as farfetched as it may seem.

With this established as a possibility, the second concept – the Causative Force periodically dissolving the universe – no longer seems impossible. After all, if the Causative Force can create something, She can uncreate what She created. And if the Causative Force can uncreate, then it is possible that She may take such an action. This is no more farfetched than the modern concept of science that the universe may implode sometime in the far future.

•

The concept of creating the universe out of nothingness is no longer just a mystery. Scientists now understand the apparent significance symmetry has as a law within which our universe exists. As such, they have developed a basic model by which our present universe could theoretically dissolve into true nothingness. This implies the reverse: the universe could logically have been created from nothingness. The process of creating and uncreating universes and why it might need to take place is dealt with in detail within this trilogy in the book *You and I Together*. The book deals with a scientific model for creation and the impact an understanding of just such a model would have had on humanity's past, on humanity's present, and on humanity's future.

The problem of temporary universes becomes one of understanding where our significance as individuals and as a species lies in all this creating and uncreating. That is where "symbiotic panentheism" comes in for it provides an answer and the logic to this very question.

#2. How do the concepts of Hinduism reinforce the concept of panentheism?

Hinduism reinforces panentheism by accepting the idea that the Causative Force periodically starts over by dissolving the existing universe and building a new one.

•

The Hinduistic concept of the Causative Force and self being identical explains why the idea makes sense that the soul came from the Causative Force and is a part of the Causative Force. If the universe were made by the Causative Force, it can, just as easily, be uncreated by the Causative Force. The soul then has one of two possibilities in terms of immortality and mortality. The soul could have the characteristic of immortality and be able to exist even if the universe were uncreated, in which case the soul would have nowhere to go but into an all present, omnipresent, panentheistic Causative Force. Or the soul could be mortal and die with the death of the universe, which is rejected by Hinduism.

•

Modern religions (since the last 4,000 years) have put forth the concept that the essence of humans is the soul and that the soul is immortal. With the uncreation of the universe, the soul would have nowhere to go but back into the Causative Force. This concept provides significance to the idea that we exist. No greater significance could be assigned to life than the significance of being a part of something so immense that it actually exists within something bigger than the universe itself. What could be more significant than being a part of an entity capable of creating the universe?

But there is something more significant and that is where symbiotic panentheism comes into the picture. Symbiotic panentheism goes even further than panentheism for it not only rationalizes the concept that the soul is significant because it is a part of the Causative Force, but symbiotic panentheism adds the idea that we as beings actually have a significant role to play in relationship to the Causative Force. The Causative Force needs the soul. The Causative Force needs you. Symbiotic panentheism doesn't just say this is so but goes on to rationalize how and why the soul could be significant to the Causative Force Herself.

This does not go against Hindu concepts; rather, it adds to them.

#3. What does Hinduism reinforce about the significance of existence, life?

Hinduism maintains that, *"...the indwelling, all-pervading Supreme Being, or Brahman, is identical with the individual self..."*

•

The concept of the Causative Force being identical with self (soul) is what gives life meaning. It indicates the source from which life came is the Causative Force. But what about the reason for our "separation" from the Causative Force? Why did we leave the Causative Force in the first place? We need patience. We can only handle one question at a time and right now we are dealing with the size of the Causative Force. The reason for our separation from the Causative Force will come when we leave religion and study philosophy.

All the major modern religions of the world absorbed the Hinduism concepts of a Causative Force and the existence of an eternal soul. Religions that evolved after Hinduism: Judaism (1000's BC), Buddhism (500's BC), Christianity (0's BC), and Islam (500's AD) ignored the Hindu premise that the Causative Force and the soul, the essence of the human being, are identical or directly connected. Western religions following Hinduism rejected the premise that you are a piece of the Causative Force. Just as a heart can be human but not be "a" human, you can be part of the Causative Force but not be "the" Causative Force.

•

How did western religions manage to rationalize this lack of connection between the Causative Force and soul? The western religions of Judaism, Christianity, and Islam were unable to overcome what they saw to be the hard side of the Causative Force: the misery, the suffering, the loneliness, the loss of loved ones, the despair, the lack of hope, the lack of meaning, the pain, the hatred, the envy, the greed. There seemed to be no logical explanation to it all.

And so western religions refused to accept the connection between the soul and the Causative Force that the Hindus offered us. Religions could not rationalize the concept that if we were pieces of the Causative Force, connected to the Causative Force, then how could we do these things to each other, how could the Causative Force do these things to us? And so western religion moved on, accepting only a part of the picture. Western religions accepted only the part of the picture they could understand regarding the connectedness between the Causative Force and ourselves.

#4. How does Hinduism help us understand what life is?

The Hindu concept of the existence of nine substances (the four atoms, and space, time, ether, mind, and soul) in the universe helps us understand that "life" is the soul.

•

Hinduism professes the idea that the universe is composed of nine substances. It specifically separates the concept of body (composed of the four atoms and wrapped in space, time, and ether) from the mind and the mind from the soul. This separation explains the essence of life.

This helps us understand that the body is just the body. Life on the other hand is not the physical body, but rather the essence of the individual is the soul itself. The mind, in turn, provides the means by which the soul is able to relate to the body's experiences within the universe. The mind provides awareness. The mind provides the means by which the soul is capable of connecting to the body and conversely, the mind provides the means by which the body connects to the soul.

•

What about the universe itself? The universe is the location, environment within which the soul can travel, experience, and learn using the body as the means of travel, the vessel of transportation and connection to the physical. The means of being capable of existing within our universe is achieved through the spiritual – the soul, the physical – the universe, the means of travel – the body, the means of connecting the physical with the spiritual and the spiritual with the physical – the mind.

The body being the vessel of travel within a universe created by the Causative Force holds the essence of a human being. The body is a vessel for the soul. The soul, traveling the universe within the body, is able to function within the universe and learn, experience, participate within the universe through awareness. Awareness being able to connect to the soul is the function of the mind.

And what of life? Hinduism teaches us that life is not our short existence in this universe as we know it, but rather life is what we experience today and what we will experience after "death." The Hindus believe that life as we know it is an experience the soul passes through. If this is true, you can be fairly sure that the complexity of creating such an intricate process has a purpose, for it would seem to be far too intricate to have been established for no reason.

#5. What does Hinduism have to offer us as individuals?

Hinduism offers us the idea of one Causative Force, having an essence, a soul, and the connection of the Causative Force and our souls. In short, Hinduism offers each of us, as individuals, the concept of being a piece of something greater than ourselves.

•

Hinduism offers us the concept of each of us being significant if for no other reason than we are a part of the Causative Force. As such, we have no choice but to demand to be treated accordingly. Likewise, you would have no other option than to recognize the same is true of others and if they to have an essence, a soul, it too is a part of the Causative Force and therefore must demand to be treated as the Causative Force. In addition, we all must protect each other, for what other option would we have other than to protect the creator of our universe, the Causative Force Herself?

•

Imagine a society where people are no longer looked upon as just people but rather as portions of the Causative Force. Abuse of any kind would no longer just be irrational, but would be totally unacceptable. Elimination of abuse and suffering would become a primary objective of people in society. Welfare running rampant? No, this does not imply that everything would be given free of charge to the individual, for this only lowers the individual's value to society to the lowest level possible, the level of worthlessness.

The environment which is a place for people to travel would no longer be a place for people to travel but would now be understood to be a place for the Causative Force to travel, for people would be understood to be nothing other than pieces of the Causative Force. As such, the environment could no longer logically be abused, polluted, destroyed for in our minds and thoughts, we would see it as belonging not to us but to others as well as to the Causative Force.

This is not implying that a person is the Causative Force. Saying that a person is the Causative Force would deny the existence of the Causative Force for She would be no greater than you. To declare yourself to be "the" Causative Force in total, would deny other people the recognition of a soul, a portion of the Causative Force. To declare yourself to be "the" Causative Force would be to diminish the Causative Force to your level of power, presence, and knowledge.

#6. What significance does Hinduism have to offer us as a species?

Hinduism offers us two basic concepts: the eternal spirit and natural order.

•

What is the difference between natural order and eternal spirit? Hinduism would imply that eternal spirits exist both within this universe and outside the universe. If such is the case, could there be any denying that you have an eternal existence? With this comes some form of significance in terms of our connection to eternity.

If we have some form of significance to eternity, we have a responsibility not only as individuals but just as importantly as a species, for the summation of us as individuals is what we have to offer as a species. This implies that we as a species must demand to be treated with the respect due the Causative Force if and when we encounter some form of alien life within the heavens. No amount of intimidation by such a life form, regardless of its apparent advanced forms of technology, knowledge or wisdom can allow us to deny our uniqueness and purpose in existence within this universe. Hinduism offers us hope in terms of having a significance for existing as a species.

•

Our significance as a species and therefore as individuals to that of impacting upon the Causative Force Herself, requires us to demand respect from others and for others.

Panentheism, supported by Hinduistic ideas, establishes the concept that we, as a species, must never submit to, must never allow ourselves to be subjugated by, other life forms, earthbound or otherwise. Likewise, we must extend the same respect to other life forms.

What we do not extend to others we cannot expect to be extended to ourselves. This could put us as a species in a very difficult situation someday. And just what types of situations could occur that would prove to be threatening to our very existence as a species? How about the cloning of genetically superior life forms other than our own? How about the creation of artificially intelligent androids that may be far superior than ourselves in terms of intelligence? Expanding our perceptions of the size of the Causative Force to the size of the Causative Force the Hindus have to offer us would be beneficial for all life forms in the universe, including our own.

#7. What significance does Hinduism have to offer other life forms in the universe?

Hinduism offers the possibility that other life forms other than our own may act as vehicles of travel for souls. Hinduistic ideas imply that souls existing elsewhere in the universe are no different in terms of purpose and significance than souls existing in a human body.

•

Significance of the soul within extraterrestrials is almost beyond comprehension for us at this point. In essence, what is being said is that no matter how powerful we become in comparison to other life forms we may encounter, we have no choice but to recognize and respect their uniqueness and their significance to the Causative Force. They, too, are a piece of the Causative Force and must be treated as such.

Likewise, we cannot allow another life forms' advanced technology, knowledge, culture, traditions or wisdom to overpower our sense of uniqueness and significance. We must maintain our individuality and respect for ourselves as a species and as individuals for we to have a significance to the Causative Force.

•

In essence, Hinduism has established the concept that there is one Causative Force to the universe and this Causative Force does not belong uniquely to us as humans. This Causative Force belongs to all life forms within the universe She created, earthbound or otherwise.

The result is the creation of a perception that all souls, earthly or otherwise, are connected and have a unique function to perform. Such a perception is undeniable if the concept of an omnipresent, panentheistic Causative Force is accepted. Accepting such a universal concept, such a universal philosophy could very well lead to an elevation in human behavior.

This panentheistically based Hindu approach would lead to the establishment of respect for each other based upon the commonality of creation and purpose for existence. It may in fact be the one and only point of commonality we find amongst each other. To establish this point before confirming the existence of extraterrestrials will be much easier than establishing this bond after an extraterrestrial encounter.

#8. What does Hinduism imply about our significance in eternity?

Hinduism not only professes that we exist in eternity but implies that we impact eternity.

•

Hinduism holds to the idea that the spirit, the soul, is eternal. Eternal existence would suggest never dying, never falling into a state of nonexistence. The idea of a soul losing its identity or a soul losing its awareness are concepts that imply the death of the soul. These ideas, therefore, are not Hinduistic. Hinduism offers us eternal existence immersed in awareness. Hinduism opens us up as a species and as individuals to the concept of maintaining our essence, our spirit, our awareness, and our individuality for eternity.

Eternity is a long time and if we maintain our awareness of what we have accomplished, the actions we have taken, we had better think long and hard about what it is that we do, for it will never go away.

•

The world under the monotheistic Hindu concepts leaves no alternative but accepting the Causative Force as the real state of existence and the world as only a learning tool for the Causative Force. Your soul, you, your essence, being eternal has no place to go but back to the Causative Force. You will be confronted with your actions, the repercussions of your actions, and the ripples they created which roll to the very ends of physical reality. You, under Hinduistic concepts, will have no choice but to accept responsibility for those actions for no one other than yourself is responsible for them.

You are eternal, and so too are the affects of the actions you initiate. Who will be waiting to confront you with the resultant effects of your actions? There would seem to be three possibilities: you, yourself; other souls, entities such as yourself; and the totality, the Causative Force Herself. The Causative Force may speak for Herself in terms of Her judgment of you, but can She speak for the individual essences you affected in either a "positive" or "negative" fashion? Can She speak for you and your essence, your understanding of what you have done?

#9. What does Hinduism imply about our relationship to the Causative Force?

Hinduism states that the Causative Force and self are identical.

•

If the world is just an appearance existing in a Causative Force, then this would provide the understanding of why the universe was molded out of nothingness. This would explain the eternal state of the soul beyond the temporary status of our physical reality. It would explain why the soul could remain should the universe be dissolved. And if the universe were dissolved, destroyed, where does that leave your soul? It leaves your soul existing within the Causative Force. It leaves your soul as being a part of the Causative Force.

We have incorporated much of the basic premises of Hinduism into our religions. Why are we so reluctant to accept this part? It would do nothing to undermine our present basic modern religions and would in fact do quite the opposite. It would unite us all under an understanding of commonality while demanding we accept, respect, and find comfort in the uniqueness of our faiths, our religions.

•

The Causative Force, we, you are a part of the Causative Force. Your wife is a part of the Causative Force. Your child is a part of the Causative Force. Your neighbor is a part of the Causative Force. A black man is a part of the Causative Force. The physically challenged, the poor, the street sweeper, the rich, the sick, the person getting ready to overdose, the person getting ready to jump off the bridge, the beggar, the soldier facing you are all part of the Causative Force.

The Causative Force fills our bodies; the Causative Force is the essence of each and every one of us. A different perspective? How can we even doubt it? A new perspective forcing us to look at ourselves, look at others differently, treat each other differently? Absolutely. A new perspective encouraging us to perceive ourselves differently and perceive others we may encounter within our universe differently? Hopefully.

Conclusion: How do the concepts of Hinduism reinforce the concept of panentheism?

They do not. Panentheism is reinforcing Hinduism.

•

Hinduism came well before the term "panentheism" was coined. Without the basic precepts of Hinduism, panentheism could not have evolved. All panentheism does for Hinduism is provide a little insight into its validity. On the other hand, Hinduism provides a lot of insight into the concepts of panentheism.

Hinduism is a major world religion influencing a large percentage of the world's population over a long period of time. And just what is it that Hinduism has offered humans existing upon this planet? She has offered us three ideas:

1. Monotheism: a belief in one Causative Force. Without this idea, Buddhism, Judaism, Christianity, Islam, etc. could not have emerged, for they are all based upon the central theme of one Causative Force.

2. The identicality of the Causative Force and the self: humans and other life forms in the universe are a part of the Causative Force.

3. The eternal soul: establishes the concept of the existence beyond life, an existence into eternity itself.

Symbiotic panentheism reinforces Hinduism by understanding through faith, observations, and logic.

•

Hinduism is so supportive of panentheism it sounds as if panentheism is just another name for Hinduism, but it is not. It is a philosophical perception that reinforces Hinduism but no more so than it reinforces Christianity, Islam, Judaism, ... prophecies, science, philosophy. It is a universal philosophy capable of uniting religion, philosophy, and science. It is a perceptual shift for humankind. Panentheism is incapable of destroying anything we hold dear, yet it reinforces our significance in the universe.

JUDAISM
1000 BC

What new concept has Judaism firmly established within the West?

Bridging the East to the West.

1. Monotheism: Carried over to the West.
2. Identicality of the Causative Force and the Self: Not understood in the West, therefore *left behind in the East*.
3. The Eternal Soul: Carried over to the West.

#0. What concepts has Judaism firmly established in the West?

Judaism:... these are the people of the Book in a unique sense...
If we ask for the general philosophy and ethical beliefs characterizing this movement the most outstanding is monotheism, a belief in the absolute and exclusive unity of God. Related to this is the belief that God has revealed Himself to man, that men are responsible for their unrighteousness, that righteousness is the way to salvation, that right will triumph in the world, that it is Israel's divinely appointed task to teach the universal Fatherhood of God, and that justice is measured out in a world to come.
Dictionary of Philosophy and Religion, William L. Reese, p. 365

•

The implication of "these are the people of the Book in a unique sense" is very direct. So the question is when was "the Book" established in terms of permanency, in terms of actually putting the teachings into writing in "book" form? Today it is believed by many that the teachings of Moses were written down approximately 1000 BC.

Judaism brought the concept of monotheism to the West at a time when western religions and Middle Eastern religions taught the ideas that some humans were gods and others were not. Judaism said, "No human is better than another." Judaism taught the concept that man, all men, were made in the image of the Causative Force. At the time when the Pharaohs were forcing millions of their fellow humans into lives of servitude and bondage, the Jews said, "Enough." At the time Europe was toying with belief in multiple gods, regional gods, and small gods, the Jews were saying, "Let's be logical. Let's accept the idea of a big God, one that created everything from the smallest insect to the universe itself. Let's make God the Causative Force of all things."

•

The desire to step off this planet and into the heavens developed in the West. The means to do so was known as technological development. This is not to say that the development of technology was "good" or "bad." This only says that it occurred and there is no denying that point. Without the unifying single Causative Force influence into western religions, western science and technology may never have occurred due to the intense competition of fragmented religious development in the West.

#1. What have the concepts of Judaism taught us about the universe within which we live?

Judaism brought to the West the principle of a Causative Force creating the universe. Thus began the western acceptance of there being more to existence than the immensity of the universe itself. In other words, our universe was smaller than the Causative Force which created it.

•

Judaism built a bridge geographically, religiously, and philosophically for the eastern idea of monotheism to pass over the religious and philosophical chasm existing between East and West. However, saying that Judaism brought the concept to the West of one Causative Force for our universe does not answer the question, "Yeah, so what?" The "so what?" is the understanding of the idea that we as humans, as individuals, are not the only possible life forms that may have significance in the vast expanse of space, that existence does not center around us as humans.

The statement of this understanding was not to be an obvious contribution of the Jews to the world. The idea that other mortal life forms may exist in the heavens and that they too may have a significance, was not something we could even begin to conceive of in 1000 BC.

•

This concept of one Causative Force was simple, yet had an amazingly profound impact upon the direction which humankind would begin heading. Humans would begin seeing the earth as a home rather than as "the" only sacred location of life within the universe. Along with the expansion of the size of the Causative Force came the expansion of the size of the universe. This may not have been an intentional outcome of the Jewish influence upon the West, but it had a major impact upon our perceptions of the significance we had or were capable of having.

The universe was growing as we humans grew. Was the universe expanding or was just the concept of the universe expanding? Whatever the case, Judaism opened up new concepts regarding the possibilities of the very size of the universe itself. We were being given new frontiers to explore without our even being aware of this happening.

#2. How do the concepts of Judaism reinforce the concept of panentheism?

Judaism holds to the concept that there is one and only one Causative Force. Judaism is monotheistic. And what of panentheism? Panentheism simply says, we are all within the Causative Force.

•

Is there a difference between Judaism and panentheism? Judaism is a religion, a belief in and reverence for a supernatural power. The Jewish concept of this supernatural power orients around the idea that this entity is so powerful and knowledgeable that this entity is capable of creating the universe itself. They believe this entity could create the universe and they believe this entity did create the universe. They go on to define the Causative Force of the universe as their 'God.' This belief, this reverence for a supernatural power, is called a religion.

Panentheism has nothing to do with a belief or reverence for a supernatural power. Panentheism therefore is not a religion. Panentheism simply is a statement that this Causative Force of religions is so big that it is everywhere in terms of the universe it created. Panentheism simply states the size of the Causative Force as being omnipresent in terms of the universe. The natural conclusion would then be: if the Causative Force is omnipresent then the only place the Causative Force could have placed the universe it created would have been within Herself.

•

Most major religions of the world agree that the Causative Force is omnipresent but oddly enough, most western religions then say that the universe does not exist within the force that created the universe.

This is done to circumvent a paradox they have created for themselves. Western religions profess their God to be perfect and they view the world to be imperfect. The concept of an imperfect universe existing in a perfect Creator is a paradox so disturbing that western religions have circumvented the paradox by creating another paradox. Western religions have decided to place the universe outside the Causative Force, a process known as transcendence. In doing so, however, they have taken us out of the arms of the Causative Force and placed our universe and ourselves along with it, into the cold of a void. Transcendency was about to establish the idea of our having no purpose, of our being 'inferior' to the Causative Force. We were about to establish the rationality for hierarchy systems beginning with the Causative Force.

#3. What do the Judaic concepts of monotheism and the soul reinforce about the significance of existence, life?

Judaism did more than expand upon the western idea concerning the size of the Causative Force; it carried with it the concept of eternity being within reach of all humans.

•

The idea that all humans have a soul which in turn is tied to eternity, provided a whole new way of looking at the individual. Now life, the individual, was not just important, but rather the individual was important because the individual was tied to eternity. How this was important was not understood. It was understood, however, that a tie to eternity would most probably not occur unless there was a significant reason. Now life in the West was beginning to take on some significance in terms of our sensing this to be true.

In short, life was beginning to have value and the possibilities were beginning to open up to the idea that the value could be important to the Causative Force Herself.

•

As we increase the idea regarding how big our universe is and in turn how big our Creator is, we enlarge what we view as the space we live within. This is important for we as humans think big. For most people, how big we think depends upon the size of the room we have to work within. Large, spacious, open rooms tend to foster large ideas.

Granted, people are capable of "thinking big" in small rooms but this takes the ability to go inward. Again, however, the size of the inner space a person sees when they look inward depends upon what they view their room to be.

The room one views when looking inward is what is called the perception we have of ourselves. If we view ourselves as not having significance to other people, to the environment, to the Causative Force, then we tend to think small. People with small perceptions of their significance are little people with self serving agendas and abusive behaviors.

On the other hand, if we view ourselves as having significance to others, to the environment, to the Causative Force, then we tend to think big. People with big perceptions of their significance are big people with universal agendas and compassionate behaviors.

#4. How does Judaism help us understand what life is?

"Life" as we observe it would only be temporary. The Judaic concept of true life would come through the immortality of the soul.

•

True life, eternal life of the soul, was becoming something we as a species sensed to be true. True life, eternal life of the soul, was becoming something the eastern religion of Hinduism was establishing as a truth of religion through the eastern world and now Judaism was bringing it to the West.

No longer was life being considered in terms of today and in terms of fifty to one hundred years. Life was now evolving into an existence of an eternal state. And what of life as a physical form? The physical form was becoming just a temporary state of being for the soul. Why this temporary state? Religions were beginning to teach us not only the concept of an eternal state of existence as opposed to the short life of a human body, but they were beginning to explain that life must have significance. The understanding that this significance must exist was radical in itself even if it couldn't explain the "Why?"

•

The understanding that life had more significance than just in this physical lifetime told us much about life. Life no longer was the body; life was the soul. Life no longer involved the pleasures of the present; life involved the comfort of the eternity beyond this physical form. Now humans had a reason, an understanding of, a purpose for living a certain type of life. Now the state of one's eternal existence was dependent upon one's behavior towards others during one's physical existence. Physical life was taking on significance because of the effect it would have upon eternity itself.

#5. What significance do Judaic concepts of monotheism and the soul have to us as individuals?

We as individuals were seeing our existence in eternity based upon our present actions. Humanitarian behavior was becoming not just humanitarian, but logical.

•

Judaism did not have the rational, logical explanation regarding the "Why?" behind how or why our existence in eternity was tied to our present physical actions. This understanding was beyond human logic for that point of our history. Our understanding of the universe was limited and a better technical understanding of our universe was needed in order to develop the understanding regarding how our actions in today's life could effect our existence after life.

This section regarding religions and their validification of panentheism has to do with the size of the Causative Force. Panentheism is not a religion; it is just a description of what religions call the size of "God," the Causative Force. Panentheism simply says religions diminish the size of the Causative Force. The Causative Force is truly omnipresent as all major religions of the world have been preaching but not practicing. The Causative Force is everywhere and that means the universe is in Her; you are inside the Causative Force Herself.

•

Understanding why we have been separated, isolated, disassociated from the Causative Force will become clear after we have left this religious matrix and move on to the science matrix. The question now, however, is what effects do the Judaic concepts bring to us as individuals? They bring to us the concept of eternal life – not just for some, but for all.

Eternal life for all individuals. All humans are equal for all humans are not human but the soul. All humans come from the same place, are here for a common reason, will return to the same place.

And just where would that place exist? If the Causative Force transcends the universe, the answer would be uncertain. If the Causative Force on the other hand is "all present," omnipresent, then there is but one place from which and to which an eternal soul could appear to travel and that would be from and into the arms of the Causative Force Herself.

#6. What significance do the Judaic concepts of monotheism and the soul have to us as a species?

If we have significance as individuals, it is very likely we have certain common traits as a species, a total group, that have some meaning or potential meaning to eternity.

•

And what of the Jews? The Jews brought to the West the concept of one Causative Force being responsible for the creation of our planet and of the universe within which the earth was located. Was this an original idea? No, but it was a new idea for the West and it definitely had an impact upon the development of the West. And what of the West? The West went on to bring the world into its present state of technological development, a state of advancement which would place our species on the threshold of stepping off this planet and stepping into the heavens.

At that time of 1000 BC, the idea of the common person being able to travel through flight was unthinkable. And where are we today? We are preparing for the common person living in space, traveling to the moon, and moving to other planets.

•

The idea of expanding the perception of our potential significance was one that allowed us to grasp the understanding that we could do anything we desired, given time, knowledge, and determination. This brought us out of a perception of limited existence. It laid the ground work for the acceptance of an unlimited physical existence. We could learn to fly. We could learn to understand the composition of the atom. We could find a way to study bacteria and viruses and, in turn, learn to conquer them. We could find a way to explore the dark side of the moon. We could learn to explore the edge, the boundary, of the universe itself.

And what of we humans? We humans, you and I, are capable of anything we put our minds to, including understanding our relationship and significance to the Causative Force.

#7. What significance do the Judaic concepts of monotheism and the soul have to other life forms in the universe?

Monotheism implies a creation of the universe by one force.

•

A Causative Force created the universe, not just the part of it humans exist within. This suggests, or forces us, to acknowledge our uniqueness. It forces us to demand respect for our uniqueness as a species. At the same time, however, it leaves us no choice but to do the same for all other life forms, souls, we may encounter in the heavens, in the galaxy, in the universe.

This demand to respect our potential to contribute to a Causative Force so large the universe itself is immersed within it, opens up a whole new way of looking at our earth as an environment, of looking at ourselves as individuals, of looking at other humans with whom we interact, and of looking at other life forms we most probably will encounter as we travel the heavens themselves.

•

The way we perceive other life forms we encounter as we travel the heavens will be of utmost importance to those life forms. The manner in which we view other life forms in the heavens will determine how we treat these life forms. Our past experience of human behavior and limited perceptions throughout our history should have taught us much. Our atrocious treatment of the Incas, Mayans, Jews, Muslims, Christians, North American Indians, Serbs, noncommunists ... goes on forever it seems.

And what of new life forms we may encounter in the heavens? What about life forms which most probably will be entirely alien to our way of thinking and appearance? We can only hope we will have a new understanding, a new perception of what life is, and what the significance of life means, before we encounter these new life forms in the heavens. Without a new perception, life may once again be subjected to inhumane human behavior.

#8. What do the Judaic concepts of monotheism and the soul imply about our significance in eternity?

Eternity existing outside our universe implies the possibility of significance beyond the universe. The concept of the soul being tied directly to this eternity implies we may have a significance tied directly to eternity itself.

•

Humans, as far back as 1500 BC [*see Hinduism*], expanded the possibility of their significance into eternity itself. Judaism played a key part in providing the bridge for the concept to spread to the other half of the world, to the West.

The concept of significance being directly tied to eternity elevated our perception of our importance, expanded immensely our view of existence, for now existence was no longer confined by the boundaries of our universe. Now humankind was able to begin thinking in terms of belonging to the whole universe rather than just our planet or our solar system.

Through an understanding of the source of the soul and the place to which a soul travels after death, we provided a view of ourselves capable of withstanding any discoveries we might make through the field of science which was to evolve later in history.

•

Science was not to become a significant influence in our society for over 2,500 years. Why the need to prepare for it now? The concept of monotheism, the soul, and eternal life were ideas that would need time to expand throughout the western world. These concepts would need time to marinate in a kettle of tradition and culture. Tradition and culture themselves needed time to evolve and age.

The concepts, traditions, and culture needed time to become an integrated part of our society worldwide. The direction we took as a species in terms of the perception we had of ourselves, our universe, and a Causative Force was just one of many that could have taken place. It was, however, one that provided a continually expanding perception of the size of the Causative Force as well as a continually expanding perception of our potential both individually and as a species regarding life in our universe as well as beyond the boundaries of our universe.

#9. What do the Judaic concepts of monotheism and the soul imply about our relationship to the Causative Force?

Monotheism and the soul are both eternal under both Hindu and Judaic beliefs. The implication is that they both are tied together in some sense. Judaism had just not figured out in what manner.

•

Judaism sensed the significance of a single Causative Force. A single Causative Force creating the universe could lead to nothing less than a realization of the idea that this single Causative Force, regardless of the name assigned Her, would belong to everyone. Judaism did not profess this Causative Force to be her God. What Judaism did profess was the idea, "...that it is Israel's divinely appointed task to teach the universal Fatherhood of God."

Fourteen million Jews in the world are not enough people to allow history to consider the ideas they profess to be firmly established within society. There is no denying, however, that the tenacity with which this religious group clung to their beliefs and purpose provided the means by which the ideas of monotheism, the soul, and eternal existence of the soul could and did take root in the West.

The West found common ground upon which it could draw its small regional groups into large powerful geographical regions whose strength through unity and advancement through curiosity would drive humanity into a realm of technological development so grand that it would allow humans to actually step off the earth itself.

•

And is this all Judaism gave humankind? No, for Judaism provided the rationale for understanding all humans were created equal. Judaism said, "God created man in His image and in the image of God created He man." If this is the case, the Causative Force created all of us equally, for no one person could be better than another since we were all created in the image of the Causative Force. Each 'image' is the same, for it is made in the same image of the one and only Causative Force.

Thus, Judaism acted as a bridge while it also provided the rationale for the equality of humankind and of other life forms we may encounter somewhere in the heavens themselves.

Conclusion: How do the concepts of Hinduism reinforce the concept of panentheism?

It does not; what is really taking place is that panentheism reinforces Judaism.

•

Panentheism is not a religion and never could be. It reinforces the idea of a Causative Force existing. It does not imply the Causative Force is "concerned" with humankind nor, on the other hand, that the Causative Force is not concerned with humankind. It has no customs, traditions, principles, dogmas, leaders, institutions or guidelines to offer people and it never will for it merely states the logic regarding the size of the Causative Force. It defines a logical size for the Hindu, Judaic, Buddhist, Christian, Islamic, atheistic, pantheistic, New Age "God."

And just what is that size? Panentheism expands the size of the Causative Force to that of true omnipresence. Panentheism says that the Causative Force is so big, the only place for the universe to be is within the Causative Force Herself.

This in turn provides the beginnings of our understanding why we do have a significance for being alive and it is tied directly to the Causative Force Herself – not to other humans.

•

Judaism has provided monotheism, the soul, and eternal existence the time needed to take root in the West. The idea is now well established in the West as well as the East. The idea is now global.

And why was this so important? We had to have a greater understanding of the source of our essence, our soul, before we could begin to relate to other souls, other humans. We had to have an understanding of the commonality of our origin before we could accept the equality of all humans. Learning to look beyond the physical aspects of the body was not to be an easy task.

If looking beyond the insignificant physical variations of color, sexuality, gender, intelligence, race, religions was to be a task almost beyond our capacities, then what of our encounters with other life forms in the heavens? Judaism was very significant indeed in terms of expanding our perceptions of ourselves to the point where it could include all life forms throughout the universe.

BUDDHISM
500 BC

*What new concept has Buddhism
firmly established within the East?*

**One must address oneself
to the elimination of suffering.**

#0. What does the conceptual framework of Buddhism have to offer us?

Buddhism: The key to the problem of salvation and enlightenment is the presence of suffering. Misery, pain, or suffering is not merely one among many other equally prominent features of experience. It is its chief and overriding feature. And all other aspects of experience also contain suffering. If one is to experience enlightenment, then one must address oneself to the elimination of suffering.

Dictionary of Philosophy and Religion, William L. Reese, p. 134

•

Now we are to find that suffering, the toleration or even the idea of just enduring injury, pain or death is something we as individuals, that we as a species, are to commit ourselves to eliminating. But why would such a commitment be so important to us as individuals and as a species that we would need to center ourselves around such an action?

As we progress in this journey, the answer will become obvious. For now, however, let us just say that the generality being stressed with this type of commitment is that "you" are as important as the rest of your fellow humans, fellow souls, presidents or kings, located here on earth or in the heavens.

Three major ideas are being stressed here: one – suffering is not to be ignored, suffering is not a necessity; two – your suffering is no more important than that of another; and three – we all have equal importance in the scheme of things.

•

The Buddhist concept does not stipulate that you are to address just the elimination of "your" suffering. Buddhism states that one is to address the elimination of "suffering," period. This statement does not imply the suffering of others is more significant than yours, nor does it imply the reverse, that your suffering is more significant than others. The concept being addressed is: all suffering being endured by others as well as by yourself must be attended to.

#1. What does the conceptual framework of Buddhism imply about the universe within which we live?

Buddhism introduced the concept that although suffering may be a natural occurrence in our universe, it does not need to be tolerated.

•

But suffering has always been with us. Perhaps, but the key word here is "has." To say that we can totally eliminate suffering is perhaps unreasonable, but to say that we are capable of addressing suffering in the hopes of eliminating a large share of it is not. The universe is a big place and we have a long way to go before we even come close to having introduced our influence into her farthest corners.

And just what influence is it we wish to impart upon our universe? What better influence than the concept of making the universe a better place, a place with less suffering and pain? Do we not understand that as we travel the universe, as we step into a region of space new to us, we leave a seed planted forever? What "seed" are we implying here? We are talking about the most potent seed that can be planted anywhere, the seed of ideas, the seed of perceptions.

Presently, the only seed we have to sow is the seed of superiority. The seed that "…man was made in the image of God, in the image of God created He man." The concept we are poised to spread is that "we," not other life forms, are "God's" creatures. Our understanding as to why this may not be true opens our behavior to new possibilities. Without a new perception regarding the significance of other life forms located throughout the universe, we may spread throughout the heavens, the abuse and the suffering relative worth generates. Relative worth is the idea that one person or life form has more value than another.

•

To bring to the rest of the universe the recognition of relative worth opens up the universe to the idea that the strong should dominate the weak, the idea that to the winner go the spoils.

But the significance of the Buddhist stance, the significance of accepting the idea, "…we must commit ourselves to addressing the suffering that exists," commits us to respect other life forms and environments in the heavens as well as our own. At the same time, it provides the rationale upon which we can argue that others in the heavens should do the same for us.

#2. How do the concepts of Buddhism reinforce the concept of panentheism?

Buddhism establishes the idea that the intolerance of suffering is so important an issue it must become a major focus in one's journey through life. Reinforcing panentheism? Absolutely, for what better way to understand the significance of the need to eliminate suffering than to make the Causative Force so big, so omnipresent, there is nowhere to put the effects of suffering we generate other than within Her?

•

Panentheism assigns true omnipresence to the Causative Force. If a Causative Force is all present, then everything that happens, happens within the Causative Force. As such, the Causative Force may become aware and even empathize with what occurs within Her.

This is truly a dramatic perception. No wonder Buddhists sense the significance of the need to eliminate suffering. With the acceptance of a truly omnipresent Causative Force, suffering is something the Causative Force Herself experiences. She feels the pain, loneliness, heartache, loss, frustration, humiliation, and depression suffering generates. No wonder Buddhists sense the importance of this issue.

Some states of suffering are caused naturally. This can be alleviated by an understanding, a deep seated sense of faith, that better things lie ahead. Some states of suffering are caused by the actions we impose upon others. These states of suffering go to a much deeper level than the suffering caused by natural events, for they occur through the intentional acts of subjugation, abuse, domination, control, intimidation, and by the simple desire to hurt each other.

Once we expand upon the size of the Causative Force and realize that we are within Her, are a part of Her, actually hurt Her as we hurt others, we will have no choice but to alter our actions towards others.

•

The Buddhist concept of dedicating one's life to the elimination of suffering is not just noble, it is crucial to us as individuals, to our species, to our environment, to other life forms in the heavens, and to the Causative Force Herself. But how do we know that what we do affects the Causative Force? If you are located within the Causative Force, what other logical possibility could there be? Even if the pain were not directly felt, would not a Causative Force feel some form of pain should Her creations intentionally murder, rape, steal, subjugate, abuse or torment others She created?

#3. What does Buddhism reinforce about the significance of existence, life?

Buddhism gives us the understanding that the significance of life and the impact it generates is so important that we must focus upon reducing suffering, the negative aspects of life.

•

The idea of all humans having a soul is tied to eternity and provides a whole new way of looking at the individual. Now the individual is not important because they are alive, but rather the individual is important because the individual is tied to eternity. This idea of being connected to eternity changed the direction of our behavior. A tie to eternity meant we needed to consider our action because our actions now might affect our state of existence later. Why this was so was not totally understood, but Buddhists sensed this to be true. As such, Buddhists further opened up the idea that life was significant and allowing suffering in life would have a major impact upon existence in eternity. In short, Buddhism further advanced the concept that life had value, significance.

•

As we increase the idea regarding how big our universe is and in turn how big our Creator is, we enlarge what we view as the potential of existence.

The Buddhist ideas were very significant, therefore, in terms of reinforcing the significance of life. Now suffering, a part of life itself, was no longer to be taken lightly or just ignored for its existence impacted upon eternity. Life under Buddhism took on a greater significance and one aspect of life, suffering, became a focal point.

#4. How does Buddhism help us understand what life is?

Buddhism tells us life is but one stage in the soul's eternal state of existence. Buddhism implies suffering can have a major impact upon this journey not only for ourselves but for others, through a process known as the ripple effect.

•

Viewing life as a physical state of existence causes us to think in terms of existing fifty to one hundred years. The length of time one exists in this physical world is not what is important. What is important is the type of ripples your actions and existence create in life.

Actions are not necessarily end results such as inventing the computer or cures for a disease. Actions are behaviors that affect life experiences of oneself and others. A sales person providing helpful advice, a priest comforting the dying, a doctor healing the sick, a short order cook providing a warm meal, a teacher preparing souls for the future, a father mentoring his daughter, a mother mentoring her son, a child showing joy, a dish washer providing a clean dish to eat upon, a park ranger providing a safe haven for hikers, and on and on it goes.

What does this have to do with the Buddhist concept of eliminating suffering? The manner in which actions are completed by individuals produces major ripples within our society. And ripples can have major impacts upon the lives they wash over. And so it is we generate or eliminate suffering through our daily actions.

•

Life is a journey. It is not "the" journey; it is "a" journey your essence takes. The Buddhist concept of addressing the elimination of suffering has as much to do with creating positive impacts as eliminating negative impacts in life. Your actions generate one or the other, positive or negative impacts. Positive impacts are impacts created by actions that do not increase and may, in fact decrease, the stress, pain, heartache, loneliness, sadness, anger ... experiences and emotions people feel while journeying.

This is not an easy task. Actions need to be viewed in terms of not just short term effects but long term effects. A young lady having built up a short term relationship with a young man may come to the conclusion that this is not the soul mate she wants for life. To lie about her feelings may make the young man happy for the short term, but over the long term, lying would be detrimental not only for him, but for her, and everyone around them as they journey life. Buddhist decisions are not easy decisions.

#5. What significance does Buddhism have to offer us as individuals?

Addressing the elimination of suffering would do nothing less than improve the environment within which we as individuals journey.

•

We as individuals travel, journey through life. Buddhism implies that life is not "the" beginning of an end; rather life is a journey we take, an episode within our existence in eternity. If you have a soul, as all major religions say, and if that soul is tied to eternity as the major religions also profess, then the time span of one day through one hundred years is but one part of your existence. It must, however, have some significance or you would not be here. Taking the journey through life, whether voluntarily or because you are forced to do so, still has the same outcome. The outcome is the result of taking the journey.

If we all work consciously to eliminate suffering, we make the journey for each individual much more pleasant and enjoyable. You expand upon your awareness as you journey. The type of awareness you take with you when you exit life is dependent upon your own actions but it also is dependent upon the actions of others. The process of addressing the elimination of suffering is really nothing other than taking actions during your journey which are intended to improve upon journeys, both in life and what is to follow life, yours as well as others.

•

The journey through life obtains an expanded significance if it goes beyond our limited time span as humans. This is where the concept of panentheism attains its importance for it reinforces the concept that the essence of the individual is the soul and it is the soul which is tied to eternity. Buddhism existed long before we began to analyze the term *panentheism.* **Therefore, panentheism reinforces Buddhism in this respect.**

Buddhism then attains its significance in its understanding of the concept of our present state of having an attachment to the eternal. As such, your awareness and experiences in your present life form moves with you into your next life form. This in turn provides the understanding of the need to reduce the suffering you undergo in this life form so as to be able to reduce your exposure to suffering in eternity.

#6. What significance does Buddhism have to offer us as a species?

Each piece of suffering eliminated by individuals improves upon someone's journey which interprets into a ripple effect that washes over society, directly affecting our species.

•

We are not alone in our physical existence. The most influential factor in our society that affects us are actions, our own actions and actions of others. By working to eliminate the suffering of others, we are essentially working to improve the environment of all the members of our species. Our actions create reactions which create reactions which create more reactions. This is known as a ripple effect.

The idea of working to relieve the suffering of ourselves as well as the suffering of others is not just a case of taking an action that helps one person, but rather it is an action that ripples through the social fabric of our species.

Through the ripple effect, suffering diminishes significantly the more people work to eliminate their own suffering and the suffering of others. There are natural events which are difficult to control at this point. Natural events, such as earthquakes, fire, famine, plagues, disease, accidents, deaths, etc. generate suffering. Our reactions to these events, the intentional actions we as a society and as individuals generate after these events, can be controlled. Understanding the concept regarding why our actions today may well affect what we experience in eternity, could generate a major positive realignment of our way of thinking. It could have significant impact on all of us, on our whole species.

•

But what of reducing the suffering of others; what has that to do with you? Once having passed through this life state, Buddhism implies you move into a new state of eternity. Panentheism implies you return to the only place there is and that is within the Causative Force. Having returned to the Causative Force, you take with you your awareness which includes your experiences. But in addition to this, you are now privy to the knowledge of the Causative Force who is omniscient. This would mean you are privy to all the suffering others have experienced. Reducing suffering in the world would in turn reduce the amount of suffering of our species that is being added to the Causative Force, thereby reducing your suffering.

#7. What significance does Buddhism have to offer other life forms in the universe?

Buddhism does not imply it is earthly suffering which is unacceptable; rather it is all suffering that is to be addressed.

•

We cannot say for sure, but the concept of suffering does not appear to be unique to our species and our planet. If suffering is a factor amongst other life forms, then Buddhism implies this suffering also must be addressed.

What new perspective of significance would stimulate the motivation needed to increase the effort we put in our attempt to reduce suffering? Presently, we view ourselves as people, human. What if we saw ourselves as pieces, portions of the Causative Force? No longer would you look at someone as just suffering; you would see the suffering as something happening to the Causative Force Herself. You would no longer be able to just pass by the suffering in a hurry, but you would have to slow down and lend a hand, for it would be seen as the Causative Force suffering.

This idea of being a portion of the Causative Force, which panentheism implies, would have no other possibility but to apply to other intelligent life forms throughout the universe. If the Causative Force is truly omnipresent, all present, there would be nowhere else for other life forms to exist but within the Causative Force. They also would be a part of, a portion of, the Causative Force.

•

But what of hostile life forms that may wish to dominate or subjugate us? We would have no other choice but to stand firm in our perception that we, as a portion of the Causative Force, have the responsibility, the obligation, to preserve our journey for it is unique and has much to offer the Causative Force. As souls journeying, we would have an obligation, a responsibility, to the Causative Force to protect our journeys, to protect the potential we have as a species.

Under panentheism, the Buddhist concept of eliminating suffering becomes significant to the Causative Force. Now, the concept belongs not only to our species, but to all life forms in the universe. Panentheism would obligate us to be just as committed to protecting the rights of other life forms to journey as protecting the right of our own species to journey.

#8. What does Buddhism imply about our significance in eternity?

Intentionally creating suffering is not something we should consciously be trying to create if it is something that is taken back to eternity itself.

•

If suffering is something we do not consider to be "good," then why would it not be something we would orient our lives around eliminating? Orienting our efforts around the elimination of suffering does not mean the end to scientific research, education, creation of parks and recreation, community clubs, hobbies, entertainment ... Orienting our efforts around the elimination of suffering means just the opposite. Human activities that have a "positive" impact would get a major boost. They would now no longer just take place. They would provide a means for us to spread positive impacts. They would obtain a major boost in terms of their significance because now we would understand that they were adding positive impacts upon eternity itself.

And what of "negative" activities of groups such as the KKK, youth gangs, drug cartels, criminal rings, slums, littering, intimidating language, spousal abuse, child abuse, sexism, segregation, hierarchy systems, social rejection etc., etc.? If we recognized that the impact of these activities actually were to be taken back to the Causative Force, would remain in eternity – a place where we were to exist forever, how could we ever again just ignore these activities? We would have no choice but to be incensed with the suffering they generate, for it would affect own personal eternity.

•

Major religions believe that eternity is where we will find ourselves after passing through this life. They also believe that the essence of the individual is the soul. If the soul is the major essence and if the soul's awareness exists in some form and if you retain some form of individuality, then the experience of the eternal soul, your awareness, becomes imprinted with your journeys. One form of journey you pass through is life as such. Are not the Buddhists the rational ones in their belief that the elimination of suffering should be the crux of our attention?

#9. What does Buddhism imply about our relationship to the Causative Force?

If Buddhists are right in their belief that suffering is something that needs our full attention, this implies a significance that may well be so immense it affects the Causative Force Herself.

•

"*Misery, pain, or suffering is not merely one among many other equally prominent features of experience. It is its chief and overriding feature.*" If suffering is so significant, would it seem logical that in some way it might impact eternity? Since existing in eternity is in essence existing in the Causative Force, then it would seem that suffering may well impact the Causative Force Herself.

Who wants to be the one consciously impacting the Causative Force in a negative manner? Who wants to be the one impacting other souls that lie within the Causative Force in a negative manner? If it is not you who wishes to do so, then what other choice do you have other than to follow the Buddhist concept of attempting to eliminate suffering?

•

Choices, free will? Some say we have "free will;" some say we are predestined. Each has their own impact to imprint upon our concept of the direction we take in life.

With predestination we have no choice; things have already been predestined. Perhaps some form of this is true, after all would we have chosen to come into a life filled with suffering, pain, abuse, rejection, envy, isolation... if we already existed within the arms of the Causative Force? However, if all is predestined, then our relationship to the Causative Force would take on the aspect of having been pre-planned. With predestination, all our suffering would be unavoidable. With predestination, your having to face the Causative Force, once having finished your journey through life, would have no impact upon your soul for where is the logic in a Causative Force holding you accountable for what She predestined would happen to you?

On the other hand, what if you are wrong? What if predestination is not the case? Then what are you to say when you return?

Conclusion: How do the concepts of Buddhism reinforce the concept of symbiotic panentheism?

It does not; what is really taking place is that symbiotic panentheism is reinforcing Buddhism.

•

Buddhism holds to the concept that suffering is one of the major causes that interferes with the intended journeys of the essence of the individual. Elimination of suffering completely will most probably never take place. That is why it needs to be the main orientation of each and every one of us. It is not a temporary task. It is an ever ongoing task.

Elimination of suffering is not to be drudgery or a guilt trip. If this occurs, you are not working at the task in the manner that is appropriate for your journey. In fact, under these conditions, you are creating suffering, for you have driven yourself into behaviors that create suffering for yourself. Find the work you enjoy doing. Find the contributions you can make to society through enjoyable hobbies, projects, recreation, volunteer work, occupations. Some actions may reduce suffering directly. Some actions may reducing suffering in the future. There is much to do and Buddhism has much to offer.

•

The Buddhist concept is simple. There has been, there is presently, there will always be (through natural occurrences) enough suffering for us to experience while journeying through this aspect of existence. Is some suffering an important part of our journey? Is some suffering needed for our souls to be exposed to? Perhaps, but the Buddhists believe there would be more than enough natural suffering left if we eliminated all the humanly initiated suffering.

Suffering has already been taken into the Causative Force from the past. Suffering that is being presently generated will enter the Causative Force. Suffering will be generated in the future that will return to the Causative Force. There has been, there is, there will continue to be more suffering. It is illogical to fear changing life for the better because there may not be enough suffering for the Causative Force. If the Causative Force is omniscient, She does not forget.

CHRISTIANITY
0 BC

*What new concept has Christianity
firmly established within the West?*

**One must address oneself
to the elimination of suffering.
The process to do so is to love one another.**

#0. What does the conceptual framework of *Christianity* have to offer us?

Life is to be lived in the light of an absolute perfection which requires of persons a similar, but proportional, perfection. They are to live with utter integrity – called purity of heart; they are to live with a wholeheartedness which excludes pride of any kind; they are to be sensitive to others – sensing the oneness of oneself and others, and ministering to human needs. They are to love one another.
Dictionary of Philosophy and Religion, William L. Reese, p. 119

•

How does one begin to eliminate suffering? One does so through love. Christianity brings the world the idea of love. Love existed before Christianity, but now Christianity teaches humankind to extend that love beyond family, lovers, and friends. One is to love all people regardless of who they are. Christianity teaches humankind to look beyond the differences that exist between each other and look towards the soul.

A black person is not black but a soul deserving of the same kind of love as a white person, for a white person is not white but rather a soul also. A woman is not a female and a man is not a male; they are both souls deserving of equal respect. A homosexual is not homosexual, an intellectual is not an intellectual, the strong are not strong, the weak are not weak, the physically challenged are not physically challenged; rather, they are all souls. Each soul came from the same place and will return to the same place.

The Christian religion teaches us to treat everyone with love, for the person is not what it appears to be. The person is a soul just as all people are. It is not at the body one must look to see the soul. It is deep within the eyes.

•

It wasn't love yourself, love your brother, love your mother, love those like you, love those who believe as you do, love those who act as you do. It was "love one another." One more step to understanding the size of the Causative Force. What does love have to do with size? Love itself has nothing to do with size, but the need for love, the reason love is so important to a Causative Force, may tell us much about Her size.

#1. What does the conceptual framework of Christianity imply about the universe within which we live?

We have two choices: to love one another in this universe or not to love one another. There are many key words in this statement, but the most significant is the word "choice."

•

Choosing to follow the teachings of Christianity leads to the development of a certain type of environment within which we and others around us will live, be they neighbor, children, spouse, friends. This environment, this atmosphere is what we call ambiance. This ambiance within which we live is created by two forces.

The first force, which develops the type of environment, atmosphere, ambiance within which we journey through life, is nature. What type of environment does nature provide for our soul's journey? She provides us with the beauty of a sunrise, glorious sunsets, cleansing rains, crisp blue winter skies, the smell of the ocean, the rush of the wind through forest tree tops, earth tones of the desert landscape, the majesty of glacial ice, the babble of a spring. Nature creates the surroundings within which we journey each day.

The second force is you and I. The second force is humanity. We make decisions regarding the behavior we take. We have the free will to choose. And what does this have to do with Christianity and the universe? Everything, for Christianity provides a simple guideline regarding how to use "free will." The guideline is told in three words, "love one another."

With these three words, billions of Christians since the beginning of 1 AD have committed themselves to the creation of developing a particular environment within which we all will travel as our souls journey through the universe. The atmosphere is one filled with love.

•

Love, hate, and the variations of what exists between. Love and hate are extremes of the atmosphere, ambiance, we intentionally create for ourselves. Christianity says to love one another. Is it any wonder Christianity is so important? Nature has done her job in creating an ambiance of wonder, beauty, and inspiration for us to journey within. The question now becomes, "What about the job we are doing?"

#2. How does the concept of Christianity reinforce the concept of panentheism?

Christianity establishes the idea that loving one another is so important an issue it must become a major focus in one's journey through life. What more important reason could exist for this than the idea that perhaps loving actions actually stay within and affect the Causative Force because She is truly omnipresent, panentheistic.

•

Christianity says God found it so important to bring the concept of loving one another to this universe that "He" sent "His" son into the world to accomplish this task. As Buddhists imply the existence of a Causative Force capable of feeling suffering, Christians imply the existence of a Causative Force capable of feeling love. In both cases, expanding the size of the Causative Force to true omnipresence would leave no place for the suffering and hatred we generate to go but into the Causative Force Herself. Under panentheism, suffering and love are elevated to a new level of significance for they impact the Causative Force Herself. Buddhist and Christian religions gain new levels of purpose through the acceptance of a truly all present Causative Force under a panentheistic perception of the size of the Causative Force.

•

If the concept of the Causative Force is one where the Causative Force transcends the universe, then it is possible that the actions we take also transcend the Causative Force, which in turn gives us a sense of relief. Relief through believing that what we do may not become a part of the Causative Force so perhaps the "bad" things we do are not so "bad" after all.

However, if the Causative Force is truly omnipresent, panentheistic, then our behavior and all of its ramifications have nowhere else to exist but within the Causative Force forever since the Causative Force is eternal. All of a sudden, we find ourselves unable to isolate our actions from the Causative Force. Panentheism forces us into a state of responsibility for eternity itself. Then what of loving one anther? Your actions become so important that the Causative Force might very well have found our actions as humans important enough to directly intervene with the direction our historically negative behavior was heading. The Causative Force may have decided to directly plant the seed of love. Not love based on conditions, but love given unconditionally to all.

#3. What does Christianity reinforce about the significance of existence, life?

Christianity clearly states that awareness not only exists in this physical state but exists in what is to follow. As such, love is a significant part of both.

•

Under Christianity, what you do in this life becomes a part of your existence, becomes a part of your eternal awareness, becomes something that is etched into your sense of being for eternity. The Christians believe "loving one another" is so important that the Causative Force directly intervened to plant such an idea into our society. This implies a significance for life. Life within this physical reality must have immense significance to the Causative Force Herself.

Christianity states that the actions you take during life are not isolated from the Causative Force. They believe the results of your actions and beliefs will follow you into the afterlife. If this concept is correct, then can there be any doubt life is significant? If we apply the concept of omnipresence to the Causative Force, the Christian perceptions and life itself become even more significant. Under a panentheistic, all present size of the Causative Force, the universe has nowhere else it can exist but within the Causative Force. You and your actions become a part of the Causative Force. Under panentheism, actions generated by love not only exist within but actually have an impact upon the Causative Force.

•

If you return to an all knowing Force and become a part of that Force, since you would be within Her, you very well may obtain access to Her knowledge. The result: you will not only be aware of what you did but you may become knowledgeable enough to empathize with the effect it had on others. The ripple effect never stops. As the wave diminishes, the diameter of the circle increases. As if this isn't enough, not only might you be aware of your own actions and their ripple effects, but so would the Causative Force. Is it any wonder that the Causative Force might consider it necessary to intervene directly with the direction of abuse and inhumanity our species initiate? What greater meaning could life have then to actually impact the eternal existence of the Causative Force?

#4. How does Christianity help us understand what life is?

Christianity tells us life is but one stage in your soul's eternal state of existence. Christianity also tells us that the best guideline you can use to make decisions regarding actions you should take in life is, "Love one another."

•

Love does not imply you give everything away. Love does not imply you are to sacrifice your journey for that of others. Love does not imply you are to be willing to live a life of misery in order to try to make others happy. To do so is to imply that your journey is of no value. The statement that your life has no value has profound negative impact.

To reduce the value of your life to a level below others is the first step in creating what is called hierarchy levels for life. What this means is, if you believe your life is worth less than another life, the process is started for one life to be judged to be of more value than another. This undermines the whole idea that the soul is not to be judged. This undermines the whole idea that "God created man in His image," for one image of the Causative Force cannot be less than another. Value systems used to judge the worth of one life over another open up the rationale for all the ...isms from racism to sexism. The Christian concept of loving one another includes loving yourself. Loving your neighbor as yourself is but one step in generating a 'positive' awareness which moves beyond the boundaries of our universe itself. The other step is loving yourself as your neighbor. Both of you have souls.

•

Actions are behaviors that affect life experiences of oneself and others, as Buddhists believe. What does this have to do with Christianity and love? Imagine everyday actions being performed with a sense of love and then imagine them being performed with a sense of jealously, hate or resentment. Love produces positive impacts that ripple through society and through the universe. Love acts to reduce suffering and impacts eternity accordingly.

#5. What does Christianity have to offer us as individuals?

The impact upon society of following such a concept as loving one another will directly affect the type of environment within which we as individuals travel.

•

There is no doubt that we sense we are traveling through life. As we do so, we make thousands of decisions regarding what types of actions, behavior, we take. Multiply this by billions of people and you have created a major impact, a major atmosphere within which we travel, a major ambiance. No longer is nature the chief source of ambiance. Humanity now becomes the major source of ambiance through which we, you and I, individuals, travel. Our souls, our essences, now journey through life immersed in a humanly created atmosphere. Now our journey through life is affected as much by each other as by natural events and observations. Loving one another becomes even more significant as our numbers, our influence upon the environment within which we all must travel, gain in significance over nature itself. We choose to create an environment of either looking out for ourselves or looking out for each other, loving one another.

•

If one senses the essence of one's self to be outside of the Causative Force (as religions say: a Causative Force is all present except She does not include the universe within Her), then your desires and needs become more important than the good of the whole. With this perception, we create an atmosphere of refusing to acknowledge the significance of other individuals. This leads to an atmosphere where everybody is out for themselves. Life is short. Grab what you can. Step on the next fellow to get what you want.

The smaller one perceives the Causative Force to be, the more acute this type of atmosphere becomes. A perception of the Causative Force being so small She does not exist, atheism, elevates a self serving perception to its ultimate. Taking another leap of size, the Causative Force is bigger than the universe but not big enough to include the universe, classical/traditional theisms, reduces the rationale for self serving actions even more.

On the other hand, by loving one another, what we are really doing is recognizing the significance of the individual. But this cannot be so unless we go beyond this eternity. This idea cannot be so unless we affect eternity itself or, to put it another way, affect the Causative Force. The most dynamic means of directly affecting the Causative Force would exist if we were located within Her, if all our actions remained within Her for eternity.

#6. What significance does Christianity have to offer us as a species?

The idea of loving one another impacts behavior we generate towards each other. It reduces suffering and improves upon individual journeys. This in turn generates a ripple effect that washes over society which directly affects our total species.

•

We are not alone in our physical existence. The most influential factor in our society that affects us are actions, our own actions and actions of others. By loving one another, we, in essence, are improving the environment for all the members of our species. Our actions create reactions which create reactions which create more reactions: a ripple effect.

The idea of loving one another is not just a case of taking an action that helps one person, but rather it is an action that ripples through the social fabric of our species. Suffering diminishes significantly the more people extend their love for one another. Natural events are difficult to control and there is no denying they can generate suffering. Our reactions towards people affected by these events, the intentional actions we as a society and as individuals generate after these events, can be wrapped in an aura of love or our actions to such events can be indifferent. Understanding the concept regarding why our actions today may affect what we experience in eternity could generate a major positive realignment of our way of thinking. It could have great impact on all of us.

•

Once having passed through this life state, Christianity implies you move into a new state of eternity. Panentheism implies you return to the only place there is and that is within the Causative Force. Having returned to the Causative Force, you take your awareness, which includes your experiences. But in addition to this, you are now privy to the knowledge of the Causative Force who is omniscient. This would mean you are privy to all the love others have experienced. Increasing love for each other in the world would in turn increase the amount of love that is being added to the Causative Force, which increases love you will experience in eternity.

#7. What significance does Christianity have to offer other life forms in the universe?

The climate through which we must travel as a species is up to us. Once we step off this earth, however, we take this atmosphere with us. As we come into contact with other planets and life forms, we will spread our influence, our sense of significance, the approach we take in terms of our behavior, to them.

•

As a totality of species throughout the universe, we develop an atmosphere, ambiance, through which we all must travel not only as individual species but as a total group. As a whole, a total group of species, we create an atmosphere through which we must travel not only as a group, but as a universe itself.

And where is all this impact going? It must be someplace very significant if it calls for us to consider "loving one another" to be the main guiding beacon for us as individuals and as a species. As we encounter other life forms in the heavens, are we to convert them to Christianity or are we to offer them the concept of Christianity to love one another? Are we to teach them that the Causative Force, in the form of a male human is what is of significance or are we to offer them the concept "He" offered us? Are we to offer them the concept that all life forms are significant in their own right, for their own uniqueness? An earthly Causative Force versus a universal one needs to be thought out before we encounter other life forms – not after the fact.

•

Do we like what we have to offer other life forms in the heavens? Do we like what we offered the Americans, North and South, when we came to these new lands back in the 1400s? Do we like what we had to offer the Jews during WWII? Do we like what we had to offer the Vietnamese and the Cambodians in the 1900s?

Panentheism would offer the concept of an all present Causative Force to all beings throughout the universe, for the universe would then be within the Causative Force – not just for humans, but for all beings. Christianity would then become universal as would Hinduism, Judaism, Buddhism, and Islam. The concepts of monotheism, the soul, eternal existence of the soul, unacceptance of suffering, loving one another, and justice would apply to all beings, all life forms in the universe.

#8. What does Christianity imply about our significance in eternity?

The concept of loving one another implies that each of us is significant, earthlings or otherwise. The soul is the soul. The soul is significant. The soul lies within the Causative Force and is a part of the Causative Force. Therefore, souls within vessels traveling this physical universe deserve the respect we as individuals sense is due the Causative Force.

•

If the universe existed within the Causative Force, and if this meant the impact of our actions remained within the Causative Force, then the ideas that Hinduism, Judaism, Buddhism, Christianity, and Islam offer would belong to all beings, not just earthly ones.

Christianity implies that our significance, the significance of the soul, is tied to eternity. Christianity also implies that eternity lies outside our universe which has a beginning–end concept. Under Christianity, the soul, lying outside the universe, has no beginning–end concept tied to it. The soul is eternal in the sense we understand eternity to be.

With panentheism, other life forms in the universe would have equal status with us. Now we would be able to rationalize what types of behaviors we should take to other beings in the universe. Now we would have an understanding of a basis upon which we would have to interact with souls, earthly or otherwise, not only as individuals but as a species.

Christianity would have a universal foundation upon which to analyze its role in the heavens. Christianity would have value which would extend to the boundaries of the universe by extending beyond the boundaries of the universe. "Loving one another" would gain a significance that not only affects this physical existence, but eternity itself.

•

Christianity, "loving one another," becomes a means to an end. The "end" is the elimination of suffering in order to reduce the impact of suffering upon eternity itself. Eternity is an experience you, I, all of us, earthly or otherwise, will have to experience. Eternity – a state of being we all are responsible for creating and the cementing factor in understanding that all religions are working toward a common cause to build an eternity we will all enjoy being immersed within.

#9. What does Christianity imply about our relationship to the Causative Force?

Christians, "they are to live with utter integrity – called purity of heart; they are to live with a whole-heartedness." This integrity is so important, one is not to live with simple integrity, but with "utter" integrity. The implication is that integrity is connected to our relationship to the Causative Force.

•

This is a journey in search of understanding. So far, there is little doubt that humankind has been gradually evolving along a path of increasing tolerance, acceptance, and a sense of connectedness not only to the Causative Force but to each other.

And now we have love to add to our sense of behavior towards each other. Why do we need a commitment to each other so intense that it actually becomes an act of loving one another? If it is another piece of the puzzle to be added to the picture regarding the size of the Causative Force, then increasing the size of the Causative Force to the largest size possible would elevate the significance of the Christian concept of love. Elevating the size of the Causative Force to that of complete totality would mean love and the effects of love would no longer be felt just in this physical universe, but would flow into the very heart of the Causative Force Herself. Love now becomes a true cementing agent to fuse the soul to the Causative Force and the Causative Force to the soul.

•

There is little doubt that Christianity, as did Hinduism, Judaism, Buddhism, and as we will see, Islam and many others, brings to the picture a reinforcement of the idea that we must be connected to each other in some truly significant fashion.

The ideas of a single Causative Force, the soul, eternal life of the soul, elimination of suffering, loving one another, and as we will see, justice, all were taking root upon our earth. But humankind was not exactly humane yet. We still treated each other as property, as a means to self serving goals, as just another way of getting what we wanted.

Something still seems to be missing. If the present size of the Causative Force does not allow us to accept other humans different than ourselves, then perhaps it is time to change something more. Perhaps it is time to change the size we assign our perceived Causative Force.

Conclusion: How do the concepts of Christianity reinforce the concept of symbiotic panentheism?

It does not; what is really taking place is that symbiotic panentheism is reinforcing Christianity.

•

Symbiotic panentheism is composed of two words: *symbiosis*, an interdependence, and *panentheism*. How is "loving one another" related to this idea? If the Causative Force is interdependent with us and we in turn with Her, and if the Causative Force is truly omnipresent, then "loving one another" is nothing less than loving the Causative Force.

Symbiotic panentheism elevates the size of the Causative Force to the maximum. Symbiotic panentheism elevates the concept of "loving one another" to the greatest level of significance. Christianity becomes a means by which the west has been given the message that the elimination of suffering is our ultimate goal. Buddhism and Christianity become soul mates under the concept of symbiotic panentheism. Buddhists are right; Christians are right.

•

Christianity does not suggest a limited love directed at just ourselves. The love here is a love extended to all. It means loving your wife, family, neighbor, countryman, and humans living across the vast seas of our planet, regardless of their race, color or creed. It means loving souls living across the vast sea of empty space which extends to the very boundaries of the universe.

Christianity does not place qualifiers on this love. It demands it be extended by you to all souls. It demands love be extended to souls you respect as well as souls you do not respect. Does this mean we, you as well as I, must respect everything other souls do? No, but it does mean we must respect the right of souls to take their own journeys as long as they do not interfere with the journeys of others.

"Loving one another" is the lesson Christianity professes each of us should give. There are no qualifiers in terms of who gets this love. It is to be extended to "one another," to all.

Islam
500 AD

What new concept has Islam firmly established within society?

Justice will not be denied.

#0. What does the conceptual framework of Islam have to offer us?

Islam: The term means "submission to God." The faith is characterized by an exclusive monotheism, the worship of Allah as the one true God, and Mohammed as the greatest of the prophets. Depending upon the degree of one's faithfulness and purity, one falls into the tortures of hell or feasting... The duties...payment of 2 percent poor tax... The ethical impulse of the movement would seem to have been powered more by justice than mercy.
Dictionary of Philosophy and Religion, William L. Reese, p. 349

•

What do Muslims bring to the world? As do Jews, Buddhists, and Christians, they continue the spread of the Hindu ideas of monotheism, the soul, and eternal life. Their worldwide influence reaches over one billion Muslims in the world. In addition, they bring a commitment to the Buddhist struggle against suffering and they bring something new into the total picture. Muslims bring the idea of justice as a part of not only this life, but the life to follow.

Justice, the idea of fair treatment and due reward in the afterlife, implies being responsible for one's actions in this life.

•

What does this idea of justice do for a Causative Force? The idea of fair treatment and due reward in the afterlife suggests that we have a responsibility in this life. It suggests that we all have a responsibility and we must all determine just what that responsibility is. However, since we are all significant, since we all have a responsibility, we must respect each person's attempt at accomplishing the responsibility each feels they have as individuals. We have no right to interfere with a person's journey in this life as long as that journey does not interfere with the journey of others.

Justice will be meted out by a force far greater, both in power and understanding, than ourselves. Justice will not be denied. Justice will be enforced in the life beyond this one. This whole concept of justice being a part of the afterlife releases us of the socially time-consuming burden involving agonizing over the just sentencing in a transgression. It would cause us to look at how to rectify the situation and how to prevent its happening to anyone in society again.

#1. What does the conceptual framework of Islam imply about the universe within which we live?

Islam tells us, beware, justice will prevail. It may or may not come in this universe but either way, it will come in the afterlife, in eternity.

•

Hinduism brings us the concepts of "a" Causative Force, an eternal soul, and the connection of the two. Judaism spreads the ideas to the West. Buddhism brings us the idea that suffering must not be tolerated. Christianity tells us to love one another, which is the first step to eliminating suffering. Islam tells us to take the concept of eliminating suffering seriously, for although justice may not prevail here on earth, there will be no escaping it in eternity. Buddhism for enlightenment, Christianity with love, Islam to avoid the repercussions, all point towards the same idea: work to eliminate suffering.

Islam, as well as the rest, does not imply these ideas are earthly ideas. It implies they are absolutes. They do not lack qualifiers. We have no right to say justice should apply in one case, but we will overlook it in another case. In other words, they are universal ideas which we are to take with us as we travel throughout the universe.

•

Under Islamic perceptions, in eternity, justice will prevail. You will face justice in regards to how well you met your responsibilities in your journey through life. But justice implies judgment and who would be willing to judge knowing they would have to face the results of "bad" judgment calls as well as the "good" ones in the hereafter?

Who will do the judging if it may imperil them in terms of their personal eternal state of being? Perhaps we should stop putting our fellow souls in jeopardy by calling upon them to judge. Perhaps it is time to eliminate, in our present life forms, the concept of judging. How do we do this and still protect journeys for which we all have a responsibility?

We could do so by accepting the Islamic concept that justice will prevail. We could start leaving justice to eternity. Now individual actions will not be examined in order to bring justice but rather to right wrongs, in order to prevent harm from being inflicted upon other journeys.

Accepting the Islamic belief that justice will prevail implies we would move from judging journeys to protecting journeys. We would move from being judgmental to rectifying wrongs imposed upon journeys, to protecting others from having their personal journeys infringed upon. The universe would now experience a nonjudgmental traveler, humanity.

#2. How do the concepts of Islam reinforce the concept of panentheism?

Islam establishes the idea that justice is so important an issue, it will not be denied. Reinforcing panentheism? Absolutely, for what better way to ensure justice than to make the Causative Force so big, omnipresent, that there is no way of escaping Her justice?

•

A Causative Force being so large, panentheistic, that all suffering stays within Her, is felt by Her. A Causative Force being so intent on reducing pain, She intervenes and plants a seed, an idea, in the minds of people on earth to change the tendency of generating such trauma, such suffering. The seed is love. To plant this seed, She is believed, by huge numbers of people, to have sacrificed something very dear to Herself.

Panentheism raises these ideas to a new level of significance and understanding, for now the idea of suffering and love become something felt by, impacting upon, the Causative Force. Under panentheism, there is nowhere else for the repercussions of the actions of suffering and love to go but into the Causative Force Herself.

So much is being said about suffering and love, but what about justice? What about Islam? Islam reinforces it all. Islam reinforces the need for each individual to strive to eliminate suffering. Islam reinforces the idea of the need to love one another unconditionally. Islam says that you will have to face the realization of the impact your actions had upon others in this life. You will have to face the realization of the impact your actions had upon the Causative Force Herself. Justice will not be denied.

•

Justice will not be denied is a concept so strongly sensed by almost a billion people that it has become the core concept of their faith. A billion people so sure of this concept that the idea of it not happening becomes something they cannot fathom. If Islamic beliefs are absolutes, they leave only one option open for a Causative Force and that is the size of true omnipresence, all presence. As such, there would be no escaping justice for there would be nowhere else for our souls to go after life but into the arms of a waiting Causative Force. The implication: think long and hard about your actions. You alone are responsible for them.

#3. What does Islam reinforce about the significance of existence, life?

Life exists. You exist. You choose the actions you take. You are responsible for your actions. Hinduism, Judaism, Buddhism, Christianity, and Islam say you will enter eternity after life. What could make life anymore significant than to know the Islamic concept was correct, you would be justly treated based upon your worldly actions?

•

Suffering exists around you and you ignore it. You will be fully aware of your actions in the afterlife, in eternity. Not only will you be aware of it, you will be aware of all the negative actions that generated ripple effects. You will be justly treated in your afterlife in eternity. This Islamic perception reinforces the impact life has upon eternity and reinforces the significance of life itself.

Suffering exists and you reach out with compassion, love. You will be aware of all your actions generated through ripple effects. You will be justly treated in your afterlife. This Islamic perception reinforces the impact life has upon eternity and reinforces the significance of life itself.

•

Now take the universe and place it inside the Causative Force. Now your actions, positive and negative, have no way out. Your actions not only affect you and your environment, but also affect others and their environments. These actions become a part of the Causative Force. Your actions actually impact upon the Causative Force. Justice takes on a new aspect. Now justice elevates the significance of life to a new level.

But what of the Christian concept of forgiveness? Islamic beliefs do not necessitate the rejection of such an idea. The Causative Force may very well forgive you for any wrongdoings you imposed upon Her just as a parent would forgive a child. This would no doubt ease your sense of empathy, but would it mean you completely forget the incident? And what of others you abused in life? Can the Causative Force override their emotional and physical pain? Can the Causative Force forgive you for them? Or do they have to do so themselves? And even if they did forgive you, could you ever forget the damage you inflicted upon them if you exist in an omnipresent, omniscient being? Empathy and justice in an eternity of total knowledge, omniscience. Can it ever stop?

#4. How does Islam help us understand what life is?

Islam tells us life is but one stage in our soul's eternal state of existence. Islam also tells us that this stage is not a fantasy. Life is real. You will be held accountable for actions within it.

•

Christians hold to the idea that life is significant and as such must be lived immersed in total, unconditional love. They go on to say that you must go through life living with "utter integrity." What does this have to do with Islamic beliefs? If justice will not be denied, then having to face the repercussions of one's actions will just be a natural occurrence that goes along with existence.

Trust is based upon truth. Truth is based upon integrity. The more integrity one has, the closer one comes to the description of "utter integrity." Therefore, to live a life of "utter integrity," one must commit oneself to a life of truth embraced in love. But why would this be so? People being distrustful of others generates an environment filled with suspicion.

Actions such as physical abuse, mental abuse, verbal abuse, lying, generating rumors, breaking confidences, dishonesty, subjugation, using others for personal gain, rape, murder, and assault, all generate an atmosphere of distrust. Suffering is generated. Suffering is not only generated by such actions, but intentionally generated by such actions. Being intentionally inflicted with pain by one's fellow soul generates a different kind of pain than that generated by natural causes. Intentionally generated pain strikes to the very depths of one's being. Intentionally generated pain strikes to the heart of the soul itself, for this type of suffering is generated by one soul against another. This type of pain is generated by the breaking of trust between fellow souls, brothers, sisters, pieces of the Causative Force. What does Islam have to say about all this? Justice will not be denied.

•

Islam says that life is but one phase in existence, for the existence of the soul is eternal. Eternal life – never forgetting, forever empathizing with the impact of one's actions. Eternity – forever being aware. No wonder Islamic believers place so much emphasis upon understanding the concept that justice will not be denied. No wonder Christians place so much emphasis on loving one another. No wonder Buddhists place so much emphasis upon working to eliminate suffering. Justice will not be denied.

#5. What does Islam have to offer us as individuals?

Islam offers us the comfort of knowing that we do not need to look for justice in this life. Islam offers us the comfort that justice will not be denied. Justice will be an eternal state of being.

•

The actions one takes, the actions one has to face, cannot be forgotten if one passes from this life form into an eternal state of being as the Muslims state. If the Causative Force is omnipresent, as they also state, then the only place for actions one generates and for the repercussions of those actions to go is inside the Causative Force. The only place the love generated or the pain experienced would have to go would be within the Causative Force if She is omnipresent, for there is nowhere else.

Are you responsible for your actions? Will you be held accountable for them? Will others be held accountable for their actions? Will justice prevail? You need to answer these questions yourself, for if you pass from this life into another, a spiritual life immersed in an omnipresent Causative Force – existing everywhere – and an omniscient Causative Force – all knowledgeable – then wouldn't you know the answer to these questions at that time? Wouldn't being fully aware of the answer and being fully capable of experiencing the pain and emotions that were the results of your actions be a form of judgment? Perhaps the Islamic idea of justice not being denied is an absolute.

•

But what of reducing the suffering of others? What has that to do with you? Once having passed through this life state, Islam implies you move into a new state of eternity. Panentheism implies you return to the only place there is and that is within the Causative Force. Having returned to the Causative Force, you take with you your awareness which includes your experiences. But in addition to this, you are now privy to the knowledge of the Causative Force who is omniscient. This would mean you are privy to all the suffering others have experienced. Reducing suffering in the world would in turn reduce the amount of suffering of our species that is being added to the Causative Force, which also reduces your suffering.

#6. What significance does Islam have to offer us as a species?

Each piece of suffering that is intentionally overlooked will be justly dealt with. This does not apply to only your individual actions, but to the actions generated by the society within which you live.

•

Being responsible for our own actions is one thing but being responsible for the results of the actions generated by the societies within which we live is another. Why would we be responsible? Why would we have to face the repercussions of the ripples societies and our species generate? How can we, individually, be held accountable for torture imposed upon other individuals if our government is a ruthless dictatorship? You are not responsible for that, are you? What of a ruthless crime organization that exists within your society or neighborhood? What of drug cartels and the suffering they generate? They exist in distant countries. What about starvation, ignorance, abuse, disease; you are not responsible, are you?

You exist in a society. Society is not a thing. Society is not an entity of its own. Society is the total sum of actions generated by the people that exist within it. Society may be ruled by ruthless dictators, but it is done so only because the people living within that society allow it to be so. Society may be governed by a vote of the people, but it is the effort or lack of effort of the people within that society that allows government to ignore the subjugation of the oppressed. Society may decide to electrocute the mass murderer, but it is the individuals in society which create the atmosphere, the ambiance, within society that allows such actions to take place. But you say, "I didn't do it! I didn't do it!!" Ah, but in the end, if there is an eternity to which we go, if we have free will, if we are not just puppets, accountability has to be reckoned with. Justice implies answering two questions, not one: "Did you do it, did you encourage it?" and "Could you have done anything to prevent the journey of others from being interfered with?"

•

But we are only human. Are we, or are we souls in human bodies? Are we capable of taking action? Are we capable of working to eliminate suffering by loving one another? Will we be held accountable? Will justice be denied or are the Islamic beliefs correct?

#7. What significance does Islam have to offer other life forms in the universe?

Islam offers all life forms the concept of justice. Islam offers all life forms throughout the universe the comfort of knowing that their pain and suffering will be addressed. Islam offers all life forms throughout the universe the right to travel unimpaired. Islam offers all life forms the right to expect to be treated with love and dignity.

•

As a total group of species, human and otherwise, throughout the universe, we develop an atmosphere, ambiance, through which we all must travel. If the Causative Force is omnipresent, all present, than all actions taken by all species throughout the universe would have nowhere else to go but into the Causative Force Herself. As such, all species throughout the universe will act together to impact upon the Causative Force and what She will be when we end our physical journey and pass on and into the Causative Force Herself.

As such, justice will not be denied. Is there anymore that can be said to better explain what will happen if Islam is correct in what her billion followers sense through faith? The perceptions sensed by the followers of the Islamic faith include eternal life and justice. These concepts do not apply to just one species. The principle applies as a truth. The principle applies to all life forms throughout the universe. Islam has justice to offer all souls.

•

Domination, subjugation, abuse, using others, lack of integrity, lack of loving behavior, all will be dealt with through justice in the state of being we occupy after this part of our journey is over. For now, we need to protect our own journeys from being completed in the manner we individually sense our personal journeys are to proceed. We need to protect the journeys of others to proceed likewise. We need to remove the impediments some souls have placed in the way of our own paths as well as the paths of others.

We do not need to worry about revenge or seeking justice for the wrongs committed against ourselves or others. But we have a responsibility to actively and aggressively make certain that wrongs committed against our journeys do not happen again and that they do not happen to others. This is what Islam has to offer all life forms, earth creatures or otherwise.

#8. What does Islam imply about our significance in eternity?

Islam holds to the idea of eternal life. The life we presently have is only temporary. But they believe there is a reason for this journey and it has significance. To interfere with this significance is to interfere with a purpose intended by the Causative Force and will be dealt with justly.

•

If Islamic beliefs are correct, if we have a soul and if that soul is tied to eternity, then traveling through one day or one hundred years is in a sense the same. One day or one hundred years is almost nothing when compared to eternity. The journey through life either has a purpose or it does not. Either way, we have to make a decision regarding the actions we take in life. But do we have to make a choice? Yes, for even if we do not make a choice, we have made a choice. By not making a choice as to whether or not we believe life has a purpose, we have decided not to address the issue and leave it unresolved. We have assigned the concept of purposelessness to our existence.

Islam, by declaring that justice will take place in the afterlife, in eternity, has taken the stand that life is important, has significance, has purpose. In addition, this purpose is so significant that justice will be an absolute in eternity. The bottom line: do not interfere with the purpose of other journeys; do not interfere with the reason the Causative Force allowed the journeys to take place. Respect the journeys of others or face the consequences of resultant justice.

•

If life has no purpose, the decisions we make have no meaning. To discuss the issue makes no sense in terms of eternal existence. Therefore, to discuss this aspect is interesting but nonproductive in terms of eternity.

On the other hand, if there is a purpose to traveling through life, then the decisions we make in life do have meaning. To discuss the issue makes sense in terms of eternal existence itself. Therefore, to discuss this aspect is not only interesting but has the potential of being productive in terms of our very eternal existence.

And what of our existence in eternity? Islamic beliefs assign justice as one of the predominant characteristics we will find there.

#9. What does Islam imply about our relationship to the Causative Force?

Islamic belief in justice being one of the primary elements of eternity implies that life in not only significant but very significant. Why else would justice be a major part of eternity, which in turn is a primary characteristic of the Causative Force?

•

But does the Causative Force pass out justice out of vengeance? Vengeance does not appear to be a necessary trait for an all knowing, all powerful, all present entity. Vengeance is usually a trait that applies to "little" entities attempting to display power.

Vengeance is defined as "the infliction of punishment in return for a wrong committed." Attempting to accomplish one's tasks in life, one's purpose, is all one can humanly do. A Causative Force expecting more of Her creations is unreasonable, especially for an entity as powerful and knowledgeable as the Causative Force.

Assisting other souls to do likewise, assisting other souls to accomplish their purposes, would seem to be an action that would reap positive rewards. It isn't a case of being idealistic; it is a case of being practical. After all, if one is to face justice for eternity, what justice, "due reward and fair treatment," would one prefer to face: justice for assisting the Causative Force or justice for interfering with the Causative Force?

•

But what of "justice?" Is it not the "infliction of punishment for a wrong committed?" No, justice is a giving process. One receives "due reward" and "fair treatment" depending upon one's accomplishment of what one was sent to do. This is not punishment; this is simply reaping the fruits of one's labors.

The ideas of a single Causative Force, the soul, eternal life of the soul, elimination of suffering, loving one another, and as we will see, justice, all were taking root upon our earth. But humankind was not exactly humane yet. We still treated each other as property, as a means to self serving goals, as just another way of getting what we wanted.

Something still seems to be missing. If the present size of the Causative Force does not allow us to accept other humans different than ourselves, then perhaps it is time to change something more. Perhaps it is time to once more change the size we assign our perceived Causative Force.

Conclusion: How do the concepts of Islam reinforce the concept of symbiotic panentheism?

They do not; what is really taking place is that symbiotic panentheism is reinforcing Islam.

	•

If the Causative Force is "all present" as Islam, Judaism, Christianity, and other traditional theisms state, then the only place for your soul to travel, once it departs this universe, is into the Causative Force Herself. This is the concept of panentheism.

If there is meaning to life, a purpose for the essence of the individual traveling within this physical reality, then for the soul to have to directly enter the Causative Force would imply the need of the Causative Force for whatever it is the soul was to accomplish while it existed within the physical universe. If there were no need, there would be no purpose. The need on the part of the Causative Force for whatever it is the soul was to accomplish suggests the Causative Force needs us. It is already accepted by the majority of our species that we need the Causative Force. Now the suggestion is being made that the Causative Force needs us. [This will be established in the sections dealing with Science, Philosophy, and Prophecy.] This interdependence is known in science as "symbiosis." But what of justice? The Islamic implication is that one had better not interfere with this interdependence of the Causative Force and individual souls. Any interference and obstruction causing the soul to accomplish its necessary goal for the Causative Force will be met with the repercussions meriting the severity of the interference, the severity of obstructing the symbiotic relationship that exists between the Causative Force and the soul.

	•

Interfering with the Causative Force Herself. Interfering with the work of the soul. Justice, "due reward," will be applied accordingly. What more needs to be said about the negative implications this could have for your own soul?

Assisting the Causative Force. Assisting with the work of souls. Justice, due reward, will be applied accordingly. What more needs to be said about the positive implications this could have for your own soul? Islamic justice says it well.

ONTOLOGY
1000 AD

*What new concept has Ontology
(debating a Causative Force without religion)
firmly established within society?*

**Perception generates behavior.
Global perception generates global behavior.
Universal perception will generate universal behavior.**

#0. What does the conceptual framework of ontology, a philosophical perception of a Causative Force, have to offer us?

An argument for God which moves from the definition of His nature as a perfect being to the conclusion that He exists. The argument has several versions.

(1) It was first formulated by Anselm (q.v. 1–3) who gave two different versions of the argument: one from "the being than which none greater can be conceived," the other from the conception of a necessary being, to the existence of that being.

Dictionary of Philosophy and Religion, William L. Reese, p. 534

•

In short, this states that "the conception of a necessary being" leads to the existence of that being. Why do we as a species seem to constantly seek a Causative Force? We perceive our universe to be filled with beginning–end items. Life begins and ends. Rivers begin and end. The atmosphere begins and ends. Our earth appears to have begun and we believe it will end. Our sun appears to have had a beginning billions of years ago and we believe it will someday come to an end. We think our galaxy had a beginning and we assume it may someday end. We even talk of "the beginning of our universe" and speculate upon when and how it will end.

Because we believe our universe had a beginning and will probably come to an end, there is a need in our minds for a force that would have originated our universe. That force we call the Causative Force. Since we conceive of the need for the Causative Force, we assume it exists.

•

Some would say we could apply the characteristic of no beginning to the universe just as well as to a Causative Force. This, however, would call for the complete reversal of the direction that science is headed. The investigative process of science is leading towards the Hindu concept that occasionally the universe ends, is "dissolved." Scientifically, it is not expressed as such, but the end result is the same as the Hindu concept.

#1. What has ontology taught us about the universe within which we live?

Philosophically, it makes sense that the universe had a beginning since everything within it seems to be based upon a beginning–end format.

•

A beginning–end format to everything within the universe implies that the vessel, the boundary, within which our universe is located likewise has a beginning–end character.

If the boundaries of our universe have no beginning–end character, then it would be entirely different from everything within it. It would be highly unlikely that the "container" would not contain some of the characteristics of its contents. For example, a bottle is made out of matter in order to hold matter.

Since the interior portion of the boundary would be within, the interior portion of the boundary of the universe would most probably have a beginning–end character just as do the items contained within the boundaries, the stars, the planets, life forms, etc. The whole of the boundary would, therefore, tend to assume the same character.

To put it another way, it would be uncharacteristic of a boundary not to have some of the most basic, primal characteristics of the items which lie within it and vice versa; it would be uncharacteristic of items within a vessel to have none of the most basic, primal characteristics of the boundaries within which they were located.

•

The universe is said to have been created from "nothingness." If this is the case, the Causative Force, if it is all present, omnipresent, would appear to need to take on some other characteristics of the universe other than time, for time itself would have been a component of the creation from "nothingness." Time would therefore appear to be a function of mass and energy.

Items within the Causative Force would logically have some of the characteristics of the Causative Force and vice versa. Therefore, applying the Hindu concepts of monotheism, the soul, and eternity; the Buddhist concept of intolerance of suffering; the Christian concept of loving one another; and the Islamic concept of justice to the Causative Force Herself may not be illogical after all.

#2. How does ontology reinforce the concept of panentheism?

A Causative Force being, as religions say, omnipresent is panentheism.

•

Panentheism did not assign the characteristic of omnipresence to the Causative Force. This was done by religions. Panentheism is not an entity. It is not an organization. Panentheism is not an institution. It is not a person. "Panentheism" is a word and nothing more. It cannot be worshipped anymore than the word "blue," "big," "short," "nice" or "good" can be worshipped. "Panentheism" is just a word that describes the size of the Causative Force, meaning She is so big, the universe must be inside Her.

Panentheism is simply a statement of size. The American Indians, the Hindus, the Buddhists, etc. are panentheistic for they all held to the concept that the Causative Force is omnipresent. Ontology would imply that if an entity is defined as being all present, omnipresent, which is what traditional religions of Judaism, Christianity, Islam, etc. do, then they cannot qualify that by saying, "But the universe is not in the Causative Force."

•

Many present day religions profess the concept of panentheism through declaring that the Causative Force is omnipresent. They then go on and say this isn't so because the Causative Force transcends the universe. But you cannot have it both ways. Either the Causative Force is omnipresent, all present, or it isn't. Either the universe is within the Causative Force or it isn't. Many religions do not want to accept the concept that the universe lies within the Causative Force because they cannot rationalize an apparently imperfect universe existing within a perfect Causative Force.

Thinking creatively, this paradox can be dealt with differently than through the elimination of the omnipotence of the Causative Force. A model of an imperfect universe being located within a perfect Causative Force can be constructed using the basic beliefs of Hinduism, Judaism, Buddhism, Christianity, Islam, ontology, and science. By reassembling these basic building blocks, a model can be built explaining a state of imperfection within a state of perfection through molding "nothingness" into "something." This is a process only recently understood by science.

Such a model is described in the book *You & I Together* in this trilogy.

#3. What does ontology reinforce about the significance of existence, life?

A philosophical perception of a Causative Force would imply significance for life. An entity to create something as complex and large as we perceive our universe to be logically implies a reason for doing so.

•

Why a Causative Force chose to create a universe and life is not something we can identify with certainty. We can, however, come up with some considerably logical reasons. These reasons would be logical based upon our perceptions. But what perceptions do we have to base assumptions upon? And what are these perceptions? They are the ideas of monotheism, an eternal soul, suffering is not necessary, loving one another, justice, logic, and observation.

•

What perceptions do we have that we can use as a foundation upon which we can start building universal philosophical perceptions? We can use perceptions which the vast majority of us as a species perceive to be true. Are there such perceptions? Certainly. The perceptions may not be held by all, nor may they be held to be the core of their particular beliefs, but they do seem to be held by the majority of us in one form or another.

The understanding of what the Causative Force is and just why it would have gone to the effort of creating a universe is therefore not an impossible task to address. It is one that can be done using philosophy to fuse basic religious assumptions that we as a species have incorporated into our society. They are assumptions science has made through observing the universe within which we perceive.

And what do our faiths and observations lead us to understand? They lead us to the understanding that there is "a" Causative Force to the universe (science). The Causative Force is panentheistic: omnipresent, omnipotent, and omniscient. The Causative Force is eternal and is tied to the soul (Hinduism), does not like suffering (Buddhism), is loving (Christianity), is just (Islam), and can grow through learning knowledge that does not yet exist (science).

#4. How does ontology help us understand what life is?

Life *is a word. What it refers to needs defining.*

•

Life is a term scientists, religious institutions, and philosophers have avoided defining. The reason for their avoidance of the task is fear. Each is afraid that if it defines the term *life* in respect to their particular area of perception, be it observation (science), faith (religion) or logic (philosophy), then the remaining two areas will criticize the one that had the courage to define it. Is this paranoia? Hardly. Each area is struggling against the other in an attempt to elevate their own importance just as we humans do.

This is not an irrational perception. Defining something as important to us as life is too large a responsibility for any one perception, be it religion, science or philosophy, to define on its own. The definition of life needs to be able to encompass all three means by which we perceive ourselves: faith, logic, and observation.

The lack of a definition for life creates problems in society that appear to have no solutions. The solutions presented are not based upon a definition of life because there is no definition. As an example, the abortion issue appears to have no solution because science, religions, and philosophy have not come to a mutual definition of life. Until science, religion, and philosophy come to a mutual understanding, a consensus, of what life is, the social dilemma of abortion will remain with us as will the social dilemmas of assisted suicide, religious conversion of aliens, creation of artificial intelligence, cloning, fetal tissue research... Defining life is crucial to our development as individuals and as a species.

•

Defining concepts is just putting the perceptions we have into words. Nothing can be proved to be absolute. Nothing can be proved to "be." Even existence is assumed to be a truth but remains unprovable nevertheless.

We have little choice but to press on with existence. There is nothing depressing about this idea. We must recognize and accept the situation of our existence in our universe as what we perceive is happening and as such, begin to deal with this concept by doing what is probably the most important task we have at hand. We must define what life is.

#5. What significance does ontology have to offer us as individuals?

Understanding what life is in terms of our universe and in terms of where our universe as an entity lies will lay the foundation for what we perceive ourselves to be as individuals and explain why we exist within the universe.

•

A philosophical definition of life will have to be broad enough to include our connection to the Causative Force even if it means no connection. Such an empty definition, however, would undermine the basic fundamentals of all religions but atheism. The fear of such a definition developing out of a cooperative effort on the part of science, religion, and philosophy need not be a concern. There is no way such a conclusion would ever be able to gain the consensus of the majority of our species. It goes contrary to the beliefs of the world's major religions. It refutes the stand of almost all renowned philosophers, and it contradicts almost all scientific observations concerning the concept of beginning–end formats within our universe.

Then what of a definition of life? The definition of life could never gain consensus unless it acknowledged a Causative Force as well as our connection to it. This type of definition would do nothing but substantiate our significance, not only in this physical universe but in terms of our connection to the Causative Force Herself.

•

A philosophical definition of life would have to be general enough to be acceptable to the vast majority of individuals making up the segments of religion, science, and philosophy, which would include the concept of a Causative Force, the essence of the individual, and the interconnection of the two.

#6. What significance does ontology have to offer us as a species?

If we as individuals have significance, then we as a total group, a species, have significance.

•

The important point here is that the significance of the individual comes before the significance of the species. It is the soul, the essence of the individual, that we perceive to have significance. To say otherwise is to deny the individual a soul. Humankind always seems to advance when it acknowledges the individual status over social structure. We have tried many times throughout history to elevate the institution or a social concept over the individual. It has always failed. We have always ended up not only reverting back to the significance of the individual, but each reversion has only increased our perception of the value of the individual.

We do not appear to be an organism capable of denying the significance of the individual, the essence of the individual, the individual soul. This would imply that the significance of our species must come through the significance of the individual. This in turn implies that our species is not where the soul lies, but rather the individual is where the soul lies. We study history, lest we forget.

•

This concept is crucial for it leads us as a species in a totally different direction than does the concept that the species is what is important. Defining life in a manner that elevates the individual over the species in no way endangers the species, for there is no denying the understanding that with the elimination of the species comes the elimination of the significance of what human individuals have to offer a Causative Force.

However, elevating the individual to a level over the species means eliminating the concept that the end justifies the means. The state does not take precedent over individual rights to journey freely, for it is the individual that contains the soul and makes the contribution. The state is just an institution intended to aid this journey rather than vice versa. The institution, likewise, does not take precedence over the individual, for it is just an institution whose purpose is to aid the soul to be in this universe; the purpose for the soul is to journey.

#7. What significance does ontology have to other life forms in the universe?

With the establishment of the significance of the individual over the state and over the institution comes the establishment of the individual over the state and the institution. This is not double speak. This is critical, for with this concept comes the recognition of the same for other life forms in the universe.

•

This is a crucial, crucial point. As soon as we take the direction that it is the species that holds the significance of life, we elevate the significance of the state and institutions over that of individuals. The elevation of the species over the individual is the recognition that existence within this physical state of the universe is important, which in turn denies the existence of the individual's access to eternity and denies the significance of the individual soul.

The only way we can reverse the behavior patterns we have taken in the past regarding our abusive actions toward different ideas, races, religions, creeds, etc., is to start looking at the individual in terms of his or her essence or what we define as the soul, what we define as life. This is crucial not only to us but to all environments and life forms we will encounter in the heavens.

•

If other life forms are out in the heavens and if they are watching or listening to us (our radio and TV waves travel away from the earth), they must be very concerned. They have much to be concerned about. Our history channels, our news broadcasts are not very encouraging. We have not yet defined what we are and as such, we tolerate and encourage much abusive behavior toward each other.

If we abuse each other, fellow humans, fellow souls, so easily, so universally, why would we even begin to hesitate abusing other life forms that may exist in the heavens? They may not appear just a little different, but may appear radically different. Why would we hesitate taking resources from another life form's planet if we don't even hesitate doing it to one of our own, those to whom we can identify physically? They must be worried indeed. How would they deal with a new species, with us, when we haven't even defined what we are or why life is important?

#8. What does ontology imply about our significance in eternity?

A philosophical acceptance of a Causative Force being omnipresent would imply our existence lies within the universe which in turn lies within this Causative Force. To put it another way, omnipresence implies we, you and I, are a part of the Causative Force.

•

Having the possibility of being eternal would force us into thinking about the connection our present state of existence has with our next state of existence – the afterlife. This in turn would create a need to elevate our behavior in this present state of being. This need to elevate behavior may come out of fear, concern or understanding of how our actions may affect our eternal state of being.

Humanity, individual humans, have always risen to a challenge. If we set our purpose for existence high, we will rise to the occasion. And what of eternity? If we are to move from here to there, from life to eternity, we would carry with us what we know. What do we want to take with us into eternity? Do we want to take the perception that we have no significance in eternity, or do we want to take the perception that we have great significance?

•

Nobody would dispute that we have some form of potential as individuals and as a species. Lowly goals elicit lowly behavior. This lowly behavior is simply the confusion generated from having no direction towards which to direct one's energy since one has already attained one's goals.

If on the other hand, one sets goals that are slightly beyond reach, the energy one has will never lack direction. This is not to say all goals should be of such a nature, for such action undoubtedly would generate defeatism. But the loftier goals, the ultimate goals, the understanding of our connection and significance to eternity and the Causative Force needs to be lofty enough so that all individuals, human or otherwise, cannot ever attain it in total, for they will assume they have the right to control all others that have not attained it.

Refusing to accept our significance to eternity leaves us where we are. Is that so bad? Perhaps we could better answer that question if we would put ourselves in the position of other life forms in the heavens looking in our direction in order to see what type of neighbors we would make.

#9. What does ontology imply about our relationship to the Causative Force?

Understanding the logic behind a Causative Force would strengthen our religious faiths and our confidence in our scientific observations.

•

We have always had some doubt about our faiths. This is understandable for they are not something we can prove. If they were provable, then we would not have to believe through faith. They would not be religions. Being unprovable is not to say they are not correct. Quite the contrary. What it does say is that we as individuals have the ability to sense what is right and what is wrong, not just in terms of behavior, but in terms of what exists. We have not denied our ability to do so and as such, we have formed religions and lived by their doctrines. In other words, we have had "faith" in our ability to sense things we cannot see or prove.

Science also has had its problems of faith in itself. Cosmology is beginning to take seriously the idea that the universe began with an explosion and is expanding. This presents the problem of what happens when it expands so far out that no star is near another. What happens when the stars burn out? But this is not the most perplexing problem science has. Their most perplexing problem now appears to be what happens when the expansion reverses itself and we begin to contract into what we were before the explosion. Science, like religion, is patient but it, too, has its doubters.

Logic, a philosophical understanding of a Causative Force would definitely help bolster the confidence in both regarding their understanding of our relationship with the Causative Force.

•

An understanding of the Causative Force would undoubtedly provide reassurances to both religion and science. This would provide reassurances to all of us as individuals and as a species as well. This understanding could, if we wanted it to, connect us logically to a Causative Force. Our connection to a Causative Force would force us into a strengthened mode of "positive behavior," a less abusive form of behavior towards each other. Defining a significant relationship with, rather than to, a Causative Force would direct us toward potentially less abusive behavior in regards to other life forms in the universe.

Conclusion: How does ontology, the concept of a philosophical perception of a Causative Force, reinforce the concept of symbiotic panentheism?

It does not; what is really taking place is that symbiotic panentheism is reinforcing ontology.

•

Argument one: If we believe the Causative Force has always existed, it would be just as reasonable to say, "No, it was our universe that always existed." It is not faith that makes such a statement unreasonable, but logic. Our universe appears to be based upon a beginning–end time concept.

Argument two: If our universe had a beginning and the initiator is called the Causative Force, then couldn't the Causative Force have had an initiator? Perhaps, but that is not what is of importance to us at this point in our universe. Then why concern ourselves about a Causative Force at all? Because our understanding, our perception of what we are, where our universe is located, determines the significance we believe we may have. It also determines the significance of what we believe other life forms in the universe may have. This perception will determine not only how we behave toward ourselves as individuals and as a species, but more importantly, it will determine how we behave toward other life forms in the heavens.

•

A philosophical perception is simply another way of saying a logical perception. Since our universe seems to be based upon beginning–end formats, it only seems logical that the universe had a beginning. From this, it only seems logical that something, some force, had to start the process. This force is what is defined as "the" Causative Force.

The existence of time implies that our universe, physical existence in time, is not the ultimate state of existence, for time implies a beginning and an end. And so it is that the need for the Causative Force arose. The argument for a Causative Force was, "first formulated by Anselm...the conception of a necessary being, to the existence of that being." Who was Anselm? Was he an atheist? No, he was St. Anselm of the Roman Catholic Church, the largest Christian religion in the world.

MODERN SCIENCE
1500 AD

*What new concept has Science
firmly established within society?*

**We cannot ignore
what we see.**

#0. What does the conceptual framework of modern science have to offer us?

> *Copernicus, Nicolas, 1473–1543 ... Architect of the heliocentric theory of the solar system.*
> Dictionary of Philosophy and Religion, William L. Reese, p. 140

•

You cannot ignore what you see, and with this idea, a new understanding developed. We were not the center of the universe. With this announcement, modern science took its place as one more means by which we, as individuals and as a species, were able to understand our position, our purpose, our perceptions of what we are. Modern science brought us the realization that we cannot ignore what we see.

Ptolemy's idea of the earth being the center of the heavens had been accepted for over 1,400 years. Copernicus made this idea a thing of the past. The earth, which humankind claimed as its home, was no longer understood to be the center of the universe. Humankind was no longer at the center. The sun was now assumed to be the center. But science was not going to stop there. Science would proceed to move the center of the universe even further from earth. As time progressed, science learned our sun was far from the center of the Milky Way Galaxy. Science would teach us our sun was only one of the millions upon millions of stars making up this galaxy. Our galaxy would then lose its proximity to the center of the universe as we discovered the existence of millions upon millions of other galaxies, all similar to our own. Millions of galaxies, trillions of stars, science was expanding our universe and with it, expanding our understanding of the size of the Causative Force. Modern science was offering each of us humility.

•

Humility is the state of being humble, not proud. It was the Christians that believe people "are to live with a whole-heartedness which excludes pride of any kind." Even so, it was to be the Christians that were to have the greatest difficulty accepting the idea that "man" was not the center of creation. Even today, we have not let go of the idea that we are, somehow, the center. We will not let go of being the center until we understand our significance is not tied to being the center of things.

#1. What does the conceptual framework of modern science imply about the universe within which we live?

Modern science leads to the understanding that the universe is big, really big, in comparison to the human body.

•

Size becomes an idea of our universe that we think we are beginning to understand. We realize we are not the center of this huge quantity of space within which we exist. Space, in fact, appears so vast, we have a sense of loss in terms of understanding just where we are within it. We don't know where we are in the universe.

With this statement, questions come rushing in. Where is the center of the universe? How big is the universe? Does the universe have a boundary? Can we step through the boundary? Are we confined to the universe? Are there other universes? Are there parallel universes? Are there nonparallel universes? Are there other life forms scattered throughout the universe? Are there other life forms within other universes? Why do we exist in this universe? Why does the universe exist? Will the universe expand to the point of breaking its boundary and explode? Will the universe ever dissolve? What lies outside the universe? How big is whatever lies beyond our universe? Did some "thing" create the universe? Did the universe have a beginning? How will the universe end? Does the universe have a purpose? If the universe has no purpose, why does it exist? If the universe has a purpose, what is it? Why do we exist in the universe? Do we have any significant impact upon the universe as a whole? Do we have significance to what may lie beyond the universe?

The questions go on and on. Modern science has not brought us to the end of questions. Modern science has brought us to the beginning of understanding why we need religion. Modern science clearly demonstrates just how insignificant we are in terms of the space the universe occupies. This space seems to go on forever and we as individuals seem to occupy so little of it. We need faith more than ever before. We need religion now more than ever. Without religion, we will lose hope in the vastness of space.

•

Modern science reinforces the need for religion as a path for us to follow.

#2. How do the concepts of modern science reinforce the concept of panentheism?

Our universe appears to have size. Size implies a limit. A limit implies something outside the limit. The universe appears to have an "outside."

Science is beginning to believe our universe has a limit and is bounded. Most religions believe the Causative Force is bigger than the universe, transcends the universe. As such, the universe is not omnipresent. The universe has size. Most philosophy holds to the logic that at this point in time, we only understand beginning–end concepts. As such, it would appear that the universe had a beginning and may have an end. All this implies size, limits, to the universe.

If the universe has size, it must exist somewhere. If the Causative Force is all present, as religions say, then the universe would exist within the Causative Force. This is panentheism. Science reinforces panentheism through its observation that the earth is not the center of the universe. The center must lie elsewhere. The sun is not the center, so the center must lie elsewhere. The Milky Way is not the center, so the center must lie elsewhere. And if our own universe has a boundary, is it not possible there are more universes? And if such is the case, is it not possible that our universe is not the center of these universes just as we are not the center of our earth, and our earth is not the center of the solar system, and our solar system is not the center of our galaxy, and our galaxy is not the center of our universe?

We are not the center. So where is the center? We have to assume the center lies somewhere outside our universe. If such is the case, then there is an outside to our universe. This opens us up to the logic within panentheism.

Science reinforces panentheism through the observation that we are not the center. Science, by searching for a center, moves the center away from us as beings. Science opens up the question, "...then what are we and why do we exist?" What an exciting time! We are on the edge of understanding our significance before we intrude upon the space of others, who most probably exist within the distant realms of space. Science has opened up the opportunity for us to define ourselves rather than have others do it for us.

#3. What does modern science reinforce about the significance of existence, life?

Modern science indicates that we, humans, do not exist at the center. This implies that ours is not the only relationship that has significance to the Causative Force. Existence, life, souls in general, must have significance to the Causative Force.

•

The humbling ideas seem to never end. No wonder the concept of not being the center was so disturbing. Now we begin to understand that we are not the center of the universe. We begin to understand that there are other intelligent life forms in space. We begin to understand we are not the center of the Causative Force's attention. We are one of many.

As we begin to realize that we are not the center of the universe, we begin to realize we are not irreplaceable as a species. No wonder Copernicus' book, *Concerning the Revolutions of the Celestial Spheres*, written in 1543, was placed on the index of forbidden books by the Catholic Church for over three hundred years, finally ending in 1853. Modern science definitely humbled us in terms of our own significance as a species. But science also opened up the idea that life may be so important, it most probably exists in many places throughout the universe.

•

So if we are not the center of attention, then what is our function? And if, as the Hindus profess, we have a soul which is eternal, then what is its purpose, and what of the Buddhist concept of our responsibility to work at eliminating suffering? And what of the Christian belief that we must love one another? And what about the Islamic concept that justice will be a part of eternity? Why is ontology able to argue the existence of a Causative Force so forcefully without involving religion? All these ideas reinforce the concept of a Causative Force being so big that we have nowhere else to exist but within Her. And if we are within the Causative Force, then all these ideas take on an elevated significance. By understanding the possibility of our being within the Causative Force, the ideas that serve as the foundations of Hinduism, Judaism, Buddhism, Christianity, Islam, ontology, modern science, become logical, become so significant, the repercussions they attempt to generate in society become logical, rational, significant to us not just in terms of today, but in terms of eternity.

#4. How does modern science help us understand what life is?

We see that we are not the center. We are not the center of the universe. We are not the center of the galaxy. We are not the center of the solar system. We can assume from this that we most likely are not the center of attention of the Causative Force.

•

We have a difficult time letting go of not being the center of focus for the Causative Force. We have had no choice but to let go of being physically the center of the universe because modern science, observations, have built such convincing arguments against such an idea.

But modern science, by proving that we do not occupy the center of the universe, opens up the possibility that we are not even the center of attention, that we are but one of many life forms the Causative Force has a significant interest in. If the Causative Force has an interest in many life forms throughout the universe, then perhaps life has significance, in some manner, to the Causative Force.

Modern science, the process of observation, the understanding that we are not the center, helps us understand that the significance of life most probably does not lie with the physical image of humanity since humanity is not the focal point. Religions, on the other hand, help us understand it is the soul that moves on after life. If the two are both correct, then the two together would imply that what we gain from life, what we add to our awareness, must be what passes into eternity. Awareness passing into eternity would seem to add to eternity.

Modern science and religion would, through the use of logic (philosophy), tend to imply that life is the passing of souls in and out of this limited physical universe for a purpose. The purpose is to learn, create, and experience in order to take such things back into the Causative Force Herself.

•

Life now takes on significance, not because it is life, not because it is human. Life now takes on significance because it is a journey. Life becomes significant because it is a soul entering a physical state of being. Life takes on a significance because it offers a purpose for that soul. Life becomes significant not to the soul, but to the Causative Force from which the soul came, to which the soul returns, and of which the soul is a part.

#5. What does modern science have to offer us as individuals?

Modern science offers us the opportunity to understand that we came from, will return to, and are a part of, the Causative Force.

•

We are actually a part of the Causative Force. What a leap, going from being the center to possibly being an actual part of the Causative Force. First religion comes along and gives us hope; we are the center of attention of the Causative Force. Then science comes along and shows us we are not at the center, but we might be within something, perhaps the Causative Force Herself. Now logic offers us the potential of understanding that we may actually be a part of the Causative Force.

But if we are a part of the Causative Force, then aren't we actually the Causative Force? Science would tell us that we are not. There is a difference between being a part of something and being that thing. Your brain is a part of you, but it cannot survive without the rest of you anymore than the rest of you can survive without your brain. Science, observation, would seem to tell us that we, as individuals, are probably not as significant a part of the Causative Force as the brain is to our body. The brain cell processes information and works with other brain cells to act as a means for the human body to survive. The brain cell is a part of the body. It is needed by the body. It, in turn, needs the body to survive. We need the Causative Force. Why would it be so difficult to accept that the Causative Force may need us? Interdependence is a relationship science has observed time and time again, to be one of the basic principles for existence. In spite of this, both religion and science have constantly rejected this interdependence as possibly being a part of our relationship to the Causative Force.

•

Science has shown us that we are not the center of the universe. We are not the center of attention of the Causative Force. Science, however, did not leave us stranded. Science may have taken one thing away but it has given us another hope. Science (observation), when combined with religion (faith) using philosophy (logic) has shown us that we may have more significance than we ever dreamed possible. Science, by shattering our dream of being the center of attention of the Causative Force, has opened up the possibility that we may actually be a part of the Causative Force Herself. We, individuals, may have significance beyond our wildest dreams.

#6. What significance does science have to offer us as a species?

If we have significance to the Causative Force as individuals, then we must have significance as a species.

•

Individual brain cells have significance to the body. As a group of brain cells working together, they may not make up the whole brain, but they act together to fulfill a purpose. As a group, they may form parts of the brain such as the medulla oblongata, the cerebrum, cerebellum, a particular wrinkle on the surface of the brain. The possibilities are enormous. We as a species may have a unique function for the Causative Force. We may not understand just what the particular function is at this point in time, but we can be certain that if we are a part of the Causative Force, we have some function, and that in itself is a greater significance for our existence than we had ever before dreamed possible.

As a species, as individuals, being a part of the Causative Force raises our level of significance over what we had before. Although this is an exciting possibility, it also should be a sobering thought. With an increase in significance of this magnitude comes an equally significant increase in responsibility. Now we would have a responsibility to ourselves, for we would be a part of the Causative Force Herself and She would be a part of us. Now we would have a responsibility to each other because those around us would be seen to be pieces of the Causative Force. Now we would have a responsibility to the Causative Force because we are a part of Her. We would now understand that what we do impacts the Causative Force, impacts our own eternity. Science opens up some heavy responsibility for our species.

•

Is it possible to begin thinking in terms of what our function in such a situation might be? If so, the key might well lie in the understanding of history and where it shows we have been heading. Some people would say it indicates we are a ruthless group. Although history has confirmed our ruthlessness, it also shows a trend. We as a species have been heading in the direction of elevating the significance of the individual, the value we place on the individual. Perhaps our purpose is to provide significance to all souls. Perhaps our purpose is to provide the understanding of the journey of life itself and the reason it needs to be protected. Perhaps we are to be the conscience of the Causative Force Herself. Perhaps...

#7. What significance does science have to offer other life forms in the universe?

If we, as a species, have significance to the Causative force, much as a part of the brain has a significance to the whole person, then perhaps the sum of souls traveling throughout the universe has the same significance to the Causative Force that our brain has to us.

•

Science, by eliminating the idea that we are not the center of the universe, opens up the possibility that we are not the center of attention of the Causative Force. This has many implications. Examining science by itself does not give us a very good picture of all the implications. When we add the ideas of religion and philosophy to science, however, some interesting possibilities open up for us as a species. These ideas become so broad in scope that they actually engulf all life forms in the universe. These ideas are so broad in scope they even engulf, embrace, life forms in other universes should we find they exist.

Religion gives us Hinduism: "a" Causative Force exists, the soul exists, the soul is eternal; Buddhism: suffering of the soul is not to be tolerated; Christianity: we are to love one another; Islam: take your life seriously for justice will be a part of eternity; ontology: "a" Causative Force is logical even without believing through faith; and modern science: we are not the center, do not ignore what you see. All these ideas point towards an all present Causative Force. An all present Causative Force would leave nowhere else for our universe to be but within this Causative Force. You being within the universe and thus within the Causative Force would imply you are a part of the Causative Force. If the Causative Force were as powerful as religions state and powerful enough to create a universe out of "nothingness" as the scientific idea of symmetry implies, then you being within the Causative Force, you being a part of the Causative Force would imply this is so for a reason. You, I, all life forms together have a purpose in reality.

•

Some say we are too lowly an entity to reason out as an important idea as purpose. But if we are a part of the Causative Force, we are not "lowly." And if we can accept we have no significance to the Causative Force, why can't we accept that we may have significance?

#8. What does modern science imply about our significance in eternity?

If we are not the center of the universe, if earth is not the center of the solar system, if our sun is not the center of our galaxy, if our galaxy is not the center of all the galaxies, then our universe most probably is not the center of the Causative Force. What does that leave us? It leaves us with the potential of being a part of something. It leaves us with the potential of being a part of the omnipresence.

•

Being a part of the Causative Force is not a new idea. Hindus have been saying that for thousands of years. The idea just never made it to the West. It was left behind. Now modern science comes along and implies what Hindus have been saying all along. Science put it in different words, painted the same picture from a different viewpoint.

But what of present western religions? They have always rejected the idea of an all present Causative Force while professing omnipresence, all presence, to be a primary part of their foundations. This paradox will be more fully addressed in the chapter titled Classical/Traditional Theisms. For now, however, let us understand that many of our older earth religions accept the concept of omnipresence, science implies such a state of being, and philosophical logic has historically found such an idea easier to defend than to refute. Perhaps traditional religions need to reevaluate omnipresence just as they had to reevaluate Copernicus' observation that we are not the center.

•

Ripples are created by actions. Ripples rush through society. Ripples wash over people, souls attempting to journey through society. Actions generated by nature are unpredictable and difficult to control at this point in time. Actions, generated by people, can be controlled by the person committing the action. We are responsible for our actions. The actions may be influenced by outside factors, but they are controlled by the individual nonetheless. Our actions are influenced by perceptions we have of ourselves and others. What more influential perception could we give to each other than the perception that we are each a piece of the Causative Force and as such, deserve the respect, love, and total acceptance we give the Causative Force Herself? We have guides: your soul is eternal, eliminate suffering, love one another, and you will be judged accordingly.

#9. What does modern science imply about our relationship to the Causative Force?

Science implies that we should not ignore what we see. What is it that we see? We see all living things dependent upon each other. We see no individual being the center of all things. We see change all around us.

•

Change, sharing attention, and interdependence are all ideas we find difficult to accept. All are actions we resist. Yet all three are confirmed as basic to everything we observe. All are underlying principles science keeps confirming over and over again. Yet all three items are concepts we struggle to withhold from our relationship with the Causative Force. We do not want to change our ideas regarding what we believe to be our relationship with the Causative Force. We do not want to give up being the center of attention, to accept that the Causative Force may need us.

Why the resistance? Accepting interdependence between ourselves and the Causative Force means accepting more responsibility for our actions. Who wants that? Sharing attention means obtaining less of it. Who wants that? Change means no longer being able to stay in the same comfortable rut. Who wants that?

For all the negatives, there are positives. Granted, accepting an interdependence between ourselves and the Causative Force does increase our responsibilities immensely. But don't forget that with increased responsibilities come increased benefits. As we accept the new significance to which we each will be elevated, we will have no choice but to improve the quality of the air, water, and land. We will strive to make our environment a place within which we all enjoy walking. The lakes will sparkle, the forests will be filled with rich colors, the air will smell crisp and clean. Taking a breath will become a pleasure, not a chore. Taking a life will mean terminating the journey of a piece of the Causative Force. As such, assisted suicide will become illogical and a means of alleviating pain will take its place. Capital punishment will be viewed as interfering with the journey of the Causative Force Herself.

•

And on and on and on. . . All intensified due to change, due to a new understanding, a new relationship, with the Causative Force.

Conclusion: How do the concepts of modern science reinforce the concept of symbiotic panentheism?

They do not; what is really taking place is that symbiotic panentheism is reinforcing modern science.

•

Modern science, understanding what we see, has been leading us away from the idea that we are the center of attention and leading us into the direction that interdependence is a fundamental characteristic of existence. If this is the case, it only makes sense that this fundamental characteristic of the universe might very well be a fundamental characteristic of our relationship to the Causative Force.

Symbiotic panentheism says exactly the same thing. "Symbiosis" means a close interdependence. "Panentheism" means all in the Causative Force. Putting the words together gives us "symbiotic panentheism," which in turn means two things:
1. The Causative Force is so big, there is nowhere else we could be other than inside Her because there is nowhere else.
2. Interdependence links us to the Causative Force; we need the Causative Force and the Causative Force needs us.

•

Our need for a Causative Force has been basically accepted by religions as being logical. A Causative Force, an all powerful, all knowing, all present Force needing us, on the other hand, has been rejected as ludicrous. But is it? Perhaps we are a means to an end for the Causative Force. Perhaps the Causative Force is so powerful, knowing, and all present that She was incapable of becoming even more so in Her existing state. That in itself created a paradox. How could an entity be truly all knowing if She did not know how to learn about things that did not exist? In other words, how could She create truly original things? Would an entity that could not create ideas that had never before existed be truly all powerful? And if an entity found a way around this problem, found a way to create, to gain knowledge that never before existed, wouldn't She become even more "aware" than She was before? Wouldn't this increased awareness be just another way of saying She was growing in awareness or presence, becoming more omnipresent?

What does this have to do with us? Science points to the idea that we may be a part of this process through the idea of interdependence, and symbiotic panentheism reinforces this concept.

ATHEISM

What new concept has Atheism
(the first size of the Causative Force)
firmly established within society?

The Causative Force is so small,
She does not exist.
No presence.

#0. What do the conceptual frameworks of atheism & pantheism have to offer us?

Atheism:
1. *The doctrine of disbelief in a supreme being.*
2. *... frequently applied to those who disbelieve in the popular gods.*
3. *... believed that religion rests on superstition.*
4. *... the philosophy of Materialism does not require a god.*
5. *Sidney Hook maintained that an "open-minded atheism" provides for a guaranteed freedom of religious belief.*
   Dictionary of Philosophy and Religion, William L. Reese, p. 48

•

Pantheism: From the Greek pan and theos meaning "everything is God." The term is to be distinguished from Pan–en–theism where the world is regarded as a constituent of God but not identical with Him.
   Dictionary of Philosophy and Religion, William L. Reese, p. 547

It is not the disbelief in a supreme being that is of interest here but rather what this idea implies about the size of the Causative Force. If there is no Causative Force, then the Causative Force is so small it has actually been defined out of existence. This implies that our universe had no beginning and will have no end.

Pantheism, on the other hand, would increase the size of the Causative Force to that of the universe. This presents the same problems as does atheism for it also implies that there is no beginning or end to the universe.

Both atheism and pantheism limit the size of a Causative Force to the size of the universe and to time. For this reason, both are considered to be non-religions by most religious faiths that exist today.

•

Science is beginning to seriously believe there are boundaries to our universe. Time may be a boundary, for science now thinks the universe had a beginning and will end. Atheism cannot explain such an idea. Science now thinks our universe may actually have a physical boundary. Our universe may actually have some form or shape. Atheism cannot account for what would lie outside such a shape. Atheism is limited and is limiting.

#1. What does the conceptual framework of atheism imply about the universe within which we live?

Atheism provides the beginning point of the debate regarding the size of our universe. Atheism says the universe is infinite in size. There are no boundaries to our universe. There is no Causative Force for our universe. Our universe had no beginning.

•

The existence of a Causative Force is more important to us as individuals and as a species than it would first appear. In fact, the existence of a Causative Force has a great deal to do with how we treat each other. Atheism begins the debate regarding the size of a Causative Force by defining that Her size as so small, She does not exist.

With no Causative Force, we have a sense that life is momentary. We live life for now rather than for what is to follow. As such, life has value only for today. This leads to actions that are directed toward self satisfaction and self-serving ends. This is not to say atheists are all self-serving. Rather, it is saying that with atheism, the concept of a Causative Force, the soul, and eternity are missing and do not add to our understanding of why we must elevate our behavior of living for the moment. The lack of the ideas of a Causative Force, the soul, and eternity establishes a universe lacking the idealism these ideas create.

The lack of understanding that something may exist beyond our universe leaves us with only a limited universe for our dreams, idealism, understanding, and logic. Philosophy, religion, and science then become limited just as do our dreams and imaginations.

•

The value we place upon the individual depends upon the significance we perceive we have. With the perception that existence only occurs in our universe, we limit our significance to just this universe. As such, we define our own significance to exist within the boundaries of this universe. This forces us into limiting our hopes, dreams, creative insights to concepts that pertain to what lies in our physical reality, in our universe.

This limitation transfers into the logic we use to determine what is and what isn't rational human behavior. If life only exists today, then the only rational behavior is behavior that leads to pleasure. Thinking in terms of elevating one's behavior because it might be beneficial in the afterlife becomes an irrational act. Under atheism, intolerance of suffering, love of one another, justice being meted out in the afterlife become irrational.

#2. How does the concept of atheism reinforce the concept of panentheism?

Atheism professes the idea that there is no Causative Force. This contradicts observations and logic and thus acts as an argument pointing in the direction of the idea of panentheism.

•

Atheism bases its rejection of a Causative Force upon the logic that if the Causative Force created the universe, then there had to be something that created the Causative Force. Put another way, an atheist might say, "If the Causative Force had no creator and still exists, then something could exist without a creator. That being true, then it is just as logical to believe it is the universe that had no creator, therefore there is no Causative Force, no God."

The problem to this argument lies in the observation we make when investigating the universe. As we make observations of things around us, we notice that everything seems to have a beginning and an end. Scientists even believe the universe had a beginning and an end. If everything in the universe had a beginning and an end, is it so unreasonable to believe that the boundary of the universe itself had a beginning and an end?

If the universe had a beginning, then something had to begin the process. The force that started the universe is what is called a Causative Force. The whole debate begins with atheism, there is no Causative Force and leads into the discussion of the idea of a Causative Force existing, which in turn leads to the idea of the ultimate size of the Causative Force, true omnipresence. This leads to the idea of panentheism.

•

The question of the Causative Force having a creator is not one we can argue at this point in time. It is interesting. It is very philosophical, but the point of our journey is to contemplate the size of the Causative Force relative to ourselves and our universe.

It appears that atheism, by limiting the boundaries of our existence, would limit our ability to behave in an idealistic manner. Due to this, it appears that atheism would establish the need for the development of something greater than what it has to offer. Atheism points us toward panentheism.

#3. What does atheism reinforce about the significance of existence, life?

Atheism initiates the concept that life is real.

•

Life being real is not a "bad" position to take. It lends validity to what we do everyday. If one did not believe that life was real, then many people would decide that putting the energy life demands of us into meeting everyday challenges would seem ridiculous.

Atheism, by declaring life to be real, begins the process of understanding the significance of life. Classical/traditional theism provides an even greater significance to life, for under the classical/traditional theism of Judaism, Christianity, Islam, etc., life goes beyond this world and into eternity. But under western religions of Judaism, Christianity, and Islam, the Causative Force transcends the universe. In other words, the universe is not inside the Causative Force. The end result of the size of the Causative Force is to expand your responsibility in life over the responsibility atheism places upon you. You now become responsible for your own actions, for they will affect you in the hereafter. Under atheism, you have no responsibility to the Causative Force for you do not have any direct impact upon Her. Is life significant? Yes, but only in a limited way.

•

Atheism differs from panentheism regarding responsibility. Under panentheism, you exist within the Causative Force. As such, you have a responsibility not only to yourself but to the Causative Force. By being within the Causative Force, you impact the Causative Force as well as yourself through your behavior. This form of existence, panentheism, places the highest form of significance upon life.

In addition, panentheism places the highest form of responsibility upon existence, life. Understanding this concept would force us as individuals and as a species into protecting life and journeys through life as the ultimate responsibility. Under the concept of panentheism, life becomes so significant that it actually impacts upon the Causative Force Herself. The value of a life, the value of existence, reaches a new height of significance which translates into new behavior patterns directed at the individual. All this is generated from the debate over the size of the Causative Force beginning with the idea of no size at all, or nonexistence of the Causative Force, atheism. Behavior in life tends to rise to the level of its responsibility.

#4. How does atheism help us understand what life is?

Life is real. Life is something that begins and ends.

•

Life being real is not an insignificant idea. It has marvelous implications. However, by itself it has major limitations. Life existing for a few days or one hundred years is insignificant in terms of the time span we believe the universe has existed. In terms of the total picture of what has happened throughout time, an atheistic approach provides hope, but it also generates much despair and pessimism. Under atheism, our significance appears to have little worth compared to the immensity of the universe.

Science continually expands our understanding of the amount of time needed to develop the universe. Under atheism, as our understanding of the amount of time needed to develop the universe increases, our sense of significance decreases. One hundred years, compared with seven days, is a long time. One hundred years, compared with fifteen billion, is a very short time and has little meaning by comparison.

Now science is considering the idea that it is possible that the universe may eventually implode upon itself. Significance, hope, now seems to lose all of its meaning under atheism.

•

But atheism has its function. The starting point atheism generates in terms of the size of a Causative Force is crucial. Every perception has to have a starting point. The starting point provides a frame of reference for debate. A starting point provides a point of reference for a journey outward from the initial idea.

Our behavior towards each other appears to be directly related to the concept we hold regarding our significance. This appears to be directly related to the concept we hold regarding our relationship to the Causative Force. And this appears to be directly related to the concept we hold regarding the size of the Causative Force.

All of this has to have an origination point and it is the atheist that maintains this point of origin. We must begin to acknowledge the significant role the atheist performs for the rest of us.

#5. What does atheism have to offer us as individuals?

Atheism offers us the idea that an individual life is limited. Limits allow for the concept of relative worth. Relative worth implies relative value. The end result: it is logical for one person to judge another.

•

Atheism offers us a definition of life. Life is what lies between birth and death. That's it, nothing before, nothing after. And why is that all? That's all because there is nothing beyond the universe. Your existence is tied to one and only one thing, the universe. There is no soul. When you die, you die. If this sounds conclusive, it is.

Keep in mind, however, that as limited as this sounds, it is nevertheless a beginning of an idea. It is the idea that you exist. This may also sound rather limiting, even insignificant, but it is a perception of what we are. Under atheism, the picture we have of what we are may seem small and limited, but it is a picture. It is the beginning of understanding the significance of the individual.

The significance of the individual is one we ourselves are defining. The definition outlines a philosophy we have regarding ourselves. The definition that defines what we are acts as the foundation for the development of a universal philosophy. This universal philosophy may grow out of an understanding a young species has regarding what their significance is for existing, but it needs answers that explain what the universe is, how the universe was created, why the universe was created, what the individual is, how the individual got here, why the individual was created, what the soul is, why the soul enters the physical universe, the purpose of a soul, and on and on. And where does the definition begin? It begins with atheism and continues from there.

•

Atheism has done us a great service. It is the first chapter in the book of understanding what we are and why we exist. Without the first chapter, the second chapter regarding the implications of classical/traditional theisms – Judaism, Christianity, Islam, etc. – would be muddied and incomprehensible.

Atheism must never be shoved aside and forgotten, for without it, we would lose the first step in understanding what we are as individuals. Without atheism, we would lose the understanding of what it is to be alone, to be without a Causative Force, and how this affects our behavior.

#6. What significance does atheism have to offer us as a species?

Atheism gives us an understanding that we have some form of commonality as a species through the physical and emotional realms.

•

Appearances now become important for we are just what we appear to be. We exist within a universe with no creator. The universe is, always was, and always will be. We, on the other hand, come and go. We have no soul under atheism. Our existence is confined to our universe.

Under atheism, the value of the individual could be argued against just as well as argued for. We have to be careful about defining our significance as a species. We will create problems for ourselves and others if we do it in a fashion that would allow one person to logically be considered better than another. Doing so only opens up the possibility for some members of our species to logically subjugate other members of our species. As a species, we are very resourceful and have always had factions who take advantage of just such perceptions.

•

Atheism opens the door to rationalize the process of subjugation. This is a very dangerous situation for our species. With that rationale in place, what are we to say should we encounter a more advanced life form in space that may want to subjugate us as a species? Could we logically say after the fact, "No, don't do that. Life is important. It is not right to subjugate others." It would be a little too late to say this for we already would have established the definition of our significance. Atheism offers our species the opportunity to not only be subjugated, but to accept it.

Finding a significance to life so airtight that no individual, no species, could find a rationale for subjugating others may not be the end we should be striving for, but if it turns out to be one of the end results of our search for understanding, is that so bad? Ask people who have been abused. Ask yourself if you would feel comfortable if the logic existed for someone to be able to subjugate you. So what can we do?

Once defining the Causative Force to be truly omnipresent, we place our universe within Her. As such, we place our souls, all souls, within Her. This elevates the significance of all of us. The final result, all souls, terrestrial or otherwise, become a part of the Causative Force. Subjugation and abuse become irrational and intolerable. In essence, with panentheism, we build a protective barrier of logic for our species, for all souls.

#7. What significance does atheism have to offer other life forms in the universe?

Sidney Hook maintained that an "open-minded atheism" provides for a guaranteed freedom of religious belief.

•

Religious freedom is an idea, a fundamental of major significance, not just to us as humans, but to life as a whole. Lack of freedom to explore one's thoughts, one's creative abilities, one's perceptions, places boundaries upon journeys that we have no right to put into place. Atheism is one of the warning posts for all of us.

But atheism holds the idea that there is no Causative Force. True, but by doing so, atheism challenges our resolve to protect the right to journey uninhibited in life both for ourselves as well as others, earthlings or not. We have the obligation, the duty, to see that this is honored for all.

What does this have to do with other life forms? Freedom to believe or not believe becomes a statement of acknowledgment that no individual, regardless of what life form it takes, has to lie about what it believes in order to please society. The individual becomes the most significant entity in our universe. Integrity of the individual becomes respected regardless of its leanings.

•

If the Causative Force is so immense, She is truly omnipresent, then wouldn't our universe and other universes be within Her? As such, wouldn't universes be a part of Her? And if universes are a part of the Causative Force, wouldn't things within the universes, being a part of the universes, also be a part of the Causative Force? As such, not only would we be a part of the Causative Force, but so would all other life forms throughout the universe. Therefore, wouldn't a failure to meet our responsibility to protect all souls in this universe and others be another way of abusing ourselves if we were in fact a part of the Causative Force Herself? Then the question becomes, who in their right mind would dare abuse the Causative Force?

#8. What does atheism imply about our significance in eternity?

Atheism defines away the concept of eternal existence.

•

The universe exists. The universe has always existed. You exist. You were born. You will die. The end. Hope for more? There is none. Significance lies in today.

•

Your actions do not affect yourself in the eternity to follow, for there is not an afterlife. Your actions do not impact the Causative Force, for there is no Causative Force.

Therefore, your responsibility lies in one area: your own state of existence. Take your responsibility seriously. Your state of being depends upon you and once you are gone, everything is gone.

#9. What does atheism imply about our relationship to the Causative Force?

Atheism says there is no relationship because there is no Causative Force.

•

No relationship. Your comfort comes from the knowledge and belief that you are not alone in this state of short term hopelessness. Everyone around you faces the same existence.

•

You are alone without a Causative Force for one hundred years. In terms of relative spans of existence, a life is insignificant when measured against the life of the universe. Under atheism, you have no significance. No significance generates all types of rational excuses for antisocial behaviors.

Defining the existence of a Causative Force in order to elevate behavior is important. But just because we do so does not make it true. On the other hand, defining the nonexistence of a Causative Force does not necessarily make that true either. So what is one to do? One could ignore the problem. One could ignore the questions regarding what the universe is, what the significance of the universe is, what we are, what our significance is. But ignoring the problem will not make it go away.

In a sense, this is what atheism does. It ignores the questions we have always been seeking answers to. Has the search for answers been unproductive? Hardly. As we have seen, what we believe to be true in terms of our religious faith, scientific observations or philosophical logic affects our behavior towards each other. Over time, we have found stronger and stronger foundations upon which to rationalize our increasing perception of the value of the individual.

Hinduism, Judaism, Buddhism, Christianity, Islam, ontology, and modern science have all added to improving the conditions under which souls journey. Now it is time to add another element. We have reached 2000 AD. We can make a choice. We can reach out to improve our significance in existence. We can define ourselves in such a way as to include all others in our universe and in any other universe that may exist. We can rationalize a Universal Magna Carta.

Conclusion: What characteristic does atheism assign the Causative Force?

Atheism asserts that Russell is correct – God has no beginning.

•

But what of the Causative Force? If there is a Causative Force, then what lies beyond Her? And for that matter, who created Her? And doesn't the idea that the Causative Force might have a creator imply that the Causative Force is not truly all present, all powerful, and all knowledgeable? And doesn't this prove that the Causative Force is not the Causative Force after all? There is no denying these arguments and questions. We are by no means done with atheism yet.

The atheist, however, has hit the target but missed the mark. The mark is not what is the Causative Force of our Causative Force. The mark is not what might possibly lie beyond the Causative Force. The mark is what *is* our Causative Force.

And what does "our" mean? "Our" does not mean exclusively "human." "Our" means "all" beings within the universe or universes, whatever is the case. And what does "the Causative Force" refer to? "The Causative Force" refers to the creator not of humankind, but rather to the creator of our universe, all universes, and what beings lie within.

•

What lies beyond God is irrelevant at this time. We must first understand what significance we have. If, as St. Anselm suggested, "An argument for God...the conception of a necessary being, to the existence of that being" is correct, then the concept of the Causative Force being omnipresent beyond Herself is not of importance to us at this point.

Omnipresence must be understood to apply to our personal essence, our existence in this physical reality. We have no idea of what lies beyond the Causative Force nor do we have any logic to apply to the beginning–end concepts and the Causative Force Herself. It is not, at this point, necessary to understand such a relationship. Omnipresence, to what may lie beyond the Causative force, has no significance to us. But omnipresence of the Causative Force relative to us does.

This then is what is being referred to as omnipresence. Omnipresence refers to the size of the Causative Force relative to us and to our universe.

Classical/Traditional Theism

*What new concept has Classical/Traditional Theism
(the second size of the Causative Force)
firmly established within society?*

**The Causative Force is so big,
She includes everything BUT the universe.
Almost omnipresent.
Almost all present.**

#0. What does the conceptual frameworks of classical/traditional theism have to offer us?

Classical/Traditional Theism: Hartshorne has pointed out that in classical theism, i.e., the medieval conception of God as absolute, the feature of divine transcendence is overwhelming in its dominance. In this view, indeed, there is only a one-way relation between God and the world, that is, the world is related to God, but God is not related to the world.
Dictionary of Philosophy and Religion, William L. Reese, p. 765

•

Classical/traditional theisms include the western religions of Judaism, Christianity, and Islam, mentioned in this text. These three, in addition to many others, speak of the transcendence of the Causative Force. In introducing the transcendence of the Causative Force, they isolate our universe from the Causative Force. They claim the universe is not a part of the Causative Force because it is imperfect and to them, it is illogical for an "imperfect universe" to be inside a "perfect being."

Although transcendence is an excellent way to explain how the Causative Force avoids our imperfection, it also contradicts the most significant characteristic these religions assign to the Causative Force, and that is the characteristic of omnipresence or the idea that the Causative Force is everywhere.

Classical/traditional religions do, however, expand upon the size of the Causative Force over the size assigned the Causative Force by atheism. Under classical/traditional theisms, the Causative Force now has size.

•

Denying the concept of the universe lying within the Causative Force is not "bad." But this denial contradicts the basic perceptions these religions wish to assign the Causative Force. This process of assigning omnipresence to the Causative Force, while at the same time excluding the universe as a part of Her, solves the irrationality of "evil" being within and, therefore, a part of the Causative Force. But at the same time, this exclusion introduces an even greater problem and that is the lack of a sense of belonging and significance. This lack of a sense of belonging and significance presents tremendous paradoxes for humankind.

#1. What does the conceptual framework of classical/traditional theism imply about the universe within which we live?

Classical/traditional theism establishes the idea that the universe is not the only existence. There is more to existence than life.

•

How can there be more to existence than life? Eastern religions gave us an answer with which western religions agree. The answer is simply that something exists beyond our universe, outside our universe. This implies a boundary to our universe. Until recently, this was accepted on faith alone for no one could conceive of a boundary to our universe. Today, the idea of our universe having a boundary is not as farfetched as it was once assumed.

Science is seriously investigating the idea that the universe began with a big bang. This implies that the universe has size; it may be expanding, but it has size. If this is true, then the next question is what is outside the universe? Many religions would say this is where the Causative Force lies. Then the question becomes just how big is this Causative Force? Classical/traditional theisms lead to an understanding of the expansion of existence beyond the universe. With this expansion of our idea of existence, the dreams, ideals, creativity, and behavior of humans rose to new levels never before dreamed possible.

Classical/traditional theisms introduced a new vision, a new perception, of what life is. We now exist outside our universe and into eternity. As such, we began viewing each other as soul mates in eternity rather than fellow humans existing for a few short decades. This new way of looking at each other changed the way we act toward each other.

•

The idea that our universe was temporary and therefore had to have a beginning lead to the need for an omnipresent Causative Force relative to the universe. Omnipresence of the Causative Force is the most difficult concept for western religions to accept in total. "Imperfection" existing in a "perfect" Creator did not make sense, therefore "transcendence" became a major element of modern religions. If "imperfection" existing within "perfection" could be rationalized, then the size of the Causative Force could be expanded once again. An expansion of the size of the Causative Force would, in turn, expand upon our understanding of our significance for existing. This would once again allow for an explosive elevation in terms of human dreams, ideals, creativity, and behavior.

#2. How does the concept of classical/traditional theism reinforce the concept of panentheism?

Classical/traditional theism expands the idea of existence to beyond the universe by establishing the concept of a Causative Force lying outside the universe. This idea leads us closer to panentheism.

•

Classical/traditional theism expands the idea of existence into eternity itself. It establishes the idea of the Causative Force, including everything except the universe. The western acceptance of an omnipresent Causative Force excluding the universe had a major impact upon us. We see ourselves outside of the Causative Force. This contradicts the idea of omnipresence, which has lead us to accept the ideas that contradictions are acceptable for if they can apply to our most fundamental beliefs, then they are okay to accept in our daily lives. Now it is okay to say all men are created equal but not to treat them as such. Now it is okay to say the environment belongs to everyone but rationalize the pollution of our waters, air, and land. Now it is okay to say everyone has the right to life but then terminate millions through capital punishment, abortions, euthanasia, mercy killings, and assisted suicides.

This is not to say classical/traditional theism hasn't improved upon our lives immensely. It just says that the contradictions of classical/traditional theism open the door for abusive human behavior. This leads to the logic that classical/traditional theism hasn't lead us all the way to the end of our understanding regarding a Causative Force. It just points the way. And the direction points toward panentheism. We have but to expand upon the size of the Causative Force even more.

•

As the major religions of the world, Buddhism, Christianity, Islam, etc. took hold, the status of humans improved. It is undeniable that many atrocious events occurred throughout our history under the name of religion.

Today, the value of a life has significantly more meaning than it did even one hundred years ago. Most of this is due to the global understanding we have of the tie life has to eternity. As we expand our perception of size of the Causative Force, we seem to expand the perception we have of the value of life. If this is the case, what would happen if we expanded it even more?

#3. What does classical/traditional theism reinforce about the significance of existence, life?

Classical/traditional theism expands upon the magnitude of existence. Now life goes beyond the universe and into eternity.

•

Atheism forces one to view the significance of life in terms of time and in terms of our physical universe. This places a limit on the significance of life. Classical/traditional theism expands our significance into eternity but shuts the door on a portion of eternity, for we exist not within the Causative Force but outside Her. This outside existence limits us, for under this viewpoint, we are not capable of being a significant contributor to the ultimate being we envision.

This expansion of our significance beyond our universe and into eternity has done wonderful things in terms of the value we place on human life. Our historical growth regarding the rights of the individual and the importance of our environment has jumped by leaps and bounds. This, however, should not lead us to complacency.

If expanding upon the size of the Causative Force caused an explosive development in the value we have of life, then perhaps we can generate another event of equal magnitude. Perhaps by expanding the size of the Causative Force, we can put into place the ideas necessary to initiate another quantum leap toward improving life.

•

This time, the leap we take regarding the value of life would apply to not only souls on earth but souls throughout space, for they also would be understood to exist within the Causative Force. In fact, the value we would then be forced to place on life, the soul, would reach even beyond the boundaries of our universe and into the concept of other universes whether or not they actually exist. We would, in actuality, be building a bill of rights for all life; a high ideal indeed, but an ideal that now becomes possible by expanding the classical/traditional theism size of the Causative Force to be truly omnipresent. This means there is no place for us to be but within the "arms" of the Causative Force. This idea might initiate another leap forward regarding our understanding of our significance, our responsibility for living. Elevating our understanding regarding our responsibilities for living would in turn elevate our behavior.

#4. How does classical/traditional theism help us understand what life is?

Classical/traditional theism introduces into the West the idea that life in this universe is only a part of what life is. Life now becomes a part of eternity. Life goes beyond this universe into eternity itself.

•

Under atheism, life begins at day one and life ends on the last day of your life. What is life? Life is existing. What is the purpose of life? Life's purpose is to exist. What happens during life? Many things, some "good," some "bad." Why does life happen? "Just because." That is enough explanation for atheism. In essence, life has no greater purpose than being just what it is, "life," something that begins and ends.

Classical/traditional theism takes a step beyond this. Life is more than just birth, death, and what goes on between the two. Classical/traditional theism goes on to say there is more. Hope now evolves that life is not the end and as such, behavior becomes elevated. The individual life takes on greater significance and so does behavior.

•

Life being unlimited by time changes the concept of what life is. Attaching the concept of eternal existence to life now adds a new possibility to life. Now life gains an appearance of having some purpose.

Why else would one leave one state of being, life before birth, in order to come into another state of being into the universe? If there were not a reason, why would you die? If your soul is eternal, leaving this existence in order to get back to where you came from would imply a need to do so. Under classical/traditional theism, hope arises, for logic springs up regarding the possibility that there is a significance to all of this.

Classical/traditional theisms such as Judaism, Christianity, Islam, and others provide hope. Existence outside this universe, however, is still uncertain. Under classical/traditional theism, the size of the Causative Force is limited to just part of the region beyond the boundaries of the universe. Under these theisms, our universe does not lie within the Causative Force. The result of this limited perception regarding the size of the Causative Force is that you still have no significant impact upon the Causative Force. This limited perception regarding the size of the Causative Force leads to limited behavior we generate towards others, for we see others as being limited.

#5. What does classical/traditional theism have to offer us as individuals?

Classical/traditional theism offers us an expanded view of our significance, offers the individual eternity and offers us hope.

•

What idea does classical/traditional theism present that provides us with hope? Judaism, Christianity, Islam provide an expanded view of the Causative Force. They expand the boundaries of existence. Under atheism, the boundary of the universe is as far as we go. Judaism, Christianity, Islam, etc. acknowledge the possibility of existence beyond this boundary. Classical/traditional theisms then establish the idea of the existence of another entity that exists outside the boundaries of the universe. Here is where they introduce hope, for they invite us to consider that we, our essence, will be able to move beyond our physical universe and move into this region of eternity.

Now the atheistic concept of temporary existence is expanded to eternal existence. Hope evolves regarding your existence for now you can understand that you may not actually die. You may live forever. The significance here lies not only in the realization that hope has evolved. Now your existence into eternity may be real. This generates the idea that your eternal existence may depend upon how you behave or what you believe. Behavior and faith in this life now become important elements regarding your existence in eternity. This idea results in a massive elevation of human behavior toward others and toward oneself.

•

A major leap in human behavior now takes place due to a perceptual understanding regarding the size of the Causative Force. The Causative Force now becomes defined from nonexistence to existing. The size now comes into question. The size of the Causative Force is defined to be almost completely omnipresent. Not completely because the Causative Force does not include the universe under the perceptions of classical/traditional theism. If the Causative Force is truly omnipresent, then "evil" would have to be a part of the Causative Force and this seems inconceivable. Overwhelming fear of such a perception drove classical/traditional theism to reject this idea and thus shrink the potential size of the Causative Force and with it your potential, my potential, the potential of all individuals.

#6. What significance does classical/traditional theism have to us as a species?

Classical/traditional theism offers our species a commonality through eternity, a commonality through the soul.

•

There is a limit to the significance of our commonality. Under classical/traditional theism, the Causative Force does not need the universe. More importantly to you, the Causative Force, therefore, does not need what lies within the universe, does not need you. Under classical/traditional theism, you need the Causative Force, but that's where it ends. This existence is a one way street.

The bottom line is that under modern day theisms, our species has no significance other than to just exist. Some would say this is enough. But is it? Our species has a tendency to be depressant if it senses a lack of purpose. As a species, we sense a need to create, be productive, advance our knowledge, and build.

Could we as a species ever be satisfied to just sit back and spend our lives merely existing for eternity? Would we ever be able to find contentment in the idea that we had no impact upon existence?

•

If most people would find little contentment in simply existing for eternity, then why aren't we looking for something more significant? What would our species find to be acceptable, challenging, inspiring for ourselves?

Atheism brings us the significance of just existing a short time with no purpose other than existing a short time. We have awareness of our impact for a short period and then our awareness is gone forever. The perception generated is that we as a species should take actions for the short term, for the results of these actions are the only ones we will be able to observe.

Under classical/traditional theism, our awareness extends into eternity. Not only do we exist, but we exist eternally. As such, we see ourselves as needing to behave accordingly. Our significance has been elevated and along with it, our behavior towards each other has been elevated. But let's not forget that under classical/traditional theism, the Causative Force is not truly omnipresent; She excludes the universe. What would happen to our behavior if we understood ourselves to exist within the Causative Force, if we understood we were a piece of the Causative Force? Is it possible we might generate a leap in our behavior?

#7. What significance does classical/traditional theism have to offer other life forms in the universe?

Classical/traditional theism holds the universe to be a finite creation within the infinite being of the Causative Force and that the universe, as such, is divine.

•

We have a choice. We can determine what religious fundamentals we want to adhere to before we step into the space beyond our solar system. We can determine religiously what size we want the Causative Force to be as a fundamental belief we adhere to in terms of our faiths. Lest we forget, it is fundamental beliefs and perceptions we have of a Causative Force that generates much of our human behavior towards each other and towards our environment.

We can determine what philosophical fundamentals we want to adhere to before we step into the space beyond our solar system. We can determine philosophically what size we want the Causative Force to be as a rationale we adhere to in terms of our logic.

We can determine what scientific fundamentals we want to adhere to before we step into the space beyond our solar system. We can determine scientifically what size we want the Causative Force to be as fundamental proof we adhere to in terms of our observations.

Faith, logic, and observations are the three means we have of determining what size we believe the Causative Force and to be the significance we ourselves play in terms of eternity. But this does not affect just us as earthlings. If we cannot expand our perceptions of eternity to include extraterrestrials, the extraterrestrials may have no choice but to protect themselves from us and the types of behaviors we initiate towards others of our own kind.

•

So which is it, faith (religion), logic (philosophy) or observations (science) that generates the greater perceptions which influence how we treat each other and ourselves? The debate is not which has the greater influence. The debate is how to restructure it. It is time all three make peace with each other and start working together. It is time. We humans grow weary. We are all tired of the abuse and trauma in society. We have no right to carry this behavior into space. The life forms out there that are aware of our behavior must be worried indeed!

#8. What does classical/traditional theism imply about our significance in eternity?

Under classical/traditional theism, we are allowed into eternity but it is a gift and the type of eternity can be bought through behavior or faith.

•

Purchase of a "heaven" or "hell" form of eternal existence offers hope. One may experience a wonderful existence after life or one may not but the fact remains under classical/traditional theism that the opportunity for one or the other is there. Many would say this is a significant improvement over the total lack of eternal awareness atheism offers.

But is our perception of eternity under classical/traditional theism really one of having to buy a particular type of existence? In a sense, it is. If one "believes," one will go to heaven. But what if one doesn't believe, cannot believe? Then the perception is that they are not working hard enough. They are lazy. Or they just profess they to want to believe, but really don't. "Believing" implies you are lying. This is followed up by the thoughts, "The atheist is lying about not being able to believe and therefore they not only will go to hell, but they will be sent there."

Some people even go so far as to say that one can do anything one wishes in life, lead the most vicious life, as long as one "truly repents" on one's death bed. Well, who wouldn't "truly repent?" Whatever the case, classical/traditional theism has definitely had a major impact upon our perception of eternity and the role we play in it.

•

Under classical/traditional theism, we are affected by eternity, but we do not affect eternity. But if we do not affect eternity, then what significance could we possibly have in eternity? Classical/traditional theism has undoubtedly expanded our perception regarding our being a part of eternity. It has elevated our significance to that of our awareness, our soul, actually being eternal. Eternity affects us. On the other hand, classical/traditional theism has come up short in terms of explaining what significance we have to eternity. This is where panentheism comes into the picture. Under panentheism, not only are you affected by eternity but you actually impact and are significant to eternity.

#9. What does classical/traditional theism imply about our relationship to the Causative Force?

Classical/traditional theism has developed the idea that "the world is related to God, but God is not related to the world."

•

Why the world is related to the Causative Force is obvious under classical/traditional theism. The world, according to most religions, was created by the Causative Force, thus the name Causative Force.

But classical/traditional theism provides no meaning for us in terms of the Causative Force needing us. In fact, the idea of the Causative Force needing us is objected to vehemently by the classical/traditional theists. The result of this objection is an acceptance of a hierarchical system between humanity and the Causative Force based upon relative worth. The Causative Force has much worth; we have none.

There is no doubt that classical/traditional theism has expanded our significance immensely over atheism for it has expanded our perception of existence into eternity. However, with the willingness to develop a hierarchical system between ourselves and the Causative Force, we establish the logic for hierarchy systems within our own society.

•

Hierarchical systems may not sound bad, but keep in mind the types of actions they tend to reinforce between us as humans. They provide the logic that some journeys are more significant than others. They provide the logic that some skin colors are better than others. They provide the logic that some genders are better than others. They simply provide the logic of judging the value of one over another. Does this have a negative impact on society? Does this create a negative impact upon the journey of others? That is not for me to say. That is for society to say; that is for you to say.

And how would we go about eliminating a logic that would allow us to value one over another? We do so by simply expanding the significance of the individual. And how can we logically do so? We expand our view of the size of a Causative Force. We make the Causative Force so big, truly omnipresent, there is nowhere else to put us but within Her.

Does this call for the dismantling of our economic systems, social systems, and religious beliefs? No, no, no. We use what works and modify what doesn't. Capitalism and democracy, for instance, have worked better than any other systems we have developed to date.

Conclusion: What characteristic does classical/traditional theism assign the Causative Force?

Classical/traditional theism assigns the characteristic of simultaneous omnipresence and transcendence to the Causative Force.

•

What is transcendence? It is the state of being independent of the material universe. It is an existence separate from the universe. It is a state of not allowing your creations to be a part of you. It gives birth to loneliness within your creation. It produces despair amongst your "children." It creates isolation and all that goes with it. It creates a perception that provides the logic allowing one to be at the mercy of another. It creates exposure to the threat of eternal punishment. It creates acceptance of not being needed. It establishes a state of nonsignificance. It permits the state of being that allows all abuse to flourish. It is a state of being we humans have allowed others to define as our condition in eternity. It is a state of being we ourselves have accepted yesterday, today, and for tomorrow, for eternity. We humans have defined our own eternity to be one of despair. Willingly, we have accepted for ourselves the hope that maybe, if we are "really, really, really good," we will get some reward. A definition. A definition we live day by day, week by week, year by year. And then we turn around and pass it on to our children as a gift, our legacy to them. Are we "satisfied" with what we have or would we like to change the legacy we have to offer our children? If we would like to change, then let's begin the process.

•

Has classical theism offered only negatives? By no means! Classical/traditional theism has immensely elevated the living conditions and perceptive significance we have of ourselves and of others. But there is no denying that negatives are generated by placing a qualifier upon the magnitude of the Causative Force.

Then back to the point, "...we have to begin the process." Where do we begin? One thing is for certain; we do not begin by destroying everything that has taken thousands of years to build. Therefore, the place to begin would be with an examination of what we have religiously, scientifically, and philosophically. Building a consensus between the three means we have of perceiving what we are and understanding our significance. Building a consensus between faith, observation, and logic. The object is to build a universal philosophy capable of being embraced by all three fields of study.

PANENTHEISM 2000 AD

*What new concept has Panentheism
(the third size of the Causative Force)
firmly established within society?*

**The Causative Force is so big,
She includes everything –
EVEN the universe.
Truly omnipresent.
All present.**

#0. What does the conceptual framework of panentheism offer us?

Panentheism: The term was first used by Krause for his view that the world is a finite creation within the infinite being of God, and that the world is a divine organism so constituted that higher organisms have lower organisms as their constituents. Indeed, organic relationships characterize the cosmologies of panentheists.

Dictionary of Philosophy and Religion, William L. Reese, p. 545

•

Panentheism is the idea that the Causative Force is "all present" and, therefore, we are inside the Causative Force. Krause was not the first to understand the concept of panentheism, but he did name the concept.

Hinduism is the most ancient of our modern religions. Hinduism gave us the broad based support of the concepts of monotheism – one Causative Force, the soul, and the soul existing into eternity. These concepts then lead to the idea of panentheism. Hindus were not the only ones to hold to this basic idea, but they were the first of our modern religions, religions that claim most of the world's population.

Who gets the credit is not the point here. The point is that panentheism assigns the largest size to the Causative Force of all theisms. Because of this, panentheism would provide solutions to many present and future social dilemmas.

•

Panentheism would require some modifications to the perceptions religions maintain, but it in no way interferes with the basics of what any of them teach. The Hindu concepts of monotheism, the soul, eternity of the soul, and dissolving universes, the Judaic concept of the universal Fatherhood of God, the Buddhist concept of addressing suffering, the Christian concept of love, and the Islamic concept of justice all could remain intact with the acceptance of an omnipresent Causative Force.

Panentheism reinforces and provides the understanding of why these ideas are so crucial to the soul itself.

#1. What does the conceptual framework of panentheism imply about the universe within which we live?

Panentheism provides the understanding our universe could be temporary. No matter how temporary our universe may seem to be in terms of philosophical or scientific concepts, our essence, our souls would now have a location, a place to exist beyond our universe itself.

•

What this says is that if the Causative Force is so big that the only place we can exist is within the Causative Force Herself, then nothing, not even the annihilation of our universe, would be able to shake our confidence in the belief that we, our souls, could continue into eternity.

As an example, science is heading in the area of confirming the Big Bang theory. This is the idea that our universe is expanding. This present day theory says that someday, this expansion may reverse itself and our universe may shrink, implode upon itself. This would lead to the total destruction of not just our solar system, nor just our galaxy, but the destruction of our whole universe. Should this idea be proven, there would be a major sense of hopelessness on our part. No possible explanation would seem reasonable as to why we exist. Our universe would be heading towards total destruction, taking our children with it.

If, on the other hand, we understood the significance of the concept that our universe is located inside the Causative Force, as are we, then we would understand that it would not be the Causative Force that was being destroyed – just our universe. The existence of an eternal soul would help us understand that the destruction of our universe would have no impact upon our soul, for our soul would continue to exist within the Causative Force.

•

The destruction of the universe would have no impact upon our souls, for they would be located within and embraced by the Causative Force Herself. Under atheism, the destruction of the universe would destroy all of us. Under classical/traditional theism, the destruction of the universe would not destroy us for our essence is understood to be the soul. However, our soul would be suspended in a void, for under classical/traditional theism, the universe is not inside Her. Only panentheism would provide an immediate location for our souls should the universe implode.

#2. How does omnipresence reinforce the concept of panentheism?

The direction we as a species have been historically heading regarding a Causative Force has been toward the idea of omnipresence. Omnipresence is another word for panentheism.

•

Omnipresence means being present everywhere simultaneously. It is simply a characteristic religions apply to the Causative Force. It is not one any person has applied. It is one that has been applied by religions for over 3,500 years or more. There are three related characteristics religions attribute to the Causative Force. Omnipresence, being everywhere, is just one of the three. Omniscience (all knowing) and omnipotence (all powerful) are the other two.

In order for these characteristics to be what they imply they are, the Causative Force would have to have abilities we profess She has. We cannot turn around once we have given these characteristics to the Causative Force and then reject the logical conclusion to which these characteristics lead us. Either the Causative Force is omnipresent or She isn't.

•

As an example, if the Causative Force is omnipresent and if She is "all just" as some say or "all loving" as others say, then how could injustice or hatred exist within a perfect Causative Force? We cannot refuse to search for an understanding to this problem just because we decide to define the problem out of existence. In other words, we cannot say the Causative Force is omnipresent and then turn around and say the universe does not exist in Her. We cannot say the Causative Force is "all present" and then turn around and place human behavior we do not consider to be "moral" somewhere outside the Causative Force. "Somewhere," in this case, is nowhere, for our religions are based upon the concepts of omnipresence, omnipotence, and omniscience. These contradictions lead to contradictions in human behavior.

This creation of a rationale for contradictory characteristics of the Causative Force then becomes part of our very essence. We begin to act in a manner that contradicts what we profess. We open ourselves up to abuse.

#3. How does a Causative Force needing you reinforce the significance of the concept of panentheism?

If a Causative Force is truly omnipresent, then you would be located within the Causative Force. The question then becomes would an entity as vast as a Causative Force allow something neutral or negative to exist within Her awareness? There would be no choice. If the Causative Force is truly omnipresent, everywhere, there is nowhere else to put you.

•

If you are within the Causative Force, there would be three possibilities regarding your purpose in terms of your eternal soul:
1. You are needed by the Causative Force, the entity within which you are located.
2. You are a detriment to the Causative Force, the entity within which you are located.
3. Your existence has not effected the Causative Force within which you are located. You are a neutral substance, tolerated by the Causative Force.

•

Under panentheism, the question is, "Does the Causative Force need you?" In other words, would your existence be one that contributes to the Causative Force within which you exist in a positive manner, a neutral manner, a negative manner or any combination of the three? All of these could be a possibility, but any of these possibilities still leads to the basic concept that you affect the Causative Force.

Even being a neutral element to a Causative Force is significant for that implies a recognition of your existence. Taking up space, taking up a portion of the actual awareness of a Causative Force, is in itself significant.

Logically speaking, however, if the Causative Force has the vast powers, knowledge, and presence that modern day religions profess, it does not seem logical that it would tolerate something existing within it if that item had no meaning. The universe, as complex as it seems, and your existence within that universe tends to imply that you must have some form of significance. If we have free will, we should give that some thought, for that would in turn imply that we each could choose the type of impact – positive, negative or neither – we have upon the Causative Force Herself.

#4. How does panentheism help us understand what life is?

Complete omnipresence, panentheism, helps us understand that life is not just possibly important; life is important. Life is significant. Panentheism implies that living our lives actually impacts, changes, the Causative Force.

•

Panentheism does not tell us if the impact we have on the Causative Force is "positive," "neutral" or "negative."

Four thousand years ago, we felt the individual had no significance. Since then, we have developed the concepts that the individual had a place in eternity, the individual was significant (Hinduism); the eternal state of the soul became global (Judaism); suffering of the individual was intolerable (Buddhism); the individual had such significance that love was intended for all individuals (Christianity); each individual was so important that to interfere with their purpose would be dealt with justly, if not in this world than in eternity (Islam); the development of the importance of the individual through logic (ontology); and the rational significance of the individual was clearly observable (science). What now?

•

We are at the beginning of the twenty first century, the beginning of the third millennium. All this time, we have been continuing the process of heading towards the recognition of the worth of the individual. We have been working relentlessly as a species towards the goal of global human rights, global individual human significance.

This process needs a perceptual boost in order to continue this momentum through the next 500 years, or through the next millennium for that matter. And where could that boost come from? It could come from a conscious decision on our part to expand the Western perception of the size of a Causative Force. What size are we talking about? We are talking about accepting the size of a Causative Force the major religions of the world have always professed but refused to embrace – panentheism. This action would do nothing less than validate the significance of our very existence in terms of eternity itself.

#5. What does the concept of panentheism have to offer us as individuals?

Panentheism is a Greek term which, when broken down by syllable, means all–in–God. Panentheism offers us a place to exist, we, you and I, within the Causative Force.

•

Panentheism is the concept that all major religions preach but do not necessarily accept. If the Causative force were truly omnipresent, then there is only one place our universe could exist, and that would be within the Causative Force Herself. The idea of being within the Causative Force is what is rejected by western religions. Existing inside the Causative Force means we, you and I, would be nothing less than a portion of the Causative Force. Imagine what this means. You are located, not near the Causative Force, but actually inside Her. All the concepts you assign to the Causative Force, whether it be eternity, intolerance of suffering, love, justice, rationality, observability, all come from, are a part of, are characteristics of the Causative Force, for they all lie within the Causative Force. All are important, for if you exist within the Causative Force, you are immersed in all these characteristics. Religions often reject each other. But why? Which characteristic can we afford to remove from the Causative Force within which we exist?

•

Eastern and western religions hold to the premise of omnipresence. Western religions, however, add their own twist to this concept. Most western religions agree the Causative Force is so big that She is omnipresent, all present. They add a qualifier, however, for they then go on to say that the universe within which we exist is not a part of Her. And why do they do such an odd thing? They do so because they have never been able to come up with a logical reason as to how "sin," how "bad" actions and events could take place in a truly loving or just God. And so it is that western religions left the true concept of "omnipresence" of the Causative Force behind. This action has caused western religions to forge ahead with a Causative Force concept less than omnipresent and that, in turn, has accentuated the major social dilemmas we have to face daily. Without true omnipresence, we cannot define life – eternal or physical. Without a definition of life, we cannot resolve the issues of abortion, cloning, mercy killings, artificial intelligence, extraterrestrial life, androids, abusive behavior, fetal tissue research, religious tolerance, and on and on.

#6. What significance does panentheism have to offer us as a species?

Panentheism offers our species the understanding that "higher organisms have lower organisms as their constituents."

•

What of "lower" organisms? Doesn't this imply that we are inferior to the Causative Force? No, no, no! The word lower here implies being "within," not "inferior to." Being a part of a whole is not a concept of hierarchy. Being a part of a whole does not diminish the concept that the "part of something" has no significance. Your heart has much significance to you. Your brain has much significance to you. Your hands and feet have much significance to you. If the question is just how much significance do you have to the Creative Force, then who are we to judge?

The point that is being made here is that with the acceptance of the concept of panentheism, you and I individually have a purpose in reality. This understanding that we have a purpose is something we never had before either as individuals or as a species. We have sensed it, but never understood it because we have always been told we exist outside of the Causative Force. We have always been told we need the Causative Force but She has no need of us.

•

We needed the message that the Causative Force was always a solid guideline for us. Religions cushioned it with an eternal existence, with a sense of belonging to one uniting Causative Force, with compassion for the misfortunes of others, with love of one another, with the knowledge that justice would have its way in the end. But the loss we felt in not belonging to the Causative Force because we were outside was always an unsettling one. The concept of not understanding that we were a part of the Causative Force always left us as individuals and as a species with a sense of uncertainty as to our significance, for if we were not a part of the Whole, a part of the Causative Force Herself, then just what were we a part of? We were in fact isolated from the Causative Force. Much of what religions had to tell us made sense to us in terms of "gut" feelings (faith, religion) but not in terms of logic (philosophy) nor in terms of much of what we saw (science).

Panentheism rectifies much of this as well as many other paradoxes.

#7. What significance does panentheism have to offer other life forms in the universe?

If we argue that we are a part of the Causative Force because the Causative Force is omnipresent, all present, then we have no choice but to argue the same for other life forms in the universe.

•

We have always related our significance in existence, both as individuals and as a species, to faith, logic, or direct observations. Most of the world now looks at its significance in existence as being attached to the Causative Force and to Her characteristics of eternal existence.

We now, for the most part, accept a limited form of an eternal Causative Force, one that is all present, omnipresent. We hold this concept with the exception that She does not include the universe because "evil" exists there. As such, we have significantly elevated the worth of the individual and the worth of our own species in terms of our right to exist on this earth and to exist along with other life forms in the universe.

Panentheism would expand upon the size of the Causative Force once again just as classical/traditional theisms expanded upon the size of the Causative Force over that held by atheism. The result would interpret into an even greater understanding of the value of the individual as well as our species. This jump would make a leap we as a species had never made before. This jump would actually leap the boundaries of different planetary life forms and create an indisputable argument for the significance of all life forms, earthbound or otherwise.

•

Making the leap of finally having a philosophy that incorporates other life forms throughout the universe provides a rationale for protecting these life forms from ourselves. On the other hand, it also provides a rationale for protecting us from other life forms. In essence, it builds a Magna Carta for all life forms in this universe. In fact, it goes even further. If we should find other universes exist, it could build a Magna Carta for all life forms in all universes. It could build a Magna Carta for the universes themselves. And with an elevation in our understanding of the size of the Causative Force would come an elevation in behavior patterns of all life forms towards each other. Panentheism is not a little idea. It is an idea that expands the size of the Causative Force to such a grand size, it actually includes all universes and all the life forms that exist within them.

#8. What does panentheism imply about our significance in eternity?

Panentheism implies that we are a fundamental part of the Causative Force. "Indeed, organic relationships characterize the cosmologies of panentheists."

•

What does the word "organic" mean here? "Organic" means being an integral part, a fundamental part, of a whole. No longer can you view yourself as existing in a void isolated from the Causative Force. Now you have no choice but to see yourself as being located "within" the Causative Force. Your actions being within the Causative Force leaves you with no choice but to acknowledge the concept that your actions within the Causative Force affect the Causative Force. You are significant enough to actually have an effect upon the very mental state of the Causative Force.

You have a responsibility. You may not be aware now of the effects your actions have upon the eternal emotional state of the Causative Force. However, if as most religions believe, if as much as philosophy rationalizes, if as the scientific beginning–end concepts have shown, you are a part of something greater than the universe, then it is very possible that you will be aware of the repercussions of your actions after this short lifetime.

If you have a soul, if you have an essence capable of surviving beyond this physical reality, you may know, you may be so aware that your awareness will interpret into empathy itself. Under the idea of panentheism, you affect your own eternity. You are responsible.

•

Under panentheism, your actions affect yourself in the eternity to follow. Your actions, through impacting the Causative Force, affect the Causative Force which affects the rest of us who have no place to go after life but into arms of the Causative Force Herself.

Your responsibility lies in three areas:
1. **The impact you have upon your own eternal state of existence.**
2. **The impact you have upon the Causative Force.**
3. **The impact you have upon the rest of us who must go back to the Causative Force.**

Take your responsibility seriously. There is a lot riding upon you.

#9. What does panentheism imply about our relationship to the Causative Force?

Panentheism implies that our relationship to the Causative Force is just that – a relationship.

•

There are many types of relationships. Some are loving and warm. Some are abusive and violent. Some are one way. Some are a two way interaction. Some are beneficial. Some are destructive. We have historically defined the relationship between ourselves and the Causative Force as a one way relationship. We did this out of logic. We did this out of our faith. We did this out of observing what was around us.

But as all of us know, one way, long term relationships lead nowhere but to resentment, disappointment, broken dreams, shattered hopes, irresolvable problems, and eventual separation. These results are reactions that we all wish to avoid in relationships we hold dear. The relationships we cultivate between ourselves and the Causative Force are ones we define. The past separation of religions, science, and philosophy has kept us from understanding the big picture. Each of the areas has one piece of a four piece puzzle and nobody is offering to be first to put their piece on the table.

Now a piece has been placed. Now the size of the Causative Force has been laid on the table for examination and been found to be just what religions have been professing all the time but refused to accept without a qualifier. Now it is time for science to bear its soul and risk putting on the table the piece of the puzzle it holds. It is time to take a breath and hope for the best. Your future, my future, the future of our children, the future of our environment, the future of other life forms in other parts of the universe may very well depend upon the actions we decide to take or worse yet, not take.

•

Panentheism. We have found a home for our soul. "Overly dramatic!" you say. Is it? Perhaps, but on the other hand, perhaps not.

Conclusion: What characteristic does panentheism assign the Causative Force?

Panentheism says the Causative Force is omnipresent (all present) in terms of our universe. There are no qualifiers.

•

A qualifier is an exception to the statement. For example, the Causative Force is omnipresent BUT transcends the universe. This qualifier is an attempt to take from the Causative Force things that are considered to be "sins" of the world. This qualifier is an attempt to take the "evil" of the world, the "bad things" out of the Causative Force. Until, however, we accept the understanding that the "bad things" of the world, the universe, are also inside the Causative Force, we will not understand why it is so important to elevate our level of behavior. We will only take our behavior seriously when we understand that the actions we consciously decide to take will have repercussions that actually become a part of the Causative Force Herself. The sense of responsibility for one's behavior only becomes important when one understands that one's behavior leads to personal repercussions generated from one's own personal behavior.

•

If St. Anselm is correct in arguing that as a species, if we conceive of a necessary being, its existence takes on a reality, then the acceptance of the concept of a Causative Force is perfectly logical. At this point, it is also worth noting that the argument against the Causative Force based upon speculation, that the Causative Force must then have a Causative Force, would have no bearing here. The acknowledgment of a Causative Force for our universe is what is at issue here. The acceptance of such a Force then leads to the discussion of the question regarding where that Force would be.

Religions once professing a Causative Force to be omnipresent, cannot then declare that She is not. The paradox of "evil" existing in a "perfect" being has to be dealt with in another fashion. That is one of the benefits of symbiotic panentheism for just as symbiotic panentheism elevates human perceptions to new levels through expanding the size of the Causative Force, it also does away with one of religion's most perplexing paradoxes which has caused them to reject the omnipresence of the Causative Force even while they proclaim it.

Religion – Conclusion

Our thoughts turn to an understanding we had not quite grasped before. If the Causative Force is truly omnipresent, then the Causative Force is located everywhere and we cannot say otherwise. As such, we must rethink the idea regarding what our significance to the Causative Force may be. Are we still an unnecessary entity to the Causative Force if we exist within Her? Are we in an interactive relationship with Her, as appears to be the case with all other entities throughout the universe? And why the emphasis on the soul, human and otherwise? Is it because the soul is what has significance? Is it because it is the soul through which the Causative Force does things it would otherwise be unable to do?

How could the Causative Force be all powerful, all knowledgeable, all present, if there is something She cannot do? In order to answer these types of questions, we have to begin thinking differently. We have to look at the big picture. If you exist in a universe that is inside the Causative Force, then you are a part of that Causative Force. If your essence is the soul, then your soul is a part of the Causative Force. If your soul is a part of the Causative Force, then your soul must have some significance to the Causative Force. If your soul has significance to the Causative Force, then it must impact the Causative Force. If the soul impacts the Causative Force, then it must impact Her in a manner in which only souls can.

It seems complicated, yet it is simple. The key is that you are in the Causative Force, you are a part of the Causative Force, so what you do is actually being done by a part of the Causative Force Herself. We have always sensed our need for the Causative Force. Yet, we have never considered the other half of the picture; the Causative Force may very well need us. This dependency upon each other is a form of "symbiosis." Each person has significance and, regardless of race, color or creed, is equal to the Causative Force. Since we may all be a part of the Causative Force, "panentheism," we have no choice but to acknowledge the significance and equality of each other. We have no choice but to acknowledge the significance of other life forms and the sacredness of each other's environment, for that is the very medium through which we journey.

The net result is that not only do we need the Causative Force, but the Causative Force needs us. We are in a symbiotic, interdependent relationship with the Causative Force.

Your need of God is only half the picture; the other half is that God needs you. Thus develops the larger picture, the picture of "symbiotic panentheism." Over the last 4,000 years, through 500 year cycles, all three now appear to have emerged in their own right. So now what? Since we are at the gate of the next 500 year cycle, what is the next step? Who is to say for sure? Perhaps it is the development of a new religion. Perhaps it will be a new form of gaining insight. Or perhaps it will be the unification of all three. Perhaps it will be the coming to terms, the establishment of the union of religion, philosophy, and science. After all, these three have been at odds and struggling to maintain the recognition they feel they deserve regarding their contribution to the understanding of a Causative Force ever since their individual emergence into the realm of human history. The struggle between religion, philosophy, and science to maintain their unique identities and significance in terms of understanding a Causative Force has been a long and, at many times, very unpleasant experience for humans. Perhaps the next 500 year cycle is meant to bring peace between the three. A union of this magnitude would no doubt go a long way towards bringing about this peace and tranquility, not only within the individual but within society.

There is much more to discuss. There is much more research that could be done. However, it is time to move on. Another field of study awaits us. It is time to examine what we have learned through the study of what we have seen.

Roger Bacon:

(2) The sciences rest on mathematics and advance only when their facts are subsumed under mathematical principles:
   a. It verifies its conclusions by experiment.
   b. It establishes truths which should not otherwise be reached.
   c. Probing the secrets of nature, it provides us with knowledge, also, of the past and the future.

–Dictionary of Philosophy and Religion,
William L. Reese, p. 63

SCIENCE
What We See

Up to this point, we have examined religious concepts from *Eastern and Western Thought – Dictionary of Philosophy and Religion*. We have been scanning through its 900 pages and have only had time to lightly explore ten of the 4,000 entries. There is much more that could be learned. With this thought in mind, it is easy to imagine the stacks upon stacks, rows upon rows, and floors upon floors of books available to us. The options regarding where to look next seem endless. The knowledge contained in these books comes from all parts of our universe, even from places seemingly alien to us.

We explored the concepts of religion first because they hold the knowledge pertaining to our oldest form of perception used to understand where we are, what we are, and why we are in terms of existence. But our search for understanding the answers to these questions needs to move into another field through which we develop perceptions of ourselves and others. Science is the means by which we form perceptions regarding ourselves based upon what we see, what we observe.

Religious studies emanate an aura of antiquity and tradition. They are wrapped in exquisitely carved stone, hand crafted windows, spires, and steeples reaching for the heavens. Science has a different appearance. It stands stark, new, and clean. The lines of science are simple and efficient. The field of science is filled with large, clear windows which allow the warmth of sunlight and the twinkle of stars to flood each room with a sense of inclusion, beckoning, "Discover what I have to tell you. Come observe and understand."

The door to the wealth of scientific knowledge is so well balanced that it seems to open on its own, leading into a long hall branching off in multiple directions. The halls are adjoined by a seemingly infinite number of rooms filled with books, blueprints, computers, pictures, and manuscripts. The center of each room is occupied with machinery, models, projection devices, and research equipment.

There is no way not to be overwhelmed by the enormity of knowledge stored within these walls. It is difficult not to be awestruck with the immensity of the seemingly endless hall stretching out before you and the diversity of rooms adjoining its spaciousness.

In order to avoid becoming intimidated by the wealth of knowledge science has to offer, we will find it useful to concentrate upon another reference book written for the general reader. The book we will use has 800 pages and over 8,500 entries. The book is the paperback reference, *Oxford Concise Science Dictionary*.

We have come a long way in terms of understanding what we see around us. The total wealth of knowledge has grown so large that it is now impossible for any one person to be an expert in all the sciences. In fact, it is impossible for any one person to be an expert in any one field of science. To assume we could pick one book to act as 'the' reference source for science makes no sense. But we have to begin somewhere, so rather than think of the *Oxford Concise Science Dictionary* as 'the' source for science, it would be better to think of it as a beginning point.

This book may be a book written for the general reader, but it is nevertheless very intimidating. The wealth of knowledge contained within its pages is mind-boggling. To pick ten concepts from this book to represent science would appear to border on the edge of lunacy. But a universal model of philosophy cannot be considered 'universal' if it cannot stand up to all means by which we develop perceptions of what we are. Religion is only one means by which we develop a perception of what it is we are and why we exist. Science, observing what exists around us, is another important means by which we develop perceptions of what it is we are and why we exist. To shirk the examination of this field of perception, based upon a sense of intimidation created by the vast wealth of knowledge this field has collected, is nothing other than shirking our responsibility.

Since accepting responsibility for one's actions is a primary outcome that the universal philosophy model of symbiotic panentheism generates, we have little choice but to examine how symbiotic panentheism stands up to the facts of science. Since we are limited to ten concepts, we may as well pick several fields of study. With this in mind, four basic fields of science stand out as excellent candidates for examination. Physics, representing the space our universe appears to occupy, is the first candidate. Mathematics, representing the container within which our universe appears

INTRODUCTION

to be located, is the second candidate. Biology, representing our life form which appears to be located within the container of space, is the third; and geology, representing dramatic change which appears to be constantly taking place within our container, is the fourth.

What concepts should be picked within the areas of physics? Since entropy deals with life and death of total systems, it seems to be a good choice to apply to space as a total. The Big Bang theory is an attempt on the part of physics to model the life cycle of the universe, which appears to connect well with entropy. Symmetry provides an interesting means of explaining how the universe could dissolve into pure nothing, which in turn allows for an understanding of how something could be created from 'nothing.' Since this would tend to summarize the ideas of entropy and the Big Bang theory, it is the third choice for physics.

Since mathematics is often difficult to understand, a concept in set theory was used. This concept is known as Venn Diagrams, which are simply pictures. Drawing pictures provides a simple yet very effective means by which we can understand where it is our universe is located. The second concept of mathematics deals with the field of geometry: 'the whole is equal to the sum of its parts.' The boundary of our universe may or may not be a part of the universe. For purposes of convenience, it will be considered as a part of the universe. Since topology is the mathematical study of surfaces, it was chosen as the second mathematical field to examine. The third choice of mathematics was the concept of space, three dimensions immersed in time.

Following physics and mathematics comes biology. Since the relationship between a life form and its environment are so important, ecology was chosen as a field of study. This was followed by the biological classification term, Homo, since humans – Homo sapiens – are the last living members of our genus Homo. Biology was then interrupted by a concept in geology called palaeomagnetism. This concept is used to represent one of the most basic characteristics of our universe: change. Finally, symbiosis was chosen as the last topic because it represents the summation of the first nine topics, but it also provides a purpose to religious concepts.

The simplicity of math and science will turn out to be the surprising aspect of this part of our journey. The ten items of math and science appear complex upon first reading, but the implications they offer in terms of understanding symbiotic panentheism are not.

SCIENCE

*What new insight has Science
firmly established within society?*

ENTROPY:
Change

#0. What does the conceptual framework of entropy have to offer us?

Entropy: In a wider sense, entropy can be interpreted as a measure of disorder; the higher the entropy the greater the disorder. ...the entropy of the universe (if it can be considered a closed system) is increasing and its available energy is decreasing.
–Oxford Concise Science Dictionary, p. 255

•

Entropy sounds complex, but it has a simple idea to offer. It states that within a closed system, a system that is located within a boundary, the system will eventually die. The more science learns, the more it appears that the life of the universe may be temporary. The life of the universe may be billions upon billions of years old, but it appears to have an ending, just as Hindus have always believed.

But how does a universe die? Entropy tells us energy is the means by which work is done in our universe. Heat, in turn, is the basic means by which energy is transferred from one item in the universe to another. Basically, heat can only pass from a higher level to a lower level. In other words, a hot item (high energy item) can warm up a colder item (lower energy item) or one could say, a colder item "steals" heat from a hotter item. As this transfer of heat takes place, work is done.

When heat has finally been spread out equally (everything is the same temperature), no heat can transfer from one item to another because everything would then be the same temperature. If no heat can transfer from one place to another, then no work is able to occur. If no work occurs, no motion, no change, no life would occur in the universe.

•

Death of the universe, death of our home, and where does that leave us? That leaves us with no place to go if our universe is not located inside something. And what are we? If we live into eternity, as religions say, then we are souls. We are souls today, souls from the past, souls that will exist into the future up to the point at which the universe 'dies.'

So, what does the conceptual framework of entropy have to offer us? It has death of the universe to offer us. Is this bad? No, but it doesn't explain the logic as to how or why the universe was here to begin with.

#1. What does the conceptual framework of entropy imply about the universe within which we live?

Because the universe is in a constant state of action, entropy would imply the universe is alive in the sense that it is constantly changing.

•

The universe is a heat exchange system. Action, change, occurs within our universe when heat is passed from place to place. The measure of the amount changed is entropy.

The whole orientation of this concept is simple. If things never change, they remain 'permanent.' The final state of the universe would be at the point heat is distributed evenly, 'equally,' throughout the universe. Combine these two ideas and you have 'permanent equilibrium.' As a simple example, if everything in our universe suddenly became the same temperature, then everything would be 'frozen' in place. There would be no heat exchange, therefore no change. Nothing would move. In this situation, nothing would decay, nothing would grow, everything would be the same. Everything would be in 'permanent equilibrium' today, tomorrow, forever.

We have never seen a permanent state of equilibrium in our universe. Our universe, and everything in it, appears to be undergoing constant change through growth or decay. Our universe is alive and vibrant.

•

Growth and decay will eventually stop as energy levels become the same throughout the universe. Change will eventually stop. If our universe is all there is, as atheists and pantheists believe, then our universe can die and with it, dies existence as we know it. This implies all the change, all the 'work' that occurred within it over the thousands upon thousands, millions upon millions, billions upon billions of years, will have had no meaning.

This does not seem logical. On the other hand, if something exists beyond our universe, the 'thing' outside itself would still exist. The significance the universe generated could possibly exist as long as the 'thing' outside existed. We refer to this 'thing' as the creator of this universe. We refer to this 'thing' as the Causative Force. Entropy implies three possible states of existence: growth, permanent equilibrium, decay. We have never observed the state of permanent equilibrium within our universe. Once our universe reaches the state of permanent equilibrium, entropy implies the universe would be 'dead.'

#2. How does the concept of entropy reinforce the concept of panentheism?

If, as entropy implies, our universe will eventually die, that would imply it had a beginning. If our universe had a beginning, this would imply there was something 'before' our universe. This would imply a creator, a Causative Force to our universe. Our universe must be somewhere or in something, for something exists besides our universe.

•

Panentheism simply means all in the Causative Force. If the Causative Force existed before our universe, then in a sense it must be "somewhere." This is not as complex as some people think. Somewhere does not have to be a place, a space. It only has to be existence of some manner or other. This existence would occupy "something" and it is within this "something" that the universe would be placed when it was created. After all, where else could the universe be put? This is panentheism. Panentheism simply states that the universe is in this "something" that created it. This "something" is "somewhere" and it is there that the universe was placed.

"Something," "somewhere" – it all sounds like a bunch of gibberish and in a sense, it is. The easiest way to say the same thing is simply to say: the universe had a beginning, therefore the universe had a creator, therefore the universe was started by a Force – the Causative Force. The Causative Force therefore exists, and the Causative Force is so big in terms of the universe that it created the universe within Herself.

•

Why couldn't the Causative Force have created the universe outside Herself? She might have, but in that case, She would not be omnipresent. This implies she is not all knowledgeable, for something exists outside Her. As such, She is not omniscient. If She is not omniscient, then this would imply she is not all powerful. The lack of any knowledge would be lack of some power, for knowledge is power. If, as a society, we wished to accept the Causative Force in terms of Her not being omnipotent, omnipresent, and omniscient, then we have to change religions drastically. Our religions are based upon the concept that the Causative Force is all three: omnipresence, omniscience, omnipotence. Religions build the beginning of our understanding of the Causative Force and significance upon omnipresence.

#3. What does entropy reinforce about the significance of existence, life?

Entropy implies life and change are interconnected, no change equals no life. Then isn't everything alive? And if so, then isn't everything sacred?

•

In a sense, everything is sacred. But there appears to be a difference between a temporary state of existence, such as the universe, and an eternal state of existence, such as a soul (eternal awareness). Entropy would imply that while the universe is in constant change, eventually that will stop. Religions imply awareness exists beyond time, beyond the life of the universe. If life is defined as a state of constant change, as entropy implies, then a 'living' Causative Force would appear to need to undergo change. If, on the other hand, a Causative Force is all present, all powerful, all knowing, it implies She cannot grow. This would imply she is not living. This is a paradox. Entropy gives us a clue as to how to get around this paradox.

If we combine religion with entropy, we come up with the following scenario. The Causative Force exists and knows everything. The Causative Force could not create 'new things' because everything was already inside and known to Her. Therefore, She took the idea of symmetry (next chapter), which already existed inside Her, and using it, created the universe out of 'nothingness' (see the book, *You and I Together*). Pieces of soul (coming from Her and returning to Her) enter this universe in one state of awareness and exit this universe in another state of awareness. Once leaving the universe in a changed state, these pieces of awareness (souls) reenter the Causative Force. The Causative Force is now changed. Life, you and I, become the means by which the Causative Force changes Herself.

•

This process seems to contradict the idea of a Causative Force being omnipresent, omnipotent, and omniscient. It does just the opposite, however. If a Causative Force is all knowing, but does not know how to create what does not exist, it is not all knowing. On the other hand, if a Causative Force is all knowing of everything there is, including knowing how to create what doesn't exist, then it already knows the process to create something that isn't. Thus, in a sense, 'new things' that do not exist already, do exist and are a part of an all knowing, truly omniscient being.

#4. How does entropy help us understand what life is?

Entropy explains the means by which the universe operates. The universe operates upon the idea of heat exchange. As heat exchange takes place, change takes place. Change is the key characteristic we use to establish if something is alive.

•

The word *alive* is a complex term. If change is part of the definition for being alive, then the universe is alive because it is undergoing constant change. Many environmentalists would say our planet is alive and our universe is alive just as we are alive. If this is true, then what makes us different from earth, plants, animals, the universe itself? Atheists would say there is no basic difference. Because we are basically the same, we should show the same respect to the earth, universe, and each other as we do ourselves.

Classical/traditional religions would say we humans are different because there is an extra element within us that is not found within the earth, soil, plants, and universe. Religions say we have a soul. They go on to say the soul is eternal and not attached to this planet or this universe. If we have a soul and if the soul goes beyond the universe, then the idea of the universe eventually 'dying,' as entropy suggests, is not a concern we need to agonize over. Entropy implies we can measure life through the means of observing if change takes place. When the ideas of entropy are combined with religion, we begin to understand life exists on many levels. There appears to be life without awareness (rocks, mountains, water...), life with temporary awareness (trees, birds, bacteria...), and life with eternal awareness (humans, extraterrestrial life forms...).

•

Entropy helps us understand life. Life now becomes definable and the soul becomes measurable. Without being measurable, the essence of human life could not be debated by science. Because of this, science could not distinguish human life from other types of life. This presented many types of seemingly unresolvable social issues, such as abortion, fetal tissue research, artificial intelligence... If, however, scientists, doctors, clergy, layman, etc. consider the essence of a human (the soul) to have left the body when the brain waves do not change (flat line brain waves), then they have no choice but to define the essence of the human to occur when the brain waves start (changing brain waves). Now the issue of abortion becomes resolvable. Entropy, the measure of change, helps us understand life.

#5. What does entropy have to offer us as individuals?

Entropy implies that change is the key to 'being alive.'

•

Science only deals with the observable and leaves the debate regarding the unobservable to religions and philosophy. The science of entropy predicts the 'death' of the universe. As such, entropy implies there was 'something' before, which implies there may very well be 'something' after. It does not seem logical that this 'something' would not exist between the stages of 'before' and 'after.' Therefore, we assume this 'something' exists now – is living now.

Entropy offers us an understanding that, although the universe may 'die,' each of us as individuals may survive this 'death.' Entropy reinforces the religious idea of 'eternal life' for the individual. Eternity is simply a state of being that came well before the universe, continues to exist, and will continue to exist beyond the death of the universe. Entropy implies the universe is temporary, which implies there is something that is not temporary. Something is eternal. Something appears to have no connection to time, for time appears to be an idea that depends upon the existence of mass. But that is another idea altogether.

Although entropy may assign a hopeless state to the universe, it will die at the same time it offers hope to each of us as individuals. By introducing the idea of our universe dying, entropy alludes to the idea of eternal existence. This suggests the possibility of something nonphysical, such as awareness, being able to transcend the physical universe. Entropy offers us a sense of hope.

•

The conceptual framework of entropy offers us eventual 'death' for our universe. If we are a part of our universe and if eternity does not exist, then the apparent conclusion would be that all individuals would eventually die away permanently. All the struggles to overcome adversity and temptation will have had no meaning, no significance. But if something exists beyond our universe, this changes.

If there is a Causative Force, as the science of entropy implies, and if the Causative Force is all present, as religions imply, then the easiest way for us to understand the manner in which we, as individuals, can escape death, the ultimate fate of the universe, is to understand that our awareness is tied to, becomes a part of, total awareness or the omniscience of the Causative Force. As such, hope emerges. Entropy brings us hope.

#6. What significance does entropy have to offer us as a species?

Entropy predicts the death of a universe. Awareness now becomes a key element in understanding the significance we may play in terms of eternity itself. Awareness of the individual becomes intensified with numbers. A species now takes on significance.

•

Entropy, by predicting the death of our universe, reinforces the idea of eternity, something existing before, after, and during the existence of the physical universe. And what is it that could possibly exist if the universe 'died?' What could exist if the universe imploded? What could exist if the Hindus are correct when they say the universe 'dissolves?' What could survive the total destruction of our universe?

Awareness would seem to be the answer. Awareness is defined as the knowledge obtained through perceptions gained in life. Once knowledge, awareness, is created, it can never be destroyed. This awareness will travel beyond the universe and eternity itself. This awareness is what we are. Will we, therefore, be required to experience the pain and love we experienced in life? Probably not, for that pain and love has already been experienced by us, known by us, and we can move on from it. What, then, of the pain and love we generated for others? Would this be experienced by us personally? We have not yet experienced the pain and love others experienced due to our actions. If our awareness transcends this physical universe, and if our awareness becomes immersed within total awareness, the Causative Force, it would seem to imply that we would become fully aware of, actually experience, the pain and love we inflicted upon others, for we will exist immersed in omniscience.

•

So what does all this mean? It means if you come into the world with some awareness, you leave with more awareness because awareness, knowledge, cannot be destroyed. Therefore, you take the awareness you gain with you to wherever it is you go. If entropy and religions are correct, you take this awareness into the Causative Force Herself and thus, you cause change within the Causative Force. Multiply this by billions upon billions of individuals that make up our species and you begin to understand how our species may affect our eternity.

#7. What significance does entropy have to offer other life forms in the universe?

Entropy is an idea that applies to our whole universe. The ideas it implies, therefore, do not apply to just the human race; they apply to all life forms in the universe.

•

"A" Causative Force, eternal life (existence beyond the universe), the soul, awareness, pain being brought into the Causative Force, love being brought into the Causative Force, all become universal ideas. Universal ideas apply throughout the universe. Universal ideas extend from one side of the universe all the way to the other side. Pain and love generated is pain and love generated. Once generated, it is known. Being known implies something or someone is 'aware' of it. It cannot ever be destroyed. It exists beyond the universe. It exists into eternity. It does not stop with humanity.

If it is possible for us to generate pain and love, it is possible for others to generate the same. As such, we owe it to each other to respect the journeys of all souls; awareness expands with having journeyed the universe and awareness moves into eternity. All souls must improve upon the potential journey the individual soul senses it must take, be they human or otherwise. We have no right to subjugate these souls nor dominate them in an attempt to force our personal impressions of what we think these journeys should be. In essence, entropy offers human souls and other life forms the initial understanding of why our journeys and journeys of other life forms are important beyond this temporary universe.

•

What is it that entropy offers other life forms? Entropy offers other life forms, all life forms, the right to journey through life unimpeded by constraints intentionally, subconsciously or naturally imposed upon them by others. This right extends to all souls, human or extraterrestrial. The only logical exception to this would be the need to prevent souls from infringing upon the journey of other souls. Infringement goes against the very right extended to individuals themselves, for it contradicts the right, the reason, a soul has for traveling unimpeded. And what of society and institutions? Do they have the right to infringe on the journey of souls? No, they are not souls. Their only function is protecting the right of souls to journey unimpeded, improving the journey each soul is intended to take.

#8. What does entropy imply about our significance in eternity?

Entropy implies our universe will die once the heat within it is evenly distributed throughout. With the death of the universe will come the death of our physical mind and body. Therefore, entropy would suggest, if there is any long term reason for existing, it must lie somewhere other than our physical body.

•

Entropy provides the basic understanding regarding why our universe is not eternal. Action takes energy. Heat, in turn, is the basic means by which energy is transferred from one item in the universe to another. Basically heat can only pass from a higher to a lower level. The whole idea behind the mechanism of our universe, the symmetry needed to create our universe, the intricacies of our universe, is absolutely wonderful. But where did the idea of this mechanism, the idea of symmetry, and the idea of different heat levels come from originally?

Some Causative Force had enough awareness to begin the process. This awareness is considered total omniscience. Total awareness implies totally embracing everything which leads to the concept of all presence. Together, all knowledge and all presence adds up to total power. Total power means having enough power to change. The mechanism for change is changing awareness itself. Our awareness changes. Our awareness is knowledge. Knowledge cannot be destroyed. We may very well be the mechanism by which total awareness, the Causative Force, changes. Entropy begins the process of understanding the significance of change. Entropy begins the process of understanding our significance to eternity.

•

Eternity is existence beyond time. Awareness is a concept; it is not physical. Physical items are connected in terms of the three dimensions of space and the fourth dimensions of time. Awareness appears to transcend all four of these dimensions. You have awareness. You have a part of you that is not connected to these four dimensions. Your awareness is unaffected by time. You are thus a part of eternity. The Causative Force is a total awareness – omniscience. Since you are a part of the total awareness, you are a part of the Causative Force. And where does the logic of all this begin? It begins with the understanding that the universe may die. It begins with entropy.

#9. What does entropy imply about our relationship to the Causative Force?

Entropy applies to a closed system. Entropy implies death is contained within closed systems. If religions are correct about an omnipresent Causative Force, then the Causative Force may be the first open system to which science has been exposed. Studying the open system of the Causative Force will require studying ourselves, for we would be a part of Her.

•

No wonder science seems to have such a difficult time dealing with the idea of a Causative Force. Science has only been able to observe 'closed,' bounded systems such as lakes, cells, stars, planets, mountains, the universe. Science, as a field of study, does not acknowledge the idea of an 'open' system, a Causative Force, because it has never seen one. On the other hand, scientists, as people, are quite capable of accepting the Causative Force because, although they work with the observable, they, as people, intuitively understand the concept of an 'open,' unbounded system, a Causative Force.

Entropy would suggest that we are a part of this open system. As such, we depend upon the Causative Force. Most religions would not deny this statement. However, entropy would suggest, if we are a part of the Causative Force, that the Causative Force is dependent upon us. How could a Causative Force 'need' humans or non-terrestrial life forms? Entropy would imply if our essence is awareness, if awareness is never destroyed, if total awareness includes our awareness (if it doesn't it cannot be 'total'), then we become a part of total awareness. As our awareness grows, so grows the Causative Force. As we change, so changes the Causative Force. Entropy suggests we are a means by which the Causative Force changes. We have an interdependent, symbiotic relationship with the Causative Force.

•

Interdependence, symbiosis, is a relationship where one is dependent upon the other. We need the Causative Force. The Causative Force needs us. But keep in mind that symbiosis is not always positive and constructive. It occasionally is negative and destructive, which we will examine in more detail later.

Conclusion: How does the concept of entropy (change) reinforce the concept of symbiotic panentheism?

It does not; what is really taking place is that symbiotic panentheism is reinforcing the science of entropy.

•

Religions imply the Causative Force is a 'living' entity.

Entropy implies change. Change is one of the means by which we identify 'life', if something is 'living.' If we have permanent significance to the Causative Force, it would imply we cause change in the Causative Force.

Combining the ideas of religion and entropy seems to reinforce symbiotic panentheism. On the other hand, symbiotic panentheism reinforces the concepts of religion and entropy. Religion and entropy are systems. Symbiotic panentheism is just two simple statements: the Causative Force is all present so we are in Her and are affected by Her. We are in the Causative Force, are a part of Her, so She is affected by us. A statement does not make a system. Two statements can support systems but they are not complex enough to be systems. Two statements can be two blocks in the foundation but two statements cannot be the complex structure built upon the foundation. Symbiotic panentheism reinforces religion and the science of entropy, not the other way around.

•

Change, a state of existence that entropy says exists for all closed systems. But if the Causative Force is not a closed system, would She have to change? Science has only observed three forms of existence: growth, decay, and permanent equilibrium. Entropy suggests that a nonchanging entity is not 'alive,' not living. The concept of permanent equilibrium, knowing everything, implies an unchanging system, a static Causative Force, a stagnant, nonliving Causative Force. This does not appear to be the concept of a Causative Force we wish to accept as a society.

This leaves growth and decay. Growth and decay are relative. Growth to one may not be growth to another. We, as individuals, will have to jealously guard our rights to determine what growth is. The concept of symbiotic panentheism would do nothing to destroy our present religions. Symbiotic panentheism would reinforce our right to determine the direction our personal journeys should go, reinforce the foundations of our religions, and reinforce the significance and rights of all souls to journey through life unimpeded by others.

*What new insight has **Science**
firmly established within society?*

THE BIG BANG:
Explosion/Implosion

#0. What does the conceptual framework of the Big Bang Theory have to offer us?

The Big Bang Theory: the cosmological theory that all the matter and energy in the universe originated from a state of enormous density and temperature that exploded at a finite moment in the past. The theory successfully explains the expansion of the universe; the observed microwave background radiation characteristic of black-body radiation...
—*Oxford Concise Science Dictionary*, p. 234

•

The Big Bang Theory is just that – a theory. Theories are not truths. Theories are guesses scientists make that are supported by observations, lots of observations. If an explanation which explains an observation is supported by only a few observations, then it is called a hypothesis. A theory is a hypothesis that has gained a greater degree of acceptance in terms of being possibly true. Theories are not always correct, however. The earth is flat, space is filled with ether, man was not meant to fly, matter and energy are totally independent of each other... are just a few examples of incorrect theories. No one is implying that the Big Bang Theory is an absolute fact. It is just that at this point, it seems to be the best explanation of what we observe occurring within our universe.

And what does the Big Bang Theory state? The Big Bang Theory simply states that the universe started out smaller in size than it is now and is expanding like a balloon being inflated. The implication is one of three things: the universe will continue to expand, the universe will reach a size of permanent equilibrium where it no longer expands and does not contract or it will contract like a balloon whose air is being let out.

•

Expansion, permanent equilibrium, decay appear to be the three choices we have. Rephrased, these three concepts become change through growth, no change, change through decay. The Big Bang Theory appears to be just another way of stating entropy. Entropy explained how the universe changes through the interaction of heat exchange and time. The Big Bang Theory explains how the universe changes through the interaction of gravity and time. The concept of the Big Bang gives a long term view of what we feel may happen to our universe, what will happen to life.

#1. What does the conceptual framework of the Big Bang Theory imply about the universe within which we live?

The Big Bang Theory offers us an understanding of what is happening to our universe. Our universe appears to be growing, expanding.

•

The implications are monumental. Will the universe ever stop growing? If not, and if it is bounded, will it explode like a balloon? If it does not explode, will it become so large that the distances between stars and galaxies become impossible to travel? If the distances become so great between the galaxies and stars, will we become totally isolated from the rest of the universe?

On the other hand, will the universe ever stop growing and just stay as it is forever, like a stretched rubber band held in place by two nails? Is there such a thing as something staying the same forever?

Then again, will the universe snap back like a rubber band and shrink back to its original size? Will the universe implode? What was its original size? Was the original size smaller than the primordial atom from which scientists think the universe started? Was there a time when the primordial atom did not exist? The questions are endless. But whatever the question, the implications remain the same. The universe appears to be in a constant state of change.

•

Change, change, change, we cannot seem to find any observations that supports the idea of a non-changing entity. We cannot seem to find any observations that support the idea that a Causative Force is constant. We cannot seem to find any observations that support the idea that the Causative Force is all present, omnipresent; all knowing, omnipotent; and all powerful, omnipotent and cannot become more so, cannot change. In spite of all our scientific observations to the contrary, religions continue to cling to the concept that the Causative Force is in a permanent state of equilibrium. Religions cannot seem to accept the idea that a Causative Force may be able to grow because it is just what they say She is: omnipotent, omnipresent, and omniscient.

#2. How does the concept of the Big Bang Theory reinforce the concept of panentheism?

The Big Bang Theory would imply the boundary of our universe is expanding into something.

•

If our universe is expanding into something, this would imply our universe is, in a sense, embraced by something. Perhaps it is embraced by its Creator. If it is not lying within its Creator, what would it be lying within? If it is lying within its Creator, the Creator is what we would call omnipresent in relationship to the universe. The universe would be finite, a part of, a piece of the Causative Force. This is panentheism. If the universe begins shrinking, the same argument applies. Expanding/contraction, exploding/imploding – the argument is still the same.

If the universe is not lying within the Creator, as present day religions profess, then it would have to be expanding into something that is not a part of the Causative Force because the Causative Force, as religions say, would 'transcend' the universe. But this argument undermines the very foundation of religion. This argument implies the Causative Force is not all present because the universe lies elsewhere. The destruction of the concept of omnipresence creates a domino effect. With the destruction of the idea that the Causative Force is omnipresence, all present, comes the destruction of the Causative Force being omniscient, all knowledgeable, followed by the destruction of the Causative Force being omnipotent, all powerful.

•

Religions need to rethink their concepts regarding the universe and its characteristics. They must begin to understand that whatever traits science assigns the universe will have an impact upon the view we have regarding the size, shape, and life span we believe the universe has. These ideas, in turn, will affect the impressions we have regarding what we believe lies outside, surrounds, our universe. This, in turn, will have a major impact upon how we view the Causative Force Herself. If religions wish to retain the concept that the Causative Force is omnipresent, omnipotent, and omniscient, then they may very well have to accept that the idea of the Causative Force knows so much, She even knows how to grow. Religions may have to accept the idea of the Causative Force being so powerful, She is able to implement the process of change, growth, for Herself.

#3. What does the Big Bang Theory reinforce about the significance of existence, life?

Life exists within the universe. The Big Bang Theory, by suggesting the universe is expanding, suggests the universe is limited in size. After all, if the universe were not limited in size, how could it expand and become bigger? If the universe is limited in terms of both size, as the Big Bang Theory suggests, and time, as entropy suggests, then the items that exist within the universe must be limited. Life must be limited.

•

For something not to be limited, it would have to have no size and be eternal. The religious concept of the soul fits these very requirements, assuming the soul is awareness and would appear to have no apparent need of matter or energy to exist. Once created, awareness just is. Awareness may need matter and energy in order to create. Awareness may need a location where it can grow, change, but awareness does not need matter and energy to continue to exist. Even the destruction, death, of the universe, whether it be through the final stage of entropy, explosion or implosion, the awareness created and the changes made in awareness will remain. Awareness created or changed remains independent of time.

•

But what of awareness? Is it really eternal? We sense eternity to be something unaffected by time. As such, the answer would appear to be, yes, awareness is eternal. If we accept the religious concepts of an eternal Causative Force, and if we accept we have a soul, essence, awareness, that is eternal, then this awareness 'lives forever.' This awareness becomes a part of the total awareness. But atheists would refute this idea. They would say there is nothing outside the universe. They would say it is the universe that is infinite. Science is strongly leaning in the direction that this is not the case. Science constantly seeks to find the boundary of the universe. Unless we are ready to discard most of our present day religions and most of science, we are going to have to direct our attentions mainly towards the implications a boundary to the universe has in terms of what significance life has. The Big Bang Theory seems to be pointing us towards specific ideas regarding the size and location of our Causative Force. The Big Bang Theory, combined with religious ideas, appears to strongly suggest that life may very well have a significant impact upon the Causative Force Herself.

#4. How does the Big Bang Theory help us understand what life is?

The body and mind are made of the same material as other objects in the universe. Just as the universe is temporary, so are the body and mind. 'Life' has a beginning and an end.

•

But religions say 'life' is eternal. Religions are referring to the soul, your essence, your awareness. Some religions are referring to a form your awareness may take once having passed beyond the limits of our universe, limits the Big Bang Theory and entropy describe. Life may leave the body, but what religions call spiritual life remains and goes elsewhere. The Big Bang Theory opens up the idea of something more permanent than the universe, to which the soul, spiritual life, may go. The Big Bang Theory changes the idea regarding living beyond the universe from being a silly speculation to being rational.

If the Big Bang Theory helps to validate the idea of 'something' existing beyond the boundaries of our universe, then by doing so, it helps validate the idea that awareness, made of neither matter nor energy, may well have a place to which it can go. An abstract idea such as eternal life does not exist in the concrete, physical sense. It cannot be measured, but we know the idea exists nonetheless. A location outside our universe may not be concrete in nature. We may not be able to measure it, but we sense it exists nonetheless. A sense of this location is reinforced by the big bang concept, for the Big Bang Theory suggests the universe is expanding into something and since the 'concrete' is what is contained within the universe, it may well be that what lies outside the universe is not concrete.

•

At last, we have another way of understanding what lies outside the universe, of understanding the eternal. Now it is awareness that takes on the sense of the eternal. It is awareness, your essence, that is understood to move beyond the boundaries of the universe. It is a little bit of awareness that comes into the universe and through expansion, change, growth, an expanded awareness leaves this universe. This increased piece of awareness becomes once again united with total awareness, expanding upon, changing total awareness. Total awareness no longer just is, total awareness now becomes a growing, changing, thriving, living entity because life, existence within the universe, makes it so. Life in the universe becomes the mechanism by which the Causative Force sustains Her own life.

#5. What does the Big Bang Theory have to offer us as individuals?

If awareness is the essence of the soul, the essence of the individual, then it would appear that your essence, soul, would need a 'place' to exist other than the universe, since the Big Bang Theory suggests the universe exists only temporarily.

•

The Big Bang Theory does not hang a curtain of despair over the universe by suggesting the universe will 'die.' At first glance, this would appear to be the case. At first glance, the Big Bang Theory seems to offer that our universe will die, our children will die, everything we have worked to build will be exterminated. Life will die out. But this is not what the Big Bang Theory offers us as individuals. If we can prove the Big Bang Theory to be correct, we will have the proof we need to believe something exists beyond the scope of our universe. If our universe is to die out, it had to have a beginning. This implies something exists in addition to what we find in this universe. This implies there is more to life than what we see. The Big Bang Theory provides us with a scientific insight as to what eternity is and where it lies.

Now it is not just religion (faith) which provides us with a sense of existence beyond time. It is science. What we observe occurring around us (science) provides the logic that eternity exists. To say eternity exists within our universe, a universe limited by time, makes no sense, but eternity existing beyond the constraints of time, beyond the boundaries of our universe, makes sense. The Big Bang Theory offers us hope.

•

If we understand eternity exists outside our universe in the form of abstract ideas, then individual awareness, an abstract idea, now is understood to be a concept that can move beyond the universe. And what scientific concept provides the reinforcement for just such an idea? The Big Bang Theory provides the understanding that there must be something beyond our boundaries if these boundaries actually do expand. Existence beyond the universe provides an understanding that all things in the universe may not be composed of matter and energy with which we are familiar. Some items may be items that exist forever. Awareness may be just such an item. The Big Bang Theory implies your essence, your awareness, your 'soul,' the individual, may be eternal.

#6. What significance does the Big Bang Theory have to offer us as a species?

If our individuality is unique, eternal, enters eternity, changes eternity through its uniqueness, then the same would be true of the uniqueness we as a species have to offer eternity.

•

The impact of billions would certainly have an impact if a single individual would have an impact. The species has as much to offer in terms of its uniqueness to eternal awareness, the Causative Force, as a single individual has to offer. The whole species cannot be represented by one individual anymore than a whole individual can be represented by one cell. After all, which cell would we use to represent us? Would we use a skin cell that represents what we look like on the surface? Would we use a heart cell to represent us as an individual? After all it helps to pump the blood, which in turn provides the nutrition our body needs. Would we use a brain cell to represent what we are as individuals, for it allows us to observe what goes on around us?

The same problem would arise in trying to determine which individual we would use to best represent our species. No one individual is typical of our whole species. The Big Bang Theory provides the understanding of the unique contribution each individual, each species, has to offer eternity.

•

Awareness, souls, appear to change as they journey within this universe. If they leave this universe, as religions and the Big Bang Theory imply, then it would appear these pieces of awareness would change the Causative Force as they move in and out of this universe. This change must be significant or it would not happen. This change would seem to have purpose, for it exists as a mechanism, a process within a Causative Force. If this is the case, if change in awareness is an important element of the Causative Force, then change created by the individual would have as much importance as change generated by a species. Change is change and the degree of change implies size or magnitude. Size is something we have basically removed as an element of the Causative Force when we say the Causative Force is omnipresent.

Thus the Big Bang Theory not only implies hope, it blows apart the idea of one individual, one species, being worth more than another, for it establishes the idea that the individual causes change.

SCIENCE: MATRIX #217

#7. What significance does the Big Bang Theory have to offer other life forms in the universe?

All life forms are equal, regardless of race, color, creed or appearance.

•

The individual contribution to eternity now becomes the contribution of a changed awareness. As an example, take the concept of color. How light is absorbed or not absorbed by matter is what causes light. Observing color changes awareness. This change in awareness has nothing to do with the color itself. The change in awareness has to do with change and change is an abstract idea separate from how light reflects off matter. This change in your awareness is an abstract event. An abstract idea is not concrete in nature like a tree or a rock. The awareness of the event is what will live into eternity, not the event itself.

Why pick color as an example? Color is one of the traits many people use to judge each other. But color is not what is of importance. Change in awareness is what is of importance. Is it really logical to expect the type of impact one's contribution would make upon total awareness to be based upon color? And just what does this have to do with other life forms in the universe? If we cannot overcome the obstacle of color when we interact with individuals within our own species, how are we going to deal with unusual shapes, smells, thought process, and value systems other life forms will surely have? The Big Bang Theory begins to elevate our understanding of the significance all life forms have to contribute to the Causative Force, terrestrial or otherwise.

•

Color is only one of many examples we use to judge other members of our species. Gender, age, sexual orientation, size, intellect, power, wealth, ethnic background... We have made great strides towards moving beyond these surface level traits for judging people, but we have much more to do. We must look for ways to accelerate the process of becoming more tolerant. If we are to step into space, we will most likely have much greater differences to deal with than just these humanly differences. The Big Bang Theory, by helping us understand the growth and death of our universe, helps us understand the concept of what may lie beyond it and the significance each life form may have to offer eternity.

#8. What does the Big Bang Theory imply about our significance in eternity?

The Big Bang Theory implies our universe is mortal, may die. As such, it implies there well may be something that exists outside of our universe, outside of time. Eternity may exist.

•

The Big Bang Theory supports the idea of an expanding universe, a changing universe. This supports the idea of a bounded universe, which in turn supports the idea of 'something' lying beyond the boundary of our universe. We are now beginning to understand time as being a function of mass. We are now beginning to understand time is created by the existence of matter and energy. We are now beginning to think time would not exist if there were no matter and energy. If the implications of the Big Bang Theory are correct in suggesting our universe, as we know it, is limited and will destroy itself, then what lies beyond it is not matter and energy and is unaffected by time. What lies beyond our universe is eternal.

If this is true, then items such as money, houses, boats, land, any physical item composed of matter and energy, would not exist there. The awareness they have to give would be there, but they would not. The awareness they had to offer each individual would be there and available to an infinite number of awareness at the same time, for there is no limit to the number of times awareness can be used. Awareness does not wear out. Awareness does not become polluted. Awareness does not have a waiting line.

•

What lies beyond the universe would not appear to be composed of matter or energy, for these items are what make up our universe. That would seem to leave the nonphysical items such as love, hate, vengeance, forgiveness, justice, injustice, suffering, recovering to be the items which remain eternal. Perhaps this is why we sense the importance of Buddhism – the need to eliminate suffering, Christianity – the need to love one another, and Islam – the need to understand justice. Perhaps we sense the abstract as being eternal. Perhaps we sense the validity of the Big Bang Theory.

#9. What does the Big Bang Theory imply about our relationship to the Causative Force?

If the universe, as we know it, is limited, will eventually die, then it may be time to reconsider our relationship to what lies beyond.

•

Western religions have always considered our contribution to the Causative Force, what lies beyond our universe, to have no major impact upon the Causative Force Herself. Their thinking seems logical to them because they see the Causative Force as existing beyond the universe, not surrounding the universe. To put it another way, Western religions see the Causative Force as existing in one place and the universe existing in another. Having established this idea, they go on to say the Causative Force is all present, omnipresent, everywhere. They completely contradict themselves.

This process has provided us as individuals, as a species, with much comfort, for it has removed responsibility from us. If we are not a part of the Causative Force, immersed within the Causative Force, we do not need to be concerned with how our 'negative' behavior affects the Causative Force because it does not take place within Her. Our behavior is independent of the Causative Force. Our behavior is not a part of Her.

On the other hand, if Western religions were to truly accept what they say about the Causative Force, if Western religions were to truly accept the 'all presence' of the Causative Force, then Western religions would have to accept the idea that we are responsible for our actions because they would be occurring within the Causative Force, were adding to the Causative Force, were actually changing the Causative Force. Our actions of love and hate are affecting, changing, the Causative Force. No wonder western religions have such a difficult time accepting the concepts of the Big Bang Theory. The ideas of the Big Bang Theory have enormous impact upon western religion.

•

Accepting the idea of our universe expanding, having a boundary lying within the Causative Force, would not change the core beliefs of any religion. It would strengthen them. It would create a greater understanding of the significance of each and every individual, species, and life form. It would change the way we interact with the Causative Force and each other.

Conclusion: How does the concept of the Big Bang Theory reinforce the concept of symbiotic panentheism?

It does not; what is really taking place is that symbiotic panentheism reinforces the concept of the Big Bang Theory, the concept that the universe may be growing in size.

•

Symbiotic panentheism assigns the characteristic of omnipresence, all presence, to the Causative Force, a limit to the size of the universe, a boundary to the universe, awareness/knowledge being eternal, and existence beyond the boundary of the universe. These ideas are suggested by the science of the Big Bang Theory. These ideas are supported directly or indirectly by what we observe around us.

It is often thought religion, what we sense, needs the support of science, what we observe, in order to gain the respect of science. Although this may have some truth to it, so does the reverse. Science, what we observe, needs support of religion, what we sense, in order to gain respect from religion. Since they both need the same thing, they should be working together rather than against each other. They should both be attempting to reinforce each other, not at the expense of truth, but rather for the common cause of finding truth.

Science is based upon perceptions of what lies within the universe. Religion is based upon the perception of what lies beyond the universe. Religion would tend to reinforce the idea of the Big Bang Theory through belief in eternity, something beyond the temporary state of this physical universe. Science, the Big Bang Theory, would tend to reinforce the idea of the religious through belief in a limited, bounded universe with 'something' lying beyond.

•

Without the religious concept of an all present, omnipresent Causative Force existing beyond the boundaries of our universe, the observations which lead to the Big Bang Theory, our universe being limited, would have much difficulty explaining what would lie beyond the boundary.

Interdependence with the Causative Force – symbiosis, and lying within the Causative Force – panentheism, leads to symbiotic panentheism. Symbiosis with a Causative Force requires an eternal state of existence for individual awareness. Panentheism requires the universe to be bounded. Both are supported by the observations which led to the Big Bang Theory.

*What new insight has **Science**
firmly established within society?*

SYMMETRY:
Matter/Energy
Anti-matter/Anti-energy

#0. What does the conceptual framework of symmetry have to offer us?

Symmetry: 1. (in physics) The set of invariances of a system. Upon application of a symmetry operation on a system, the system is unchanged.
   –Oxford Concise Science Dictionary, p. 709

•

The Causative Force, awareness, able to create 'some-thing' from 'no-thing.' This sounds like an impossible task. Entropy and the Big Bang Theory both imply change must and does constantly take place. Both imply what lies beyond the universe may not be physical, may not be affected by time, may be eternal, may be abstract (not made of matter or energy). Both suggest two things: change could occur within this 'thing', if it occurred in an abstract form and our universe, matter and energy, did not exist at one point.

These ideas would seem to validate the idea of the universe being 'created.' How could the abstract, the nonphysical, the invisible, the untouchable, ideas, emotions, awareness, 'create' something composed of matter and energy when matter and energy did not exist? Would this even be possible? If the 'Creator,' what we refer to as the Causative Force, were all knowing, omniscient, She would know how to do so. If the Causative Force were all powerful, omnipotent, She would have the power to do so. If the Causative Force were all present, everywhere, omnipresent, She would do so within Herself, for there would be no other place to put Her newborn creation.

Only recently has science advanced the concept of symmetry enough to be able to speculate upon this question. Symmetry is recognized, in the physics community, as one of the basic principles existing within our universe. With symmetry as a base, the idea of totally dissolving matter and energy universes becomes logical, thus the reverse, creating universes of matter and energy, becomes logical.

•

The concept of dissolving universes is a Hindu concept. Hindus aren't the only ones that have held this belief. Now science has begun to understand the physics involved. Asimov's explanation of dissolving universes is explored in depth in the book, *You & I Together*.

#1. What does the conceptual framework of symmetry imply about the universe within which we live?

If, through symmetry, four universes could exist as parallel universes and be completely dissolved into 'nothingness,' then it seems only logical that four universes could be created from nothingness.

•

Our universe is composed basically of matter and energy. The symmetrical, opposite of matter would be anti-matter. When matter and anti-matter collide, they dissolve into pure energy. We know matter exists in our universe. We see it, feel it, and smell it. We have also seen signs of very small traces of anti-matter. We have seen its effect within cloud chambers and particle accelerators. Mathematics and physics have both established the existence of anti-matter. Theoretically, if there were two universes, ours filled with matter and energy and another universe filled with anti-matter and energy, and if our universe should pass through the other universe, then the matter in both universes would completely dissolve and revert to pure energy.

This new universe of pure energy would be lacking its symmetrical counterpart. If, therefore, there were two more universes, one composed of matter and anti-energy and the other composed of anti-matter and anti-energy, then using the same process of one passing through the other, a universe of anti-energy would result.

At this point, the four universes would have dissolved into two. The last step needed to completely dissolve the universes would be to pass the cloud of energy through the cloud of anti-energy. Asimov discussed this process in the 1950's. He speculated that the results of mixing equal amounts of energy and anti-energy would result in both being completely dissolved, leaving 'no-thing,' not even space.

•

Religions have been saying this for thousands of years. The newcomer, science, has been rejecting this idea as ludicrous ever since it came into the picture 500 years ago. Scientific evidence is now beginning to accumulate which verifies these strange, previously unexplainable beliefs. The universe now appears to actually have been created from 'no-thing' other than a 'knowing' abstract idea very possibly aware of and intentionally creating.

#2. How does the concept of symmetry reinforce the concept of panentheism?

Panentheism is the concept of awareness, 'some-thing' nonphysical, occupying the existence beyond the universe.

•

If the universe can be dissolved and recreated as Hindus believe, and if the universe was made from something that preceded the universe as religions believe, then it follows that something preceded the universe. But why couldn't the universe just appear in empty space?

Even empty space is something. Often we think of empty space as nothing, but, in fact, it is something. We think of it as surrounding us; we see it in the heavens between our planet, the sun, and the moon. We picture it when we dream of star ships traveling distant galaxies. We think of empty space filling the void between atoms and molecules. But empty space exists and gives form to our universe. Empty space provides a place within which our universe itself can unfold.

If the universe were created, it would have to be able to be placed somewhere. Space itself would have to be created. All of this creating, 'making room for' this universe, providing the 'initial push' for the universe to begin, would take an originator. Something had to initiate the idea of the universe. This 'something' is what panentheism describes as an all present, omnipotent being. Panentheism does not put qualifiers on the condition of all presence and accepts this characteristic in total.

•

If the Causative Force had no beginning, why couldn't the universe just begin to exist on its own? Religion basically does not discuss the question of whether or not the Causative Force of our universe had a creator of Her own. This question is way beyond our means of understanding. The point being made by religion is simple: our universe had a creator, a Causative Force. Now science is beginning to lean towards the idea that everything in our universe, the boundary of the universe itself, had a beginning. Science and religion are beginning to come together.

#3. What does symmetry reinforce about the significance of existence, life?

Will there be any impressions left of the universe, and of the life that existed within it, after the universe has completely dissolved?

•

The Big Bang Theory suggests that our universe has a boundary, is limited, and is a closed system. Entropy suggests that closed systems powered by heat exchanges, such as those operating in our universe, constantly undergo change until they eventually die. Symmetry suggests that universes can be created out of nothing and reduced back to nothing. Life, existing within this universe, is a part of the process. As the universe evolves, so evolves life. As the universe dies, so dies life. When the universe and the space it occupies completely disappear, so, too, will life. The physical will no longer exist.

If there is nothing outside the universe, the universe would make no impression upon what exists after the universe 'dissolves away' because there is nothing outside the universe.

On the other hand, if there is something outside the universe, if this 'thing' created the universe, if She placed the universe inside Herself because either She was omnipresent or She did not want to risk losing what was to evolve out of this physical universe, then a mark would be left by this creation, this universe She created. Pieces of the awareness of the Causative Force, having been thrown into the universe, would undergo change while existing within the physical form of a physical universe. This changed awareness would have no place to go but back to the creator within which the universe was located. The result: our awareness would flow back to the total awareness that exists outside this physical universe. Therefore, our awareness, being changed, would change the total awareness into which it returned.

•

Life and awareness changes. If the whole is equal to the sum of its parts, then as pieces of awareness change, so, too, does the sum of awareness. Changing total awareness, if awareness is eternal, means changing eternity.

#4. How does symmetry help us understand what life is?

Life is often thought of in terms of physicality. But the physical exists only temporarily. The physical can be destroyed. The physical can be reduced down to nothingness through the process of symmetry. However, the nonphysical is the eternal part of life we call awareness.

•

While journeying through this universe, your awareness changes. Awareness exists within your mind and body. Awareness is carried by your physical mind and body. Living life changes your awareness. When your body and mind are worn out, die, return back to ashes, does life die? Does your awareness die?

Your awareness may not be very great in comparison to all awareness that exists, but if your awareness can die, then so can other pieces of awareness. This is a major statement, for if pieces of awareness can die, then so can pieces of the Causative Force, because the Causative Force appears to have some sense of awareness. If pieces of the Causative Force can die, then eventually, the total awareness of the Causative Force could die, piece by piece. The idea of the Causative Force being able to die is contrary to every idea we assign to Her.

However, if the Causative Force cannot die, its awareness cannot die. If the awareness of the Causative cannot die, awareness cannot die piece by piece. If awareness cannot die, your awareness cannot die. If your awareness cannot die, a part of you cannot die and is eternal. If the Causative Force is all knowing, totally aware, then your piece of awareness must be part of the total awareness, part of the Causative Force. Symmetry demonstrates how the universe could dissolve. As such, symmetry demonstrates that the physical is not what is eternal. If the physical is not eternal, then the only thing left to be eternal is the abstract part of you – your awareness.

•

Anything that exists for a limited time and then totally disappears – including any memories of it, any ripples it generated, any influence it had – is not eternal. Compared to eternity, it just 'is' for a short period of time. Awareness appears to be the only hope we have for eternal existence.

#5. What does symmetry have to offer us as individuals?

Having become part of awareness, the part you play will become fully recognizable in an all knowing state of existence when becoming, once again, a part of eternal awareness.

•

Symmetry offers us more than the death of our physical universe. Symmetry helps us understand the logic regarding the creation and destruction of the universe. Symmetry helps us understand that life is not the physical. The physical is literally nothing, not even emptiness. Life, therefore, must be something other than the physical. Life must be the abstract. Life must be the soul – our awareness.

If, in fact, it is awareness that remains once the physical has dissolved, then it would appear our awareness will add to the total awareness, the all knowing, that already exists. Omniscience is awareness of total knowledge. Omniscience is the characteristic we, in our society, globally assign the Causative Force. Your awareness becomes a part of the Causative Force.

•

But what if you forget things, such as appears to be the case of people with Alzheimer's? People with Alzheimer's disease do not simply forget. Their brains lose the ability to hold memory from being literally destroyed by the disease.

Under present day theisms, the problem of the loss of awareness becomes glossed over and a leap is made to the end result; the soul returns to be 'near' the Causative Force. But with the understanding that awareness is your essence – not the body nor the brain – things begin to become clear. With this understanding, your awareness becomes a part of the Causative Force once your awareness leaves the body. With the global picture of a universal philosophy, such as symbiotic panentheism, your awareness may become lost to the physical part of your brain, but it remains a permanent part of total awareness. This concept complements present day theism very well.

The implications of this idea are phenomenal. Be careful with people; they will remember forever. Some brains may not be capable of remembering today, but their souls – awareness – are never destroyed. Upon leaving this world of 'imperfection,' awareness will live forever. Your awareness will have to confront other people's awareness for eternity.

SCIENCE: MATRIX #226

#6. What significance does symmetry have to us as a species?

Just as we will remember everything we did as well as everything that happened to us as individuals, we will become fully aware of what our species contributes to the whole.

•

We impact our surroundings in more ways than just through our own selves. We are a part of many parts. You impact your surroundings as an individual. You are a member of your species, the human race. As such, you impact your surroundings through the manner in which you tolerate, encourage, and contribute to how your species acts as a whole. If you work for an organization that aims only for profit and, in the process, contributes to the extermination of other species, you are partly responsible for their extermination. By working for that organization, you provide the ability for the organization to exist. You cannot shrug off this responsibility by stating you are one of many. The 'many' are composed of individuals, and you are an individual.

So what does this have to do with symmetry? Symmetry shows us that religions may be correct after all. Our universe is capable of being created and dissolved. Symmetry shows that our universe could have been created from nothing and could dissolve to nothing. The only thing that would possibly remain is the abstract, nonphysical awareness. As such, the actions taken by our entire species, of which you are a part – have a definite role to play. Our actions as a species become a part of the total awareness that exists outside the universe. You will have to stand with the other members of your species and face up to what you, as an individual and as a member of a species, contributed to the total awareness.

•

With your actions, total awareness will expand and grow. You are unique as a member of your species. Being unique, you have something unique to contribute to the whole. The same applies to your species. As a whole, your species is composed of the sum of its members. Each member has a contribution to make. As a whole, our contributions are the sum of our uniqueness. As we control our unique contributions, we control our species' unique contributions. As individuals, we are responsible for our species' contribution to the whole.

#7. What significance does symmetry have to offer other life forms in the universe?

Symmetry has to offer other life forms in the universe the same thing it offers you: responsibility, understanding, purpose, and hope.

•

Your responsibility for your actions goes far beyond what is taking place in front of you. Your actions affect not only what is occurring here and now, but ripples through society. Your actions ripple to the very ends of the universe. The ripples you generate actually pass through the boundary of our universe and become a part of eternity, known as the butterfly effect. This effect goes far beyond New York City and Singapore. You are a member of the universe. The universe is full of souls traveling and gaining awareness. The soul's final impact lies not within this universe but outside of this universe, for the soul is not physical. The nonphysical, abstract awareness goes beyond the physical universe. The physical aspect of the universe is shown by the physics of symmetry to be only a state of temporary awareness.

We are a part of our total species and the impact our species makes upon awareness. The same applies to all souls throughout the universe. What total are we talking about? There are several totals involved: the total impact you make as an individual, the total impact of your species, and the total impact of all souls in the universe.

•

If we all affect eternity, we should start thinking like a universal team. It is time to start thinking as a universe. A universal philosophy helps us understand the part we play in terms of the impact our universe is to make. Understanding the function of our universe and our function within the universe makes us a member of a universal team. As such, we need to understand the rules by which we must function. We need the teamwork concept in place *before* we meet the other members of the team. If it's not in place, much conflict will occur. Without a basic understanding of this universal function, the desires of the individual may overpower the concept of loving one another.

#8. What does symmetry imply about our significance in eternity?

Symmetry implies the universe could well have been created from nothing but awareness. As such, it is eternity that is the real essence of what exists – not the temporary state of your physical being.

•

There is no doubt you feel pain – physical as well as emotional. There is no doubt you feel love – physical as well as emotional. The point is, however, that without your being capable of having awareness of these events, they would not exist for you. Without awareness, you would not exist.

As an example, if your parents were stranded on a deserted island far away from everyone and you were born ten years later, no one would know of your existence but your parents. If they died and you went on to live eighty years before you died, no one but you would be aware of your existence. Others would have had no awareness of your existence. But to yourself, there would be no doubt of your existence. If you stubbed your toe, you would feel pain. If you basked in the warm sun, you would feel warmth. As you gazed into the night sky and saw the twinkling stars, you would sense awe.

Your awareness would exist. What you experience would exist as awareness. Once your body stopped functioning, the awareness you experienced would still be awareness. Does this awareness become a part of total awareness? If the awareness does not become a part of total awareness – what we call all knowing – then total awareness is not truly total because your awareness is not a part of it.

•

If we wish to retain the concept that the Causative Force is omniscient, then we appear to have no choice but to accept the idea that the Causative Force includes you. You are a piece of the Causative Force. The physics of symmetry leave us no understandable choice but to accept the concept of something existing beyond the universe, for the universe appears to be only a temporary state within something much bigger than itself. The only apparent way out of this conclusion would be to reject the idea of symmetry, which science is not willing to do at this point.

#9. What does symmetry imply about our relationship to the Causative Force?

Through the concept of symmetry and the closed system of the bounded universe, nothingness is nothingness.

•

Doesn't this imply what lies outside the universe also remains unchanged? Doesn't this destroy what the concepts of entropy and the Big Bang theories were implying, that all things change? Doesn't this destroy the concepts that even the Causative Force changes and that we, you and I, change total awareness, the Causative Force Herself?

Oddly enough, the answer is no. Symmetry implies a closed system, such as a bounded universe, is unchanged. We are not sure what lies outside our universe, but if it is the Causative Force, then the Causative Force may be an open system within which the concept of symmetry may not apply.

•

Symmetry applies to closed systems – systems with boundaries. Religions adhere to the idea that the Causative Force lacks an end and a boundary. When we speak of a Causative Force, we speak of a force that is all present. This means the Causative Force has no boundaries.

The open ended system of the Causative Force can be changed for change is a part of a living entity, as entropy implies. Couldn't the Causative Force be surrounded by something? Perhaps, but the Causative Force would still be the next stage of our existence – eternity. We don't know what lies beyond eternity. This is a new frontier for speculative thought.

Your responsibilities lie in the manner in which you affect the awareness of yourself, your species, and your contribution to life. The Causative Force grows with either negative additions of hate, jealousy, sadism, masochism, subjugation, domination, and abuse or the positive additions of love, compassion, and joy. Is this a war? No doubt about it. It is a war over who and what we want to be in eternity.

Conclusion: How do the concepts of symmetry reinforce the concept of symbiotic panentheism?

They do not; symbiotic panentheism reinforces the concepts of symmetry, the concept that the universe could dissolve into what it was before – a nonphysical state of awareness.

•

Symmetry implies the universe is only temporary. What the universe came from was the Causative Force – an abstract awareness. Having awareness, we are a part of total awareness. As our awareness grows, so changes and grows the total awareness that exists, so grows and changes the Causative Force. Symmetry is the first primitive step in understanding the logic behind how our universe could have been created from nothing, leading to the potential size of the Causative Force. The Causative Force is truly all present, truly omnipresent. The result leads us to understand where the created universe must have been placed. If the Causative Force is omnipresent, then the created universe had to be placed within the Causative Force, for the universe and its members are both present and knowing.

Symmetry, along with entropy and the Big Bang Theory, provides an understanding of a relationship we may have with the Causative Force. You and I may be part of the total awareness of the Causative Force if She is total knowledge and total awareness, creating an interdependent, symbiotic relationship.

•

Going from something, our universe, to complete lack of matter and energy is possible through symmetry by combining energy with anti-energy. Symmetry provides the understanding of how to dissolve the universe, which leads to a better understanding of creation.

*What new insight has **Science**
firmly established within society?*

Set Theory:
Venn Diagrams

#0. What does the conceptual framework of set theory have to offer us?

Venn diagrams: set theory: ... the rectangle represents the universal set E, circles represent sets or subsets. These diagrams are called Venn diagrams, after John Venn (1834–1925), who invented them.
  –Oxford Concise Science Dictionary, p. 654

•

Set theory offers us the ability to draw what we think. Let's use a dot to represent your eternal awareness, your soul. We can then use a circle to represent the universe, and a box – a rectangle – to represent the Causative Force.

There are lots of ways to put these drawings on a piece of paper. In order to better think about the different situations, let's use separate sheets of paper to draw Venn diagrams of different situations.

Venn diagram #1: Draw a dot. Draw a circle around the dot. In this situation there is no eternal awareness, there is no Causative Force, only you and the universe exist. This is a drawing of atheism.

Venn diagram #2: Draw a dot. Draw a circle around the dot. Draw a box in such a way that the circle is in the box and the box is in the circle. This is very difficult, if not impossible, to draw. This is pantheism, which says you exist, the universe exists, and the Causative Force exists (but is the same as the universe).

Venn diagram #3: Draw a dot. Draw a circle around the dot. Draw a box somewhere off to the side so that the circle and dot are not inside the box. This is classical/traditional theism – Judaism, Christianity, Islam, etc. These theisms say you exist in the universe. They all agree there is a Causative Force separate from the universe. You are not a part of the Causative Force.

Venn diagram #4: Draw a dot. Draw a circle around the dot. Draw a box so that the circle and dot are inside the box. This is panentheism. Panentheism says you exist. The universe exists and you are a part of it. There is a Causative Force and you are inside the universe, which is inside the Causative Force. You, like the universe, are part of the Causative Force.

•

Can you prove that the drawing of panentheism is correct? No, but you also cannot prove any of the other drawings. And that is the point; we have the free will to choose the foundations upon which to build our societies.

#1. What does the conceptual framework of set theory imply about the universe within which we live?

Whichever picture or Venn diagram you chose as the perception you have of the Causative Force, the soul, and the universe, one thing stands out in all four: the universe exists.

•

Mathematics, with the use of Venn diagrams from set theory, clearly implies that the universe exists.

Venn diagram #1 and #2: With atheism and pantheism, the universe exists but appears to be dependent upon your existence. Under an atheistic and pantheistic drawing, the universe appears to be temporary and everything seems to end, at least in terms of your awareness, when you no longer exist.

Venn diagram #3: With classical/traditional theisms, the universe may die, but something exists after the universe dies. Now we begin to understand how the universe could have been generated, but we still cannot understand why we exist nor what purpose the universe could possibly have in terms of what lies beyond it.

Venn diagram #4: With panentheism, the universe takes on even more significance for it exists within the Causative Force. By being located within the Causative Force, it becomes a part of the Causative Force. As such, even if the universe dies, the significance it had for existing is kept as a part of the Causative Force. Its apparent worth seems sacred and eternal, for it is a piece of the Causative Force Herself. We may not understand its exact purpose, but now we can see its purpose must have something to do with the Causative Force if for no other reason than the understanding that it lies within this Force.

•

Atheists, pantheists, classical/traditional theists, and panentheists have been given their various names based upon which Venn diagram they believe to be the most logical. If you subscribe to the idea that the Causative Force is all present, there doesn't appear to be any other choice about where to put the universe than inside the Causative Force, making it a piece of Her, diagram #4. This idea reinforces Hinduism, Judaism, Buddhism, Christianity, Islam, etc., and their beliefs regarding an all present Causative Force. There are only four diagrams; you have to choose one, for it acts as a foundation upon which to build your principles and morals. This foundation becomes the cornerstone of all your behavior.

#2. How do the concepts of set theory reinforce the concept of panentheism?

There appears to be basically four Venn diagrams we can draw of the location of the Causative Force. As we go from Venn diagram #1 to Venn diagram #4, the size of the Causative Force increases.

•

Venn diagram #1: Atheism allows for no Causative Force at all. This concept answers no questions regarding how our universe was created, as the basic physics ideas of entropy, the Big Bang Theory, and symmetry imply happened, and as present day theistic religions profess.

Venn diagram #2: Pantheism provides for a Causative Force but it holds to the idea of the universe and the Causative Force being the same. How can something that exists create itself? This forces us to discard all our religious beliefs and traditions.

Venn diagram #3: Classical/traditional theism provides us with a belief in the worth of the individual, the existence of the eternal soul, and the existence of a Causative Force, but provides no logic as to why the three have significance to each other.

Venn diagram #4: Panentheism, as do present day religions, believes in 'a' Causative Force and claims the Causative Force to be omnipresent and omniscient. If such is the case, the only Venn diagram to support such a concept is the fourth drawing where the dot (your essence) is in the circle (the universe), which is in the box (the Causative Force). This is the only diagram that allows for the boundaries of the box to be extended into infinity and leaves the system unchanged. Panentheism is the only concept of the four allowing the Causative Force to actually become truly all present.

•

Only the universal philosophy model of symbiotic panentheism provides the religious, scientific, and philosophical logic of the interrelationship of the three.

#3. What does set theory reinforce about the significance of existence, life?

Set theory allows us to visually see the significance of life.
•

Venn diagram #1: Atheism, in picture form, shows why life is insignificant. Life exists but for the moment. Once life is over, everything is over for you. When one gets to the core of the significance of existence, if it has no meaning to you, does anything have any meaning to you? With atheism, hope does not exist.

Venn diagram #2: Pantheism, in picture form, shows us the same results as Venn diagram #1. This is why pantheism and atheism are often considered, in general, to be the same concept.

Venn diagram #3: Classical/traditional theisms, in picture form, provide something neither atheism nor pantheism can provide. They provide a sense of hope. They provide a sense of the soul existing beyond the temporary state of the universe. But these religions, by holding to the picture of a less than all present state of the Causative Force, leave the state of the soul in question once it has left the physicality of the universe or once the universe no longer exists.

Venn diagram #4: Panentheism, in picture form, provides an even greater sense of hope, for there is nowhere else to go once leaving the physical state of the universe, but into the arms of the Causative Force. How reassuring or how unsettling depending upon the type of life one leads. And therein lies the logic behind people taking responsibility for their actions. Therein lies the argument for forgiveness and the understanding of why vengeance is not an idea we must seek out.
•

Only with Venn diagram #4, a dot (your essence) within a circle (a physical universe) which in turn is inside a box (the Causative Force) is there no doubt about what you are. You belong to something for you are inside something. To be included in the Causative Force leaves little doubt as to your life's significance. Life exists within the Causative Force. The concept of interdependence, a symbiotic state, begins to evolve.

#4. How does set theory help us understand what life is?

The whole is made up of the sum of its parts.

•

Venn diagram #1 & #2: Atheism and pantheism provide a clear picture of what they believe is in store for life. Life exists in the circle of the universe. Entropy leaves no option but for the universe to reach a final point of death. The Big Bang Theory implies two possibilities for the universe. The universe will either continue to expand until items within it become so far apart, so diluted, the items within it, including life, become insignificant. Or, the universe will contract back into its primal state and destroy all that presently exists within it. The implication: life is a thing, a temporary physical state of being.

Venn diagram #3: Modern day theisms leave some sense of hope of life having significance beyond the universe. There is something that exists outside the universe. But the certainty that life does have significance beyond the boundaries of the universe is unable to be stated as an absolute. The possibility exists of life being snuffed out just as the universe could be snuffed out. The possibility exists for both life and the universe to totally disappear, without having any affect upon the Causative Force, for neither the universe nor life exist within the box representing the Causative Force. The box, the Causative Force, and the circle containing the dot, the universe with you in it, are totally separate from each other. No direct relationship, no direct connection, no interdependence is implied.

Venn diagram #4: Panentheism, the dot within the circle within the box, is the only representation providing no doubt as to what life is. Life is a part of something.

•

Life exists as a part of something greater than itself. In mathematics, elements of a set interact with each other. Permanently remove one element of the set and the set no longer is what it was before. Remove yourself from diagram #4 and the Causative Force is no longer what it was, for without you, the Causative Force has lost its characteristic of being omnipresent, omniscient, and omnipotent.

#5. What does set theory have to offer us as individuals?

In mathematics, we call the whole 'the set' and we call the parts 'the elements.' Thus, we could say the whole is the Causative Force and the elements are what lie within it.

•

Venn diagram #1 & #2: Atheism and pantheism provide no place for you to exist but within the circle, for the box and the circle are the same. No place exists outside of either. You are a part of the universe but you have no relationship to something greater than the universe, for there is nothing other than the universe. What happens to the universe happens to you. Under atheism and pantheism, there is nothing outside the universe so the universe has no significance to anything greater than itself. Therefore, if we find the universe to be temporary, you become temporary. Under atheism and pantheism, you have no more tie to eternity than does any physical object. You are temporary and your significance is temporary.

Venn diagram #3: When looking at modern day theisms, four possibilities become apparent. You may have no essence. You may be nothing other than physical and thus be destined to end up just as the physical ends up. You may have an essence that is capable of leaving the universe should the universe eventually die. In this case, the other three scenarios become possible. Your essence could enter the Causative Force, your essence could wander aimlessly outside the Causative Force, your essence could enter another box (location), keeping you totally isolated from the Causative Force. Although hope exists for the first time, people remain fearful of the next part of their journey. Your eternal existence becomes a gamble.

Venn diagram #4: Panentheism places your essence within the universe and the universe within the Causative Force. This makes you an element of the whole, a portion of the Causative Force. There is no possibility for you to be excluded or isolated from the Causative Force.

•

Only under the concept of panentheism do you automatically become a part of the whole. Only under panentheism does the probability of entering the Causative Force become complete. Only under panentheism does the significance of the existence of the individual become an absolute.

#6. What significance does set theory have to us as a species?

The species is a total summation of the actions of its members. The species takes on a uniqueness generated by its members.

•

Venn diagram #1: Atheism offers the individual a sense of responsibility only to one's self. Once the individual dies, all significance for the species dies. Awareness is dead.

Venn diagram #2: Eternal existence of the universe is temporary, as religions and the sciences believe. Pantheism offers the species a sense of responsibility only to itself. Once the species dies, all significance for the species also dies.

Venn diagram #3: Eternal existence is a possibility, for something exists beyond the universe. But the Causative Force exists separate from the universe. Doubt exists as to where your soul will go, what your soul is, and what the purpose of your soul is. Doubt also exists as to the value of your fellow humans and to where your soul will finally come to rest.

Venn diagram #4: The Causative Force exists and nestles the universe, and you along with the it, in Her arms. No more doubt. Your body may die, but your awareness, soul, will not. The universe may die, but the awareness generated within it will not. There is no doubt where that awareness would go – into the arms of the Causative Force. You and what you help your species become would be part of the total, a part of the Causative Force.

•

Set theory offers a clear depiction of just what we are, where we are, and why we are. Set theory offers our species purpose, responsibility, hope, and the elimination of doubt.

#7. What significance does set theory have to offer other life forms in the universe?

The universe takes on a uniqueness generated by the sum of its total parts. Life forms within this universe generate an atmosphere of its own just as do members of a species generate a uniqueness specific to that species.

•

Venn diagram #1: Atheism offers life forms nothing to travel within other than one's own body. The time span for travel is the present – today. Once death occurs, all else perishes.

Venn diagram #2: Pantheism offers life forms the universe within which to travel, for it is possible for the essence to continue beyond the body in which it travels through the time span of existence and the life of the universe. If the universe dies, all that lies within it dies. And since pantheism believes nothing exists beyond the universe, so, too, dies everything including the Causative Force.

Venn diagram #3: Modern day theisms offer life forms eternity within which to travel. What one is to travel within is uncertain. If the universe dies, your essence would have to find a way into the Causative Force or travel outside the Causative Force – what is called 'hell' by religions and a 'zombie' state by science. Entrance into the Causative Force would have to be sought, earned, merited, justified. People holding the key could control your actions. You, your journey, becomes something others can manipulate.

Venn diagram #4: Panentheism offers life forms freedom. True freedom from subjugation, intimidation, abuse, fear, and uncertainty others can subject you to. Set theory draws a picture of the three basic characteristics of the Causative Force: omniscience, omnipotence, and omnipresence. The picture describes panentheism.

•

This may answer the question regarding where our universe is, but why would the Causative Force create life forms and put them in a universe within Herself? There must be a reason and, as we shall see, there is a logical possibility.

#8. What does set theory imply about our significance in eternity?

It would only seem logical for something, as knowing and as powerful as we assume the Causative Force to be, to have a reason for creating a universe and life, and then to place it within Herself.

•

Venn diagram #1: Atheism would refute the argument since it states simply that there is no creator. Atheism states the universe is, will always be, and has always been. But science and religion both find this to be an inadequate response. This does not resolve the questions and fundamentals science and religion have put into place.

Venn diagram #2: Pantheism would refute the argument since it states simply that there is no creator other than the universe itself, since the Causative Force and the universe are one. Therefore, the universe is, always will be, has always been and, if it turns out to be that the universe had a beginning, then the universe created itself. Once again, science and religion both find this response difficult to embrace.

Venn diagram #3: Modern day theisms would also refute the argument. Modern day theisms do not believe the universe is inside the Causative Force for the universe is, as they say, 'imperfect' and to them it is not logical for an 'imperfect' object to be inside a 'perfect' being. But science does not recognize the concept of 'perfection' and would refute the modern day religious argument. Venn diagram #3 may provide life with the sense of hope, but at the same time, it creates dissension between what is believed and what is observed.

Venn diagram #4: Panentheism embraces the argument of our being within the Causative Force, thus embracing science. Panentheism embraces the concept of an omnipresent Causative Force, thus embracing religion. Panentheism holds to the idea that what seems to be 'imperfection' is not imperfection, but a process of learning.

•

Panentheism provides the logic behind the introduction of the concept of hope and fuses the warring factions of science and religion.

#9. What does set theory imply about our relationship to the Causative Force?

Set theory clearly demonstrates an inescapable relationship between the universe, the essence of life, eternal existence, and the Causative Force.

•

Venn diagram #1: Atheism provides no understanding of the relationship between the universe, the essence of life, eternal existence, and the Causative Force because atheism rejects the existence of the Causative Force.

Venn diagram #2: Pantheism also provides no understanding of these relationships because, with pantheism, nothing exists beyond the universe. The universe is as big as it gets. But, as Einstein showed, time is believed to be related to mass and energy. Time is tied to the concept of beginning/end concepts. Time is believed to be a characteristic of our universe. Since pantheism holds to the idea of there being no outside to the universe, time will remain dependent on our universe. Since the science of entropy, the Big Bang Theory, and symmetry indicate a beginning and end to our universe, time would have a beginning–end characteristic. The only way to resolve the issue of time having no beginning or end is to show the universe has no beginning or end. That would force us to dismantle all the scientific theories we have in place today.

Venn diagram #3: Modern day theisms allow the present scientific theories to stay intact, but create a whole host of other dilemmas to be resolved. The social dilemmas are addressed in detail in the book *In the Image of God*. The scientific–religious clash created by modern day theisms' belief in the universe being located outside the Causative Force pits individual against individual, species against species, the species against the environment, life form against life form, and humanity against the Causative Force.

Venn diagram #4: Panentheism brings harmony to the whole.

•

Harmony comes through understanding that the whole is equal to the sum of its parts and every member of a set has a purpose.

Conclusion: How do the concepts of set theory reinforce the concept of symbiotic panentheism?

They do not; symbiotic panentheism reinforces the concepts of set theory, that sets and subsets are members of a larger set we can define.

•

Venn diagram #1: Atheism depicts existence as being the universe and all things within it. Creation is not a topic of discussion with atheism because there is no Causative Force. Atheism provides no answer for the question, Why? Atheists believe it is not up to them to answer this question. It is up to others to do so.

Venn diagram #2: Pantheism depicts existence as being the universe, all things within it, and some type of causative process, but the process remains within the universe. The universe created itself. Pantheism contradicts the scientific concepts of entropy, the Big Bang, and symmetry. Pantheism contradicts classical/traditional theisms. Pantheism leaves unexplained the concept of creation, time, life, death, and purpose. Pantheism provides only one reason to the question, Why? The answer pantheism provides is simple, "Because we say so."

Venn diagram #3: Modern day theisms accept the scientific implications of entropy, the Big Bang, symmetry, and set theory. But modern day theisms do not allow for the full acceptance of their description of the Causative Force. Modern day theisms do not totally accept the concept of omnipresence they assign to the Causative Force. Although modern day theisms provide some meaning to the reason we should rely on the Causative Force, they do not explain why the Causative Force would even bother to create life or the universe within which life exists. The question, Why?, still goes unanswered.

Venn diagram #4: Panentheism not only accepts the scientific implications of entropy, the Big Bang, symmetry, and set theory, but it allows for the full acceptance of the concept of a truly omnipresent Causative Force. Panentheism is the only Venn diagram to allow for the significance of the next six topics of science.

•

Symbiotic panentheism is the only concept to reinforce rather than undermine all three areas we are exploring: science, religion, and philosophy.

*What new insight has **Science**
firmly established within society?*

Space:
The Null Set
Nothingness

#0. What does the conceptual framework of space have to offer us?

Space: A property of the universe that enables physical phenomena to be extended into three mutually perpendicular directions. In Newtonian physics, space, time, and matter are treated as quite separate entities. In Einsteinian physics, space and time are combined into a four-dimensional continuum (see space-time) and in the general theory of relativity matter is regarded as having an effect on space, causing it to curve.

Space-time: In Einstein's concept of the physical universe, based on a system of geometry devised by H. Minkowski (1864–1909), space and time are regarded as entwined, so that two observers in relative motion could disagree regarding the simultaneity of distant events. In Minkowski's geometry, an event is identified by a 'world point' in a four-dimensional continuum.

–Oxford Concise Science Dictionary, p. 678

•

These concepts may seem complex, so let's simplify them. In essence, what is being described with the definitions of 'space' is that there exists a 'place' within which the physical items of mass and energy can be placed. Said another way, you think you exist. You think the universe, composed of the planet earth, the sun, the stars, the galaxies, and all the interesting 'stuff' such as black holes, comets, novas, light, exist also. The definition of space simply agrees and makes room for these things, creating a place within which these things can exist.

•

Why include a definition of space-time? This second definition is included because we had always thought of the universe being composed of matter, things you can touch such as wood, glass, plastic, and energy, things you cannot touch such as light, heat, magnetic fields. We had never been able to associate time as a property of matter and energy. Minkowski began dabbling with the mathematical ideas of geometry and Einstein began dabbling with the mathematical ideas of physics. What fell into place, at least with formulas and scribbles on paper, was the idea that the universe was not three dimensional, but rather four dimensional. Space now had length, height, depth, and time. Space, a theoretical location, was created within which a universe could be placed.

#1. What does the conceptual framework of space imply about the universe within which we live?

Space is emptiness. Space is a location for physical matter, energy, and time. Space is where the substance of our universe was put. Space is a void. But a void cannot be put inside a void. Therefore, space, a void, and the universe would appear to have been placed within 'something.'

•

Sounds complicated, but the basic idea can be simplified. In the chapter on Set Theory – Venn Diagrams, a picture was drawn regarding the four choices from which we can pick in terms of where our universe was placed. These were choices because none of them could be proven as fact. Therefore, one has the option of choosing based upon simply a desire for one of the four, or one can choose based upon the information we have gathered as a species throughout our religious history of beliefs, our scientific history of observations, and our philosophical history of reason. The second option, choosing based upon concepts we have gathered as a species, is the most difficult. This trilogy just begins to validate the diagram of panentheism.

Let's take a break and take the simpler option. The simpler option is to choose based upon which diagram is easiest to draw. At first glance, it would appear that the easiest choice would be to choose the most simplistic drawing: atheism. But atheism does not include a Causative Force. The drawing appears incomplete based upon what science and religion has told us. The second drawing, pantheism, is the most difficult to draw. The third drawing, classical/traditional theism, requires us to draw both the concepts of 'inclusion' and 'exclusion.' You are inside the universe but the universe is outside the Causative Force. Panentheism turns out to be the easiest to draw.

•

Panentheism continues the concept of inclusion and, thus, is the easiest to draw. Changing one's philosophical perception from inclusion to exclusion is not only difficult, it raises more questions than it answers.

#2. How do the concepts of space reinforce the concept of panentheism?

Space, having to have a location, implies it is inside something which is exactly the definition of panentheism: all within the Causative Force.

•

Space having a location inside something is the easiest Venn diagram to draw in terms of ideas generated by the drawing. Space having a location inside something is reinforced by and reinforces Hinduism, Judaism, Buddhism, Christianity, Islam, ontology, and the modern science of entropy, the Big Bang, symmetry, and set theory. As we shall see, we have just begun to explore the dynamics of panentheism, for it goes on to reinforce and be reinforced by topology, ecology, zoology, geology, and vast areas of philosophy.

Mathematics often refers to the whole as equal to the sum of its parts. The reason we have a problem understanding the whole of which the universe is a part may be due, to a large degree, to the idea we have of the universe being separate from a creator. Most of our religious, scientific, and philosophical ideas point us in the direction of the universe having a beginning. So understanding the concept of a Causative Force, for most of us, is not the problem. Understanding the idea regarding where space exists generates the problem.

Diagrams #1 & #2, atheism and pantheism, show a universe with an outside. They do not provide a description of what surrounds our universe. Diagram #3, classical/traditional theisms, have the same problem. Only diagram #4, panentheism, resolves this problem. This is not to say panentheism provides all the answers. Panentheism does not resolve the issue of what lies beyond the Causative Force within which the universe and the individual may lie. But panentheism does provide us with some answers and, in the future, entropy may give us even more answers.

•

The idea of space being created within the Causative Force is panentheism. The idea of creating space within the Causative Force reinforces the idea of panentheism. The idea of creating space outside the Causative Force contradicts the foundation upon which modern theims rest, the concept of an all present, omnipresent, force.

#3. What does space reinforce about the significance of existence, life?

The concept of space implies a location for the universe to exist. But just as it implies a location for the universe, it implies a location for itself.

•

A location for space is a different idea than a location for the universe. A location for the universe works from the edge of space inward. It creates a place into which we can put the heavenly bodies, matter, energy, and life. A location for space works from the edge of space outward. It creates a place into which space can be placed without time. Does this contradict the idea of symmetry? After all, symmetry implies the universe could have been created from nothing and nothing would seem to need no space since it was nothing. In this case, however, nothing is expanded into a form. Nothing is changed from an abstract form to a physical form. This form would require a location. But to build space, space must be placed somewhere.

What about life? Isn't the essence of life awareness? What does space have to do with awareness? In the universal philosophy model of symbiotic panentheism, awareness needs a place, needs space to move around and explore, travel, journey, create. To constantly bump into, be submerged in, the all knowing leaves no ability to think creatively, for everything is already known. Therefore, awareness must get away from itself. One possibility is to open up an empty space within yourself. This space would have to be inside the Causative Force, for the Causative Force is omnipresent. Inside this space, emptiness and symmetry would be let loose to allow for the creation of matter, energy, anti-matter, and anti-energy.

•

To put it more simply, a Causative Force that is all present, omnipresent, could remain all present if She would create space within Herself. By creating space, She could get away from Herself and experience what She had never experienced before. Gaining experience, new knowledge, is a form of changing. It is learning and growing. Life becomes the means of doing so. Space allows for the characteristic of growth to be assigned to a Causative Force.

#4. How does space help us understand what life is?

Space is the idea which connects life, the universe, and the Causative Force. Life is located within the universe. The universe is located within space. Space is located within something. This something may very well have created the initiating force behind space and the universe that lies within space.

•

This something doesn't need a name, but it is easier to talk about it if we give it a name. Since we are discussing an initiating force we may as well call it the Causative Force. And since we are discussing 'birth,' we may as well call 'it' a 'She.' Life created within a universe, a universe created within space, space created within what? Where is the universe? We come back to this question, for it appears to be the foundation of basic questions such as, why was the universe created? Where are we? Where is the universe located? This sense of location, this sense of belonging, gets at the very heart of the question, what is life? One cannot begin to understand what life is and how one is to behave until one begins to understand what the individual is and what the environment is that surrounds the individual.

We say our total universe lies outside the Causative Force, yet we believe the Causative Force is omnipresent. We contradict ourselves over and over. Religions constantly tell us we were made in the image of God, but we refuse to accept the Causative Force's ability to do so in a perfect manner. Will we continue this process of contradiction by refusing to accept a perceptual shift of what we are? Life exists within the universe, which exists within space, which is inside its creator, inside the Causative Force. With this understanding, life would then have to be defined as a piece of the Causative Force.

•

If we accept the idea of the Causative Force being omnipresent as religions state, and if we accept the idea that space exists, we have little choice but to accept the idea that we exist within the Causative Force. If we accept this idea, we have little choice but to accept the idea that we are a part of the whole, we are a part of the Causative Force. If we accept the idea of being a part of the Causative Force, we have little choice but to accept the responsibility that goes along with it.

#5. What does space have to offer us as individuals?

Space offers us not only the recognition of being a part of the Causative Force, but the awesome responsibility that goes along with such a position.

•

Accepting ourselves as existing within a universe which is located within space which is located within the Causative Force, forces us to reevaluate ourselves and what we are. No longer can we look at ourselves as superior to others, for how could one piece of the Causative Force be worth more than another? Man, woman, black, yellow, physically handicapped, world Olympian, mentally retarded, intellectual, schizophrenic, mentally stable, mentally unstable, bashful, outgoing, short, tall, handsome, homely, rich, poor... what's the difference? A piece of the Causative Force is a piece of the Causative Force.

If we accept ourselves as being a piece of the Causative Force, we would have little choice but to acknowledge the environment as being the place through which the Causative Force travels. The result of such a perception would require that we, as individuals, accept the environment as belonging to all others as well as ourselves. The environment would be viewed as a sacred place having a specific function to the Causative Force and would need to be treated as such.

Accepting ourselves as a piece of the Causative Force would require that we, as individuals, no longer abuse, subjugate, dominate, take actions which produces personal gain at the expense of others, force ourselves and our ideas upon others or intimidate others. These actions could no longer be tolerated. We would now have some understanding of the reason why this was not acceptable behavior, because it was not being done to 'someone' but rather to 'something,' and that thing would be none other than the Causative Force Herself.

•

Elevating our status to the level of becoming a part of the Causative Force is not 'sugar and spice and everything nice.' Being given the status of the Causative Force is an awesome responsibility. It requires us, as individuals, to set goals we know we cannot attain, spend our lives attempting to attain them, and then to find peace within ourselves knowing we did our best, even though we may not attain what we set out to do.

#6. What significance does space have to us as a species?

Space offers our species not only the recognition of being a part of the Causative Force, but the awesome responsibility that goes along with such a position.

•

Accepting our species as a part of the Causative Force requires that we, as a species, accept the concept that other species are also a part of the Causative Force. Each species has a purpose. As we traveled through history, we learned of the functions various species on our planet were to perform. As we find new species of life throughout space, we will need to be very careful how we define their function, for they are pieces of the Causative Force. Do we even have the right to define this function at all? Isn't it the species itself that should define this function?

Accepting ourselves as a piece of the Causative Force requires that we, as a species, accept the environment as belonging to *all* species. The environment is a place within which the Causative Force travels within individuals. Regardless of which species the individual belongs to, the environment is as much theirs as ours, for they are pieces of the Causative Force.

Accepting our species as a piece of the Causative Force would require that we, as a species, accept other species in the heavens as being likewise. We would have the obligation of protecting other species from ourselves. We would have the obligation of preserving their journeys as we do our own. Intruding upon their cultures, traditions, beliefs, and customs would have to be examined very carefully. Imposing our belief systems, social behavior, primal drives, and motivations would be denying the new species we encountered the opportunity of following its own path and contributing its own uniqueness to the Causative Force.

•

Accepting our species as a piece of the Causative Force would require that we, as a species, honor the right of all species to develop unhampered. There will be many perplexing dilemmas we will have to face in terms of what ideals we support. We will need an understanding of what we stand for and why in order to deal with these dilemmas. A universal philosophy will help us decide what actions to take.

#7. What significance does space have to offer other life forms in the universe?

Space offers other life forms the same magnificence as it offers us. At the same time, it also places upon other life forms the same responsibility as it places upon us.

•

Accepting ourselves as a piece of the Causative Force would require that we, as individuals, no longer allow ourselves to be abused, hampered, subjugated, dominated, taken advantage of, and forced to accept principles and morals we object to. It means we, as individual life forms, no longer allow others to commit acts against us that go against our personal beliefs. It means that we, as individual life forms, not allow ourselves to be forced into being something we are not just because others try to force us. We would understand that we are all unique, we are all a part of something greater than ourselves. We would understand we are unique pieces of the Causative Force and have the right and obligation of standing up for our unique journey in life.

What does this have to do with other life forms? If we expect this type of attitude from ourselves, then we should not be surprised if we encountered the same type of attitude from other life forms we encounter in the heavens. This would mean we should expect to find major resistance confronting us should we decide to intimidate or force upon other life forms our particular way of thinking be it in the realms of religion, government, science, mysticism, logic, perceptions of purpose or philosophy.

•

Doesn't this contradict the idea of a universal philosophy? No! No one knows what the 'correct' universal philosophy is and that is just the point. Other life forms will or should want to protect their own journeys and perceptions. If symbiotic panentheism should prove to be the universal philosophy we choose to follow because of the logic, knowledge, traditions, and religious aspects it is based upon, then we would have no choice but to respect the decisions of others to follow their own paths. In other words, we should not be surprised if other life forms violently resist any actions we take to subjugate and intimidate them. On the other hand, we have the obligation to vehemently resist if other life forms attempt to interfere with our unique journey through life.

#8. What does space imply about our significance in eternity?

Space implies a location; a location implies something exists beyond space. Time appears to be what we call a function of mass and energy. Once we remove mass and energy from the location of space, it would appear that time may disappear. Time may very well not be a characteristic of what remains. Eternity is the lack of time. Space provides the understanding we have of where time exists.

•

Time, eternity, mass, energy, existence, nonexistence, appear, disappear... It seems confusing. It is not intended to be; it just gets confusing the deeper we examine the details. Simply put, what we are saying is mathematicians and scientists think time exists. They think it is something that is connected to matter and energy. Our universe is immersed in the idea of time. Without matter and energy, scientists and mathematicians believe it is possible time would not exist. If there is no time, then there is either nothing left or there is eternity. Nothing left would suggest no awareness would exist. But can something that existed be totally destroyed in terms of having its presence eliminated? If the universe should dissolve away tomorrow, would the fact that it had existed also be totally dissolved or would the fact that it existed in some form always remain, since it had existed at one point?

Another way of saying this is, can the fact that you exist ever be erased from the total sum of awareness? Just because your body dies, do the accumulation of your experiences and impacts also die or do they become a part of total knowledge, all knowing, omniscience? If your awareness also dies as you die, then the all knowing is not all knowing, for it does not know what it is you experienced or learned. And if the all knowing does lose your knowledge and experiences, then it is not all knowing and, therefore, it is not omniscient.

•

If your experiences and knowledge do not become a part of the Causative Force, the Causative Force is not omniscient. Therefore, the only way the Causative Force could exist eternally, as an omniscient, all knowing being, would be if you are a part of the Causative Force. This would require that you, your awareness, your soul be tied but to eternity – not to time. You, your awareness, would seem to be a part of eternity.

#9. What does space imply about our relationship to the Causative Force?

Using Venn diagrams, pictures, we can see that under atheism, pantheism, and classical/traditional theisms, awareness enters nothing as it enters the universe. It is only under panentheism that the awareness enters something. Under panentheism, awareness enters the Causative Force and becomes part of the whole.

•

Space being the region within which our universe was bounded would imply our universe was inside a 'container' and you are inside the universe. Space would seem to be inside 'something' since it does not seem likely a void would be created within itself. It would seem that as the universe evolved and grew, so, too, would this form, this entity within which the universe was located.

Within all this creating, life forms could evolve and within life forms' essence, awareness could be placed. This could allow awareness to travel away from itself, uninfluenced by Her total awareness which existed outside the universe. This could allow the small pieces of awareness to travel uninfluenced in its journey to create 'newness.' This could allow the total, the whole, omniscience, omnipotence, omnipresence to create without influencing Herself as She did so. Parts of the whole could get away from Herself in order not to influence this creation of newness. The whole would now have a means of removing parts of Herself from Herself without becoming less than the sum of Her parts, for all the parts would still be within the whole. Life would take on significance. It would appear life and the Causative Force were more than just aware of each other. It would appear the Causative Force and life were a part of each other, interdependent upon each other, existing in a symbiotic relationship.

•

If the universe is reducible to nothingness – space – and if space is nothing but a location, it can be reduced to nonexistence. That leaves only the abstract – awareness – to exist. If awareness continues beyond the eradication of all else, you and your awareness have no option but to remain eternally, as does everyone else's awareness. Upon leaving the universe, you would have no option under panentheism but to become part of what it entered as it left the universe. Your awareness would become a part of whatever it was that surrounded the universe.

Conclusion: How do the concepts of space reinforce the concept of symbiotic panentheism?

An Einsteinian space took on an appearance of curving, and curving implied a directional change, even if only from the viewpoint of the observer. The directional change, curving of space, implied the possible existence of a limit, a boundary. A boundary, in turn, implied an outside, which implied the universe was not the outer limits of our ability to think. A boundary opened up the ability for the creative side of humanity to start thinking in terms of what lies beyond the universe. This creative side brings us back to religion.

•

The problem of the universe lying outside the Causative Force, rather than within the Causative Force, forces us to try to visualize what lies in the emptiness between our universe and the Causative Force. When we try to visualize this space, we had to draw a picture of classical/traditional theism. This picture, a dot in a circle located outside of a box, placed both you and the universe outside the box. At this point, we became confused as to what lies between the circle (the universe) and the box (the Causative Force). With diagram #4, the confusion goes away. Panentheism resolves the paradox of a Causative Force being considered as all present, omnipresent, yet not including the universe. Panentheism resolves the issue of how a Causative Force could be omnipresent, yet not necessarily be 'within' the universe. Panentheism also resolves the issue of dissolving universes, yet leaves the Causative Force intact. And it resolves the issue of imperfection being within a 'perfect' being.

•

Symbiotic panentheism may sound simple enough, but it would not be an easy task. This concept presents many challenging dilemmas in terms of standing up for and protecting our own rights to travel uninhibited and doing likewise for other species. How and when, for instance, do we resist life forms who are intimidating, subjugating, forcing themselves upon others in the heavens? How do we protect the journeys of the weaker without interfering with the journeys of the strong?

SCIENCE

*What new insight has **Science**
firmly established within society?*

TOPOLOGY:
A Container

SCIENCE: MATRIX #250

#0. What does the conceptual framework of topology have to offer us?

Topology: The branch of geometry concerned with the properties of geometrical objects that are unchanged by continuous deformations, such as twisting or stretching. Mathematical approaches employing topology are of great importance in modern theories of the "fundamental interactions".
  –*Oxford Concise Science Dictionary*, p. 734

What are 'fundamental interactions?' If the interactions that exist between a Causative Force and what She creates is not fundamental, what is?

•

Geometrical objects are made up of points, locations. A point, in terms of mathematics, is so small, it has no length, height or depth. A point does not exist in the physical sense; it is an idea, a concept, an abstract 'thing.' Mathematics deals with the abstract, with non-physical ideas, and examines how these non-physical, abstract ideas interact. Science then takes these laws and applies them to the physical universe. On the other hand, if science finds the abstract ideas of mathematics do not fit our universe, it will reject these ideas and send mathematics back to the drawing board to rethink its ideas. Some ideas are so theoretical and advanced that science is unable to prove or disprove them since they seem to have no direct connection with our universe in terms of what we understand at this point in time.

Einstein proposed the idea that light did not always travel in a straight line as science had always thought. Einstein, using mathematics, demonstrated the path of light will curve due to the pull of gravity. It wasn't until much later that scientists were able to prove his assumptions and his mathematical model. Because of the solid logic supporting Einstein's statements, science accepted this mathematical model until direct observation could prove or disprove the model.

•

If science is willing to use solid, logical, abstract ideas of mathematics and apply them to their investigations concerning the universe, why shouldn't they do the same regarding religious and philosophical abstract ideas?

#1. What does the conceptual framework of topology imply about the universe within which we live?

Topology is an area of mathematics that deals with 'the properties of geometrical objects that are unchanged by continuous deformations, such as twisting or stretching.' Doesn't this sound familiar? Science twists and stretches the concepts of religions. Religions twist and stretch the concepts of science. Both try to discredit the other.

•

Science and religion should work together to reinforce each other in order to reinforce us, individuals, who have to face and travel the journey of life. We need reinforcement, not confusion and infighting. Life is difficult enough to deal with without having to choose principles with which one is going to side. Principles should be as close to absolutes, 'universal truths,' as we are able to get. Why should we have to choose between 'what it is we see' and 'what it is we inwardly feel?' Science and religion are not living entities. They were developed by us, for us, as tools to help us understand what life, what the universe is, where the universe is, and why both we and the universe exist.

Topology is a field of study that attempts to define 'universal truths' in reality. Science and mathematics now have a specialty area of study intended to help them understand what 'truths' may exist in the universe. The 'truths' they are seeking are independent of the forces of the universe. If what we see – science, and what we believe – religion, have any validity to them, then why aren't we seeking out the 'truths' that apply to both? Why are we constantly allowing the two to continually bicker amongst themselves? This causes the core issues regarding what life is and why it exists to remain in a state of confusion. There is a lesson to be learned from topology: maybe there are 'universal truths' to be found within our universe.

•

Science and religion are both attempting to be the primary player in our ability to understand what we are. As such, science and religion not only beat up on each other, but beat up on philosophy, the tool necessary to unite the two. Philosophy, the investigation of causes and laws that underlie reality, lies languishing and broken on the sidelines of the debate. And who suffers the consequences for such behavior? We, the individuals seeking desperately to understand, are the victims of this war.

#2. How does the concept of topology reinforce the concept of panentheism?

Topology is a field of mathematics that opens up entirely different ways of looking at things which exist around us. Panentheism does the same.

•

Topology can take a strip of paper and change it from a two-sided figure (top and bottom) to a one sided figure (top only). Take a strip of paper, make a loop, and tape the loop together. Color the inside red and the outside green. Now take another strip of paper, make a loop, twist it once and then tape the loop together. Color the top red and, as you do so, pull the loop around until the entire top is colored red. As you will see, the inside and outside are now entirely colored red and there is no place to color green. This is called a Mobius strip.

Your first impression is that this seems a waste of time. But one must remember that mathematics delves into the realm of the unknown. Theoretical mathematics deals with the concepts that seem to have no value to us because they deal with ideas of which we have little or no understanding.

But topology has come much further than a one-sided Mobius strip. Topology is now toying with the idea of a four dimensional bottle (length, width, height, located in time) having only three dimensions. This bottle is called a Klein Bottle. It is a container that would appear to have no inside if you were outside the container. It is a container that would appear to have no outside if you were inside the container. Once again, the sound of familiarity rings loud and clear. Our universe appears to be just such a situation.

•

We appear to be inside a universe located in a container of space with no way out. The Causative Force appears to be outside the container with no way to get inside. I am not saying this is 'the' explanation of what is occurring in terms of the Causative Force, the universe, and ourselves, but it is an interesting perception. Such an idea would reinforce the concept of panentheism as opposed to any of the other three ideas of theisms: no Causative Force as put forward by atheism, the Causative Force being the same as the universe as put forward by pantheisms, and a Causative Force not including the universe as put forward by classical/traditional theisms.

#3. What does topology reinforce about the significance of existence, life?

A topological concept of a universe having universal truths would imply that life may just as well have universal truths connected to it. Life having significance could be one of those truths.

•

Why do we find it so difficult to believe life has significance? Stars, mountains, and rivers are 'things' in our universe which appear to have no awareness. As we look at other objects in our universe, we see countless reminders of objects having no awareness of what seems to be taking place around them. As we look at life forms on earth, we see endless examples of life that seem to have some form of awareness, but only in a limited sense. The awareness of a bug seems to be limited to what is occurring around it. A bug does not appear to have a sense of the universe. It lives from day to day with a seemingly inbred understanding of a need to survive. The bug, however, does not seem to consciously plan for next week or for the third, seventh, 100th generation to follow it. Living objects seem to be different than nonliving objects but life still seems to have little significance in terms of intentionally and consciously affecting the universe. Because we have so few examples of life forms using their awareness to consciously and intentionally impact 'their' eternity, we find it difficult to accept the idea that we, awareness, could be capable of having eternal significance, immortality, which is a different form of significance than that tied to time, mortality.

Topology should give us hope, for it confronts just such a problem within the field of mathematics and science. It attempts to find universal truths unaffected by the distorting forces of the universe. If mathematics and science can logically attempt to seek out such truths, what is illogical about science and religion doing the same? What is illogical about science and religion both exploring hypothetical concepts about the significance of life that reach beyond the distorting forces of our universe?

•

Mathematics and science seek universal truths to guide them using a special field of study as a tool. The field of study is topology. Science and religion have no reason not to do the same. The field of study has already been established. The field of study would seem to be philosophy.

#4. How does topology help us understand what life is?

Topology, having only recently been recognized as a respectable field of study, attempts to find universal truths within the universe unaffected by the distorting forces of the universe. If we can accept this concept as logical, we should find it easier to accept doing the same in terms of finding universal truths about life.

•

Many philosophers, scientists, and religious leaders would be quick to point out that the concept of a soul, an abstract concept of life, deals with the abstract and not the physical. As such, they would be quick to point out that topology centers its attention on truths regarding physical items in the universe, truths that would extend beyond the universe. There is no doubt that the topic of concern regarding this trilogy deals with the abstract, the nonphysical. But the truths topology seeks to find, truths which extend beyond our universe, deal also with abstract, nonphysical concepts. Topology, should it find universal truths, in actuality is doing nothing less than philosophy attempts to do. Topology attempts to find truths existing beyond time in order to help us better understand the universe within which we must exist as a life form. We are conscious of the possibility of an abstract existence called eternity. If topology should find universal truths, they would appear to be truths which would apply to eternal existence.

Philosophy has been attempting to do the same thing for thousands of years with little success because of the lack of information. Religion has provided information for a long time in terms of what we sense to be true. Science is a newcomer into the arena of understanding what we see. Philosophy needs an understanding of both what it is we sense and what it is we see in order to accomplish the task of developing a human consensus in terms of what we are and why we exist.

•

Topology initiates a scientific understanding of 'universal truths' that are unaffected by the universe. But topology also acts as a model of the role philosophy is to play in terms of the search for 'universal truths.' Philosophy is the tool to fuse the information science and religion provide regarding what life is.

#5. What does topology have to offer us as individuals?

Topology offers us hope. Topology offers us the idea that perhaps there are universal truths that reach beyond the universe itself.

•

Topology is a field of mathematics that has such a firm belief in universal truths that it seeks to actually find them. The term 'universal truths' is misleading. Universal truths really refer to truths that extend beyond the boundaries of our known universe. Since time appears to be a factor of our universe, universal truths would appear to be concepts that reach beyond time, concepts that describe eternity itself. We associate life as being limited by time. If universal truths could exist, then it is possible that the essence of life, awareness perhaps, could be associated with just such concepts as universal truths. Topology gives us the understanding that science and theoretical mathematics are now beginning to acknowledge the possibility of eternal existence. This acknowledgment may not be one they are boldly announcing, but it is one they are quietly accepting by searching with topology.

What if topology finds universal truths exist unaffected and undistorted by the forces of our universe? Then topology would have discovered the existence of truths in the area that lies beyond our universe. Topology would then become the first field of science or mathematics to do so. But this wouldn't make topology the first field of study to do so. Religions have been discussing universal truths for thousands of years. Mathematics, on the other hand, may well become the first field of study dealing with direct observation of the universe around us which is capable of proving truths which describe eternity. Such an accomplishment would be the first step science or mathematics would have taken to reinforce the field of religion. Hope of an eternal existence could become re-ignited by one of the least expected fields of study – theoretical mathematics.

•

'Could become' should actually read 'has become.' Topology does not need to actually find universal truths. Just the fact that this field has evolved within the analytical areas of math and science should be enough of a statement to make us realize that even mathematics and science are now beginning to give some validity to the idea of eternity.

#6. What significance does topology have to us as a species?

Topology offers us a second area of hope. Topology offers us the idea that perhaps being contained in a limited universe is not as negative a concept as we might first believe.

•

Many scientists and philosophers would automatically dismiss any idea mentioning the concept of the universe being bounded. These philosophers and scientists would do so on the basis that any model professing such an idea, or any model willing to even entertain such an idea as a possibility, would itself be too limiting and, therefore, unworthy of their consideration. This process is another example of rejecting the value different fields of study may be able to contribute to a universal model of philosophy. Knee jerk reactions of automatic rejection are based upon a desire to maintain one's own status either in a sense of reputation, power, financial support, academic notoriety, etc.

Boundaries aren't necessarily physical, nor are they limited to a single level. Boundaries can be created by forces unable to escape themselves, forces which turn in on themselves. Einstein suggested just such a scenario for our universe. Einstein felt it was possible that our universe may be curved due to the effect of gravity. This would create a boundary based not upon a physical boundary, but upon what appears to be an abstract force.

•

There are many other means of creating a boundary. Scientists studying vacuums now believe there may be different forms of emptiness. This potentiality for nothingness opens up entirely new concepts for modern science in terms of the structure of the universe. Layering now becomes a possibility for our universe, the first layer possibly being what we are presently capable of observing. Closed systems could become systems we perceive to be open only because we cannot 'see' the total picture. We have to be careful about rejecting the possibility of anything. What we can do, however, is formulate a model of our universe and ourselves based upon the most logical information we have been able to gather. This information would be the fusion of our perceptions based upon what we sense – religion – what we see – science – and what we can logically deduce – philosophy. Topology offers us hope for universal truths, hope through containment, and hope through example.

#7. What significance does topology have to offer other life forms in the universe?

Just as topology offers us hope as individuals and as a species, topology offers the same hope to other life forms throughout the heavens.

•

Since Hinduism, religions have been professing that the essence of life is the soul. The soul is not mortal. The soul is immortal. The soul is not limited by time. The soul is eternal. Put in scientific terms, this would be expressed as: the essence of life is abstract. The essence of life is awareness. Various perceptions of awareness may be influenced by the stretching and twisting deformations of the forces within the universe, but the very 'existence of awareness' remains what it is: awareness existing. Therefore, the idea of the existence of awareness is a universal truth. Awareness exists and the fact that it exists remains unchanged by the deforming forces of the universe. This scientific statement is simply a statement of the fundamentals of topology.

Religion was the first to discover a universal truth through a process we call a sense of what is. The newcomer, science, is just now beginning to verify what religions have been saying for thousands of years through the process of seeing and observing what takes place around us. The field of study it is using to do so is mathematics – topology in particular.

Topology offers us hope from the scientific point of view, that maybe, just maybe, we are more than just temporary beings. Topology offers us hope that perhaps religions are correct, perhaps we are a direct part of eternity, perhaps we are a form of a universal truth. As far-reaching as this may be for us, let us not forget it is not a truth pertaining to only us. It is being professed as a universal truth, which means it applies to all life forms.

•

Topology offers the individual hope. Mathematics now joins religion as a believer in the concept of something possibly existing beyond the universe. Mathematics is the purest form of science; it is the language through which science speaks. Mathematics is so convinced of the idea that universal truths exist that it has established topology as a field of study dedicated specifically to the concept of seeking these very truths.

#8. What does topology imply about our significance in eternity?

Topology gives us insight into what type of container, boundary, may enclose our universe. It is here that the idea of a Klein bottle provides some rationale into our universe having an outside, even if we cannot see the boundary.

•

Mathematics is a language. It is perhaps the purest form of language in our universe. Through mathematics, we begin to understand things in our universe that we have never seen or known to exist. It is through mathematics that scientists and mathematicians speculate about what exists and then begin to search for these building blocks and events in our universe. Mathematics points into the darkness of the unknown science, then lights up the path with the flame of knowledge until the treasure, mapped out by mathematics, is found.

Topology may very well be just such a map. Topology has recently begun to examine the idea of a container capable of causing the forces within it to bend in on themselves. The container would have no physical boundary but would be bounded nevertheless. The container is called the Klein bottle. (Many interesting sites exist on the internet dedicated to explaining the Klein bottle.)

The Klein bottle itself is not what is important here. What is important is the understanding it provides regarding the idea of something being bounded within itself by a non-existing boundary. Restating this idea, topology opens up the possibility that a region, a space, could exist that, when viewed from the outside, would appear to have no inside and when viewed from the inside, would appear to have no outside. In short, it would be possible for an entity, the Causative Force, to create a place within Herself that She could enter. This space would provide a place for the Causative Force to get away from Herself in order to create newness, in order to create without being influenced, interrupted or disturbed, in short: symbiotic panentheism.

•

Opening up the possibility of the Causative Force creating within the universe substantially expands upon our potential significance to the universe itself. Being a part of a process through which a Causative Force learns and grows increases our significance to eternity immeasurably. We, as individuals, as a species, as a life form in the heavens, have never been given this type of status.

#9. What does topology imply about our relationship to the Causative Force?

The Causative Force created the universe, our reality. How far beyond the concept of our human understanding of a Causative Force may be limited only by the life span of our universe.

•

Topology explains how it may be possible for time to exist within a bottle, a universe, but not outside the bottle. Topology searches for universal truths unchanged by the forces of the universe itself, applicable to multiple universes, and existing beyond time. Topology searches for the eternal. Religions search for the eternal. What's the difference? They both search for the same concepts. It is time for the teamwork to begin.

The Big Bang Theory puts forth the idea that the universe is expanding. This would imply one of two things. Either the universe actually is expanding, which implies it is expanding into something, or the universe appears to be expanding within a portion of itself. This may imply the universe is bounded and constant, but its contents, the stars, galaxies, etc., flow within a container that varies in dimension, such as a topological Klein bottle. This could cause the appearance of expansion and contraction.

Either case suggests something exists in addition to the universe. This concept is none other than what religions have been professing for thousands of years: there is something beyond time. Immortality may well be the first universal truth we are able to prove and our essence being tied to this immortality may be the second universal truth we are able to prove.

•

Topology offers us the first formal field of mathematics and science that reaches out to the ideas religions have been professing for over 3,500 years. Mathematics may not be doing so intentionally, but it is doing so nonetheless. Topology may not acknowledge the soul, awareness existing beyond time, a Causative Force or an eternal existence for the soul, but topology is moving in that direction, illustrated by the fact that it is studying universal truths.

Conclusion: How do the concepts of topology reinforce the concept of symbiotic panentheism?

They do not; what is really taking place is that symbiotic panentheism reinforces the concepts of topology: the concept that the universe could be contained, the concept of universal truths, and the concept of awareness possibly being immortal.

•

Topology would appear to suggest the idea of something existing beyond our universe. In fact, topology, through its search for what lies within our universe but is unaffected by the forces within our universe, would seem to imply that our universe is submerged within something, some universal truths. This is panentheism.

Topology would appear to suggest that universal truths exist and are unaffected by the forces of our universe. Topology further suggests that these universal truths, inside and outside our universe, are related in some fashion to each other. These universal truths interact with each other in some interlocking fashion. This is the concept of symbiosis.

This model, symbiotic panentheism, developed long after the formation of topology, strongly reinforces the field of topology.

•

At this point, it would be difficult to offer any other suggestion than those entropy offers. The universe would appear to be either a closed system or an open system. If it is a closed system, it would be bounded and it would eventually need to come to an end. A closed system would appear to be a negative concept for our species. Our species perceives itself as being able to do anything, given enough time. Combined with the idea of a bounded universe, this would imply our species will eventually exhaust all of our options. The end result: hope would transform into a state of apathy and depression.

This scenario, however, is not the only option open to us. Granted, it is the option atheism, pantheism, and classical/traditional theisms have to offer us under their perceptions of our universe existing independent of the Causative Force.

However, if we combine the topological concept of universal truths being contained inside a universe with the concepts of entropy, the Big Bang Theory, symmetry, Venn diagrams, space, and symbiotic panentheism, we get something entirely different for our species. These ideas offer our species endless, infinite options in terms of the role we play in continual creation. Hope now becomes eternal.

SCIENCE

*What new insight has **Science**
firmly established within society?*

ECOLOGICAL NICHE:
Belonging

#0. What does the conceptual framework of ecological niche have to offer us?

Ecological niche: The status or role of an organism in its environment. An organism's niche is defined by the types of food it consumes, its predators, temperature, tolerances, etc. Two species cannot coexist stably if they occupy identical niches.
                                  —*Oxford Concise Science Dictionary*, p. 234

•

The status or role an organism plays in its environment is usually set first and then the organism develops to fill the niche – not the other way around. Plants use sunlight to convert the sun's energy into stored food to be used later when the sun is not shining. Plants do not have to move about; they are able to store the excess energy in a form that allows them to survive periods when the sun is hidden by clouds during the day and darkness at night. Plant-eating animals developed to use the excess food the plants produced. They learned to move about in order to go from one plant location to another. Animal-eating animals developed to use the energy stored in plant-eating animals. They developed the ability to move fast in order to catch the slower moving plant-eating animals.

This process continued up the food chain with niches becoming more specialized. And then we come to humans. Humanity appears to be the most sophisticated animal on earth. Humanity is unique for many reasons and its relationship within ecological niches is just one interesting example. Ecological niches for plants and animals are created by nature, but humanity appears to have created its own niche.

•

We may have evolved over a period of millions of years. The point being addressed here is not evolution of our species, but rather the evolutionary development of our ecological niche. We may have started by filling an ecological niche, but we now seem to be in a niche of our own making. We appear to be the only life form in our solar system searching for meaning. We have developed our societies in such a manner that we are capable of seeking knowledge for knowledge's sake. Or is there another reason? We may not appear to be filling an ecological niche within this physical universe but perhaps we are filling a niche created by the very existence of the universe itself.

#1. What does the conceptual framework of ecological niche imply about the universe within which we live?

"An organism's niche is defined by the types of food it consumes, its predators, temperature, tolerances, etc." As we examine living organisms, it would appear that living organisms fill niches developed within the universe. By studying the niche, we can begin to understand the organism.

•

Most animals evolve in order to fit into an ecological niche located within the universe. Humanity, on the other hand, seems to have used ecological niches to sustain itself while it evolved into what it is. We did not evolve into a niche and then stagnate there. We moved on with our development in order to continue to higher levels of development. Each level brings us more knowledge about the universe. Each level brings us a greater appreciation for the value of the individual. Each level whets our appetite for the next level of development. We are never satisfied with the level we have mastered. We are continually in the process of seeking new ideas, new knowledge, new experiences, new levels of control over nature, social development, survivability, exploration, and understanding. No matter how successful we seem to be in terms of filling a particular ecological niche, we strive to move on and find new challenges and adventures both as individuals and as a species. We are never content.

A zebra is a zebra is a zebra. It does not appear to ever consciously seek out new ecological niches to fill. It does not appear to consciously develop itself in order to move into a different environment. For the most part, it stays within the niche it evolved into. It may, on rare occasion, mutate to fit a new niche, but it does not consciously seek to do so.

We, on the other hand, relish the thought of diving to the far depths of the oceans, walking on the moon, and communicating with parallel universes we do not even know exist. If all living things fill niches, then what is our niche? It appears our niche may be tied to something other than niches formed within the universe itself.

•

Studying a niche created by the universe is one way to understand a living organism. Studying a living organism is one way of understanding its niche. Humanity's constant search for eternity may well be able to tell us something about the limits of the universe itself and what lies beyond.

#2. How do the concepts of ecological niche reinforce the concept of panentheism?

Biologically speaking, organisms evolve to fill niches. We appear to have evolved with a primal need to explore, learn, and touch the face of the Causative Force Herself.

•

We believe the universe exists, life exists, and life evolves to fit ecological niches within the universe. If biologists are correct in these theories, then it appears biologists have two options available to understand the interrelationship of the environment and the living organisms within that environment.

Biologists can study the environment in order to understand life forms or biologists can study the characteristics of life forms in order to understand the environment. If we believe we are tied to eternity, immersed within eternity, then we should be able to study eternity to understand our function within it. But at this point in our development, we are unable to see, touch or measure eternity. Because of this, we cannot study eternity, our environment, in order to understand ourselves. We, therefore, must use the second option; we must study ourselves in order to understand eternity.

Taking this approach, we see that humankind seems to have some innate drives. We are constantly seeking to fill a role – the role religions define. We are constantly attempting to satisfy the needs of what we perceive is our 'creator.' We constantly attempt to abide by the laws of the Force which created the universe. We constantly seek to find the edge of our universe in order to verify our idea of something existing beyond our limited physical world. We call this existence outside the universe *eternity*. We sensed the existence of just such a place long before Einstein formulated the mathematics explaining the relationship between time, matter, and energy.

•

Niches exist within the environment, not independent of and separate from the environment. And if we also fill an ecological niche, it seems we are defining that niche by our actions both past and present. Studying human actions in order to understand that niche leads us to an apparent conclusion that our niche is tied to something beyond the physical world of our universe. All organisms are immersed within the niche they fill. If we were created to function as a part of eternity, then we must be immersed within eternity. This is panentheism.

#3. What does ecological niche reinforce about the significance of existence, life?

Niches reinforce the concept of belonging. Organisms are members of the universe. Organisms fill a place created within the universe.

•

Does humanity belong and, if it does, to what does it belong? Organisms fill ecological niches within a universe and, when studied, the niche they fill can be understood both generally and in great detail. The same concept applies to life. Even if a life form were removed to an environment totally alien to them, biologists could gain great insight into the nature of the surrounding within which that life existed just by studying the life form. The same applies to humans. When studying the human biological organism, both body and brain, one could learn much about the individual's and the species' environment. But one would have little insight into the motivation, drives, conscious needs, and desires on an intellectual level unless one also examined the accomplishments, hope, dreams, and knowledge the human organism had established

There is far more to the human organism than described by the physical niche it fills. There is the spiritual side of humanity, the idealistic side, the aspect of humanity wrapped in dreams, hopes, and sense of connection to something beyond the boundaries of the universe. The physical aspect of the universe creates ecological niches that living organisms with 'local' awareness fill. But humanity seems to have more than local awareness. Humanity seems to have a sense of, a possible connection to, a form of universal awareness that goes far beyond the physical universe within which we function.

•

We acknowledge the existence of our universe as an absolute in terms of perceiving its existence. In addition, we acknowledge the existence of life existing within the niches created by the physical aspect of the universe. Both define each other. If there is more to existence than the physical universe and life, and if life and the universe exist within 'something' that lies beyond the boundaries of the universe, then both the universe and life would seem to have a function within and to this 'thing' within which they lie. Studying the two, life and the physical aspect of the universe, should help us understand what lies beyond the universe. But we need more information than what we observe about life and the universe. We need to also study the strong sense of purpose of humanity.

#4. How does ecological niche help us understand what life is?

Defining a niche tied to what lies beyond the universe could help us understand what life is.

•

We have studied life by looking at it from a viewpoint located within the universe. We have studied physical niches in the universe in order to understand how life evolved to fit these ecological niches. This means of studying life comes from a perspective of time. As such, we study life as a beginning–end concept.

We have, however, never studied life from a more distant view. Our species senses it is directly tied to a niche beyond the universe, to eternity. If this is the case, why can't we study this abstract niche in order to understand how awareness, human awareness, evolved to fit this niche? To do so would force us to make assumptions about the afterlife and then apply them to life in order to corroborate our perceptions of the afterlife. This corroboration would come through a confirmation of how well our perceptions of an afterlife meshes with what life in the universe actually is and functions. This is a risky action, for if our assumptions regarding the afterlife do not lead us back into life as we know it, we would have to change our model of the afterlife.

•

If we define life to be a certain way, does this make it necessarily so? Nothing is an absolute. Even existence itself is not an absolute; we all may be nothing but participants in a dream. In spite of this possibility, we accept existence as an absolute. To define the afterlife in terms of what we see around us and then reinforce it in terms of verification through what we believe, is as legitimate a process as any we have in place. It is one we have accepted for hundreds of years in the scientific field. This is exactly what we do today. We define what life is because there is no one else to do it for us and, even if there were, would we want someone or something else defining our life?

Defining a niche for life and for ourselves tied to what lies beyond the universe is different. It raises the significance of all life, for it elevates life from a level of mortality to a level of immortality. This elevation has already been accepted by religions, but to have science and philosophy also accept it would provide a great deal of support to the concept. Religion alone has been unable to fully accomplish this task. However, the three working together to support the idea of our connection to eternity would go a long way toward helping us elevate our behavior within the universe.

#5. What does ecological niche have to offer us as individuals?

Defining the location of our ecological niche as being outside of our universe offers us a sense of purpose and a marker by which we can measure our behavior.

•

We are an organism. But are we? Our body is certainly physical. Our mind is certainly physical. Our body and mind work in conjunction together as do the body and mind of other organisms. Ecological biomes depend upon heat, as does our body. Ecological biomes depend upon water, as does our body. Our universe works upon a heat exchange system, entropy, as does our body. Our universe may die and so may our bodies.

Looking to the past, we have little option but to be certain that death will occur. We accept this as a 'truth.' But because we sense eternity, the logic of 'something' not being connected to time, we sense the possibility of our connection to eternity.

The past does not provide us with any insight regarding the logic of the idea that eternity exists. Looking into the future has provided us with this insight. As we gazed into the starry heavens, we sensed an understanding that all things must come to an end, even the heavens. As we allowed this thought to settle over us, we realized that if this were true, then it only makes sense that the universe had a beginning if it can end. But it does not make sense for the universe to create itself through the process of spontaneous generation. Spontaneous generation, the process of an organism being created out of thin air, is a concept science discarded hundreds of years ago. Rejection of spontaneous generation as a means of the universe by its own accord leaves only one other option – creation – and this concept is a process that elevates the significance of the individual, for this process implies purpose.

•

Spontaneous generation is an excellent way to explain the sudden appearance of something you cannot otherwise explain in terms of its origin. But using spontaneous generation as a valid explanation defies all the lessons science has provided us. Using the concept of spontaneous generation does our species a great injustice, for it stifles our search for knowledge, it inhibits the growth of our understanding, and it belittles the very faiths we have preserved over time.

#6. What significance does ecological niche have to us as a species?

The concept of an ecological niche offers us the opportunity to define a niche for ourselves, incapable of being 'bettered' by any other species, earthbound or otherwise. With a visionary definition, we will never have to worry about being replaced by a competing species.

•

The definition of ecological niche is very blunt in prophesying the future for the human race. "Two species cannot coexist stably if they occupy identical niches." We persist, as a species, in trying to find a role for ourselves in terms of what our function is in terms of what lies outside our universe. We constantly look to our present and our past in order to define this function. We have never been able to develop a model most of our species would agree represents what we are as a species. All our models have been based upon subjugation and domination. All our models have been based upon power struggles, personal gain, competition, value judgments, and bettering one's life.

Some feel religions do not do this. Don't they? The past has given us: "I'm Christian and I will go to heaven; you will go to hell. I'm Moslem and Mohammed was a greater prophet than Christ. I'm Roman Catholic and you're only Protestant. I'm Buddhist and I take offense to your use of the term 'God.' I'm a ... and you're an atheist, so I don't want to associate with you. I'm a man and can be a church leader; you're only a woman." It goes on and on, with even children saying, "My church is better than your church." The future perpetuates the past.

If we continually look back to define what we are, it will take us a long, long time to raise our level of thinking regarding what we are and what our function for living is. Our level of behavior is based upon our perception of what it is we are and what our purpose for existence is. In order to make quantum leaps in terms of our behavior, we have to make quantum leaps in terms of our perceptions of what it is we think we are. To make this quantum leap, we have to stop looking backwards and take a new approach by looking forward.

•

If looking to the past has been unable to provide us with a universally acceptable model of what we are and why we exist, then why not look to the future? We can analyze what we see ahead for us and try to reinforce it if we like what we see, or change if we don't.

#7. What significance does ecological niche have to offer other life forms in the universe?

We appear to have the ability to define our own niche. If we define our niche to be so basic that it takes on the same aspect as other animals on the food chain, we will undoubtedly be confronted with many other life forms competing for control of the same niche.

•

Being able to define our own niche opens up many possibilities for us as a species. To take the most obvious path, to define ourselves as the top of the food chain, to define our niche as the highest order of animal life, will leave us in a position of having to compete for that position with many other life forms.

The most secure option for our species would be to raise our level of significance to that attached to what lies beyond our physical reality. Doing so requires defining ourselves in terms of accepting our ability to comprehend a form of existence beyond our physical reality. As such, we would be able to tie our significance to eternity rather than to mortality. This would require that we accept all awareness capable of such universal thought and to be tied to this omniscient awareness.

We would have to share such a position, such a status. This would mean we would have little choice but to accept the soul as an entity not of a human nature, but of a nature connected, directly coming from a being, an entity, outside the universe. We would have to accept human souls as pieces of the same entity, as would be true for all life forms throughout the universe.

•

Defining a niche for ourselves so significant that no other life form is 'better' means defining a niche to be so significant that all other life forms take on the same status of invaluable significance. But can we ever accept other humans who differ from us as equals? We can if we start looking at them in a different manner. We can if we stop seeing them as the body and mind with different needs and desires, and start looking at them as bodies and minds whose needs are simply the function of the biological organism. We would need to learn acceptance for these differences and look more towards the soul. It is the soul's journey we would need to protect.

#8. What does ecological niche imply about our significance in eternity?

If niches are a fundamental relationship between the physical aspect of the universe and the living portions of the universe, then wouldn't niches be fundamental relationships between the physical aspect of the universe and the abstract aspect called 'awareness' within which universes exist?

•

Niches in the physical universe all seem to be temporary. It is most likely that our genus and species, Homo sapiens, are temporary also. However, we have what seems to be a special type of awareness. We seem to be the only living species on earth capable of contemplating a 'place' without time, a place called 'eternity.' But we not only contemplate such an existence, we contemplate how our actions might affect our eternal existence.

In short, we have mentally developed a niche for ourselves outside temporary existence that we observe located within the physical universe. The amazing thing about such a development is that this creates a niche tied to eternity and we then become an integral part of that niche. We become an integral part of eternity.

•

Most life forms we have seen do not build their own niches; they develop to fit niches that already exist. Humanity seems to be unique because we appear to be able to evolve to fit higher order ecological niches within the universe. Even now, we appear to be ready to slip into an ecological niche conducive for space traveling organisms. This is an exciting time for our species. But as exciting as it may seem, we do not want to lose track of the concept that we may also be evolving into understanding what lies beyond the boundaries of our universe.

Is it just a coincidence that these two leaps, space travel and an understanding of a universal philosophy, are evolving at the same time or is it possible one cannot occur without the other? If it is imperative that we have a universal understanding of the significance of our lives as well as the lives of others before we explore the existence of other life forms, then we should not ignore this development. On the other hand, if this understanding is not a prerequisite of space travel, perhaps we should give it serious thought anyway in order to prevent our past from repeating itself at the expense of innocent life forms we may encounter.

#9. What does ecological niche imply about our relationship to the Causative Force?

Ecological niches are something biologists have defined in order to better understand the interrelationship between three fundamental aspects of existence: the niche itself, the organism itself, and the interrelationship that exists between the two.

•

Within the confines of our universe, we study physical niches because the universe is physical in nature. Life forms within the universe appears to have awareness and intelligence capable of sensing the physical environment. They seem to interact with the physical environment around them. They appear to have a conception of time. There is a time of day to get food, to sleep, to reproduce, and to move on. What sets the time and rhythm for action is the physical niche to which they are tied. Change their biome and the animal dies. Take a seal out of its niche and put it in the niche a fox fills and the seal will die.

But humans seem to be able to adapt themselves to almost any niche. We are capable of living in tropical rain forests, cold mountain climates, hot desert regions, and the airless atmosphere of the moon. Humans do not seem to be confined to 'a' physical niche. Our level of awareness also seems to be different. Other life forms on the earth seem have an awareness limited to time; humans seem to have an awareness capable of focusing on time, but they also appear to have an awareness capable of focusing on eternity – the absence of time.

We appear to be tied to an abstract ecological niche as well as to physical ecological niches. Physical ecological niches involve the environment within which the organism is immersed, the organism, and the interrelationship between the two. An abstract ecological niche also involves three aspects: an abstract concept of eternity within which our universe is immersed, the organism, and the interrelationship of the two. What is this environment of eternity called? Religions call it the Creator. Symbiotic panentheism calls it the Causative Force.

•

The environment, ecological niche, within which the universe appears to be located may well be total awareness, omniscience, the Causative Force.

Conclusion: How do the concepts of ecological niche reinforce the concept of symbiotic panentheism?

We can choose our niche. We are one of the few, if not only, animals on earth capable of doing so. What niche do we want to fill? We can choose one that already exists or we can create our own based upon the idealism that reinforces the diversity of religions we have, based upon what we see – science, based upon logic – philosophy, or based upon all three.

•

We need to start looking forward into the future. The further into the future we can project, the greater the quantum leap we will make in terms of what it is we think we are and what purpose we believe we have. The greater the quantum leap we make in this area of understanding, the greater the quantum leap will be in terms of our behavior towards each other, ourselves, and our environment.

Why not make the leap of understanding that we not only may exist in eternity, but we may be a part of an ecological niche *involving* eternity, a part of the niche involving the Causative Force? We may very well have an important function to the Causative Force. We may be significant not only to the physical universe, but to eternity.

•

We seem to be attempting to fill a niche within something outside our universe, surrounding our universe, something within which our universe is located. Even a subject as basic as ecological niches reinforces the idea of panentheism: all being within a Causative Force. Ecological niches also reinforce the idea of symbiosis: we interact with the Causative force.

Studying the organism to understand its environment seems to be a round about way to understand the environment of the organism. But this is not so in the situation where the environment of the organism is invisible to the organism. If the essence of humanity is tied to eternity and if eternity is something we are unable to 'see' at this point in time, then our only option to study eternity would be to study the organism tied to it. To study eternity, we would have to study the organism, humanity, in order to understand our environment. Interestingly enough, when we do so, it appears that symbiotic panentheism is one explanation, perhaps the only explanation we have at this time, of the interrelationship we have with eternity.

SCIENCE

*What new insight has **Science**
firmly established within society?*

PALAEOMAGNETISM:
Change

SCIENCE: MATRIX #270

#0. What does the conceptual framework of palaeomagnetism have to offer us?

Palaeomagnetism: The study of the magnetism in rocks. During the formation of igneous or sedimentary rock containing magnetic minerals the polarity of the earth's magnetic field at the time becomes frozen in the rock. Studies of this fossil magnetism has also revealed that periodic reversals in the geomagnetic field have taken place.
        –Oxford Concise Science Dictionary, p. 526

•

The earth's core is thought to be composed of molten material containing a large amount of the element iron. As the core rotates, a magnetic force field is created. This field can be measured with a compass. Flip the earth and the needle of the compass will change directions. If there were some manner of recording such a movement permanently, we could study the history of the earth's rotation. This is where palaeomagnetism enters the picture.

Palaeo means 'old.' Palaeomagnetism simply means old magnetism. The earth has an interesting method of recording the alignment of its north and south poles. Molten magma seeping to the surface of the earth contains iron. As this iron slowly cools, the crystals it forms line up with the north and south poles and become permanent records of the direction of the poles literally etched in stone. Scientists, studying these records, have discovered evidence that our earth has shifted on its axis from time to time, which would be a major traumatic event. We would not be able to stop such an event, but we could prepare for it physically and psychologically. Either one has its own benefits and potential for reducing the trauma our species would face.

•

The earth shifting on its axis is a major event. The forces involved are enormous and would create cataclysmic geological events around the world. If it has happened before, it can happen again. This is but one of hundreds of cataclysmic events our species may have to face. We must prepare ourselves psychologically for just such events. We must establish a tremendously strong sense of purpose and direction for our species if we are to minimize the damage such an event would have upon our present civilization.

#1. What does the conceptual framework of palaeomagnetism imply about the universe within which we live?

The universe is in a constant state of change. We cannot change this; it is a part of the process known as entropy. We can, however, change our approach to cataclysmic events of change.

•

Earthquakes, hurricanes, floods, and tornadoes are minor cataclysmic events creating major upheavals in society and individual people's lives. Events such as these are excellent test runs for the more traumatic cataclysmic events we will have to face at some point. Examples of such major events would include pole shifts, large meteor impacts, global epidemics, and ice ages.

Presently, we react to small worldwide cataclysmic events with a sense of awe and wonder over the power of nature and science: monsoons in Asia, earthquakes in Mexico, epidemics in Africa, nuclear meltdowns in Russia. We view these events as isolated occurrences deserving our attention for the full two minutes they are being aired on TV. Many people point to organizations such as the Red Cross, the United Nations, and world governments as examples of our compassion and united front intended to address such events. But would such minor efforts provide us with the expertise to handle an event such as a pole shift?

This is not negativism; this is fact. We are missing the point of these minor cataclysms. We are missing the opportunity to put into place global social structures capable of dealing with major traumatic events, tested by minor traumatic events. If our present civilization is to survive events such as a large meteor impact, it will have to learn how to deal with such an event before it happens. The more localized events should be looked at as practice runs for the much bigger events to come. Palaeomagnetism gives us solid evidence that worldwide cataclysmic events, such as pole shifts, occur from time to time. We need to start preparing ourselves.

•

Preparing ourselves for major cataclysmic events is not an exercise of desperation, nor is it a means of demeaning the trauma and effect the less traumatic events create. Trauma is trauma, devastation is devastation, emotional loss is emotional loss. But the event, once having occurred, may as well be used for a greater purpose. In fact, the victims would find themselves to be the recipients of the training and experience we gain.

#2. How do the concepts of palaeomagnetism reinforce the concept of panentheism?

Palaeomagnetism clearly shows us that change occurs throughout the globe in various degrees. Change appears to be a natural state of our planet, our solar system, and our universe. Natural states of the universe would imply natural states of a Creator.

•

Palaeomagnetism is not the only indicator we have of cataclysmic events in the universe. Astronomical observation has provided us with the ability to see stars expand and burn up any planets that may lie in their path, stars explode, and galaxies collide. The simple event of a planet shifting on its axis is nothing by comparison. To prepare for this may seem to be a major task, but it is nothing compared to preparing for the death of our star.

As a species, we have evolved out of various ecological niches. We are one of the few, if not only, life forms on earth that has evolved to the point of being able to fill a niche existing beyond the universe within which we travel. This is nothing less than accepting the concepts that something does exist outside our universe, that our universe is immersed in something outside of it, and the idea of panentheism, all in 'something.' If this turns out to be the case, we, the last living representative of the genus Homo, have little choice but to accept such a development and do everything in our power to preserve our species. This will take planning, not in terms of how to deal with what has already occurred, but in terms of what may occur in the future.

This is not a debate of evolution or creationism. In either case, whether we evolved to the level of having a purpose or were created for a purpose, the end result could be the same. We, Homo sapiens, may be important to what lies beyond the boundaries of our universe. Therefore, we have an obligation to preserve our species and continue to advance for the purpose we believe we have.

•

If we are to continue our progress, we must begin to understand what this niche may be. We are not advanced enough to know for certain what this niche is, but we are advanced enough to begin making educated guesses regarding this niche and attempt to accomplish the task we assume we have.

#3. What does palaeomagnetism reinforce about the significance of existence, life?

In spite of pole shifts, meteor impacts, and ice ages, life continues to struggle to exist. Life senses its own significance and demonstrates its commitment to this significance through its determination to preserve itself.

•

Life is filled with the need to cope with change. As old ecological niches are destroyed, new ones are created and new life forms emerge to fill these niches. This occurred with the genus Homo. Now, however, all the branches of our genus have died out except one, Homo sapiens – modern man. We have a decision to make in terms of the significance of our genus. We either recognize its significance in terms of something greater than a planetary significance or we resign ourselves to whatever planetary cataclysms may occur.

If we begin to think of our significance as being tied to the universe, we will expand greatly upon our ability to survive planetary cataclysms. As individuals and as a species, we have already begun the process of expanding the perception we have from regional significance to global. We could go even further by expanding our perception of ourselves as having global significance to universal significance, a leap of true faith.

•

We are capable of thinking in terms of abstract concepts that may lie beyond the universe. To tie our significance to such a location is nothing less than what religions have been telling us. Science is just now confirming the logic of such a possibility. And philosophy, rationality, may not have begun a full scale assault upon such a problem, but it is recovering from a major physical assault upon its identity by both science and religion. It needs time to compose itself. It needs time to heal. Science and religion could both extend a hand of acceptance, recognition, and tolerance. This would go a long way to help philosophy emerge as a major contributor towards this evolutionary leap for our species.

#4. How does palaeomagnetism help us understand what life is?

If we do not commit ourselves to expanding our view of the significance of life, if we falter in our ability to prepare ourselves for major cataclysmic events and die out as a genus and species, we need not feel guilty. Life will most likely go on without us.

•

This may sound depressing and sarcastic. It is not. It is a statement of hope. What it implies is that life is not just life. Life is something not just of this universe. Life is something eternal. Now whether or not this applies to all levels of life is as debatable as the statement itself. But if awareness is abstract and eternal as religions imply, then our existence will continue well beyond any extinction our species and genus may face. Other life forms, earthly and otherwise, would go on to accomplish the purpose life forms are to accomplish.

Wouldn't that be a sad turn of events for our species and genus? To lose the opportunity to participate in such a magnificent significance because we were not wise enough, not far sighted enough, not open minded enough to expand upon the perception we had of our significance in order to survive global cataclysmic events would be a sad event indeed. We are so close to making this leap. We are so close to being an entity worthy of universal travel that to lose this opportunity due to our narrow-mindedness while we professed our open-mindedness would be the ultimate of Greek tragedies. If such is to be, at least all will not have gone for naught. At least we could become a source of universal historical tragedies for other cultures and civilizations throughout the universe.

•

It appears that a tone of despair has been set in place, but that is not the case. To be an example for other cultures and civilizations, studying life forms as models of what not to do is no little accomplishment. To have established ourselves as an archeological example of how close organisms can get to preserving their species through the process of diffusing through the glory of the heavens can be just as beneficial as making the step itself. In fact, it can be more beneficial to others if it acts as the alternative to having that species step into the heavens as a dominating, subjugating, non-compassionate, egocentric, intolerant species. But life is flexible, life is capable of growth, life is capable of changing its perceptions. We can change if we want to. All we have to do is commit to doing so.

#5. What does palaeomagnetism have to offer us as individuals?

Palaeomagnetism offers an understanding of just how fragile we as individuals and as a species are and it offers the hope that perhaps there is more to life than just life.

•

Science would say life guarantees us nothing. We know we will die. We know just as surely as we came into being that we will lose our tie to our present life through the process of death. Life is not meant to be eternal. Religions would object to this statement. Religions would say life is eternal. Religions would say life does not exist in the form of the body or mind but rather in the form of the soul. There is nothing wrong with either of these two statements as long as the word 'life' is defined.

Science and religion do not disagree with each other in principle, only in definition. Science says life is the physical; religion says life is the spiritual. Both would probably agree that awareness is the key to either definition. Science says life ends when awareness ends, as indicated by a flat brain wave. When the brain wave goes flat, the plug is pulled on the life support system. And then what? Science leaves this open ended and never defines what occurs.

Religion agrees with the concept of awareness being the essence of the individual. It agrees it is okay to turn off the life support systems of the individual once the brain wave is flat since the body and brain at that point no longer register awareness. Both seem to be saying that awareness is the key.

If there was a Causative Force that initiated the formation of the universe, and if this Causative Force was aware of what She was doing, then the Causative Force has awareness. If the Causative Force has awareness and if She has total awareness, then the awareness of the individual must be a part of Her. If this awareness is or becomes a part of the Causative Force, then the individual would never die. Life would be eternal and nothing, not even the annihilation of billions of individuals caused by the shifting of the earth on its axis, could change the fact that the awareness of the individual would remain.

•

If awareness exists and if the Causative Force is truly omniscient, then the awareness of the individual can never be destroyed. Your responsibilities in life never end regardless of what the future offers.

#6. What significance does palaeomagnetism have to us as a species?

We are in a fragile situation. Our species, the whole genus of Homo, is confined to one planet. We could be wiped out by one swift natural event. Palaeomagnetism gives us evidence of just one of many natural events that could cause this.

•

Palaeomagnetism supports the theoretical idea that the earth flips on its axis from time to time. A small shift of the earth causes earthquakes. A small movement of the earth's molten interior causes volcanoes. Imagine the cataclysm caused by the whole earth shifting. Such an event could conceivably wipe out all of modern man, the last living representative of the genus Homo.

A meteor struck the earth during the time of the dinosaurs. The dinosaurs found themselves unprepared for such an event. This was not the typical meteor. It was large enough to create geological events greater than what would be created by a shift of the earth on its axis. This meteor strike caused so many volcanoes to erupt and threw so much dirt into the air that sunlight was unable to penetrate the dust clouds for months. The earth was in darkness, which caused the plants to die, which caused the plant-eating dinosaurs to die, which caused the meat-eating dinosaurs to die, which lead to the death of the dinosaurs.

It may sound ludicrous for us to think that dinosaurs could have prepared for such an event, but what about our species? Is it ludicrous to think we should begin such preparations or are we also too primitive intellectually to begin preparations for such an event? Are we destined to die out and make room for a new experimental species nature may be developing or have we developed to the point of being capable of controlling our own fate?

•

We have come a long way as a species. We appear to have the ability to think ahead. How far ahead seems to be almost unlimited. What kind of thinking would it take to get us to seriously start preparing for cataclysmic events such as pole shifts and meteor strikes? To begin thinking seriously about how to deal with cataclysmic events, we would have to begin thinking about and understanding our relationship to what may lie beyond the universe itself. We would have to begin developing a universal understanding. We have to explore who we are and what our purpose is within the universe. We would have to begin developing what Steven Hawking calls a universal philosophy.

#7. What significance does palaeomagnetism have to offer other life forms in the universe?

Our species may die out at any time. We should act accordingly. We should be prepared to leave a legacy to other life forms should they discover the remains of our extinct species.

•

This is not negativism; this is an objective. Our species could die out at any time. We are not spread throughout the heavens enough to preserve our species should a major cataclysm occur to our earth or to our solar system. Someday, someday soon, we will be better protected from a cataclysm that could annihilate our species.

But what about other life forms in the heavens? We are on the verge of stepping into space and exploring our own galaxy. Next will come the explorations of other galaxies. We almost surely will encounter other life forms. If we envision the possibility of a major cataclysm being able to wipe out our species, then what of other life forms in the universe? Wouldn't they also have to prepare for traumatic events? More importantly, don't they also have to prepare themselves for encounters with dominating, subjugating, self-righteous cultures and civilization that may be driving through space in a quest to conquer territory and expand their empires? And haven't we as a species encountered just situations here upon our own planet? In fact, aren't we guilty of just such actions? If you disagree, then ask the North American Indians what their opinion is. Ask the remaining ancestors of the Mayan and Incan civilizations. Ask eastern civilizations whose morals and cultures are being transformed through telecommunication exposure with western civilizations. Palaeomagnetism opens our perceptions to the fact that we, Homo sapiens, may become the invincible cataclysm for other life forms in the heavens. We must prepare in order to avoid this possibility.

•

Ah, but that is different, you say. Is it? What makes us think the same thing would not happen to civilizations of other life forms we would encounter in the heavens? What makes us think we would not turn out to be 'the' cataclysm other life forms could not overcome as we inundated their numbers with diseases such as small pox, tuberculosis, AIDS, and the common cold? We'll be careful, you say. But will we when we see the priceless wealth alien civilizations control, wealth beyond our imagination?

SCIENCE: MATRIX #278

#8. What does palaeomagnetism imply about our significance in eternity?

Eternity holds importance – not the temporary state of the universe. Can we prove this? We cannot prove it anymore than we can prove we exist.

•

I'd rather put my faith into what I can see, you say. Fine, entropy tells you the universe will eventually die and all life will die with it. The Big Bang Theory says the universe will eventually die by imploding or it will die through eternal expansion. Thus, the Big Bang says all life will eventually die. Symmetry says the universe could have been created from nothing and could eventually dissolve back into nothing. Symmetry says all life may eventually die. Science has discovered what religions have sensed for thousands of years. There is an end to all things. So put your faith in what you can see. It is no different than putting your faith in religion. Both say life will end.

But if all things come to an end, then this would mean the Causative Force would end. No, no, no. Religions have professed this to be a false statement. Religions have taught the concept of an eternal soul, eternal awareness, for thousands of years. Now science joins the ranks of religions. Science now believes time is a function of matter and energy. As such, science now believes that without matter and energy, time would not exist, life as we know it would not exist.

Both religion and science, however, seem to agree that awareness is the measure of life – not the physical body and mind. It is awareness that is used as the measure to determine when life has ended in the physical sense. But awareness is not physical. Awareness is an abstract, nonphysical 'thing.' And it is awareness we speak of when we discuss the idea of a Causative Force. If the Causative Force is a form of awareness, then we are a form the Causative Force, for we have awareness. Just as importantly, other life forms with awareness would also have to be a form of the Causative Force. As such, we must not become the cataclysm that destroys the unique contributions these alien life forms have to offer the Causative Force.

•

We are responsible for our actions. We must make choices. We need a guide, a universal guide. We need a universal philosophy to assist religions in their attempt to guide our behavior as we travel the heavens.

#9. What does palaeomagnetism imply about our relationship to the Causative Force?

If we have awareness, and if awareness is indestructible once created, and if our body and mind are real, and if we are located inside the universe, and if the mind and body act as a means of travel for our awareness, and if they provide the means by which we can allow our awareness to experience and learn, and if the Causative Force has awareness, and if the Causative Force has total awareness, then we have significance.

•

We become significant; we become a means by which the Causative Force learns. Let me rephrase that statement. We either are significant or we aren't. Whether we become aware of our significance or not is not the point. As we learn, our awareness grows and if the Causative Force is total awareness, then the Causative Force grows as we grow. As eternity expands, Her omniscience and omnipresence expands. We may be more important than we ever thought possible. We may be significant beyond our wildest dreams. We may have the vital function of having a significant relationship with the Causative Force.

If this relationship is as important as symbiotic panentheism suggests, we should be very careful, for our actions as individuals and as a species would impact upon the awareness of the Causative Force.

•

If this train of thought is correct, then we can assume it would not have been very intelligent of a Causative Force to find a means such as this to increase its knowledge, power, and presence, and then assign this process to just one life form. Considering the intelligence most religions would assign to a Creator and the intelligence science would assign to a Causative Force, we most likely would not be the only life form in the universe assigned a function as important as assisting the Causative Force to grow in its magnitude.

Our species, the only living representatives of the earth genus Homo, may find itself set back by a major cataclysm such as a pole shift or global warfare. We may find ourselves set back by a collapse of our present civilization. We may annihilate ourselves or be annihilated by natural events. Whatever the case, we can be fairly certain that life will go on and the interactions will continue between life and the Causative Force.

Conclusion: How do the concepts of palaeomagnetism reinforce the concept of symbiotic panentheism?

Change can happen quickly; we must prepare psychologically, morally, and physically for major catastrophic events if we are to leave a legacy for life in the future.

•

We must prepare not only to survive, but we must prepare what we wish to leave as a legacy should we not survive. We may be satisfied to leave a legacy of fossilized bones, concrete office buildings, ribbons of asphalt, and idle TV sets as our legacy. If that is our desire, a large meteor striking earth tomorrow would grant our wish.

But if we wish to leave life forms a loftier legacy, then we had better start working on it. Palaeomagnetism is one concept that shows life is unpredictable. As far as the legacy we may wish to leave behind, what better legacy than an understanding of a relationship the Causative Force may have to the universe, to life, and to various species. Symbiotic panentheism would do just that. But symbiotic panentheism is not what is important here; what is important is what symbiotic panentheism represents. Symbiotic panentheism represents the first intense effort to develop a model of a universal philosophy. This is not a religion; this is a philosophy, a universal philosophy. This is a model which would act as a foundation to religions, science, and philosophy.

Palaeomagnetism shows us we should not take life for granted. We should prepare for the inevitable. Our planning should start with the thought that the unexpected could occur tomorrow. In addition, we need to do some long term planning. If we move into the coming centuries and begin dispersing into the heavens, what is it we would take with us? What is it we would be offering and what is it we would like to offer other life forms in the heavens? What human legacy would we like to leave behind as we travel throughout the heavens? What would make us proud to leave behind?

•

What better legacy to offer than an understanding of a universal philosophy embracing all life in the heavens. Why not finish what we had been working on throughout our history? Why not complete the Magna Carta embracing all life forms and reaching into eternity itself?

SCIENCE

*What insight has **Science**
firmly established within society?*

HOMO-:
Sapiens – Last of its Species

#0. What does the conceptual framework of Homo- have to offer us?

Homo: The genus of primates that includes modern man (H. sapiens, the only living representative) and various extinct species...
  —*Oxford Concise Science Dictionary*, p. 346

•

Science uses Latin to name animals for the purpose of classification. Latin is used because it is what we call a 'dead' language. This means it is a language that is not spoken by any present day cultures or races. Because it is not used anymore, the meanings of the words do not change; the meanings stay the same from millennium to millennium.

The sciences name organisms by using two words, the genus name and the species name. The genus name is capitalized and the species name is not. 'Homo' is the Latin word for 'man' and 'sapiens' is the Latin word for 'modern.' Thus, science classifies us as an animal under the name Homo sapiens or modern man. What is interesting here is the *Oxford Dictionary* statement that we are the only living representative of this group. If we should die out, there is no other organism in the genus Homo to replace us.

Should we die out, so, too, may three unique aspects humankind has to offer the universe:

1. Modern man appears to be the only existing earth-bound genus capable of leaving earth on its own. We appear to represent earth's only living species capable of joining other life forms in the quest to explore the heavens.

2. Modern man appears to be the only existing earth-bound genus with the ability to create its own ecological niche. This capacity is critical if a species is to travel throughout the heavens exploring the ecological niches of others.

3. Modern man appears to be the only existing earth-bound genus capable of filling a niche tied to what exists beyond the universe.

•

Stated in another manner, modern man appears to be the only earth-bound genus capable of filling a niche unaffected by time.

#1. *What does the conceptual framework of Homo- imply about the universe within which we live?*

We appear to be a unique organism within the confines of our earth, for we define what lies beyond the universe and then adapt our behavior accordingly.

•

Filling a unique niche in itself is not unique. All animals and plants appear to have unique characteristics about them. This uniqueness is what allows living things to sustain the continuation of their species. We, on the other hand, seem to be the only living species on the earth capable of leaving this planet on its own. We appear to be the only species on earth capable of thinking in terms of what lies beyond the boundaries of our universe and then set out to connect ourselves directly to this entity. We have been connecting ourselves to this entity for thousands of years through the realm of religious perceptions and thought.

But what about the second and third means we use to draw conclusions regarding what we perceive ourselves to be? What about science and philosophy? As a species of Homo sapiens, we have repressed the development of scientific and philosophical perceptions. We have done so historically through intimidation, actions and threats of physical torture, actions and threats of mental torture, excommunicating members of our own species from 'the rewards of heaven,' and sentencing the souls of our own brothers and sisters to the 'fires of hell.'

This process of repression worked well for a limited period of time. But science deals with the concrete and the observable aspects of the universe. Attempting to force members of our species to disbelieve what they see did not last long. Try as they might, religions were unable to repress the facts that our observations revealed. The concept of the earth being the center of the universe, for example, could not sustain itself against all the evidence to the contrary.

•

Philosophy, on the other hand, was more easily repressed than science, because philosophy did not deal with the concrete. The *American Heritage Dictionary* defines philosophy as "love and pursuit of wisdom by intellectual means and moral self-discipline." Religion gained the upper hand over philosophy. It was able to draw most of the intellectual ability into its own camp. The means of doing so was power – power over the soul through excommunication and the power to sentence the soul to 'hell.'

#2. How do the concepts of Homo- reinforce the concept of panentheism?

We appear to be the only life form on earth capable of grasping the concept of a place beyond time, a place beyond our universe – eternity. We appear to be the only life form on earth capable of adjusting our behavior to the concept of this abstract existence.

•

We are unique. We have a unique awareness. We are aware of not only our own environment but the whole earth, the whole universe, and even what may lie beyond the universe. Religions have been describing this existence for thousands of years. Now science is on the verge of joining the search for and understanding of eternity.

Science has evolved to the point of not only understanding matter and energy, but understanding the concept of anti-matter. The next apparent step is understanding Asimov's concept of anti-energy. This is simply the process of finishing the establishment of the concept of what physics calls the principle of symmetry. If symmetry proves to be an accurate observation of our universe, then it would go a long way toward understanding how the universe could dissolve into nothingness and how it could have been created out of nothingness. As significant as the understanding of such a process may be, what is even more significant is the implication this would have for science. It would imply an existence before the universe. Since matter and energy would most likely not be an element of such an existence, time would most likely not be an element of such an existence since it is a function of matter and energy. We may well be immersed within something timeless, eternal. This is simply what panentheism states.

•

The universe is immersed within eternity. Time is immersed within the universe. Humanity, the genus Homo, is immersed within the universe. The genus Homo appears to be able to think in terms of eternity. The genus Homo has awareness. The essence of the genus Homo appears to be its awareness. Awareness is an abstraction incapable of destruction. Total awareness, omniscience, includes all awareness. The essence of individuals may be a part of the whole that lies beyond the universe, the location within which the universe is located. The concept of symmetry appears to leave the awareness of humanity nothing to interact with in a timeless manner other than the Causative Force.

#3. What does Homo- reinforce about the significance of existence, life?

Entropy tells us all closed physical systems eventually die. But what of open systems, what of abstract systems? Are they also subject to the laws of physics?

•

If the Causative Force is an abstract entity, having no physical body or form, then the laws of physics may or may not apply to Her. At this point, we cannot make any accurate determination regarding this point. We do, however, have a better understanding of the existence of an eternal universe. It is presently believed that our universe is not eternal. It is believed our universe bounds time. The physical aspect of the universe is believed to be controlled by the laws of entropy and the laws of entropy state that eventually the universe will perish.

So there it is. The universe may eventually die. But are all things in the universe subject to the laws of the universe or are they applicable only to matter and energy? It appears matter and energy may die, but the other abstract items may remain. What are abstract items? Love is abstract. Hate is abstract. Emotional pain, despondence, fear, greed, envy, happiness, admiration, union, tranquillity, and esteem are all abstractions. But the essence of these abstractions lies not in themselves, but within the awareness that senses them. Awareness appears to be the unit capable of providing a place for other forms of abstractions.

The basic unit of abstraction appears to be the awareness of the individual. Human awareness appears to exist within the body and mind. Homo sapiens appear to have another level of awareness other life forms on this planet do not have. We appear to be aware of the eternal. We appear to be aware of the idea that the universe may not be the ultimate form of existence.

•

We have not just recently acquired this form of awareness. We have had the sense of this type of existence long before modern science even considered the idea of an existence beyond the physical boundary of reality. We have had this sense of an eternal existence long before Islam, Christianity, Judaism, Buddhism or Hinduism came into existence. We have had a sense of life being significant beyond death perhaps even before we began burying our dead.

#4. How does Homo- help us understand what life is?

To say life is life is not enough. Life deserves to be defined, for life is the essence of us all. Life is the role we play in the environment within which we are immersed.

•

If we, as Homo sapiens, are to define life, we have little option but to understand the environment of life. To understand life, we must understand what life is immersed within. A drawing is the easiest manner to discuss the concept of 'immersion.' A dot, you, exist in a circle, the universe. Very few people would question this drawing. What of the universe? Continuing the drawing, one can put the circle inside a square representing the Causative Force or one can put the circle outside the square representing the Causative Force.

Present day theism, the drawing of a universe outside the Causative Force, leads to only one logical perception, a door must be opened to enter eternity. And if a door to eternity can be opened, then a door to different types of eternity can be opened. Heaven and hell become logical. Conflict, violence, and war begin over who will control the keys to the doors.

The drawing of a universe inside the Causative Force leads to only one logical perception; no door must be opened to enter eternity. You already exist within eternity. You become responsible for your own eternity. Once leaving this universe through death, you have no place to go but into the arms of eternity. This drawing, panentheism, frees all Homo sapiens from the tyranny of others.

Homo, man, appears to be the only life form on earth capable of thinking in terms of eternal life. We are so sure of it; our whole history is filled with desperate actions intended to gain entrance into it. Our history, the whole history of Homo sapiens, the 'saint' and 'sinner' mentality, should provide us with some sense of confidence that life is more than the physical; life, awareness, is eternal.

•

Modern day Christianity, Judaism, and Islam are immersed within the concept that the Causative Force is omnipresent, but that we are not in the Causative Force. This contradictory concept is the cornerstone for power. The ultimate form of power over Homo sapiens lies not with money but in control over the door to eternity. In the end, eternity holds significance to our genus and species – not money – for we believe life is eternal.

#5. What does Homo- have to offer us as individuals?

The genus Homo, man, has a unique ability to think originally. To do so requires one to 'think out of the box.'
•

Take this literally and a simple picture comes into focus. First the dot representing individual awareness becomes visible as one floats backward away from the earth. Floating much further away, a circle, the universe, becomes visible. Many dots, awarenesses, inside the circle become the focal points. An interesting perception becomes evident. The abstract points of individual awareness appear to be confined within a physical container. This physicality, this container, must be suspended within something. To gain a better perspective, float even further away. Still nothing. Keep going, float even further away, still nothing. Your abstraction cannot seem to float outside what the universe is suspended in. We are going to have to apply a slightly different twist to our thinking by stepping out of our awareness and floating above it. This is 'thinking out of the box.' We appear to be the only life form on earth capable of performing such a task.

Leaving our abstractness floating still further away from the circle filled with dots, we see something surrounding the circle, surrounding the universe. We see abstraction bathing the sphere of the universe. Total awareness, omniscience, seems to be the substance within which the universe is floating. Upon closer examination, it appears that bits and pieces of abstraction are confined within the container, the universe. The ability of man, the genus Homo, provides us with the potential to literally 'think out of the box' and see the significance of the individual lying outside the universe and in eternity.
•

This opens up the concept of the first of three forms of existence. This opens up the concept of the individual. We, the genus Homo, can see the individual as a separate entity, separate even from the Causative Force. Separate not only because it is within the universe while the Causative Force is outside the universe, but separate also because it has its own identity, awareness, uniqueness, and individuality. You exist. You exist as an individual while at the same time being a part of something greater than yourself. The whole is equal to the sum of its parts and you are a part of the whole. While in the universe, you may be temporarily separated from what it is you are a part of, you are a part of it nonetheless and nobody has the power to take that away from you.

#6. What significance does Homo- have to us as a species?

Sapiens are the last remaining species of the genus Homo. So in our case, if we allow our species to die, we are responsible for the death of our genus as well as the death of any unique contributions it had to offer what lies beyond the boundaries of the universe.

•

The first type of existence, individuality, is offered two types of freedom. First, our ability to think abstractly offers us the ability to think of ourselves as being independent, free of what lies beyond the universe and second, we have the ability to think of ourselves as being independent, free of the universe within which we are located. We, as individuals and as a species, are immersed in the concept of freedom. The rights of the individual, freedom of the individual, is one of the most sought after rights we have aspired to gain throughout our history. This ability to think of freedom from being controlled either by a Causative Force or from the confinement of our universe appears to be generated by the unique ability of our genus, Homo, to think in an abstract manner. This characteristic is not unique to one individual or a few individuals. It is a characteristic of our species.

We may exist within the space of the universe, but we definitely think of ourselves as not being confined by space. Take away space and we still see our essence as existing. Take all awareness out of space and we still see space as existing. We see the two, awareness and space, as two independent entities. Unless we are willing to throw away what our faiths tell us, our observations point toward, and our rational arguments center around, we have no choice but to accept the concept that our genus is unique in some very basic way. We appear to be the only life form on earth capable of connecting our existence to abstract existence.

•

We, as the genus Homo, are about to leave the earth. We can leave with one of two philosophies. We can leave earth to subjugate and dominate in order to establish our kingdom as a species so that certain individuals may reign supreme. Or we can leave earth to learn about the heavens and expand the Causative Force. The first is more exciting but short-lived. The second is more idealistic but projects further into the future We have a responsibility to make this choice. If we do not consciously make the choice, we will go into space as we are, a species oriented around animalistic, territorial behaviors, the first of the two philosophies.

#7. What significance does Homo- have to offer other life forms in the universe?

If we jump into the heavens oriented around a significance based upon what lies within the universe, we will be striving to subjugate and dominate and we should expect the same from others in space.

•

A second type of awareness now enters the picture. Others exist other than just you. You are not 'the' Causative Force. Others exist. We know this to be true in terms of Homo sapiens. There are billions of us on this planet, billions of pieces of awareness. If we, Homo sapiens, are capable of abstract thought, it would only seem reasonable that there would other life forms capable of doing the same. If our individual awareness adds to total awareness, it would only seem reasonable that other life forms could contain awareness that could do the same.

Looking at the overall picture from the viewpoint of a Causative Force, it would only seem reasonable to create many life forms capable of providing a variety of learning experiences in order insure the continuation of learning experiences should one species or another become extinct. In short, if our genus Homo has a significance beyond the confines of what lies within the universe, we must assume others do also. If awareness has a significance to the Causative Force, then this significance would be too important to entrust it to just one species. The significance of this idea lies in the concepts we as a genus are developing. We are on the verge of developing the understanding that we are not only related to other humans through the soul, but we are related to all life forms in the heavens whose significance lies in the abstract. Homo sapiens are on the verge of offering brotherhood to all life forms. Subjugation and domination can now become irrational.

•

Homo sapiens are on the verge of expanding our understanding of life. We have been seeking the answer to the question, 'What is life?' since far back in our history. We are on the verge of defining life without using the restraints of time. We are on the verge of finishing the Magna Carta of life. This understanding, this definition, is what is more commonly referred to today as a universal philosophy, written with more than our species in mind. Is such a universal understanding of what we are unique? We have no way of knowing at this time but it is unique to us. It is the means by which we can go into the heavens without being shackled by our old behaviors oriented around the need to dominate and subjugate.

#8. What does Homo- imply about our significance in eternity?

If we jump into the heavens with the belief that our significance lies outside the universe, we will be striving to elevate all beings to an equal status and we could rightly expect the same from others in space.

•

This concept places a whole new level of responsibility upon individuals, our species, and all life forms as a whole. It now becomes a possibility that eternity may be actually molded by what we do. This brings up the concept of a third type of awareness – the sum of the individual parts, the substance which fills the spaces between individuality, what we, individual awareness, is immersed within.

Symmetry offers us an understanding that 'good' and 'bad' may not be the symmetrical counterparts of each other. The symmetrical counterparts of 'good' and 'bad' may be their ripple effects. We are a symmetrical animal split down the middle with mirror images. But does our behavior have to have a mirror image of 'good' and 'bad' or could it be that our behavior generates a mirror image – good behavior generates good ripples and bad behavior generates bad ripples?

Actions generate ripples of 'positive' and 'negative' behavior patterns that flow throughout society. Good and bad actions never really die. They exist forever. But you say if I do something good, it is soon forgotten. No, no, no. It may be forgotten in the sense that nobody will remember you did the action, but it generates reactions that flow through society forever. Think of the negative actions one abusive act of greed can generate and the ripple of rage it can start surging through society. The ripple of rage does not stop with the victim. Think of the positive actions one honest act of love can generate and the ripple of compassion it can start surging through society. These actions and their ripples become a permanent part of every piece of awareness both directly and indirectly touched by it.

•

What happens to these pieces of awareness? They are pieces of abstract essences that become part of 'total awareness' upon exiting the confines of the physical universe. There is no way for them to be destroyed without destroying awareness altogether; without destroying the Causative Force.

#9. What does Homo- imply about our relationship to the Causative Force?

The last remaining species of Homo- is ourselves, humankind. We are the last members of our lineage. Knowing this, what are we going do with ourselves? Are we going to settle for what we have, what we have always been, or are we going to set our sights high and reach for the unreachable? We can improve eternity, what lies beyond the boundaries of our very universe, and strive to improve the Causative Force Herself.

•

What existed before and what will continue to exist after the universe is the definition of the Causative Force. Complete annihilation of the universe would call for the annihilation of all things that are made of matter, anti-matter, energy, and anti-energy. What of awareness, the abstract, nonphysical essence? Life based upon the perception that the dot (your awareness) and circle (the universe) is inside the Causative Force, leads to only one logical perception: there is nothing one can do to escape eternity. One is responsible for one's actions because the results of one's actions are already within the Causative Force and there is no 'taking back' the actions that are already committed. Words cannot explain away one's actions. We evaluate actions and behavior – not rhetoric.

•

Don't be afraid of eliminating suffering; suffering generates painful ripples as its mirror image. We appear to be here to learn and learning generates errors. There is no need to worry that there may not be enough suffering for everyone to share once entering total awareness. The past has generated volumes of human trauma, the present is immersed in trauma, and the future will generate natural trauma even if could eliminate all humanly initiated trauma. Trauma is a part of our universe. There has been, is, and will naturally continue to be enough trauma to satisfy any primitive need we may carry with us as we exit this physical universe and enter the world of the abstract.

Conclusion: How do the concepts of Homo- reinforce the concept of symbiotic panentheism?

They do not; what is actually taking place is symbiotic panentheism is reinforcing the concepts of the significance of our genus and species, Homo sapiens.

•

No ecological niche tied to time, mortality, seems to 'fit' our species or ourselves as individuals. The interrelationships we see around us, that we study through what we call science, tend to indicate all things interact in some form or other. All things seem to fill a niche. We are of a physical nature and would, therefore, seem to fill a physical niche. Awareness is of an abstract nature and would seem to fill an abstract niche. Awareness of existence outside the universe is abstract; the existence outside the universe would seem to be abstract. Therefore, the abstract nature of humanity would seem to fill a niche within the abstract concept of total awareness outside the universe. Isn't this what religions have been telling science ever since science has emerged as a means of understanding our place in the universe? Is science rejecting religion or is religion rejecting science? The feud has been long. The feud has been a bitter one. It is time to end the feud and unite the two bickering parties. There is so much to do and there may be little time, as palaeomagnetism purports. The universe may only be temporary, but we could be eternal and we need to act accordingly. We, as the genus Homo, whose only remaining members are us, Homo sapiens, need to prepare for eternity. We may be responsible for eternity itself.

•

Under symbiotic panentheism, no one controls the keys to the gate to eternity, for one does not have to enter eternity; one is already in eternity. Symbiotic panentheism sets life free of the oppression generated by the few who profess to hold the keys. But just as wonderful as this may sound, it has its drawbacks, for now you must take responsibility for creating your own form of eternity. You are responsible – not someone else. You will truly reap what you sow. Our species is not responsible for itself. Our species does not have its own awareness. The effect our species makes is only a summation of each individual. You are responsible for the species. You are responsible, not some individual that attempts to dictate.

Symbiotic panentheism may set you free from the tyranny of others. Symbiotic panentheism may allow you to establish your own heaven and hell in eternity, but it also makes you responsible for having done so.

SCIENCE

*What new insight has **Science**
firmly established within society?*

SYMBIOSIS:
Interdependence

#0. What does the conceptual framework of symbiosis have to offer us?

Symbiosis: An interaction between individuals of different species (symbiants). The term symbiosis is usually restricted to interactions in which both species benefit but it may be used for other close associations. Many symbioses are obligatory (i.e. the participants cannot survive without the interactions); for example, a lichen is an obligatory symbiotic relationship between a blue-green bacterium and a fungus.
–Oxford Concise Science Dictionary, p. 709

•

So much is being said here: "An interaction between individuals of different species...usually restricted...but may be used..." The number of different types of relationships are enormous, ranging from the extremely negative to the extremely positive. But one thing stands out in terms of its consistency.

The third edition of the *American Heritage Dictionary* defines species as, "A fundamental category of taxonomic classification." Taxonomy is then defined as, "The classification of organisms in an ordered system that indicates natural relationships." Natural relationship is the key word. The operative idea for the concept of symbiosis is *natural relationship*.

What is a natural relationship? The *American Heritage Dictionary* defines natural as, "present in or produced by nature." Nature is then defined as, "the forces and processes that produce and control all the phenomena of the material world." Relationship is defined as, "the condition or fact of being related: connection or association."

A symbiotic relationship does not have to be one involving physical life forms. It is simply a natural relationship between symbiants, related life forms having some form of connection or association where they depend upon each other to some degree. Spiritual or living abstract life forms could exist in a symbiotic relationship.

•

It is interesting to note that, for thousands of years, religions have been telling us we have some form of connection, association with an abstract entity that produced the universe. Over time, our perceived relationship with the Causative Force has changed. There is nothing to date indicating that our understanding of this relationship is complete.

#1. What does the conceptual framework of symbiosis imply about the universe within which we live?

As far as we know, most organisms involved in a symbiotic relationship do not recognize their interdependence upon each other.

•

Termites eat wood for food, but termites cannot digest wood. Termites, however, are not aware of this fact, so they continue to eat wood. Wood is made up of a substance called cellulose. Bacteria in the intestines of termites eat cellulose as food. These bacteria do not appear to know they are in the intestine of a termite. They do not appear to be aware of the organism providing them with a continual supply of cellulose. They just go about their business of life and eat the cellulose the termites continually supply them. The waste product produced by the bacteria as it breaks down cellulose is what the termite uses as its food. Should either the termite or the bacteria die, the other dies. Neither appears to be concerned with the welfare of the other. Neither appears to be aware of their symbiotic relationship between each other. This is a symbiotic relationship.

Homo sapiens have an innate sense of a close association between themselves and the Causative Force of the universe. As individuals, we not only have a sense of a relationship existing between ourselves and the Causative Force, but we make a conscious effort to live our lives based upon this relationship. Religions have been telling us for thousands of years of this close association but they have not defined it as a symbiotic relationship. They would rather not accept this terminology, for this would imply the Causative Force is dependent upon you and I. But if you and I are within the Causative Force, then are we not a part of the Causative Force. And if we are a part of the Causative Force, then the Causative Force, if She is dependent upon us, is still not dependent upon anything other than Herself. The universe, however, now obtains significance, for the universe becomes a part of something. The universe becomes an integral part of the Causative Force.

•

Why else would our universe exist if not as a function of what it is located within? If our universe does not have a function to the Causative Force, then give us a better reason why it exists or stand aside and let us get on with the task of developing a universal philosophy to explain this function, our function for existing. It is time to move on and finish the task.

#2. How do the concepts of symbiosis reinforce the concept of panentheism?

Symbiosis is a relationship between two living entities. The relationship can be of a physical nature as between the termite and the bacteria. Or the relationship could be of an abstract nature as may exist between the Causative Force and awareness of the individual.

•

And just where is awareness of the individual located? It is located within you, within me. Where are we located? We are located within the universe. Very few people would disagree with any of these two concepts. But then the question becomes, just where is the universe located? Here is where significant disagreement begins to surface. Modern day theism, such as Christianity, Judaism, and Islam, would say that the universe is located outside the Causative Force; we are not a part of the Causative Force. But if this is the case, then where is the universe located? Modern day theism cannot answer this question because they say the Causative Force is all present. Then they go on to say the universe is not located within the Causative Force. They do so because that would mean we, you and I, are located within the Causative Force and this would imply that you and I are a part of the Causative Force, which modern theism does not accept. But if the Causative Force is everywhere and if the universe is not in the Causative Force, then that leaves no place to put the universe.

Panentheism provides a place for the universe. Panentheism places the universe within the Causative Force, which opens up the concept of an interactive relationship between the Causative Force and ourselves. And what of symbiosis, the concept of a close relationship between two living entities? Symbiosis opens up the understanding of why we exist. Panentheism says we exist within the Causative Force and symbiosis says there is a reason we exist within the Causative Force. We and the Causative Force need each other just as the termite and the bacteria need each other.

•

If the universe is within, then it must affect what it lies within – a symbiotic relationship. The degree of impact is questionable; the point of interaction is less so. The abstractness of the relationship between abstract entities causes a hazing of the boundaries between the two as compared to the boundary of physical life formed by a cell wall, cell membrane or skin.

#3. What does symbiosis reinforce about the significance of existence, life?

If we interact with the Causative Force as symbiosis implies, then the significance in life lies in the manner in which we interact with the Causative Force.

•

"Symbiosis is usually restricted to interactions in which both species benefit." This phrase clearly indicates that symbiotic interactions do not necessarily benefit any of the parties involved, let alone both. The AIDS virus infects the human body and destroys the body's immune system to create an environment within which it can reproduce and thrive. By destroying the immune system, the body becomes easy prey to all forms of diseases and cancers. The process of suppressing the immune system of the body may, in the short run, work to the advantage of the AIDS virus, but in the long run, it destroys the human body as well as the very environment within and upon which the virus lives.

If we may be in a symbiotic relationship within the Causative Force and if we have free will, this would imply we have the ability to impact the Causative Force in either a positive or negative manner. What does 'positive' or 'negative' mean? It could be argued that no one knows for sure, but the fact that we recognize the concept of positive or negative behavior indicates that behavior may be one or the other. If behavior could be one or the other, positive or negative, if we have the free will to choose one or the other, then why would we choose the negative knowing it might impact the Causative Force and impact the eternity into which we assume we will once again be immersed? How are we to avoid actions that may impact the Causative Force in a negative fashion? In other words, how are we to avoid creating an eternity filled with what we call the 'negatives'? Guidelines would help.

•

Interestingly enough, these guidelines have already been in the process of being established over thousands of years of introspection, open debate, sacrificing material wealth for idealism, suffering mental and physical punishment, and even violence by the masses. All this sacrifice and blood letting was endured by many throughout history in order to preserve the very concept of 'positive' behavior and protect of what is called the rights, liberty, and pursuit of happiness of the individual.

#4. How does symbiosis help us understand what life is?

Life is a continual process of discovering, learning, exploring, growing, finding significance, establishing harmony, and seeking truth.

•

We cannot all be the ones on the cutting edge of discovering new truths, but those who are on the cutting edge of finding new truths could not be there without the rest of us. It is the rest of us who maintain and advance social structures capable of bringing members of our genus and species to the cutting edge of our knowledge and creative thought. Religion, science, and philosophy all develop our understanding of what we are and why we exist. All three delve into the means by which we gain a perception of what it is we are.

All three indicate that life is more than just the present, that something exists beyond the universe, that something existed before the universe, that we are tied to more than time, and that we have the ability to choose. All three do not hold to these concepts in the same manner nor in the same degree, but all three are growing within their own rights and all three seem to be heading toward the same concept. Religion, science, and philosophy understand that life, in the form of the body and mind, is physical and thus tied to the concept of time. Life in the physical form is temporary. At the same time, all three seem to be headed to the understanding that life in the form of awareness is abstract and thus not tied to the concept of time. Life in the abstract form is not temporary. Life in the abstract form is eternal and capable of growth. The direction of growth is up to us, not as a group but as individuals. We have free will.

•

To affect the Causative Force by affecting Her growth is not to be taken lightly; it is the greatest form of significance we have yet assigned to life. If life is connected to the eternal, and if we have free will, then life would appear to have the ability to impact eternity. If such is the case, then life is more than just a daily drudgery. Life is the process of molding the very eternity within which the essence of the individual would once again be immersed. This is a big responsibility, for with this concept of a symbiotic relationship between the individual and the Causative Force, one builds the very environment within which one will eventually be living in an eternal state of existence.

#5. What does symbiosis have to offer us as individuals?

If life does take on a symbiotic relationship with the Causative Force, then it would appear that you would be a part of this. What other form of significance is greater than this?

•

Your awareness would be one of three forms of awareness that would exist. These three forms of awareness will be explored in the section of the matrix covered by philosophy. But for the time being, if your awareness were destroyed upon your physical death, then some awareness would have been destroyed. This may represent a very small aspect of total awareness but it represents some awareness nevertheless. With the existence of eternal, total awareness, the death of your awareness would become the death of a part of total awareness or what religions call omniscience. This would imply a part of the Causative Force could be destroyed. No aspects of religions, science or philosophy accept such a possibility, such a state of being for the Causative Force. Even atheism does not hold to the concept of a Causative Force slowly dying. If this is not a possibility for the Causative Force, then it would imply that your awareness could not die. To accept otherwise would create a need to revamp every concept we presently have of a Causative Force.

It is difficult to imagine that we could, would or should cut off all our efforts in the past and begin all over again in terms of understanding what the Causative Force is, what we are, and why we exist. If we do not wish to start all over in regards to our understanding of what significance the individual has, then we have little choice but to accept the logic of omnipresence, an all present Causative Force. This would leave little choice but to accept the concept that the individual lies 'within' the Causative Force and thus is a part of the Causative Force. Since all three, religion, science, and philosophy, imply the Causative Force is not tied to time. This would leave little option but to assume the Causative Force is an abstract entity immersed within eternity itself. Your awareness would be part of the whole awareness. You, as an individual, gain an elevated position in eternity. You become a means by which eternity grows. You become significant.

•

Panentheism leads to an understanding of a symbiotic relationship to eternity. Symbiosis leads to a logical understanding You, everyone, becomes important within society due to your significance to eternity.

#6. What significance does symbiosis have to us as a species?

Our species has existed for thousands of years. Our experiences over these thousands of years have molded us and our beliefs as a species and as individuals. To discard everything we have learned over the millennia would be ludicrous.

•

The suffering has been enormous. Blood has covered the fields, colored the waters, seeped deep into the earth. Wails of despair and desperation have reached to and through the very boundaries of the universe. Tears have been so numerous they would cause the greatest floods to pale. The sadness, fear, yearning, pleas for mercy, ... cannot be ignored. And why is it that the negatives are the ones being stressed here? Because it is not the wonderful, warm, and awe inspiring events we want to reduce significantly. It is the future negative aspects and experiences of our species we want to reduce. It is the future painful actions of our species we want to push aside in order to make room for the positive. It is the future despair and despondence we want to squeeze into a box and set aside in order to allow the positives to become substantially dominant in our society as we drag our social presence throughout the heavens.

But what of the negatives? They have molded us and shaped us. How can we let these go? Aren't we afraid we will lose what these negative experiences had to offer us if we reduce their occurrences in the future? There has been so much pain and suffering in the past, how could it be that there is not enough to last forever? How could it be that if all awareness becomes a part of total awareness, that there would not be enough pain and suffering for all pieces of awareness to share when these pieces are once again immersed within the total sum of awareness? Knowing our history as a species, how could we ever believe we have not contributed more than our share of the negative? How could we ever believe we must suffer more for the good of the whole? Our species has suffered enough. We may have done this through self infliction, but we have suffered it nonetheless. It is time to move on and this can only be done through understanding where we are located and why we exist.

•

But never forget, for we have no right to let all the suffering endured by members of our past go in vain. We must not ignore the suffering in our past.

#7. What significance does symbiosis have to offer other life forms in the universe?

Just as symbiosis offers us, as individuals and as the life form Homo sapiens, a new understanding of our significance, it offers the same elevated form of significance to all life forms in the universe.

•

This is truly one of the most exciting aspects of a universal philosophy. This is what 'universal' means. Universal is not a concept tied to life existing on this planet. Universal is a concept tied to the universe. Universal is a concept which exists as close to truth as we are able to draw. Universal is a concept which we will find existing not only in the open spaces of the universe but seeping into the small cracks and crevices marking the 'perfectly' smooth surface of the container bounding this universe. Universal is a concept we will clutch to our chests as we sense fear and doubt with the unraveling of the secrets of the heavens within which we live. Universal is a concept we will undoubtedly ponder over, time and time again, as we reflect upon our past and recall the horrible events of the past we inflicted upon each other. Universal is a concept which will allow us to forgive ourselves for all the atrocious actions individuals, our whole species, committed against the Causative Force using the name of the Causative Force as an excuse.

And what is a universal truth? It is most likely something abstract rather than physical. It is most likely something characteristic of what this physical universe is immersed within. And if this is the case, if this 'truth' is truly universal, it applies to, belongs to all life forms in the universe, not just to us.

•

If we examine our history as a species, we seem to have been driving towards one particular goal. Our whole orientation seems to have been obsessed with an attempt to understand the significance of the individual person, not the species. We have shed much blood to establish this. All civilizations have collapsed as they wondered too far from this concept or if they were not able to expand upon this concept. We have been building upon a Magna Carta for the individual throughout our history. We cannot, we must not let go of this concept. It is a worthy endeavor. It is an endeavor immersed in blood. It is an endeavor immersed in pain and suffering. It is perhaps the only endeavor we have to be proud of as a species. It is perhaps the only worthy or acceptable endeavor we have to offer life forms in the heavens.

#8. What does symbiosis imply about our significance in eternity?

A symbiotic relationship existing between ourselves and the Causative Force offers us an understanding of what we are and why we exist. We, you and I, may very well impact, grow eternity itself.

•

We have sensed a significance in terms of the universe. Our power and influence over nature has grown magnificently over time. We have advanced from being able to kill large animals with spears and stones to being able to create holes in the ozone, warm up the globe, convert the vast oceans into pools of waste, level every city on the globe with one massive launch of rockets, and now, we are so powerful we can wipe out every man, woman, and child on this planet with the release of life forms engineered by us, Homo sapiens.

Our significance appears to have grown to new levels of magnificence. But what if we step back past the moon and watch, then this new growth seems less impressive. If we step back past the solar system, the influence we have in the universe seems even less impressive. And if we step back past the galaxy itself, a system of millions and millions of stars, our significance appears so infinitesimal it becomes almost insignificant. We, trying to find significance, look to making an impact upon the physical as our means of leaving our mark upon eternity. Yet by doing so, we lose track of the understanding of how large the finite is. As contradictory as it may seem, we may never be able to find our significance in the physical. There are two reasons for this. First, we have little comprehension of the vastness of the physical. Second, the physical may very well not be permanent since it is permeated with a concept called time and time, being a state of beginning–end, is, by its own definition, limited. If the physical is not the place we will find our significance, then we have little option but to look towards the abstract, towards eternity, to find our significance.

•

Where does our significance lie? Science has been obsessed with finding the answer to this question using observation. Philosophy has been performing all forms of contortions trying to use logic to find the answer to this question. And ironically, religion, having lost faith, has resigned itself to accepting the statement, 'I know because I have faith,' as one of its most basic axioms. None of them understand that they cannot find the answer alone, for the understanding lies not in one or the other but in all three.

#9. What does symbiosis imply about our relationship to the Causative Force?

A symbiotic relationship with the Causative Force implies we may have the ability to impact, the ability to mold the Causative Force. You have great significance. You may be responsible for the end product of what the Causative Force becomes.

•

We come back to it again and again. Responsibility, responsibility, responsibility. With each increase in significance the individual gains, comes an increase in the level of responsibility we have. Along with responsibility come benefits. As our responsibility as individuals increases, so does the understanding of the value of freedom for the individual.

Now comes an understanding that we, you and I, may actually mold and sculpt the Causative Force Herself. An understanding of such an existence elevates the need to take care of the environment for the environment becomes 'the' location of learning for the Causative Force. The location of learning exists not just for today but for a vast expanse of time during which the Causative Force learns and grows.

The individual becomes not an individual but a part of the Causative Force Herself for it is 'in' the Causative Force. Symbiosis describes how and why the individual is significant to the Causative Force. No longer can we treat these pieces of existence, individuals, as just 'living things.' Capital punishment, the killing of pieces of the Causative Force, becomes as ludicrous as murder. Refusing terminally ill individuals the medication to relieve pain and suffering means forcing a piece of the Causative Force to suffer as we wait piously for the final hours to arrive. Allowing yourself to be abused by a dominating, intimidating, self serving spouse or boss means subjecting the Causative Force to this abuse. Your awareness of your suffering becomes a part of total awareness. Allowing ourselves to participate in actions which generate negatives become absolutely illogical and insane.

•

You are responsible, not someone else. You can only affect what you can affect but, on the other hand, you cannot shuck the burden of responsibility by saying that you are not responsible. You cannot unburden yourself of your responsibility by wanting to believe you cannot affect what you know is taking place. You know what you know and yes, you are responsible.

Conclusion: How do the concepts of symbiosis reinforce the concept of symbiotic panentheism?

The idea of panentheism, you and I being 'in' the Causative Force, leads to the understanding of why we are significant. Symbiosis provides this understanding of why we exist, why we would be 'created,' why we would travel through a realm known as 'reality.'

•

But what of negatives and positives, are they really negative and positive under symbiotic panentheism? Negatives or positives are considered to be negative or positive by 'our' standards. And what in our society sets these standards? Religions sets these standards based upon what we sense. Science sets these standards based upon what we observe. And philosophy sets these standards based upon what we can reason. So if positive and negatives are not absolutes, how do we choose which will be which? We use our history of blood letting and suffering to guide us. We use our awe of what we see as beautiful in the universe to direct us. We use our logic of where glory and idealism lie to light up the correct path. We use our beliefs and faiths entrenched in tradition and blood to hold us close to the path. We take comfort in our past and where it seems to have been leading us. We stand tall and strong in our belief in ourselves and what we have to offer. We stand by our principles and beliefs in what we perceive universal truth to be. Ah yes, 'universal' truth, and just what is that? That is what we must find. That is what we must come to agreement upon before we can stand by it. That is what science, religion, and philosophy must help us find. We will never find universal truth in philosophy, science or religion for each has only a piece of the perception. Science, religion, and philosophy must join hands in their effort to help us find this perception of universal truth, a universal philosophy by opening themselves up to the others.

•

Science, having faith in what it sees; philosophy, having faith in what it reasons; and religions having faith in faith, all have lost faith in 'truth.' But is there really 'truth'? In the end does it really matter? We behave according to what we perceive 'truth' to be. We define 'truth.' As such, is it not better to take a 'universal' approach to 'universal truths' in the hope that if there are 'universal truths' we have defined them correctly? If universal truths do exist, our behavior may affect our final state of existence, the final state of existence of others, the final state of the Causative Force Herself. And if we are wrong, if there is no 'universal truth,' no eternal existence, then we would, in essence, have lost nothing.

Science – Conclusion

There appear to be three forms of existence which we can confirm through observation: growth, decay, and permanent equilibrium. Decay is not a state most of us would like to impose upon the Causative Force. Permanent equilibrium, however, cannot be found within the universe. That leaves only growth as a state of existence. No one can say for certain that one of these three forms of existence are the only possibilities for the Causative Force, but no other options have been offered. Until another option is offered as a viable form of existence, we can only discuss these three. Western religions hold to the state of permanent equilibrium as the state of existence for the Causative Force. They do so dogmatically. They refuse to release this concept for they feel it goes to the heart of their beliefs. But it does not go to the heart of their beliefs. It only goes to the heart of the means by which they retain control and power over their followers. Permanent equilibrium is an irrational concept that contradicts what they profess. It contradicts the idea that the Causative Force is all knowing, all powerful, and all present. If a force is all knowing, it would have to know how to increase its knowledge, or it wouldn't be all knowing. If a Force were all powerful, it would have to have the ability to increase its knowledge. And lastly, if a Force were all present, it would have no choice but to increase its knowledge within itself since it was everywhere and, thus, there would be no outside to the force.

Science, subconsciously, understands this paradox, this contradiction. As such, science has been rejecting western concepts of religion based upon the irrationality of the contradictory stands western religions have been taking. Religion, on the other hand, has been rejecting science because the logic it uses as its base would act to erode the three basic contradictions religions feel a need to maintain: 1. the Causative Force is all knowing but does not know how to grow, 2. the Causative Force is all powerful but does not have the power to grow in knowledge, and 3. the Causative Force is all present but we, Homo sapiens, and the universe within which we live, are located outside the Causative Force, are not a part of the Causative Force.

SCIENCE

So there is the conflict. There lies the power struggle – a basis for abstract territorial disputes generating abuse, attempts to subjugate, actions intended to dominate, and suffering, all in the name of power. We are entering into a new age. It is time to mend the fences, heal the wounds, and take the best of both worlds. It is time for religion to accept the observations of science and the concept that the universe has a function, as do all things we study within it. It is time for religions to accept the universally observed characteristic of the universe, symbiosis, and apply it to the relationship between life and the Causative Force.

But just as it is time for religions to reevaluate their dogma, it is also time for science to accept the fundamental concept of religion, something exists outside the universe. It is time for science to accept panentheism and apply it to understanding the relationship of the universe and how it interacts to what it is immersed within.

It is time for philosophy to use its ability to reason and join the two, science and religion, through the process of its ability to speculate in a rational manner. The universe is most likely immersed within something. We have a relationship with this 'something' in some fashion or other.

Palaeomagnetism tells us change will come. There is no holding it back. Major global trauma will come. We must begin to prepare for it in order to reduce the magnitude of the trauma. Being prepared may not prevent the occurrence, but it certainly can prevent further trauma from rippling throughout society. The after shocks of an event are often more traumatic than the event. Humanity has a great ability to abuse itself as a whole and as individual members. We must begin to establish an understanding of what we believe we are and why we believe we exist. It is through such an understanding that we can draw together rather than splinter apart before a major global catastrophe occurs.

Where does this bring us? It brings us to philosophy, for science may provide us with clues about our future through observation, and religion may provide us with clues about what we are, but it is philosophy – the tool of reason – which must be used to unite science – the concrete – with religion – the abstract. How are we to process the thousands of years of philosophy into a few pages? We must do so as we did in science and religion. We must use a reference book written in terms of generalities so we all can follow the initial logic. We must stick to the concept that a universal philosophy is not universal if its basic principle cannot be understood to the general population.

Roger Bacon:

(3) But experiment concerns external experience. Also to be considered is internal experience with respect to which divine illumination is possible. Here, philosophy passes beyond experimental science to theology. Leaving behind its imperfect knowledge of created things, it turns toward its true end, which is knowledge of the Creator.

–Dictionary of Philosophy and Religion,
William L. Reese, p. 63

Philosophy
What We Reason

We have religion, science, and philosophy to help us develop perceptions of what we are and why we exist. Why would we ever decide to throw any of the three out when they each have contributions to make? They each uniquely address the three means of perception we have available to us. We sense what appears to be through intuition, faith, religion. We see what appears to be through observation, measurement, science. We rationalize what appears to be through reason, logic, philosophy. One does not necessarily lead to another. What we sense may not be observable. What we see may not be logical. What we reason may not be sensible.

We must not give up any one for another. Each is unique in their own way. Each has something special to offer. Each represents a special means by which we are able to understand ourselves and others. With religion, we use faith to tell us what we are, what the universe is, what a Causative Force is, and how the three are interrelated. With science, we use observations to tell us what we are, what the universe is, what the Causative Force is, and how the three are interrelated. With philosophy, we use reason to tell us what we are, what the universe is, what the Causative Force is, and how the three are interrelated.

The order of development of each is not surprising. Religion deals with faith, our intuitive ability to 'sense' what is even if we cannot 'see' it or cannot find any logic to it. As such, religion would be the most difficult to prove through observation or logic. In order to remain strong and not be pushed aside, it would need to establish deep roots. History, culture, tradition, and custom would all need time to develop. They would be the means of identifying with this field and they would provide the deep roots necessary to allow religion to survive the onslaughts of science and philosophy.

What area would then be the second area to develop? It should be the second most difficult area to maintain – logic. Philosophy began long before modern science established its foothold (*see Science Introduction*). Philosophy, using reason to understand what we are and why we exist, may seem to create a stronger foundation than faith but it is also wrapped in abstraction rather than the physical. Both needed a great deal of time to develop and establish a strong base.

The third area allowing us to understand what we are and why we exist would be the easiest area to accept. And what area is so easy to understand that it took only 500 years to develop rather than the 3,500 years religion took and the 2,500 years philosophy took? It would be the realm of what we can analyze through direct observation – the arena dominated by science.

We are working on a puzzle. Because this is a puzzle being solved, the sequence of putting the pieces together may not always be the same, but the end result should be.

Philosophy may not have evolved last but since it deals with logic, we will use it last in order to put the religious portions of the puzzle together with the parts of the puzzle science provides. In other words, we will use logic, reason, philosophy, to put the pieces together.

Reason would imply that religion may be correct, the Causative Force may indeed be all present, omnipresent, relative to our universe as was discussed in the religion portion of the matrix. If this is correct, the universe would have no place to be but within the Causative Force. And what then of yourself? If you are in the universe, you must be in the Causative Force, a part of the Causative Force, a piece of the Causative Force. Religion's insistence upon the Causative Force being omnipresent is one of the pieces of the puzzle. Panentheism, the perception of size, was the first puzzle piece discussed in the matrix.

But the size of the Causative Force is only half the picture; the other half is why the Causative Force needs you. Thus develops another piece of the puzzle, 'symbiosis.' It is science in this matrix that brings us the concept of the whole being the summation of its parts. Science also underscored the idea of the whole being less than what it is should any of its parts be missing. And thus it is science that brought us the concept of the parts interacting with and impacting the whole. It was the science section of this matrix that discussed the concept of symbiosis.

Combine religion – a perception of abstraction, a perception of the size of a Causative Force, panentheism – with science – a perception of the physical, a perception of interactions, symbiosis – and one gets symbiotic panentheism. One can put the two, religion and science, side by side but they will quickly fall apart once the pressure which keeps them together is

INTRODUCTION

removed. Religion and science tend to repel each other because the two are so different. One deals with the unprovable, what we sense, what we believe, the abstract and the other deals with the provable, what we see, what we observe, the concrete.

If our essence and if the essence of the Causative Force revolves around awareness, then a portion of ourselves lies in abstraction. This is unprovable; this is religion. On the other hand, if our body/mind and if the 'substance' of the universe is based upon the physical, then a portion of ourselves lies in the physical. Building a model fusing the abstractness of the Causative Force with the physicalness of the universe, will take some form of glue.

We, you and I, lie somewhere in the middle. A part of us seems to lie in the abstract and a part of us seems to lie in the physical. We have been torn apart many times by conflict and violence attempting to establish one over the other. One way to overcome our past history of violence and abuse may be to build a model gluing the two aspects of ourselves – abstraction and the physical – together. How do you glue abstraction and the concrete together? It would appear the only glue available to do so is reason or philosophy.

Over the last 4,000 years, through 500 year cycles, religion, science, and philosophy now appear to have emerged in their own right. Since we are at the gate of the next 500 year cycle, what is the next step? Who is to say for sure? Perhaps it is the development of a new religion. Perhaps it will be a new form of gaining insight. Or perhaps it will not be the development of something new but rather the unification of what we already have. Perhaps it will be the coming to terms, the establishment of the union of religion, philosophy, and science. After all, these three have been at odds with each other throughout our history. These three have been struggling to maintain the recognition they each feel they deserve regarding their own particular contribution towards the understanding of a Causative Force. Each has been struggling to overcome the other two ever since they emerged upon the scene of human history.

The struggle between religion, philosophy, and science to maintain their own unique identity and their own dominance in terms of understanding a Causative Force has been a long and, many times, very unpleasant experience for humans. Perhaps the next 500 year cycle is meant to be one of peace between the three. A union of this magnitude would no doubt benefit all of us, terrestrial and otherwise. Perhaps the next 500 year cycle is meant to bring peace to all of us through the process of bringing religion and science together by using reason.

Philosophy

*What new insight has **Philosophy**
firmly established within society?*

Unified View

#0. What does the conceptual framework of philosophy have to offer us?

Philosophy: Philosophy has two important aims. First it tries to give people a unified view of the universe in which they live. Second it seeks to make people more critical thinkers by sharpening their ability to think clearly and precisely.
–World Book Encyclopedia, p. 345

•

Let's begin by discussing the first aim of philosophy. First, it tries to give people a unified view of the universe in which they live. Philosophy has shrunk from this aspect of its responsibility. Philosophy has become so entrenched in the concept that we cannot *know* 'truth' that it has refused to tackle the problem of finding 'truths.' We may not be able to know truths, but we certainly can develop what we perceive truths to be based upon our intuitions and faiths – religion, our observations and experiences – science, and our logic and reason – philosophy. If we attempt to establish truths based upon only one of these three means of developing perceptions, then we develop a truth favoring one of the three: religion, science or philosophy. This type of truth is immediately rejected by the other two on the basis of bias. Since our perceptions are based upon how we incorporate all three fields, any truths must be able to be incorporated within the scope of all three.

As for the second aim: ... it seeks to make people more critical thinkers by sharpening their ability to think clearly and precisely. This also is the responsibility of philosophy. Philosophy has the responsibility to develop a unified view, a universal philosophy, so airtight that no reasonable person could refute the concept based upon any reasonable argument, be it from religion, science or philosophy. A unified view, a universal philosophy, has to be so basic, so fundamental to the general layman, that it cannot be refuted through any use of common reason.

•

To develop a unified view and to make people better critical thinkers is the responsibility of philosophy, for philosophy incorporates reason. Without reason, all three – philosophy, science, and religion – fall apart. Therefore, the concept of a unified view must begin with reason and fuse itself with universal religious concepts and universal scientific concepts.

#1. What does the conceptual framework of philosophy imply about the universe within which we live?

Philosophy becomes a means by which we gain the broadest possible picture of ourselves and our environment, both on a microscopic and macroscopic basis. Philosophy, by its very purpose, implies an outside as well as an inside to our universe.

•

Philosophy is the attempt to understand the function of the universe in terms of what lies within it and what lies outside it. By doing so, it leads us to an understanding of what we may be, what our function is, within the universe as well as to what lies outside the universe.

This process is accomplished through an attempt to establish a unified view of the universe. Many great thinkers have left their mark upon the field of philosophy over the last 3,000 years. But just as surely as they have left their mark, they have left their doubts about the ability of philosophy to accomplish its task of developing a unified view of the universe. This is not a negative statement; rather, it is a statement of growth, for just as a humans grow through self examination, so do specialty fields of knowledge. Knowledge we gain as a species is nothing more than perceptions we gain based upon our efforts as individuals to understand what it is we perceive through faith, observations, and reason. It is no wonder our basic fields of study go through similar stages of development as their architects. There is little doubt that humans are the most soul searching life form on this planet. Since humans are the engineers of their own fields of study, it only follows that philosophy would go through much soul searching in terms of its ability to accomplish its own function. But eventually, one has to stop searching and get on with life, and so it is with philosophy.

•

Self doubt, soul searching, hesitation, fear of failure, whatever excuse one wishes to place upon the lack of success of philosophy to accomplish its goal, the fact still remains that philosophy has not developed a unified view of the universe. It is time for philosophy to stop worrying about being condemned to 'hell' by religions and being ridiculed by science. It is time for philosophy to have faith in itself and use what it has observed as being successful for science. It is time to build a model of a unified view of the universe. The mere fact that we perceive the universe exists should be enough for philosophy to understand it can be modeled.

#2. How do the concepts of philosophy reinforce the concepts of panentheism?

The very concept of being able to develop a unified view of the universe implies the universe is 'an' entity. This, in itself, implies the universe is within something, which is the definition of panentheism.

•

A unified view of the universe has been abandoned by philosophy over the recent centuries. Philosophy has fallen behind, it has shirked it duties, it has fallen prey to the worry over hell, it has missed the boat, it has forgotten it is the foundation to both religions and science, it has been shattered into a million pieces, it has lost contact of a global need. It has forgotten its aim. Its purpose is to provide a unified view of the universe. It is only through this understanding that we can begin to understand what we are, as individuals and a species. How can we step into the heavens until we have an understanding of this concept? In its lack of confidence, philosophy has avoided its primary aim and concentrated instead on the second aim, clarity of thought. The reason clarity of thought is so important is not for the sake of thinking clearly, but rather because thinking clearly is the best means we have to understand our faiths and our observations. It is only through clear thought that we can develop logical models of the universe. It is only through clear thought that we can build a unified view of the universe. Thus, the second aim of philosophy – clear, critical thinking – is the means by which we can accomplish the first and primary aim of philosophy, a unified view of the universe.

•

Philosophy is so afraid it may be wrong if it builds a unified view of the universe that it has avoided the task altogether. But by now, philosophy should realize that science builds models with the view that these models are only temporary. These models are only intended to explain what we know today and, in fact, are intended to be modified and even discarded as we learn more tomorrow. Any unified view of the universe which philosophy builds today should be looked at as temporary. Any unified view of the universe is intended to 'best' explain what faith and observation hold to be true. As such, it is a unified view, a universal philosophy, which must act as a foundation to what we already believe and see. It cannot be developed on its own, but rather must take what is 'known' to build the model. It is not called a unified view because it destroys, but because it unifies. It is time for philosophy to get back on task and build a model, and possibly two, three or four models, just as in science.

#3. What does philosophy reinforce about the significance of existence, life?

If philosophy establishes a unified view, a universal philosophy, it has no option but to recognize the significance of life since it is a part of the whole.

•

If life is within the whole, it is a part of the whole. Life cannot have more significance than the whole of which it is a part. Few of us would object to the concept that we, a life form, are a part of the universe. If we accept this, if we ever come to the understanding that the universe may eventually die, then the only conclusion we can draw is that life will eventually die. The only way around this is to accept the idea that life is a part of something greater than the universe. This is the reason we intuitively feel that the significance of life lies not in the physical but in the abstract concept of the soul. Granted, this may not be the case, but we have to make a choice one way or the other. There is no in-between that we can presently conceive of. Selecting one or the other is not a moral question but a question of choice.

Our history of searching and suffering for idealism, religion, science, reason, love, and compassion has been in the realm of confirming and protecting the concept of the abstract, the soul, being the important essence of our species. We could give this all up. We do have the choice. But why would we do this? Why would we reject everything our ancestors have done for us to protect our ability to think of ourselves in the most idealistic fashion? Perceptions mold behavior and maintaining the most idealistic perception reasonably possible will generate the most idealistic behavior for our species. To choose to lower our perception of the significance of life being limited to physical reality would generate a lowering of our behavioral standards and few would suggest this would be a 'positive' course of action.

•

If we have the ability to choose a perception of the significance of life, it would most probably be a type of perception beneficial to all life forms, earth bound and otherwise. Development of such a perception, a unified view, is where philosophy should be headed. Philosophy needs to renew its commitment to understanding what the universe is, why it exists, what we are, why we exist, what life is, and what the purpose of life is. In short, philosophy needs to refocus upon the concept of a unified view, a universal philosophy.

#4. How does a philosophy help us understand what life is?

If we have the free will to choose the perception we have of life, we have the free will to choose how we define life – verbalize what we understand life to be.

•

Many would object to the idea of our defining life. They believe such an action is blasphemous. However, if we look at how we define life presently, we would quickly discover that we do not do so. The most significant aspect of our existence, life, is not defined. You will find characteristics that tend to describe life. You will find generalities about what living things can do, but one will not find a definition of life. Curiously enough, biology, a major branch of science, has devoted itself to the study of life; however, biology doesn't define this elusive concept. In fact, it does not even understand what it is studying.

We haven't obtained a unified view of life that faith, observation, and reason all embrace. Interestingly enough, these three have come to agreement upon when the essence of the human is no longer present in the body, when the essence of the individual has left the body. They have all come to agreement that this can be identified as the point at which the brain wave of the individual becomes 'flat lined.' The body may still function with the aid of technology, but the individual is declared 'dead,' not alive.

It would seem only logical that they would then agree upon when the essence of the human enters the body. It would logically appear to be the point at which the brain waves begin to function. The time this occurs is approximately ten weeks into the pregnancy. It is a very definitive point in fetal development and is subject to scientific measurement. Do the three, religion, science, and philosophy, agree upon this definition for the beginning of life? No, they do not agree because they have not come to a consensus upon a definition of life.

•

The definition of life has eluded them because they do not have a unified view regarding what life is. And so we remain in conflict. Society remains in conflict. Conflict over principles remain the major stumbling block we have to developing a long term, stable society capable of leading us into a form of peaceful coexistence with the universe and its life forms. Why all this confusion? Life has not been defined because philosophy has lost track of its primary aim, partly due to itself and partly due to the actions of religion and science to suppress philosophy.

#5. What does philosophy have to offer us as individuals?

Religion has faith to give individuals. Science has observations to give individuals. But what of philosophy? Philosophy has reason to give individuals.

•

It would seem that reason would be the strongest of the three. But faith is difficult to shake, which is why it is called faith. Observations are difficult to deny, which is why the expression 'seeing is believing' is so widely accepted. Reason, on the other hand, is based not upon faith nor upon observations, but rather upon both. Philosophy must take both into account while favoring neither of the two. Philosophy has attempted to create a niche for itself rather than be the common foundation of both science and religion. This process has lead to a flow chart starting with nothing at the top and then branching downward to the three categories of religion, science, and philosophy. This type of flow chart leads to competition amongst the three to climb to the top. The competition for power between the three is heated and nasty. It does not benefit any of us.

The flow should be different. It should be symmetrical and create a box capable of being rotated upon any of its sides. One side is science, a second is religion, a third is philosophy, and the fourth is a unified view of the universe. Religion, science, philosophy, and a unified view must be strong enough to support the others. What is it that lies outside philosophy, science, religion, and a unified view? It is what is. It is what could be called the Causative Force. And what lies within the box? The universe does. And where are we, the individual? We, you and I, individuals, are inside of it all. In fact, we are expanding the size of the box by using any three of the sides to expand the remaining side.

•

The wall of the box composed of the unified view has been our weakest link. It is time to work on this wall through the process of building a united view. There does not need to be one united view. There could be many. When science built a model of the universe, it did not create one theory. It built several, the steady state theory, the Big Bang... Philosophy needs to use its specialty, reason and clarity of thought, to assemble a strong unified view based upon 'truths' religions and science establish as their foundations.

#6. What significance does a philosophy have to offer us as a species?

We may be individuals and we may be responsible as individuals, but there is no denying that our actions as a whole species have a dramatic impact upon our environment.

•

As a species within the universe, we are subject to existing. There appear to be only three states of 'being' within our universe: growth, equilibrium or decay. Since permanent equilibrium does not appear to be a natural state of existence within our universe, that leaves only growth or decay. Each state of being leads to different ends. Growth leads to life and decay leads to death. Science would say, over time, death will win out. Religion would say, over time, life will win out. There you have it, pessimism and optimism. But there is a third vote to be taken. Philosophy, reason, has not voted. Philosophy has waited timidly on the sidelines. Philosophy has had ambivalent feelings. If philosophy does not stand up and vote, then history will continue its present course and our species will find itself once again faced with major global trauma. This is not a statement of doom, for our species has always managed to overcome such trauma and rise above it. In fact, the trauma has always been a means by which we have cleared away the old to make way for the new and the new has always helped us to grow as a species.

This cycle of growth, three steps forward and two steps back, has been predictable in history. Is this cycle inevitable or is it manageable? It would appear that it is inevitable if things stay as they are. It does not appear that we have put anything in place which would allow us to circumvent this process of cultural decay in order to make way for the new. What would it take to do so? No one could say for sure, but perhaps it would be the institution of a unified view regarding what we are, why we exist, what the universe is, and why it exists.

•

Creating a unified view capable of embracing the basic 'truths' science and religion seem to offer would certainly be a form of growth in our perception of who we are. Most collapses of civilizations initiated an environment capable of providing a growth in perceptions evolving around just such objectives. Why not initiate the growth voluntarily rather than through the natural process of collapse? After all, it is our choice.

#7. What significance does philosophy have to offer other life forms in the universe?

The major aim of philosophy is to develop a unified view of life. The operative word here is life, *not human life, but life. Such a goal offers us hope. But that is not the end of it. Such a goal offers other life forms in the universe the same hope.*

•

We have just reached the point of stepping into the vastness of the heavens. Previously, our perceptions generated behavior that affected only our species and 'lower' earth bound life forms. An earth oriented Magna Carta for life is okay for an earth bound organism, but such a limited Magna Carta has tremendous negative implications for life forms we could encounter as we explore the heavens.

To understand what this means, step back in human history to 1492 AD. At that time, Columbus stepped on the American continent. He brought with him a perception, a unified view, a universal philosophy, which existed for that era in our history. The unified view was simple, as all unified views are required to be. The established unified view existing in Europe at the time hinged upon two concepts: the Caucasian race was superior to other races and non-Christians were heathen, uncivilized, and no better than animals. With this universal philosophy in place, this unified view, Europeans were able to rationalize the actions of stealing the land, the environment, the home of others, and claiming it for themselves. It was not only logical but morally correct to kill over two hundred and fifty million Mayans, Incas, Iroquois, Sioux, Arapaho, Apache, Blackfoot, and Navaho. This was not a proud moment in our history. But it did have some things to teach us, such as killing was wrong. The lesson it held for us was: as we perceive ourselves, so we shall behave.

•

If we enter the heavens with too narrow a point of view of what we are and why we exist, it may have tremendous repercussions upon other life forms in the heavens. It could also have tremendous repercussions upon ourselves. We may not encounter life forms less advanced than ourselves, but more advanced than ourselves. These life forms may not look too kindly upon Homo sapiens intent upon establishing the perception of human superiority.

#8. What does a philosophy imply about our significance in eternity?

Using philosopy to define life can take on one of two forms. The definition can incorporate the concept of limited time – death – or it can incorporate the concept of unlimited time – eternal life.

•

Two concepts: death and no death. There is no alternative option being put forward in our society today. We cannot 'prove' either. We can prove death of the physical body, but the physical body is just made of matter and energy. Matter and energy are components of our universe. Matter and energy are components of what we believe is a closed system and, thus, affected by what we believe to be true, entropy. Matter, energy, and time are all interconnected. Matter, energy, and time are all limited, or so we presently believe. And if our perceptions of them are correct, then they all will come to an end.

But religions do not hold to the concept that the body is the essence of life. Religions hold to the concept that the essence is the soul, an abstract item. Science only applies entropy, the death of systems, to what we call reality, the physical aspect of existence. Science acknowledges the abstract – love, happiness, joy, hate, jealousy, greed – are concepts the physical essence is able to comprehend. Science has never claimed to know what happens to these abstract creations when the physical essence dies. Science only assumes it knows.

•

Abstract concepts, such as love and hate, have been created within the individual. Their existence can be measured through scientific observation. But the abstract cannot be proven to die once it has been created. When absolute proof is unavailable, choice becomes the option. Choice, yes choice, your choice, my choice, our choice, comes into play. So often we allow others to choose for us and then find ourselves unhappy with the choice others made. We allow this to happen because we do not accept the concept that we can make the choice. We allow it to happen because it is easier to let other people make the decisions for us. We allow it to happen because we've been told over and over again we have no choice in the matter. We've been told others know better than we. And we believe it. We believe them. We have so little self confidence in ourselves. We do not question. It is time to start thinking and develop a unified view. Any unified view must incorporate death or eternity as its basis, for we know of no other option for existence. Since neither can be absolutely proven, it is your choice to make.

#9. What does philosophy imply about our relationship to the Causative Force?

Growth or decay is controllable. What is not controllable is the fact that it will happen one way or another. We cannot defy the forces of nature. We either grow or decay. As a species, if we grow, we live; if we decay, we die. By insisting upon clinging to our present perceptions, be they of the Causative Force or otherwise, we will not grow.

•

But why couldn't we just stay as we are? This is called a state of permanent equilibrium and nothing we have observed within the universe supports the idea that this state of existence is possible. Everything in the universe points to the concept of change. We have a choice. We can control our destiny. We can choose how to change or we can do as we have always done in the past and wait for random change and then attempt to adjust to it.

'God,' the Causative Force, is not the point of this book. The concept of the degree of involvement between ourselves and the Causative Force is not what this trilogy is all about. The point is to develop a model of a unified view to act as an example for philosophy to use in order to get back on track of finding a unified view. The point of developing a unified view is to develop growth voluntarily as a team of Homo sapiens rather than accidentally as a series of random events. Symbiotic panentheism acts only as a starting point, a model, of how to do this. If it turns out to be 'the' model we wish to use to advance the concept of a universal model, fine. But either way, the point remains: we can either intentionally develop a perception of ourselves in what would be viewed universally as growth or decay or we wait for the occurrence of random events to change us. Either way, change is inevitable, for it seems to be a universal condition of our universe, the reality within which we function.

•

Much of our dramatic growth in history seems to have been generated around perceptions we have of ourselves and our relationship to eternity, to the Causative Force. Much growth has taken place in this area, but this in no way implies that there isn't much more growth that can still take place. The growth of a perception of what we are, what life is, is a form of abstract growth. Technological growth has been in the forefront for a long time. Perhaps it is time to help the abstract catch up.

Conclusion: How do the concepts of philosophy reinforce the concept of symbiotic panentheism?

They do not; what is actually taking place is symbiotic panentheism is reinforcing the concepts of the significance of philosophy.

•

Philosophy has lost its respect in the eyes of the common layman. People often say, "Why should I listen to philosophers? My ideas are as good as anyone's." The battle for influence between science, religion, and philosophy has been long and hard. Science and religion have beat upon philosophy for so many centuries that philosophy, the ability to use critical thinking, the ability to understand the universe, ourselves, and what lies beyond has taken on the aspect of an endeavor in futility. But it isn't just religion and science that has done this to philosophy; it is philosophy itself. Philosophy has become so unsure of itself, it has accepted its fall in the eyes of men as being reasonable. Philosophy has no confidence in itself. The majority of intellectual thinkers of our species have taken to the fields of religion and science. The idea of some people in society being more capable in the field of critical thought centered around picturing the whole is an incorrect, invalid concept.

Philosophy must get back on track. Philosophy must get its self respect back. Philosophy must get its self confidence back. It must do so not for its own sake, but for the sake of our species. Philosophy is one of the three means by which we as individuals and as a species obtain a self perception. And it is through perception that we understand what it is we think we are, what other people are, what life is, what the universe is, and why we exist. Our perceptions of who we are, what we are, and why we exist act as the foundation of our behavior both as individuals and as a species.

•

Perception is based upon faith, observation, and reason and reason is the field of philosophy. It is only through reason that we can unite the three. Faith and observations left alone will constantly stay at odds with each other to some degree or other. Clear thinking is the only thing that can unite what we have learned through faith and observation. Its means of doing so? A unified view of the universe using the knowledge we have gained from reason, faith, and observations leads to understanding and peace.

PHILOSOPHY

*What new insight has **Philosophy**
firmly established within society?*

Philosophy, Religion, and Science: Reality and reality

#0. What does the conceptual framework of philosophy, religion, and science have to offer us?

Philosophy and Science: Philosophy and Science have always been related in some ways. Both of them seek a knowledge of basic principles, and both try to be systematic in their investigations. But science tries to gain knowledge about a specific subject matter, and philosophy concerns itself with the laws and structure of all reality.
–World Book Encyclopedia, p. 345

Philosophy and Religion: When we speak of philosophy as a world-view, we must include religion in that world-view. Religion then becomes a part of philosophy or one philosophic position in a larger system.
–World Book Encyclopedia, p. 346

•

The key word in this paragraph is not science, religion or philosophy. The key word is *reality*. Science seeks to understand it in bits and pieces by studying 'specific subject matter' through observation. Religion seeks to understand it in bits and pieces by accepting certain basics through faith. Philosophy seeks to understand it by assembling the bits and pieces science and religion gather together. Philosophy then generates an overall picture, a unified view based upon the pieces we have at any particular point in time.

Piece by piece, little by little, biology, physics, chemistry, sociology, anthropology, archeology, mathematics, the arts, and the humanities receive observable pieces of the puzzle. Hinduism, Judaism, Buddhism, Christianity, Islam, New Age spirituality, atheism, and unity receive intuitive pieces of the puzzle. It is then the responsibility of philosophy to put the pieces of the puzzle together. Religion and science deal with the pieces, the microcosmic view, and philosophy deals with the total, the macroscopic view.

•

This in no way diminishes the value of science or religion, for without their contributions, philosophy has nothing with which to work. Philosophy has little option but to humble itself before the significance of each of them. On the other hand, the pieces of knowledge that science and religion have hold little value in terms of the big picture unless they are put together to understand the whole.

#1. What do the conceptual frameworks of philosophy, religion, and science imply about the universe within which we live?

Science observes the concept of things having a beginning and end. There appears to be an initial force to all things. Religion accepts the concept of 'a' Causative Force and has moved on from there.

Philosophy, on the other hand, has become bogged down in a paradox of its own making by continually second guessing itself and asking how we can develop the big picture of what we know when we may never know for certain.

•

Why are we so afraid of moving forward with finding truth? We are only human. Truth is the best we can reason it out to be. Philosophy is the process developing the best possible unified view using what we have uncovered through religion and science. But philosophy cringes in uncertainty, unsure of its ability to find truth about ourselves, the universe, what lies beyond the universe, and the interrelationship of the three. Philosophy has not accepted the concept that we will most probably never know truth as a certainty while we remain within this universe. But the best perception of truth we are capable of understanding is still worth seeking. Philosophy should take heart in the concept that it is possible that the Causative Force Herself may not know truth in terms of an absolute. Philosophy needs to move on. Philosophy needs to do its job and when confronted with the question, "How do you know for certain?" reply, "We don't know for certain, but can you give us a better explanation?" The universe is waiting; we are waiting. Although truth may not be proven to be an absolute, we can develop a unified view from what we do know.

•

The universe appears to be ever changing. If the universe lies within the Causative Force, then it may be that the Causative Force also changes as the universe changes, as we change. As such, truth itself may grow. We may have an awesome responsibility. We may be responsible for the development of truth itself. If such is the case, we have an obligation to start working on what type of truths we would like to see emerge in eternity, the region within which our universe lies.

#2. How do the concepts of philosophy, religion, and science reinforce the concept of panentheism?

Science: searching for the boundary, outside, of our universe.
Religion: adamant in its belief, faith, that the universe was created.
Philosophy: unable to shake the overwhelming logic that our universe had a beginning and will most probably come to an end.

•

Science, by searching for a boundary, is searching for an outside, something bigger than our universe, something within which our universe is located. If science finds this location, this non physical existence, this abstraction within which the universe lies, science will most likely call it something other than the Causative Force. In essence, however, that is most likely what it will be. If it is not an abstraction, then it would most likely not be the boundary of our universe, but just another layer of it, a further expanse of the mechanism we call the universe.

Religion holds to the fundamental belief through faith of the creation of the universe, a more omnipresent state of being exists than that of time and mortality. Religion was the first of the three realms to reach this conclusion and, therefore, religion was the first to name this essence. But the name is not what is important; it is the idea of its existence. And if it doesn't exist, if the universe has no creator, nothing greater than itself, then why are science and philosophy so obsessed with understanding the concept of creation and why we exist?

Philosophy holds to the same premise as do science and religion but not because of what it sees nor because of what it believes. Philosophy holds to the concept of a state of being outside of a universe limited by matter and energy because it is the most reasonable, logical concept available which explains the very limits matter and energy impose upon themselves.

There it is, all three obsessed with the concept of an existence outside the mechanism called the universe. All three obsessed with greater Reality. In essence, all three are searching for panentheism.

•

All three are seeking the essence of panentheism, seeking to learn of its nature, seeking to learn of the significance of our reality to this greater Reality. All three seek to understand what reality is submersed within, and the interrelationship between the three.

#3. What do philosophy, religion, and science reinforce about the significance of existence, life?

Religion: life exists, why?
Science: life exists, why?
Philosophy: life exists, why?

•

Life exists in reality, but why, why, why? Science hasn't told us. It doesn't know. It views things in too much of a microcosmic sense to ever be able to theorize a reason for life. Most religions haven't told us why. They don't know. Western/Middle Eastern religions tell us what to do, and even tell us to do so because 'we have been told to do certain things.' Still the question remains, Why does life exist? Why was life created? Why did life evolve? What significance does life play in the greater scheme of things? How does life existing within reality affect the greater form of Reality that exists beyond the boundaries of our universe?

Science and religions of the West/Middle East have not been able to answer these questions. They have been dabbling in the examination of themselves in relationship to our existence within the universe. They have been dealing with the microscopic view rather than the macroscopic view. It is philosophy that must put together the microscopic bits and pieces science and religion have accumulated. It is philosophy which must fuse the abstract with the concrete in order to rationalize why it is we exist, were created, evolved.

•

Philosophy, religion, and science are all obsessed with essentially the same question, 'Why?' Philosophy, religion, and science – reason, faith, and observation – are all seeking an answer independently. But the answer most probably does not lie in one or the other; pieces of the answer most probably lie in each. The fusion cannot take place from too close a proximity. It will have to be assembled from a more distant viewpoint from outside the universe. This point of view must originate from the point of abstraction. The only area of the three capable of such a perspective is philosophy. Philosophy has little choice but to step forward and begin the task it was developed by the West to do. It must begin assembling the puzzle.

#4. How do philosophy, religion, and science help us understand what life is?

Science: life – consciousness, awareness in reality.
Religion: life – the soul, awareness in reality.
Philosophy: life in reality, which is in Reality.

•

In essence, philosophy, religion, and science have constructed the idea of two realities:
1. Reality (upper case 'R'): what exists beyond the universe and would exist should the universe dissolve.
2. reality (lower case 'r'): the universe within which we currently exist.

Religion and science did not intentionally set out to create these two types of reality. They emerged as a natural result of both. Religion intuitively understood the concept of a creator. Science is beginning to understand the concept of time, limited existence. The two realities, reality and Reality, are most likely not separate from each other.

•

A creator does not have to be physically greater than Her creation. But by definition, She is greater than Her initial creation and if that creation is a part of Her, within Her, She remains greater than Her creation as long as that creation remains within Her.

Religion: Life is eternal. We cannot ask religion to relinquish this position. To do so would be asking religion to annihilate itself. Philosophy has no option but to include this aspect within its unified view if it is to be truly unifying.

Science: The universe exists. We cannot ask science to relinquish this position. To do so would be asking science to annihilate itself. Philosophy has no option but to include this aspect within its unified view if it is to be truly unifying.

Philosophy: Most religions sense something greater than the universe. Science is seeking the boundary of our universe. As such, philosophy must now begin to study Reality. Philosophy has little choice but to begin building a model depicting reality within a greater Reality. It appears that reality, our universe, is a part of something other than itself or life most probably could not be eternal.

Life is in reality, which is in Reality. Until we understand the model and its dynamics, we will remain in a state of confusion.

#5. What do philosophy, religion, and science have to offer us as individuals?

Religion: existence in Reality through faith.
Science: existence in reality through observation.
Philosophy: fusion of the two through reason.

•

Religion, science, and philosophy are the three basic means we have of obtaining a perception of what we are as individuals. A model of the individual, the universe, and what lies beyond can be constructed using any one of the three. The dynamics behind the model can be spelled out in all three cases. But the models will all be different from each other and each will be based upon only one perceptual view. Three views, one built upon faith alone. The past results: conflict, infighting, violence, intimidation, fear of death, arrogant attitude... Another view built upon observation alone. The past result: doubt, skepticism, constant insecurity, fear of death, defiant attitude... The third built upon pure logic alone. The past result: no absolutes, no solid foundation, fear of death, doubtful attitude... None of the three have been sufficient by themselves. Combining two may prove to be better than any one alone but still not the best means we have of building a model of reality within Reality.

Science, philosophy, and religion are each capable of developing a model of the individual, the universe, and what lies beyond the universe, but none can develop a stronger model than the three together.

•

Science, philosophy, and religion may be unique in the contributions they have to offer us as individuals, but none of them can stand alone against the other two. To bring peace and harmony amongst the three will take a cooperative effort. To provide the strongest foundation, the greatest cohesive bond for us as individuals dispersing throughout space, will take a united approach from the three. Without a united view, we will disperse as a divided, competitive group of individuals sending mixed messages to whomever we come into contact, be it other life forms or ourselves as we once again bump into each other in the vast distances of space.

#6. What significance do philosophy, religion, and science have to offer us as a species?

Science: the whole is equal to the sum of its parts.
Religion: a part of the whole is less than the whole.
Philosophy: reality is less than Reality.

•

We are presently bound to the planet earth. We presently are in a constant state of turmoil over social issues, religious issues, infighting between religion and science, science and philosophy, philosophy and religion. The feuding prevents us from coming to terms over issues each attempts to dominate from their particular point of perception. So it is abortion, capital punishment, fetal tissue research, assisted suicide, genetic research, sexual harassment, bigotry, and abusive actions remain major issues of debate. We have not resolved these issues because we have not established a unified view addressing why we exist. What is the significance of our species to reality and Reality? Do we have an active role to play in terms of what lies beyond our universe? We do not have a universal philosophy in place that brings together the most basic and cherished perceptions, tenets, axioms, and principles religions, science, and philosophy use as the base of their perceptions.

The process of fusing the most basic perceptions to which the fields of religion, science, and philosophy adhere will allow the development of a means to resolve the basic differences dividing us. Until we join the three in a united front, accepting the concept of ourselves belonging to something greater than ourselves, we will most likely never provide a united front as a species.

•

The concept of 'united we stand, divided we fall' does not apply only to geographical territories. It applies to us as a species. Religion, science, and philosophy must unite. Their union will provide not only a source of strength to individuals of our species, but to our species as a whole. We will be struggling for our survival in the vastness of space. As long as our species stays clustered upon one planet, we remain susceptible to any number of catastrophes capable of annihilating our total species. We will need all the strength of faith, all the absoluteness of observation, and all the logic of reason we can gather together in order to survive not only the random species-threatening events that occur throughout nature, but also the intentional acts that may occur – humanly generated or otherwise.

#7. What significance do philosophy, religion, and science have to offer other life forms in the universe?

Religion: a Causative Force created the universe, reality.
Science: a Causative Force initiated the universe, reality.
Philosophy: a Causative Force is the dynamic behind reality.

•

The process of developing a unified view can orient around the physical world. If things continue as they are, a unified view most likely will orient around the concept of our species being superior to others in some way. If the observation of superiority is not observable, then we will believe it through faith. Without philosophy taking the lead, without reason acting as the foundation for the overall unified view, our past behavioral tendency to place ourselves above others will continue to dominate our perceptions and our past history will continue to repeat itself.

'Good,' you say. But is it? Our past has been entrenched in the concepts we have observed around us: survival of the fittest, only the strong endure, crush or be crushed, violence, violence, violence. But is that the only way to survive? It may be true that survival depends upon strength, but on the other hand, is strength the reason we were created? Is strength the reason we exist or is it the means by which we protect ourselves so we can fulfill our purpose?

If we have a purpose other than to be strong, then that purpose, if truly universal, may apply to other life forms within the universe. What is that purpose? As life forms aware of abstraction itself, we have the ability to define this purpose based upon what we see, what we believe, and what seems logical. As such, we can create a unified view inclusive to Homo sapiens only, or we can create a unified view incorporating other life forms. We can make it a self serving philosophy or we can make it so broad it will incorporate vast numbers of others throughout space. To make it truly universal, we most likely will have to attach it in some logical manner to a greater Reality than our reality, our universe.

•

The broader we make our model, the longer it will serve us in the future. Change generates turmoil. The broader we make our model, the less radical any future modifications will be. Less radical future modifications mean less turmoil and upheaval for future generations. Let's choose ourselves this time rather than wait for change to occur. But let's not just choose; let's choose wisely using science, religion, and philosophy.

#8. *What do philosophy, religion, and science imply about our significance in eternity?*

Science: the universe being initiated does not exist in isolation.
Religion: the universe being created is not the ultimate.
Philosophy: the universe, reality, is tied to Reality.

•

We have a unique view to offer eternity. At this point, we do not yet know for sure what it is, but we seem to be the only life form in this solar system with the capacity for an altruistic abstract perception embracing the rights of the individual, be they human or otherwise.

This concept seems to be entrenched within us as a species. Our whole history appears to have been headed in this direction. There is no doubt that our history has been filled with atrocious actions indicating just the opposite, but upon closer examination, our species has made valiant sacrifices to repulse the permanency of all such actions. The heroism, the self sacrifice, the willingness to give up everything one possesses, including one's own life, in order to protect the rights of the individual to journey life unimpeded by others has been a magnificent story to watch unfold.

Our history as a species is not one of despair and negativism; it is one of hope and glory. Our history is not one of a glass half empty, but rather one of a glass half full and rising.

We are continually adding to our history of compassion for life, love of nature, and understanding of our significance to Reality by existing in reality. The longer science searches, the closer it comes to concluding that our universe, our reality, is limited. Science is beginning to understand that we, Homo sapiens, are but one of many life forms capable of abstract awareness that may be a part of total abstract awareness. Our universe may very well not exist in isolation. Life forms within this universe may well be only one of many life forms throughout Reality. Religion senses this larger Reality, understanding that our existence within the smaller reality may have a part to play within the greater Reality.

And philosophy may be on the verge of getting back on task and develop its first unified view, a model of a universal philosophy explaining our significance in eternity.

•

A unified view would be a means of providing a foundation underneath all three – science, religion, and philosophy.

#9. What do philosophy, religion, and science imply about our relationship to the Causative Force?

Religion: the ultimate to be truly ultimate must be omnipresent, all present, or it is less than the whole and therefore not truly ultimate in scope, but rather just a part of some other whole.

Science: an initiator must keep what it initiated within itself if it is to remain omniscient, all knowing, relative to its creation.

Philosophy: without reality, our universe, Reality becomes less than what it is – less of an entity. We are an integral part of the whole.

•

Science: We cannot be a part of something unless we are a part of something. We could be the whole 'thing,' but if such is the case, then there is no outside to our universe. If such is the case, the search to find the Causative Force of our universe, reality, would have to take a different turn. The search for the Causative Force would have to go inward. No one is saying that is not a possibility, but for now, that is not where we are searching because that is not where science feels the limits of reality lie. Rather, science feels the limits lie within Reality, what lies beyond our universe.

Religion: We are less than what lies beyond the boundaries of our universe. Western/Middle Eastern religions hold to the concept that although the larger Reality lies outside our universe, our universe is not a part of Her. So there we stand, stranded and no place to go unless we submit to the 'keepers of the keys.' If we don't, we will be given free entrance to the 'fires of hell.' Western/Middle Eastern religions expand the size of Reality over that of atheism and pantheism but leave the greater Reality stripped of its total potential, for with them, the greater Reality does not include our universe.

Philosophy needs to enter the debate and attempt to bring some resolution to the picture of Reality using a macroscopic viewpoint. The three, together, can bring us to an understanding of our relationship to a Causative Force and to Reality itself.

•

This macroscopic viewpoint is not one that judges the pieces of the puzzle science and religion have gathered together. Using what we know today, philosophy's job is to make sense of our relationship to Reality.

Conclusion: How do the concepts of philosophy, religion, and science reinforce the concept of symbiotic panentheism?

They do not; what is taking place is that symbiotic panentheism is reinforcing the concepts of the significance of philosophy, religion, and science.

•

Science: symbiosis states that all elements within the whole impact upon the potential of the whole, all elements within the whole make the whole what it is, and any element removed from the whole diminishes the potential of the whole. Science tries to understand the whole, the dynamics of the whole, the relationship of reality to Reality, and what part we play within the two. No part of the whole can exist without affecting the whole. 'Negatives', 'positives,' whatever words we wish to use, have the same basic results. They both create change. And we, you and I, are a part of it. You and I together have a purpose in reality and, therefore, in Reality.

Religion: panentheism states that Reality exists outside our universe and is omnipresent. Whether or not this Reality itself is a closed or open system (*see Entropy*) is beyond our comprehension at this point. However, understanding the concept of our reality lying within the greater Reality is not. If the Causative Force is what we lie within, then it is the Causative Force we impact. If we do not lie within the Causative Force, the entity within which both we and our Causative Force lie within is truly 'the' Causative Force. Whichever case, we lie within something.

Philosophy: symbiotic panentheism states that the union of science and religion is symbolized by the ring of reason. The butterfly effect is alive and well and you and I are the butterflies.

•

Philosophy is not to repaint the pieces. Rather, philosophy is to direct the assembly of the pieces using the advantage it has of being able to stand back and view the construction of the picture from a distance.

There should be a place for everyone. The picture will not be complete if it throws away pieces of the puzzle science and religion have worked so arduously to discover. No unified view should ignore blood spilled in the past that saturated the soil of our planet earth, discolored our rivers, lakes, and oceans, and fell from sky. The picture we obtain of the Causative Force, Reality, will indubitably be painted upon a canvas of red that can only accentuate Her character.

Philosophy

*What new insight has **Philosophy** firmly established within society?*

Confucianism: Order over Disorder

#0. What does the conceptual framework of Confucianism have to offer us?

Confucianism originated in 500 BC; society could be saved if it emphasized sincerity in personal and public conduct; the key to orderly social life was the gentleman; [the gentleman] was to think for himself guided by definite rules of conduct; a gentleman also studied constantly and practiced self-examination; when gentlemen were rulers, their moral example would inspire those beneath them to lead good lives; virtuous behavior by rulers had a greater effect in governing than did laws and codes of punishment.

–World Book Encyclopedia, p. 756

•

Confucianism is an eastern philosophy just as Hinduism is an eastern religion. East or West, it does not seem to matter. We are both headed in the same direction. The East through Hinduism led the way for religion with the global perception of a Causative Force. The West through the ancient philosophy of the Greeks led the way for philosophy. But leading implies going somewhere. The question is where? The answer appears to be toward an understanding of ourselves, our universe, and the cause of our universe.

The key concept of Confucianism appears to orient around the statement, '[the gentleman] was to think for himself guided by definite rules of conduct.' This was the means by which an orderly society could preserve itself and it was through an orderly society that humankind could achieve its purpose.

What was humankind's purpose? Why was the universe created? What is the soul? What are the definite rules of conduct? How are we to sense the 'way' if we don't know what our purpose is? Confucianism had a major impact upon the lives of billions, but it still fell short of a unified view. It began with the construction of the framework but it lacked the foundation, the understanding of the answer to the question, Why?

•

This in no way diminishes the positive impact Confucianism had and still has upon society. It simply implies Confucianism, like everything else, would be much stronger if it had a foundation of understanding to support it.

#1. What does the conceptual framework of Confucianism imply about the universe within which we live?

Confucianism with its orientation of living one's life oriented around 'definite rules of conduct' implies the need for order in an ever changing environment.

•

Our universe is permeated with change. Its very beginning is believed to have been initiated with a horrendous explosion. There appears to be nothing we can do about change but to live with it. But upon closer examination, the universe appears to also follow specific natural laws as it undergoes change. Order appears to be the underlying theme of the universe. Without order, randomness loses its meaning.

Society acts in much the same manner. Order must exist for the purpose of allowing the ramdomness of the individual to flourish. Confucianism orients around the premise of effective leadership being based upon a leader who follows 'definite rules of conduct.' Confucianism does not define these rules of conduct. Confucianism simply makes the statement: 'the key to orderly social life was the gentleman.' And then goes on to define the gentleman as one who 'thinks for himself guided by definite rules of conduct.'

A particular order of conduct was not what was being pushed by Confucianism. What was being put forward was the concept of a definite rule of conduct – the concept of order. Confucianism was implying order was the key and that we have the free will to choose our rules through self examination and constant study. Society could choose to define who we are through the process of establishing rules of conduct. The rules of conduct were to be determined by leaders within society. The key to the behavior, however, was consistency; that's why they are called rules. They could not apply to everyone except for the leader; they had to apply equally to everyone including the leader.

•

Confucianism emphasized the concept of establishing the rules and then following them. But society has had a problem determining what these rules should be. They change so often and become so complex it seems impossible to understand them. The reason they become so complex is because many different spheres of influence attempt to establish their influence upon law. Simplification can come about with the establishment of laws based upon what it is we think we are, why we exist, and why life exists.

#2. How do the concepts of Confucianism reinforce the concept of panentheism?

Confucianism implies a need for order, yet we live in a universe filled with apparent disorder. But is it? Or is it simply order hidden in disorder separating us from what lies beyond the Causative Force?

•

We are an orderly creature. Our societies are based upon order. Our understandings become understanding when the solutions are explained in an orderly manner. Our language is based upon order. Our families and societies are based upon order. Our very existence is oriented around order.

If the universe is a closed system (*see Entropy*), then the creation of a universe which appears to be based upon universal laws of physics, would seem to have been derived from a process of orderly thought, an orderly form of awareness. It would appear Confucianism, through its strong emphasis upon a reliance of 'definite rules,' is indicating the Causative Force Herself may retain this form of existence.

Interestingly enough, religions have indicated that the Causative Force is just that, the Causative Force. The implication is the Causative Force is the leading force behind the universe. As such, the Causative Force is not just omnipresent, but a leader to Her creation. Confucianism is implying the rules we sense we are to follow are the same rules the creator of our universe would need to follow if She is to be the most effective form of leader. And what is it religions profess are rules of conduct we need to follow? They are understanding one entity comprised of its many parts (Hinduism), we are responsible for our actions (Judaism), the elimination of suffering (Buddhism), unconditional love (Christianity), and justice for all (Islam).

•

But the characteristics of the Causative Force is not what is being addressed by the question being put forward. Rather, one and only one question is being submitted and that is how does Confucianism reinforce the concept of an omnipresent Causative Force, in other words reinforce panentheism? Confucianism implies that the Causative Force, by being a leader in the greatest sense of the word due to Her supposed perfection, would need to lead by example and that is nothing less than what religions have been telling us has been taking place throughout our history.

#3. What does Confucianism reinforce about the significance of existence, life?

Order is what is being stressed by Confucianism. Order is implied as the state of existence through which society thrives. It is not the order that is important but rather what can take place once order is established.

•

Life either has significance or it doesn't. If life has no significance, then that is the end of this discussion. But we are not privy to the absolute fact regarding whether life has significance or not. However, we do and have always suspected life did have a purpose, was worth protecting, was worth sacrificing in order to establish and maintain the concept of significance lying within the individual.

Confucianism implies life has significance and order is important and must be maintained in an unbiased manner to be effective. The rules of conduct are only as effective as the example the leaders at the top display in following these rules.

But just how far does the top go? Eastern and Western religions would both say the 'top' goes well beyond our universe and into the abstract form of existence within which our universe is immersed. As such, Confucianism would imply that even the Causative Force would need to abide by the most basic principles if in fact we are made 'in the image of God' as religions, for the most part, imply or outright state.

Science also is heading in the direction of an outside to our universe. Scientists have no idea how many shells exist around our universe, nor how many universes may be directly tied into ours, but they nevertheless keep searching for the end, the boundary of the universe. And why does science keep looking for this boundary, the limit to our universe? Like religion, science senses the answer to the questions regarding what it is we are and why we exist may well lie outside – not inside – the universe.

•

So there it is, everybody searching for the same thing. Religion and science developing the pieces. And philosophy? Philosophy has not yet begun to take responsibility seriously and so our rules and laws remain entwined and tangled within the jumble of the puzzle pieces strewn upon the table. Until philosophy gets its act together and begins assembling the puzzle, the fear of Confucianism will remain a reality and significance, life, existence, society will remain in a state of confusion and conflict.

#4. How does Confucianism help us understand what life is?

Life and existence are as different as they are alike.

•

Life and existence are simply states of being. Assuming we do exist, there would appear to be three forms of existence: existence with no awareness – rocks, water, existence with awareness – birds, frogs, and existence with awareness of awareness – humans. Only one of these states of existence appears to have awareness of its existence, awareness of its ability to love, to hate, to find happiness, and to seek out and fulfill a purpose it senses it has for existing.

Existence generated by a body, existence with awareness generated by the mind, and existence with the capacity to be aware of what it means to be aware generated by a soul, the essence of the individual. It is only existing in this third level that the abstract concept seeking purpose to life becomes a driving factor for existence.

This is not to say that an entity must have a central nervous system in order to be aware of awareness. It is not to say a central nervous system is the key to life. On our planet that may be true, but who is to say what curious forms of existence we will find in the heavens?

•

This is not to say that only the level of existence having awareness of awareness is to be respected. The environment is a place with a purpose and as such deserves the respect due just as such an existence. Existence having no purpose needs no respect. The reason we treat our environment with such disdain comes back to our lack of understanding regarding purpose. We have no idea why we are important. We have no idea what our purpose in existing is. We lash out at our environment as if it is what has no purpose when, in actuality, we are lashing out at our environment in frustration over our inability to place purpose in our own existence. If we could make the leap from sensing we had a purpose for existing to seeing a model which explained our purpose, then we would extend respect to the environment because we would see it as a place within which we existed. Respect for the environment would come as a natural outgrowth of our understanding what our purpose is for existing.

Confucianism, the concept of, 'society could be saved if it emphasized sincerity in personal and public conduct,' is saying to save society, we need the big picture. We need to understand a model of why we exist if we are to understand the 'definite rules of conduct.'

#5. What does Confucianism have to offer us as individuals?

Confucianism does not offer us 'the' rules. Confucianism offers us the concept that a definite set of rules are necessary.

•

Which set of rules is up to us. The rules establish the order. The rules establish what we think of the individual, define what it is we think the purpose of the individual is, and form the model of what it is we think life is. And so we go about setting up rules and laws in society to outline conduct acceptable to society and to fine tune our rules and laws, they eventually become so complex that we lose sight of the individual altogether. The society and institutions then become what is important – not the individual.

This complexity gains momentum the further it gets from its point of origination. The point of origination is the concept of setting up rules so society can be saved. This does not imply Confucianism is the cause of our problems in society. Quite the contrary. What is does imply is that we are at fault. You and I are at fault. Society is not a living entity of its own. Society is composed of you and I. Society is composed of individuals. You and I are the ones lacking the foundation of our purpose and, as such, the rules and laws we create lack a foundation. We build rules and laws for society, not the individual. We set up rules and laws upon a nonexistent understanding of what life's purpose is.

You may not know what the purpose of life is. That is what is so exciting about philosophy. Philosophy is the field that builds the model, any model it wants to build, and then turns the model over and over in its hands as it examines the model. Philosophy feels the model, applies the model, projects the model into the future, applies the model to the past, and theorizes what the model could do for the present. Philosophy builds rules and laws based upon these theoretical models and then examines the results of just such laws and rules. But it is one thing to build a model and another to build a model acceptable to individuals in society.

•

Confucianism implies laws and rules are necessary for an orderly society. But Confucianism does not state what these rules and laws ought to be. That is left up to us. By leaving this up to us, Confucianism implies we have the freedom and the free will to build the model of our choice.

#6. What significance does Confucianism have to offer us as a species?

Society has not been what our species has been striving to protect. Society has been the tool through which our species has been striving to elevate the perception of the value, the significance, of the individual.

•

We have so much to be proud of as a species. We have tenaciously retained the concept of individualism. The essence of the awareness lies within the individual, not society. Millions have given up their life's journey in order to solidify the rights of future individuals to journey unimpeded in life. This has not been a recent development. Blood has been spilled for this cause ever since our history began. The blood trail began as a trickle and has become a river. The blood trail is not finished. The establishment of the rights of the individual as the foundation of our species has not been locked into place.

The reason we have not finished giving blood for this concept is because we have no foundation to place under the idea that it is the individual that holds significance. We have fought for this idea. We have died for this idea. But the idea is built upon a foundation of sand and just as soon as we finish expanding the idea to include others throughout the world, the idea begins to slip as the foundation of sand begins to erode away, undermined by members of our own species. And what do we do as the foundation slips away? We sit and watch until it becomes a major crisis. We cannot see the foundation begin to erode because the foundation is not visible to us. We have no foundation, no unified view because philosophy has not built one for us.

•

The foundation is what we must work on. This is philosophy's responsibility. Philosophy is the field within which we build models of what we believe the Causative Force is, what the universe is, what we are, how the three interrelate, and what the function of each is. Philosophy can build any model it wants, but if it is to be acceptable to society, it must follow certain guidelines, 'definite rules of conduct.' These guidelines are established in terms of what we believe and what we observe. How can this be when religions seem to contradict each other and science and religion quarrel? That is why it is called a unified view. It is not religion and it is not science. It is a model meshing the two, fusing the most basic concepts of each, through the glue of reason – philosophy. It is a model that acts as the foundation and, like all models, it would change with time.

#7. What significance does Confucianism have to offer other life forms in the universe?

This model building is the basis of Confucianism. The models established, set in place a foundation of logic upon which our 'definite rules of conduct,' rules and laws, can be built.

•

Confucianism does not set any particular rules. Confucianism simply states that a society cannot remain orderly, cannot save itself, without having established what these rules are. Many would say that Confucianism implies a certain amount of humanitarianism. The argument stems from the belief that the Confucian idea of 'studying constantly and practicing self-examination' naturally leads to humanitarianism. But humanism is just that – humanism. What we may get out of study and self examination may be entirely different than what another life form may derive from the same process.

We, Homo sapiens, appear to be evolving towards establishing the rights of each life form, including ourselves, to develop in their own unique manner. This is an area of potential conflict, for other life forms may be evolving around the concept of aggression and dominating others while we are evolving around the concept of the right of all life forms to remain free and independent. This is going to force us to make choices. The choice, to maintain our own independence and freedom, will be one of those choices that most likely will not come easily when we are confronted by an aggressive, oppressive life form. We may see the color red for a long time to come but it will be a lot easier to accept if we know why we are giving blood. A model connecting us to something greater than physical existence could provide us with a foundation capable of transcending our species. Such a model would move beyond humanism and fuse us with other life forms as we travel throughout the heavens.

•

A practical model of what it is we are and why we exist has much to offer different individuals, different species, and different life forms. The model we as humans build, has no choice but to be practical and thus accepting of what it is we, as billions of individuals, have been striving to establish ever since history began. And what have we been striving to establish? The right of the individual to journey unimpeded, respect for the individual, equality for all individuals, and respect for the individual's home – their environment.

#8. What does Confucianism imply about our significance in eternity?

Confucianism has its own unique foundation. One piece of the Confucian foundation is composed of the idea of studying constantly and practicing self-examination.

•

Constant study and self-examination takes a lot of work. There is no logical reason to expend all this energy unless there is more to life than what we see. Without something more than physical reality, all this effort would seem to go against the laws of nature. All this expense of energy would appear to be inefficient. Why go against the natural process, as indicated by the path of least resistance, unless there is a reason to expend this energy?

We as a species are comprised of a mass of individuals who have always sensed the existence of a 'higher order' than physical reality. We have two choices. We can either acknowledge our past and place faith in the intuitive ability of the great bulk of individuals to sense where our purpose lies or we can reject this idea and begin from scratch. But why would we begin from scratch? Why would we ignore what our forefathers have fought so bravely to protect? What would make us think we know better than the billions that came before us? And if we accept the first choice, the choice of acknowledging what those that came before us had to say, then we have little choice but to incorporate into our model, not only freedom and free will, but the concept of eternity, our ability to enter it, our being a part of it, and through all this, the logical implication of our being able to impact eternity.

•

Therein lies our significance to eternity. Therein lies our foundation, a unified view upon which we could very well build our rules and laws. Therein lies the basis upon which the Confucian concept of order could evolve. But this model, symbiotic panentheism, is only one of many philosophy could build. Each would be valid in its own right. Theoretical models need to be created by theoretical philosophy just as theoretical physics is toyed with by theoretical physics. But the model of a unified view needs to be strong. If this model is not strong, we may once again find the foundation slipping away. Once we are scattered through the heavens, we may not be able to rebuild the concepts of freedom and free will and we may find a new foundation being imposed upon us by some life form other than ourselves. This time when we build the foundation, we had best think long term and of affecting eternity itself.

#9. What does Confucianism imply about our relationship to the Causative Force?

When gentlemen were rulers, their moral example would inspire those beneath them to lead good lives. Virtuous behavior by rulers had a greater effect in governing than did laws and codes of punishment. Is there a difference between leaders, rulers or gods? Only in degree.

•

Webster's Dictionary defines the word *lead* as, 'to guide on a way esp. by going in advance.' A leader then is one who shows the way through example. A leader does not attempt to control. A leader abides by the concept of, 'Do as I do.' Leaders build respect for themselves through the respect they show for the journey of others. Leaders use example as their means of influence.

Webster's also defines *rule* as, 'a prescribed guide for conduct or action.' A ruler then is one who dictates the way through proclamation. A ruler attempts to control. A ruler abides by the concept of, 'Do as I say, not as I do.' Rulers do not build respect for themselves; they build contempt through the lack of respect they have for the journeys of others. Rulers use laws as their means of influence.

Webster's defines *god* as, 'a powerful ruler.' A god then is one who not only dictates the way but has power: the ability to enact or produce the effect. A god does not merely attempt to control; a god does control. A god abides by the concept of, 'Do as I say, not as I do, or else!' Gods do not build respect for themselves; they build fear of themselves through the ability they have to punish others who do not abandon their own personal journeys through life in order to follow the demands dictated. Gods use punishment as their means of influence.

Webster's defines *God*, the Causative Force, as, 'the Being perfect in power, wisdom, and goodness who is worshipped as creator and ruler of the universe.'

Confucianism would imply the relationship between ourselves and a Causative Force would be the most effective form of relationship, a relationship based upon 'leadership,' a relationship based upon respect. And what greater form of respect can be shown than through permitting free will, the ability to chose independently?

•

Determinism or free will? Confucianism would tend to imply this relationship is based upon free will, a symbiotic relationship.

Conclusion: How does Confucianism reinforce the concept of symbiotic panentheism?

It does not; what is actually taking place is symbiotic panentheism is reinforcing the concept of Confucianism.

•

Confucianism came long before the term *symbiotic panentheism*. Symbiotic panentheism is simply a modern term to describe the logic behind the concept of Confucianism. Panentheism is a concept of relative size. Panentheism is a concept of the Causative Force being so large that the universe must lie within Her and therefore is a part of Her. We, being a part of the universe, are therefore a part of the Causative Force. Under the symbiosis aspect, we interact with the Causative Force because we are a part of Her and occupy a niche within Her (*see Niche*).

In science, the higher one goes up the energy pyramid, the fewer species one finds on the upper levels, the more species one finds on the lower levels and, therefore, the more individuals affected. This progress up the ladder can reach into the universe, through the boundary of the universe, and into what lies beyond, into the realm of the Causative Force Herself.

Confucianism implies the most effective means of governing is through example, not through dictating or subjugation. Wouldn't 'virtuous behavior' and 'perfect power, wisdom, and goodness' equate into the same thing? Wouldn't 'creator and ruler of the universe' equate into the highest form of this concept? If Confucianism is a valid concept, it would appear it may apply to the Causative Force as well as ourselves.

•

Leader, ruler, and god are all degrees of the same thing. So what about 'God?' Which relationship would Confucianism imply the Causative Force would establish with life forms within Her creation, the universe? Would She be a leader, ruler or god? Confucianism would hold to the idea of the universe being 'ruled' through the order of 'natural laws.' But Confucianism implies that we, you and I, the individual, is capable of acting independent of the Causative Force and, as such, if the Causative Force is a 'perfect Being,' She would act in the most effective manner, which according to Confucianism would, 'inspire those beneath them to lead good lives.' The implication is the Causative Force would not impose its ability to be a 'god' but rather would allow for a relationship based upon free will. If such is the case, it is up to philosophy to build such a model for us to examine.

Philosophy

*What insight has **Philosophy**
firmly established within society?*

Taoism:
Living Close to Nature

#0. What does the conceptual framework of Taoism have to offer us?

Taoism began in China, probably around 300 BC; a life in harmony with nature; the word is also used to mean reality as a whole, which consists of all the individual ways.

–World Book Encyclopedia, p. 27

•

Tao (pronounced 'dow') is a Chinese word which means 'way.' The way to live one's life is based upon remaining in 'harmony with nature.' In order to do so, one must understand nature. There are several means of understanding nature. One can search for understanding through the detailed examination of what lies outside one's self or one can search for understanding through the detailed examination of what lies inside one's self.

The West attempts to understanding nature by looking outward. The West dissects nature, bit by bit, piece by piece. As each piece reveals its secrets, the piece is further broken down to gain an even deeper understanding regarding the nature of nature Herself. The dissection process is conducted by the western field of science. We are to the point of having broken the atom into such small subatomic particles that in order to understand them, we are attempting to build cyclotrons contained in a circular underground tunnel fifty miles in diameter. This is not to imply this is a waste of time and resources; it is simply a statement of the progress we have made in obtaining an understanding of what lies within our universe in order to better understand what lies beyond our universe. The West examines what lies outside ourselves and outside our awareness by observing our physical universe.

The East, on the other hand, takes a different approach. The East tends to look for understanding of what lies beyond our universe through examination of what lies within ourselves. This process is enacted through meditation.

•

Western philosophy orients around the external; eastern philosophy orients around the internal. The two are distinctly different but equally important in the quest for understanding.

#1. What does the conceptual framework of Taoism imply about the universe within which we live?

'...reality as a whole...'
•

When the Taoists developed their concepts of sensing the whole, the idea of an outside to our universe was not a common point of discussion. The Hindus held firmly to the idea but many groups looked skyward and saw the universe, the seemingly eternal, an endless existence.

Either way, nature is our home. It is the niche we occupy in our present state of existence (*see Niche*). In addition, nature provides us with the means by which we can begin to understand what lies beyond our universe through the process of understanding the universe and what lies within it. If we can understand our universe, we may gain valuable insights as to what it is our universe lies within.

Understanding the concept of the size of our universe would imply a great deal regarding our relationship to the Causative Force. Because we have been so historically obsessed with understanding what our relationship to the Causative Force is, using a comparison of the size of our universe to the size of the Causative Force would appear to be an excellent place to begin building a unified view or universal philosophy explaining the characteristics and interrelationship of three entities: the essence of the individual, the universe, and a Causative Force. Defining the size of the Causative Force relative to the universe could provide an understanding of four questions: What is the universe? What are we? What role does the universe fill in regards to the Causative Force? Why do we, you and I, exist?

Taoists believe nature provides us with the most efficient means of sensing the size and location of the Causative Force. Taoism keeps us focused upon the big picture, the whole, while the West dissects the whole into a myriad of tiny pieces. Taoism sets aside the high paced life of the West and replaces it with simplicity and getting back to nature.
•

What better way to get to know the artist, the creator of a piece of work, than to immerse one's self within the total work of the artist? The analogy applies directly to the Taoist way of thinking. What better way to get a sense of what the Causative Force is and where She lies than to immerse one's self within nature and leave the cold analytical ways and fast paced life style of the West behind?

#2. How do the concepts of Taoism reinforce the concept of panentheism?

'...reality as a whole, which consists of all the individual ways.' Taoism is simply saying the whole is the sum of its parts; total awareness is nothing less than the summation of all awareness.

•

The concept of panentheism is nothing less than Taoism. Panentheism holds to the concept of the whole being composed of its many parts. Total awareness is the summation of individual pieces of awareness. The perspective of the size of the universe may be somewhat larger than it was around 300 BC when Taoism first began but the principles are the same. We may now be thinking in terms of the universe being a part of what it is immersed within but that in no way makes the concept of the whole being composed of its parts any less meaningful. Panentheism is not a concept of the 20th century. Tillich, Northrop, and Whitehead had no monopoly on this concept. Hinduism and Taoism embraced the basic concept long before the word *panentheism* existed.

So why all the emphasis on panentheism now? The term has been examined and rejected so leave it alone. Just because the West has seen the concept and rejected it does not make it any less significant or any less useful. If we were to discard the concept of eternity, it would not make the significance and potential impact of the concept of eternity any less potent. Panentheism was rejected because the concept of an imperfect being existing within an assumed perfect being was irreconcilable in the western mind. Rather than put the idea on hold, labeled 'pending,' it was labeled 'irrational' and thrown in the trash.

The old saying, 'One man's garbage is another man's treasure,' may well apply here. Sometimes we must revisit what it is we have discarded in order to find missing pieces of the puzzle. The Taoist perception of the whole being the sum of the many individual pieces may be more than just junk; it may be one of the key missing pieces we need for a unified view.

•

Hinduism held to the Taoist concept of the whole being equal to the sum of its parts long before Taoism existed. Taoism entrenched this concept into its foundation long before geometry, entropy or ecology used it as their base. The point seems to be that this idea is so universal in the fields of religion, science, and philosophy, it may be one of the fundamental building blocks to a unified view.

#3. What does Taoism reinforce about the significance of existence, life?

If life is a part of the total and placed in isolation of the total in order to prevent the contamination of creation of the new, then life has more significance than we had ever imagined. To exist in order to influence the growth, the actual direction of a Causative Force elevates life to a level never before defined by the West.

•

In the past, we have defined ourselves to be members of 'the superior race.' We have defined ourselves to 'know the mind of the Causative Force.' We have claimed to be the 'chosen ones.' We have defined others to be heathen, mentally handicapped, perverted, intellectually inferior, physically inferior... and each perception led to physical and mental violence of phenomenal proportions.

On the other hand, our history is not all negative. We have defined ourselves to be members of the same flock, all human, brothers through the soul. We have established the emancipation proclamation, the Magna Carta, and claimed equality for all men. We have held to the concepts of being our brother's keeper, all one with nature, and 'do unto others as you would...' These items also led to physical and mental violence of phenomenal proportions, but in these situations, the product was quite the opposite from the first examples.

The difference in the end result appears to emanate from the initial starting point of reference. In the first paragraph, one individual was viewed to be a 'lesser' being than another. In the second paragraph, one individual was viewed to be equal in status to all others. As we elevated the perception we had of each other and the perception we had of ourselves, we significantly elevated our behavior toward others. In addition, as we elevated our perceptions of what we are, we lowered our level of what we would tolerate in terms of behavior directed at ourselves and others in society.

•

The Taoist process of sensing nature to better come into contact with our sense of purpose, to retain what it is we are all about and not allow the glitter and fast pace of western life to obscure our vision of the bigger picture has much merit and is by no means a technique we should lose. It has far too much to offer us as our life styles are subjected to the temptation to accelerate and speed past the roses.

#4. How does Taoism help us understand what life is?

'... the word is also used to mean reality as a whole, which consists of all the individual ways.' The implication is that we have to be 'true' to ourselves, for this sense of truth is the only means we have of following what we sense is our path in life.

•

Taoism is based upon the concept of the whole being the sum of all individual ways. If life is an individual way and the whole is the sum of these ways, how could we ever presume to speak for the whole? But some would say that the whole has spoken and told our fathers before us that such and such behavior is acceptable behavior. That is all well and good, but what right have we to force others to conform to our beliefs and sense of direction? A woman is a woman and just because a man likes being a man and senses being a man is right for him, he has no right to force a woman to undergo the surgery required to become a man. A Caucasian is white and although Asians outnumber whites by two to one in the world, gives them no right to force whites to subject themselves to the process of changing their physical appearance to conform to the physical appearance of an Asian.

If we accept some differences, why can't we accept all differences? Life is a journey intended to be taken unimpeded by others. We may offer options, we may offer assistance, we may counsel, but we have no right to interfere with a journey; it is sacred. But just as we have no right to interfere with a journey, we have an even greater responsibility to understand that right to journey unimpeded and, therefore, we have a responsibility to protect that right for all individuals. To do this we may have to go to the extreme of isolating some individuals in order to prevent them from interfering with the journeys of others. The right to journey life unimpeded takes precedence over the individual's journey. The principle takes precedence over the action. Taoism teaches that the whole is the sum of its individual ways. Life lies in the individual.

•

The simplicity of Taoism teaches us tolerance, not the Western complexity of law and order. Taoism recognizes the whole as being the sum of the individual ways. Through this understanding, Taoism provides the simplistic acknowledgment of the rights of the individual over the demands of conformity imposed by society.

#5. What does Taoism have to offer us as individuals?

Assuming Taoism is correct, assuming life is to be lived in harmony with nature, what significance could this imply about existence, life?

•

Assume for a moment we are a piece of the Causative Force by way of being located within the Causative Force. Assume also we are isolated from the Causative Force through the vastness of space. It we were to seek out a means of feeling a closeness to the Causative Force, one would have two options. One could search within or one could search without. The East chose the first, searching within through meditation. The West chose the second, searching outside through the scientific process.

We have already examined the western approach in the section on Science. The eastern approach of meditation is attempted in the West through a process of prayer, reaching out to the Causative Force. The eastern approach is one of reaching in, sensing the presence of the Causative Force through meditation. Taoists felt the best way to accomplish the act of connecting to the original force, the Causative Force, was through the simplicity of nature. One needed to shuck the artificial layers of society, the fast pace and material distractions of society, if one was to obtain a sense of connection to the whole. The ultimate goal was to make the contact.

But the question remains, Why is this important? Taoism is unable to answer this question. Taoism, like science, religion, and other philosophies, needs the base that explains the reason to this question. With a base established, Taoism survives for a long time and continues offering us a means of staying in touch with and understanding the 'big picture' as we continue to examine the intricacies of its smaller parts.

•

If we are in the Causative Force, we are a part of the Causative Force. If we are journeying with free will, we may have the ability to influence the growth of the Causative Force (symbiosis). What better way to sense one's purpose as an individual than to come into contact with the whole, the Causative Force, than through the whole of Her creation, nature? Through this contact, the sense of oneness with the Causative Force, one can sense the correctness of one's decision in terms of the direction one should take in life. This sense of direction provides us with a sense of comfort and confidence as we go about our hectic, daily lives.

#6. What significance does Taoism have to offer us as a species?

'...the word is also used to mean reality as a whole, which consists of all the individual ways.'

•

The West brings out the best in our potential to gain knowledge of our environment through observation. The West turned its efforts toward developing our ability to finding the small – the basic building blocks, and finding the large – the boundary of the universe. The West has made great strides in the field of science, the field of understanding both the large and small of the universe. As such, the West has moved its expertise of examination far from the essence of the individual and this has brought about what is known as the fast paced life for individuals in society. The faster life becomes, the more we, as individuals, appear to lose our sense of orientation, direction, and purpose. We are being swallowed up by the complexity and size of the universe itself.

The western approach of resting on the 'seventh day' has helped us to retain some control over our fast paced life, but the 'seventh day' is rapidly losing its influence to the need for more time to fulfill what is perceived as our obligations to economics, society, and family.

Taoism offers us the ability to return to a sense of purpose. Taoism offers us a process of being able to give our weary bodies and minds a rest from the complexity of life while our essence, awareness, takes time to reconfirm its intuitive sense of orientation, rejuvenate its intuitive sense of direction, and secure its intuitive sense of purpose.

Our species needs this sense of purpose, orientation, and direction just as much as the individual. We must look to individuals to understand what appears to be our purpose as a species. Taoism tells us that it is individuals who comprise the species and, as such, it is the overall direction the majority of individuals of our species are taking which we wish our species to take.

•

The big picture concerning what lies beyond the universe, why we exist, and what connection and purpose we have in regards to the whole picture of existence is an elusive concept. Taoism provides us with the concept of meditation, looking inward in order to sense the whole as we immerse ourselves within nature. This process prevents the materialism and fast paced life style of the West from distracting us.

#7. What significance does Taoism have to offer other life forms in the universe?

'...reality as a whole, which consists of all the individual ways.'

•

The Taoist concept of sensing one's purpose through contact with one's natural environment from which one's ancestry evolved (or was created), is critical. If one does have a purpose, if life has purpose, then it is quite possible that the most natural means of sensing this purpose is to immerse one's self within the natural environment from which one's physical being emerged. This process would need to occur for different lengths of time and different frequencies for different people and different life forms.

Although the frequencies and time spans may differ from individual to individual and from life form to life form, the principle remains the same. Connecting, sensing, feeling, however one wishes to express it, the process of understanding the purpose of one's journey through this physical universe, can most efficiently, intensely, confidently be done through immersion of one's self within one's natural environment. Taoism, by underlying this point, leads us to understand the significance of unique environments for unique life forms throughout the heavens.

We as individuals, as a species, as life forms have little choice but to take this responsibility seriously. If we do not, we destroy a major aspect of a life form, be it our own or another. If we are a part of the Causative Force, if we are a piece of the Causative Force, then the action of destroying environments is not as much an action taken against life forms but an action taken against the Causative Force. Symbiotic panentheism places a major responsibility upon all of us, terrestrial or otherwise.

•

Symbiotic panentheism blended with Taoism adds much purpose to Taoism. By acknowledging the specific need for nature, Taoism leads us to understand why nature is so important. Taoism, on the other hand, gains respectability with symbiotic panentheism for its message becomes a message not intended for just our species, Homo sapiens, but for all life forms throughout the universe. The homes of life forms throughout the universe are to be respected for what they are, natural niches within which life forms may immerse themselves to maintain their sense of purpose.

#8. What does Taoism imply about our significance in eternity?

Taoism implies we can connect ourselves to a sense of purpose. We can, by removing the distractions on the outside in order to concentrate on the inside, find peace with ourselves.

•

Just what is peace? Peace is a sense of understanding that there is purpose to life. Peace is sensing one is fulfilling that purpose, one is on track, one is doing what one is intended to do. But isn't this predestination, determinism, fatalism? How can one sense what does not exist? If everything is predetermined, then why is it that so many people feel they can obtain a sense of what is 'right' and 'wrong,' 'good' and 'bad,' 'to be done' and 'not to be done,' 'the correct thing to do' and 'incorrect action?' Taoist concepts only have meaning if freedom is a natural state. There are two forms of freedom: freedom from one's peers and freedom from the Causative Force.

Freedom from one's peers releases one from having to be subservient to the whims of others. One may lead one's own life. One has the ability and latitude to choose one's own actions. Freedom from the Causative Force is nothing other than the existence of free will. Freedom from having to be subservient to the whims of the Causative Force. One may lead one's own life. One has the ability and latitude to choose one's own actions. Without both forms of freedom, freedom from members of one's own species and freedom from what occupies the abstraction of existence without time, one is not free. Without freedom, attempting to stay in contact with one's self, one's sense of purpose, has no meaning. Determinism totally undermines the concept of Taoism, remaining in contact with one's self, one's purpose in order to choose that path.

•

Taoism implies we have a significance to eternity itself; we can impact eternity. If we could not, then attempting to connect with one's self, with abstraction, with a sense of purpose, would have no meaning since everything under determinism would already be pre-determined. If everything were predetermined, then being in contact or not being in contact with a sense of one's self and one's purpose would change nothing. Taoism tenaciously resolves to connect with eternity, the inner self, through nature, exemplifying the concept of our significance to eternity.

#9. What does Taoism imply about our relationship to the Causative Force?

'... the word is also used to mean reality as a whole, which consists of all the individual ways.'

•

It can be said that the West provides us with places to meditate. True, the West has its innumerable houses of worship in every community, but they are unavailable. They are all locked up to protect these places of meditation from disrespectful members of society. The West has its beautiful cathedrals reaching to the heavens. True, but they are filled with the unending procession of humanity streaming through its doors in an insatiable desire to see the wonders of the human potential to pay homage to its Creator. The West does have its regimented clockwork of opening the doors to its places of worship for four hours every seventh day, but meditation, the process of connecting individual awareness with the Causative Force, the whole, cannot be done through regimentation of conformity and communalism. The western approach of connecting with the whole has its place in terms of what lies outside the individual, but the western approach does not have the ability to maximize the potential of the individual to connect the essence it senses within itself to the essence of awareness, abstraction which lies outside itself. This outer essence lies beyond the boundaries of our universe. This outer essence of awareness from which the universe came, from which the individual came, from which the individual is isolated lies outside the individual but can only be reached by digging deep within the individual.

This is where Taoism comes into play. Taoism provides us with the process of maximizing our potential to sense our connection with a Causative Force. The means of doing so? Shucking the distractions of the West and immersing ourselves in isolation within nature.

•

This Taoistic process gives our inner essence, our souls, the opportunity to connect with the greater whole through the process of communing with nature, immersing ourselves within nature. Taoism is a process of letting go of the materialism and distractions of the West. Taoism is a serious means by which we can give our bodies and minds over to something we trust, nature, in order to allow our abstract to freely indulge and bask in the sense of connection to its origination without the worry of suspicions and distrust life imposes upon the indivdiual.

Conclusion: How do the concepts of Taoism reinforce the concept of symbiotic panentheism?

They do not; what is actually taking place is symbiotic panentheism is reinforcing the concept of the significance of Taoism.

•

The two, the East and the West, complement each other very nicely. To give one greater value over the other is to lose sight of the significance each has to offer. The West provides us with our understanding of what lies outside our essence, the external. The East provides us with the understanding of the internal essence and its sense of connection with the whole of existence, not just within the boundaries of the universe but well beyond this boundary and far into the realms that lay beyond the temporary border of our physical universe.

Taoism provides us with the understanding of why our environment is important to us, not in terms of the physical resources it has to offer but in terms of the 'church' it is for our inner essence, a place for meditation, a place for us to take refuge from the high paced life of the West. The environment is the physical home for our soul as we travel through this aspect of our existence. We have an obligation to keep it clean not just for ourselves but for the myriad of other souls that will be claiming it as their own and using it in their own efforts to remain connected. It's difficult to make a connection when smelling the fumes from rotting garbage, viewing dead fish along the river bank, tasting oily water from a bubbling stream, listening to sonic booms amongst the rustle of the leaves, and stepping on rusted cans littering the forest floor.

Taoism provides the reason for the environmentalist, the sense of purpose for the environmentalist, the connection of the environmentalist's work to the Causative Force Herself. Taoism has much to teach us.

•

The East brings out the best in our potential to gain knowledge of ourselves through meditation and intuition. The East has turned its efforts toward developing our ability to find the one small thread of an umbilical cord that was not cut as we were thrown into the isolation of the vast expanse of space known as the universe. This umbilical cord pulsates with the scientific sense of individual awareness, with the religious sense of total awareness, and with the philosophical sense of the whole being equal to the sum of its parts.

PHILOSOPHY

*What new insight has **Philosophy** firmly established within society?*

Ancient Philosophy: Nature of Reality

#0. What does the conceptual framework of ancient philosophy have to offer us?

The period of ancient philosophy extended from about 600 BC to the 500's AD. The earliest Greek studied the nature of reality, and suggested various theories about the universe. Some said the universe was made of a single substance. Others said that everything in the universe was alive ... maintained that numbers were the realities, and all other things in the universe were imitations of numbers.
　　　　　　　　　　　　　　　　　　　　　　　　　　　–World Book Encyclopedia, p. 348

•

　　The ancient philosophy oriented its perceptions around three concepts: substance, life, and abstractions. The universe was being divided into three distinct categories. The process would accelerate until it finally became a case where three distinct branches of perceptual study developed: religion – life, science – substance, and philosophy – abstraction.

　　These three branches became rivals in a power struggle over legitimacy. Ancient philosophy gave us a direction, initiating a debate that was to take place for thousands of years. The debate? What is reality? Is it substance, life or abstraction? Is there a difference between the three?

　　It was not the debate that was important, but the product of the debate. As we struggled to understand ourselves and our purpose for existence, our perceptions would change, and as our perceptions regarding who we are and why we exist changed, so changed our behaviors. It was the behavioral change that was the product of the debate and which began to define us as a species as well as our overall behavior as a species.

•

The further our perceptions extended regarding the size of existence, the more compassionate we became. As we moved from being geographically centered to earth centered, to solar centered, to galactic centered, to universe centered, we reached to expand the value of the individual. This was a type of direct relationship. As our perceptions regarding the size of what lay outside us, our universe, expanded, the value of what lay inside us, the individual, expanded.

#1. What does the conceptual framework of ancient philosophy imply about the universe within which we live?

Religion: life, '...universe was alive'
Science: substance
Philosophy: abstraction

•

In ancient times, we had a 'living' universe and today we have a 'Causative Force,' Mother nature. In ancient times, we had numbers being reality and today we have 'figments' of one's imagination. In ancient times, we had earth, air, fire, water and today we have matter, energy, anti-matter, anti-energy.

We think we have come so far, yet, upon closer examination, have we really? At first glance, the answer would seem to be, 'No.' Our understanding of the universe still orients around the concepts of substance, life, and abstraction – science, religion, and philosophy. But now our understanding of the intricacies of each has grown. As we begin to better understand each realm of perception, we appear to be gaining a better insight regarding how the three are interconnected and how they may reduce to the same basic, universal building blocks.

In ancient times, earth, air, fire, and water were separate substances. Now, matter and energy are understood to be two forms of the same thing: $E=mc^2$. In ancient times, we had gods of love, darkness, the sea, lightning, the overlord... Today, we have one Causative Force with many potentials. In ancient times, we had a three dimensional object having three dimensions. Today, we can theoretically reduce three dimensional objects to two dimensional objects (*see Topology*).

With matter's universal building block of a quark, life's universal building block of the cell, philosophy's universal building block of 'I exist,' we appear to be drawing closer to reducing science, religion, and philosophy to a universal perception. Religion, philosophy, and science were not separate entities during the time of the ancients. It was only after the ancients that they separated. They are still separate, but the movement seems toward union once again, a 'unified view' of a living universe.

•

Union, separation, union once again? Perhaps. What would this union be called? What better name than a unified view or a universal philosophy? And that, in itself, defines who should coordinate the project, for that is the very definition of the function of philosophy.

#2. How do the concepts of ancient philosophy reinforce the concept of panentheism?

Science: substance, '...the universe was made of a single substance'
Philosophy: abstraction
Religion: life

•

Today, we can scientifically visualize how the universe could be reduced to nothing and thus be created from nothing. Now we can scientifically visualize how awareness could leave a Causative Force and go back to a Causative Force (*see Symmetry*). Science is on the move and its movement appears to be directly towards a union of itself with faith and reason. The movement has begun towards a unified view, not of science, religion or philosophy, but of all three. The movement has begun towards a consensus of opinion of the three fields: science, religion, and philosophy. The movement has begun towards a consensus of perception fusing the three means we have of developing perceptions of ourselves: faith, observation, and reason. All appear to be moving towards the perception that there is a greater Reality than our reality, that our universe lies within something greater than itself and the material of which it is composed, and that our reality lies in a Causative Force, which is the definition of panentheism. If these three areas merge to build a model of existence and a temporary consensus as to why we, you and I, exist, then they will have brought themselves back to where ancient philosophy left off. Under a unified view, the three will have found a means of expanding the respect they have of each other and being able to work together. The means of allowing religion and science to remain independent of each other while fusing the results of their work is the very objective of philosophy.

•

We are, in essence, returning to the same mode as the ancient philosophers. Is there a difference? Absolutely, for in ancient times, life, substance, and abstraction were seen as distinctly different concepts with no means of understanding how they could be the same – but believing they were nonetheless. Today, we are drawing nearer to understanding how they can be the same while we continue to sense that they are distinctly different. We are beginning to understand how something physical can be generated from something non-physical.

#3. What does ancient philosophy reinforce about the significance of existence, life?

Philosophy: abstraction, '...numbers were the realities of the universe
Religion: life
Science: substance

•

If numbers were the true reality of the universe, then numbers such as 1, 2, 3... were elements of such a universe. It was not the number itself that was the entity; it was the concept. The written numeral was a hieroglyphic, a piece of chalk spread out on a piece of slate leaving the impression of a number symbol. If it was the concept of the number, not the numeral that was the essence of reality, then even the ancients recognized the perception of existence being a summation of its parts. The concept of oneness, the number one, was in essence the concept of the individual. The concept of twoness, the number two, was the concept of two individuals, and so forth. This would lead to the concept that the whole had no choice but to be the total of all the numbers, thus the whole was equal to the sum of its parts. Total awareness was equal to the sum of individual, unique, aware essences.

Ancient philosophy subscribed to the basic perception of what we think we understand today. The only difference lies in the details. Ancient philosophy could not place pieces of the puzzle made up of entropy, topology, Homo, ontology, Islam, Christianity... because they did not exist. Today, philosophy can use these pieces to construct more of the puzzle to give us a more complete view of the whole picture. Before philosophy can do this, however, philosophy must decide to do so, and modern philosophy has not made the decision to do so.

The ancient philosophers still have much to offer us. The ancient philosophers, like old craft masters, have an understanding to offer us that the primary purpose of philosophy is to develop an ongoing unified view, an ongoing living, universal philosophy.

•

The process of developing a universal philosophy, a unified view, is nothing less than what the ancient philosophers did thousands of years ago using the information they had available to them. The process they used was one of combining the three means we have of perceiving what it is we are and why we exist: faith – religion, observation – science, and reason – philosophy.

#4. How does ancient philosophy help us understand what life is?

Religion: life, '...universe was alive'
Science: substance, '...the universe was made of a single substance'
Philosophy: abstraction

•

Life seemed to be the primary focus of ancient philosophy. 'The universe was alive,' a living universe was made up of one substance – essence, a living universe is an abstraction. The ideas are really Hinduism without the name and the means of functioning best within life was basically concluded to be what modern religions say today: reduction of suffering – Buddhism, love one another – Christianity, and justice – Islam. They then went on to say the means of reinforcing our adherence to these concepts is by thinking clearly – ontology, and by observing what goes on around us – science.

Ancient philosophy provided the base and we have, over time, proceeded to reinforce their concepts. This is not to say they had all the answers, for they were as perplexed as we are today. They no more understood the total picture during their times than we do. That can change, however, if we start asking more universal questions, such as, 'What is life and why does it exist?'

But one may say we have been asking these questions forever. That's true, however, we have not been accepting the concept that the answer may never be fully understood. All we can hope for is answering the question to the best of our ability for any particular point in time. We must then realize that temporarily accepting this model will allow us to move on with the task of gathering more knowledge in order to further understand life and its relationship to the whole picture, our relationship to the whole, and how we can best accomplish our perceived purpose for existing.

•

If the universe is alive, filled with life, and if the universe is made of a single substance, then the essence of the universe would appear to be composed of life. The most complex form of life we 'know' is human, a physical being filled with abstract emotions and reasoning. The implication is that life is the abstract sense of awareness. This leads to the idea of total awareness being composed of its parts, individual pieces of awareness, individuals, you and I together.

#5. What does ancient philosophy have to offer us as individuals?

Science : substance, '...the universe was made of a single substance'
Philosophy: abstraction, '...numbers were the realities of the universe'
Religion: life

•

If the universe is teeming with life, then the universe is a niche for living things. But niches do not exist in isolation. Niches exist within a greater picture, niches exist as a part of a whole (*see Ecological Niche*). As a living being within this universe, we are a part of the universe, yet we are also a part of what the universe is a part of. If the universe is made of a single thing, a form of abstraction, then we are a part of the greater abstraction. We are a part of the Causative Force. We are a part of what we define as the abstraction within which our universe is immersed. But wouldn't this perception make us the Causative Force? No, it wouldn't make you 'the' Causative Force anymore than your foot is you, no more than a cell of your body is you. We can say the foot is human, we can say a cell is human, but we cannot say the foot, the cell, is 'a' human, 'is' you. But wouldn't the perception of being a part of the whole give us the power of the whole? Does a cell or a foot have the ability to do what you do? But doesn't that make us a part of the whole, which gives us no control over our lives and existence? That would be the case should the Causative Force be as limited and simplistic a life form as we humans are. This primitive perception of a Causative Force, however, was rejected by us thousands of years ago.

•

If the universe can be destroyed, so can life if it is just a form of matter, energy, anti-matter, and anti-energy. But the ancients did not feel we were four items. Rather, they felt the four could be eventually reduced down to one substance. By saying the one substance was the concept of numbers, they were saying the one substance was your essence, my essence, the essence of others, life was a form of abstraction. Why do we exist in this state, in this universe, separated from the whole while remaining within the whole? That is one of the primary questions we need to address in order to understand, for with understanding comes direction. Focused direction is the key to accelerating the progress we make towards becoming proficient at what it is we define as our function and responsibility in life.

#6. What significance does ancient philosophy have to offer us as a species?

Philosophy: abstraction, '...numbers were the realities of the universe'
Religion: life, '...universe was alive'
Science: substance

•

Part of ancient philosophy felt that numbers, concepts, and individual abstractions were what made up the universe. Many of them also felt the universe was 'alive,' not as stone existing within a greater entity, but rather as a living, thriving entity teeming with individual pieces of responsiveness and interactions. They thought of the universe interacting within itself.

They did not think of the universe interacting with what lay outside itself because they had no idea something could lay outside the universe. This was understandable, for they did not have much of the knowledge we have today. Had they had this knowledge, their general perceptions of interactions and a living universe imply that they would have accepted the idea of a universe interacting with not only what lay inside itself, but with what lay outside itself.

Ancient philosophy, as does philosophy today, basically held to the idea of being responsible. Responsibility is the key. Some would say that we as individuals are not very responsible, but how can one act responsibly if one does not understand what one's responsibility is? How can we expect individuals to act responsibly for life when we haven't even defined what life is? How can we act responsibly and direct our energies towards accomplishing the task set before us as rational living entities when we have not even defined what that task is, why life exists in the first place? And if the behavior of our species is a summation of its parts, the summation of individual actions, how can we expect our species to act responsibly if the parts, you and I, don't even know why we exist and what our purpose is for living?

•

It is crucial that philosophy gets back to the task ancient philosophy was attempting to accomplish. Philosophy needs to once again begin the process of defining what it is we are and why we exist. Our behavior as individuals and as a species is dependent upon just such a definition and as long as the definition remains undefined and in chaos, so does the overall behavior of the individual and our species.

#7. *What significance does ancient philosophy have to offer other life forms in the universe?*

Religion: life, '...universe was alive'
Science : substance, '... the universe was made of a single substance'
Philosophy: abstraction, '...numbers were the realities of the universe'

•

Responsibility, responsibility, responsibility… This is not a concept for just ourselves as individuals, nor for us as a species. It is a concept involving all life forms within our universe. A definition of life is nothing other than a simple statement providing the rational foundation for behavior. It does not say what the behavior should be; it provides the rationale for the behavior society sets in place. Religion provides the guidelines for behavior based upon faith. But this guideline for behavior needs a base upon which it can rest. If religions give the reason and emphasize one behavior over another simply, 'Because we said so' or 'Because the Causative Force said so' or 'Because if you don't you will go to hell and if you do you will go to heaven,' then they are setting the base of their argument upon a foundation of sand. The foundation has no solid substance to it because it does not go to the heart of the matter and answer the question, 'Why are our actions so important to what lies beyond our universe that our actions can determine our eternal state of existence?'

Religious descriptions of behavior are just that – descriptions of behavior. They have been very influential in our historical development and their influence and guiding principles are by no means irrelevant, but we have reached a point in our development when reason is taking its rightful place in our thoughts. As such, it is rapidly approaching the time when religion needs to strengthen its foundation or find itself resting upon a crumbling structure. Religion needs science – observation, the concrete, and religion needs philosophy – the tool capable of building the molds and forms within which the concrete can set. These two – science and philosophy – provide the fundamental foundation for religions, which guides our behaviors as individuals and as a species.

•

At this point, if we should encounter other life forms within the vast expanse of space, we would not be able to answer the most important question they may ask of us. The question, 'You and we are living things. What does being alive mean to you?' The answer to such a question will define for them how individuals of our species will interact with them.

#8. What does ancient philosophy imply about our significance in eternity?

Science : '...the universe was made of a single substance'
Philosophy: '...numbers were the realities of the universe'
Religion: '...universe was alive'

•

And what of science, the concrete? Doesn't the 'concrete,' the observable, take precedence over the intuitive, over faith, over religion? If ancient philosophy's perception of the abstract being the basic component of existence is correct, then it doesn't. If ancient philosophy is correct in its intuitive perception of existence being able to be reduced to a basic fundamental form of abstract awareness, then science, the study of the concrete, the study of the observable, would be nothing other than a study of one aspect of a state of being. Science would be the study of a state of being defined by an existence within a universe (or many) composed of matter and energy.

Science would be the study of the part of eternity that exists in time. But time is thought to be endless. No, time *was* thought to be endless. Now science feels that time is a product of the existence of matter and energy. If that is the case and if matter and energy cease to exist, then time will cease to exist for any individual pieces of awareness that exist within that universe. So it is, that the concrete moves over and makes room for the abstract, moves over for reason. So it is that the intuitive, what we sense through faith outlives the concrete through the logic of reason. So it is that we, an abstraction, become fused with eternity, affect eternity itself, through our presence within Her.

•

Eternity may very well be the Causative Force Herself. Ancient philosophy intuitively felt we were a part of this. Our being connected to eternity was most probably through a process of belonging, being a part of the whole, for the whole is not complete without all of its parts. The whole becomes lesser with the deletion of any part of itself.

To belong to eternity, to expand upon eternity through belonging, to add to eternity through observation, faith, and reason, to change eternity itself are significant reasons to direct one's behavior in a specific direction. And what direction should that be? That is the function of religion to define using the fundamental model of a unified view produced by philosophy.

#9. What does ancient philosophy imply about our relationship to the Causative Force?

Philosophy: abstraction
Religion: life
Science: substance

•

Ancient philosophy, with its concept of the universe composed of a single substance, the universe being a living entity, and existence being a form of abstraction, implies that by being a part of something, we have an interactive part to play with that something. We are not alone and She is not alone. We are companions to each other, comforting each other, providing for each other, wedded to each other.

The universe is made up of a single substance; the universe is alive. It all sounds so familiar. Even today, we have not let go of these ideas. Some of us say the universe is but an abstract idea, the universe is all there is, matter and energy are the essence of existence, the living earth, the living universe... Has it really changed? If it hasn't really changed, then what would this imply about the ideas ancient philosophy has to offer us, the generation of technology? What would it tell us about our relationship with the Causative Force?

The advances we have been making are not confined to the arena of change. Our advances have also developed within the arena of constancy, remaining the same. We have been solidifying our constancy through our ability to verify two things: one – what we have always sensed as a species and, two – our ability to expand what we can see of the total picture. As our knowledge grew, the basic picture remained fairly constant, but our ability to see more of this picture grew. Oddly enough, as the total picture grew, our intuitive perception, what we have always sensed as a species, only seemed to be reinforced. That is why we seem to have changed little in terms of our perceptions today as compared to the perceptions of ancient philosophy. The picture is more complete, the details are more vivid, the understanding is more in focus, but the overall basic foundation is primarily the same. The basic foundation: we exist, the universe exists, something – a Causative Force – initiated the universe, life existing within the universe most probably interacts with, and may in fact be a part of, the Causative Force Herself.

•

Perhaps it is time to deal with these issues, accept the existence of this relationship, and move on until it can be proven otherwise.

Conclusion: How do the concepts of ancient philosophy reinforce the concept of symbiotic panentheism?

They do not; what is actually taking place is symbiotic panentheism is reinforcing the concepts of the significance of ancient philosophy.

•

Ancient philosophy dealt with gods who took actions directly affecting the lives of humans. But ancient philosophy went a step further by acknowledging the ability of humans to directly affect the lives of the gods. They accepted the concept of an interactive relationship.

It may be considered a stretch to interpet this as a symbiotic relationship, but the ancient philosophers would be the first to admit they had no idea of the exact amount of time the gods were involving themselves with us. The degree to which we as individual humans and as a species influenced their lives also would have been unanswerable. Regardless of how much of their time the gods spent involved with us, ancient philosophy believed we interacted with the gods.

Ancient philosophy sensed we were capable of changing the lives of the gods, the actions and reactions of the gods, and how the gods interacted amongst themselves. It was believed we could affect the Causative Force. In short, this was a form of symbiosis.

And what of today? Western/Middle Eastern religions have rejected this concept of a two way interaction and embraced instead a one way interaction. Some would say moving to a one way interactive relationship with the Causative Force is an advancement in understanding. But perhaps this was not an advancement, but rather a regression. There is no reason we shouldn't reexamine our having let go of this symbiotic relationship with the Causative Force. After all, we have retained the ancient concepts of a Causative Force, immortality of the Causative Force, the potential for immortality of a mortal being, the existence of the universe, and the existence of the individual. Combine this with the understanding that the gods controlled what lay beyond man's reach, which implies something actually did lay beyond man's reach, and you have a rudimentary form of symbiotic panentheism – a unified view.

•

The West, with its ancient philosophy, and the East, with Hinduism, were defining basically the same thing: symbiotic panentheism.

PHILOSOPHY

*What new insight has **Philosophy**
firmly established within society?*

Early Christian Philosophy: Philosophy and Theology Split

PHILOSOPHY: MATRIX #350

#0. What does the conceptual framework of early Christian philosophy have to offer us?

The Christian era in philosophy lasted until about the 1400's. Philosophy came to depend more and more on reason, and became separated from theology. Religious leaders did not accept reason as a proper criterion for religious truths.

–World Book Encyclopedia, p. 349

•

Ancient philosophy provided our species with a unique concept: the idea of using philosophy to fuse our intuitive perceptions of faith with perceptions developed through observation. Ancient philosophy opened up the door to developing a unified view, a universal philosophy, which would be an ongoing, ever-changing view based upon faith and observation fused with reason. It was understood that this model would undergo constant revision as we expanded our knowledge and understanding.

Ancient philosophy was in the process of fusing knowledge we gained from science and religion with philosophy. Up until this time, the majority of the world separated these three from each other. Until the time of ancient philosophy, perceptions we had of our significance were generated by the strongest of the three at any particular point in time. As such, our perception of our significance for existing was analyzed in terms of one or the other of the three, not in terms of the overall picture. No particular model was able to captivate our total enthusiasm as a species and as individuals.

The ancient philosophy direction of developing a unified view would not last long, violently subdued and suppressed by early Christian philosophy. Once again, history was to repeat itself and reestablish the concept that the strongest survive. Religion, being stronger and more influential than science and philosophy, demonstrated its dominance over the other two. A unified view was repressed for another 1,500 years.

•

Early Christian philosophy was attempting to offer us significance for existing but instead found itself offering us an existence within a physical reality located outside a Causative Force. We were about to be defined as being located within what was considered to be a void.

#1. What did the conceptual framework of early Christian philosophy imply about the universe within which we live?

Philosophy came to depend more and more on reason, and became separated further and further from theology as it became less able to cope with the relentless questioning of the logic of its dogmas.

•

The universe was about to be dissected and examined in terms of its parts, rather than as a whole. Science, religion, and philosophy were about to conduct intensive independent examinations of reality, the individual, and larger Reality. Reason is only one of three means we have of establishing what it is we think we are and why we exist. Reason and observation had been rejected for centuries as means of developing legitimate perceptions of what the universe was, and why it existed. Religion claimed to be the sole means of answering these questions.

Early Christian philosophy, believing deeply in faith, rejected science in order to preserve dogmas of faith from having to undergo change – the natural state of all things in the universe. Fearing what religions could do to us, philosophy was rejected in order to avoid the 'eternal flames of hell.'

Reason – philosophy, and observation – science, had been beaten back so completely by early Christian philosophy that they were barely visible in society. Later, as science and philosophy timidly emerged, they naturally shied away from religion and each other. The religious oppression and intimidation of the past left its mark. Science and philosophy were about to emerge and grow in a vacuum. All three, philosophy, science, and religion, were about to become completely separate entities from each other. Instead of them working together to help us understand what life is and its significance as ancient philosophy had done, they were to shy away from each other in order to avoid intruding upon each other's turf.

•

The avoidance of intruding upon each other was not to be established out of respect, but out of fear. Early Christian philosophy dominated society and refused to return to a united view. For the next fifteen hundred years, the task of building a unified view to better understand what the universe is and why we exist within it, would be avoided like the plague. A unified view of reality and life would be one of the few things to remain in the dark ages.

#2. How did the concept of early Christian philosophy reinforce the concept of panentheism?

The universe was a physical entity and the Causative Force was an abstract entity. Together, they would rationally create a whole, a summation of the parts, but religion within early Christian philosophy was not about to surrender any of its turf and acknowledge such a concept.

•

Science, believing what we saw, was not recognized as an authorized means to understand our universe, let alone our significance within it. If what we saw was not an acceptable means by which we would gain insight into the Causative Force, then there was no way reason was to be treated any differently. So it was that panentheism was about to be not just ignored, but intentionally confined within a box. This innocuous box would be placed in storage for thousands of years. This box, Pandora's box, was to rest upon the shelves of the taboo.

Why would panentheism, the concept of a Causative Force being so large that She was truly omnipresent, be so threatening to early Christian philosophy? The reasons are too numerous to list in this matrix; however, a brief examination may be interesting considering religion's adamant position regarding the sanctity of an omnipresent characteristic for a Causative Force, while at the same time rejecting the idea of the universe being located 'within' the Causative Force.

An absolute rejection of the location of the universe being 'within' the Causative Force was and is necessary if one is to keep control of the keys that unlock the gate allowing entrance into the Causative Force. Control of these keys grants the power to gain and keep control of who will and who will not enter into the Causative Force. By definition, panentheism would automatically place all life, you and I, within the Causative Force. No one could keep us out of eternity. No group could prevent another group from entering. Panentheism says we exist in the universe, which in turn is within any entity that is all present, omnipresent. By religious definition, this is the Causative Force.

•

Through its absolute resolve to crush ancient philosophical concepts of uniting science, philosophy, and religion and to suppress panentheism through a conscious process of reducing it to an unknown state of existence, early Christian philosophy brings to mind Shakespeare's statement, "Me thinks thou dost protest too much."

#3. What does early Christian philosophy reinforce about the significance of existence, life?

Early Christian philosophy rejected the concept of omnipresence while professing to believe in it. All the while, however, this philosophy adamantly held onto the concept of the significance of life.

•

The concept of the individual possessing a quality known as eternal existence was a fundamental premise of early Christian philosophy. This was a complex issue and the scholars of the day were unable to determine a rational reason to explain it. If the scholars were unable to explain the rational for such a model, how could one expect the common individual to do so? Since we had no conception regarding the reason why life 'existed,' our only alternative was to rely upon someone to tell us 'why' eternal life must be.

We, as a species, as individuals, find it hard to give up hoping. As such, we accepted the process of letting others tell us why we existed. We sought out the most logical source of hope. We sought out faith, religion. Thus it was that religion was once again able to provide a model explaining the significance of life. Western/Middle Eastern religions built a model based upon the separation of 'good' and 'evil,' built upon the separation of 'heaven' and 'hell,' based upon the separation of the universe and the Causative Force.

So it was that omnipresence grew over atheism (a Causative Force not existing) and over pantheism (a Causative Force is the same size as the universe). Western/Middle Eastern religions expanded the Causative Force to a size larger than the universe but not large enough to have the universe located within it. The Causative Force grew but maintained the potential to grow even more. Behavior improved but maintained the potential to improve even more. Significance of life grew but maintained the potential to become even more significant.

•

Life gains significance each time we increase the size of the Causative Force. As such, it would seem only logical that we would want to increase our understanding of the size of the Causative Force to the greatest possible size we are capable of generating. Today, we have advanced science to the point of understanding the possibility of our universe having a boundary. The implication is that our universe may have an outside and, therefore, may in fact be located within something.

#4. How does early Christian philosophy help us understand what life is?

There are two statements we can make regarding our universe – our reality: our universe either exists within something or it does not. In either case, our definition of what life is becomes quite different.

•

If life exists, then the definition of life would most probably have to be derived from and account for either one of these two perceptions.

If life exists within the Causative Force (panentheism), then hope rises up and engulfs all individuals equally. Significance becomes absolute and rational rather than a possibility beyond our understanding. On the other hand, if life does not exist within the Causative Force because there is no outside to the universe, then hope begins to die out and eventually loses the warmth and comfort it had to offer us. Without an existence outside the universe, time becomes a major factor of our existence, for it permeates our universe. With no outside beyond our reality, time, being a function of matter and energy, becomes a characteristic of all living things and, thus, immortality becomes an irrational concept. In short, if nothing exists beyond the boundaries of our universe, immortality becomes illogical since time permeates our universe. With the elimination of the rationality of immortality, religions would lose their significance. Early Christian philosophy was not about to entertain any suggestions leading to this possibility.

So it was that early Christian philosophy expanded upon the size of the Causative Force over what western/Middle Eastern pre-Judaic faiths believed. Early Christian philosophy established the size of the Causative Force to be greater than physical reality, our universe. With the increase in size of the Causative Force came an elevation of the significance of the individual followed by an elevation of behavior.

•

Early Christian philosophy offered us an understanding of something greater existing than life. Something greater than the universe existed, and we had the opportunity to be a part of it if…. With philosophy questioning the qualifier, 'If …,' philosophy found itself in direct confrontation with religion, which refused to give up its control over the keys to the gates of 'heaven.' Religions, unwilling to be questioned, created a split between faith and reason. Religion moved on with its own existence ignoring scientific or philosophical perceptions contradicting religion.

#5. What does early Christian philosophy have to offer us as individuals?

Early Christian philosophy offered us, as individuals, the understanding that we all were to be givers of and recipients of a concept called 'unconditional love.'

•

The concept was of 'unconditional love,' not unconditional acceptance (*see Christianity*). Early Christian philosophy established the notion of Christian principles being acted out, not just verbalized. The foundation of this idea was literally sealed in blood through the ultimate actions of the individual the Christians called Christ. He reinforced this principle through the sacrifice of his life for others.

Early Christian philosophy focused its thoughts and works upon the basic concepts of its founder. Its founder and greatest teacher was felt to be two things in one. To Christians, Christ was a part of the Causative Force while at the same time Christ was a man – an individual. Without knowing it, early Christian philosophy offered us, as individuals, the potential of being both. This idea was very unsettling to early Christian philosophy. The question became, 'How could imperfection, evil, be located within a perfect being?' The easiest way of avoiding this topic was to proclaim it to be blasphemous and then reject it. Religion could do this, but philosophy could not. So religion walked away from the question and proclaimed the Causative Force to be omnipresent. Early Christian philosophy proclaimed the universe to be outside the Causative Force. And so the two remained intact for hundreds of years.

•

If the Causative Force is omnipresent, all present, then the universe must be within the Causative Force. If the universe is within the Causative Force, the universe and everything within it is a part, a piece, of the Causative Force. Therefore, you are a part of the Causative Force, as was Christ. As such you, as did Christ, have a responsibility to society, others, and yourself. You are responsible to see to it that all people, regardless of race, color, creed, health, physical capability, mental capability, sexual orientation, past history, personal beliefs, etc., are treated no less than we would treat the Causative Force Herself. And lest we forget, the environment is nothing less than the home of each and every one of us, the home of the Causative Force Herself, and thus deserves the same respect.

#6. What significance does early Christian philosophy have to offer us as a species?

Early Christian philosophy held fast to the Judaic concept: '...and God created man in His image, in the image of God created He man.' Could the Causative Force create something perfectly without it actually becoming that item?

•

If the Causative Force truly personifies the characteristic Homo sapiens have persistently attributed to Her, then She is truly omnipresent, omniscient, and omnipotent. As such, if She decided to create 'man' in Her image, She should have no problem knowing how to do so. She should have the ability, power, to do so and She most likely would do so within Herself because there would be nowhere else to place Her creation since She is presumed to be omnipresent, all present.

Would 'man' then be a piece of the Causative Force? This question is seldom discussed willingly in a rational fashion by people of 'faith.' The only reason, however, to ignore such a discussion is out of fear of having to change one's perceptions. But there is no change that needs to take place regarding Christians and their perception of Christ. The perception of panentheism still provides Christians with the ability to hold fast to their teachings. This new perception still allows for rationally acknowledging the purpose for Christ's coming – humans were on a behavioral path accelerating inhumanity of each of us to the other. The Christian concept of someone needing to bring the message of unconditional love still has its merits. If anything, our being a part of the Causative Force amplifies the need for such an action.

A unified view would not diminish the significance of Christian philosophy, nor of its rationale for who Christ was, why He came, and what it was He did. A model of a unified view would embrace this concept, just as it would embrace concepts of Hinduism, Judaism, Buddhism, Islam, ontology, and science. Christian philosophy would offer our species a plank of unconditional love built into the model of a unified view, a universal philosophy.

•

Any universal philosophy is just a model. Any universal philosophy model would not diminish the concepts of Christianity. What it would do is elevate our perception of what it is we think we are and why we exist, which in turn would elevate the need to improve the behavior of our species.

#7. What significance does early Christian philosophy have to offer other life forms in the universe?

Are there other life forms in the heavens capable of abstract thinking? Are there other life forms with the capacity to understand the concepts of eternity, existence beyond the boundaries of our universe – our physical reality, our being within a greater being, the concept of a Causative Force?

•

Early Christian philosophy had much to offer all life forms in the heavens. The concept of unconditional love was most likely not intended for Homo sapiens alone. Nowhere did it say, 'Love Homo sapiens as thyself.'

Although early Christian philosophy did not address the issue of unconditional love in terms of other life forms in the heavens, they, interestingly enough, analyzed it in terms of the generic sense. The message was clear and left clearly generic. The message was not left as unconditional love only for a select few, nor as unconditional love only for your fellow humans.

The message was also not unconditional acceptance. Tough love is very much a part of the general work established by early Christian philosophy. Unconditional love was not a case of accepting every type of behavior being acted out. Quite the contrary, the point was to not only give unconditional love but to take the responsibility to make sure all members of society were being treated in this fashion by yourself, by other members in society, and by society itself. Actions of abuse, hate, prejudice, intimidation, coercion, whether self inflicted, inflicted by others or inflicted by society, were actions to be eliminated. People's journeys were to be respected and assisted and it was your responsibility, my responsibility, to make sure this was accomplished.

•

The implication of Christian philosophy is that unconditional love belongs to all, not just humans. But Christian philosophy oriented around the idea of Christ coming to our planet, to earth. What possible reason could exist for such a visit to our planet? Perhaps the idea of Christ coming to this planet was significant in itself. Perhaps it provides some understanding and insight as to the significance we have as a species. Perhaps our evolution towards recognizing the value of the individual was a significant one. Perhaps, perhaps... but that will be up to religion to decide.

#8. What does early Christian philosophy imply about our significance in eternity?

Early Christian philosophy was oriented around understanding the idea of the actual existence of a Causative Force.

•

Early Christian philosophy was very much concerned with faith and reason. However, faith and reason were not given equal status. Faith was 'the' primary basis upon which religion was founded. Reason, on the other hand, was divided into two camps. Reason, which reinforced or unconditionally confirmed what religion professed, was embraced with open arms. Reason of this nature was used to demonstrate the rational nature of religion. Reason, which appeared to undermine or contradict religion, was rejected emphatically and absolutely. This type of reason was used to demonstrate the need for unquestioning faith. Religion had not learned to embrace one of the traits it so dearly admired, the trait of humility. Religion was unable to say, 'We don't know.' Any appearance of uncertainty, whether it be from the institution, the leaders or the members, was considered to be a sign of a lack of faith punishable by fire and brimstone.

As a result of the process of conditional acceptance, religion and reason split, causing each to disregard the other. Divided, religion and philosophy began their own independent investigation of existence, significance, purpose, immortality, and eternity.

The fact that philosophy would not lose interest in the very questions religion had persistently placed its energies and efforts said much about the concept of eternity. If philosophy had reemerged into its own and taken a different direction than religion, one may have concluded that the concept of eternity may not have been as significant to us as individuals and as a species as we had thought. But philosophy did not reemerge and begin establishing a concept completely separate from the concept of eternity. Philosophy was very much interested in eternity and the role we may play regarding eternity.

•

Not only did philosophy emerge as an independent process of examining eternity through the fields of cosmology and metaphysics, but science shortly afterwards emerged independent of religion and began an obsessive search for the outer and inner limits of our universe, our reality. Science began to examine what lay beyond the universe, what lay beyond the concept of time. Science began looking for eternity.

#9. What does early Christian philosophy imply about our relationship to the Causative Force?

Early Christian philosophy was concerned with the interaction of the Causative Force to reality – our universe. With the split of reason and faith, however, faith was no longer held accountable to reason and was able to subscribe to unreasonable arguments in the name of faith. In a sense, this was a form of religious poetic licensing granted by religion.

•

Other areas of perception were unwilling to acknowledge this process of granting religious poetic license. Thus, observation/science and reason/philosophy ignored religions and moved on by themselves. The end results for all three were surprisingly similar although attained by entirely different means.

Religion, using religious poetic license granted to itself, decided to declare the Causative Force to exist, to be omnipresent/all present, and humans to have an essence connected to this timeless concept of eternity. Religious poetic license allowed religion to ignore reason and observation and declare this Causative Force to be omnipresent, but then turned around and stated that reality was not within Her. Thus, religion was able to separate 'evil' from its picture of a 'perfectly good' being. Purpose for life emerged. Life existed for the purpose of singing praises and bolstering the ego of the Causative Force, an omnipresent, omniscient, omnipotent being. One of many more paradoxes arose, that of an all present, all knowing, all powerful being needing the reassurance that it was just that.

Philosophy, reason, began its search for eternity, the Causative Force, and an understanding of our relationship to this abstract Force. Within a thousand years, philosophy began evolving toward the concept of an omnipresent Causative Force, panentheism. And with it came a purpose, aiding the Causative Force to grow.

•

Science, observation, began its search for eternity, what lay beyond the universe, the abstract Force which initiated our universe, our reality. Within a short 500 years, science began evolving towards the concept of entropy – all physical realities must, at some point, come to an end. This implied there must be a beginning; we were created. Action and reaction, cause and effect, beginning and end, a Causative Force and Her creation interacting. Science was also coming to the same conclusion.

Conclusion: How do the concepts of early Christian philosophy reinforce the concept of symbiotic panentheism?

They do not; what is actually taking place is symbiotic panentheism is reinforcing the concepts of the significance of early Christian philosophy.

•

Symbiotic panentheism simply states: The Causative Force is omnipresent and whatever exists within the Causative Force must have some form of impact upon Her as well as She affecting what is inside Her, a symbiotic relationship.

Given the behavior they exhibit and the frailties of the human species, early Christian philosophy had a problem with the idea of humans being a piece of the Causative Force. Symbiotic panentheism does not imply the Causative Force has to be all present in terms of its location 'within' the universe nor does it imply a human being has all the knowledge, power, and presence of the Causative Force. Quite the contrary; this model of a universal philosophy, a unified view, goes as far as to say these very pieces of the Causative Force are almost totally amnesiac of their origin and past experiences 'within' this ultimate entity.

Also keep in mind that the model being examined within this trilogy is not professed to be 'the' model. The point of the trilogy is to develop a process for the creation of a model that is the most accurate model we are capable of creating at this particular point in time using faiths, observations, and logic we have been able to gather as a species. Early Christian philosophy is definitely a part of this.

•

We can no more ignore the perceptions of early Christian philosophy than we can the faiths of one billion Muslims, one billion Hindus, three hundred million Buddhists, three hundred million atheists, tens of millions of Jews or eight hundred million people who have no particular religious orientation. All views must be respected and the only way to do that is to build a foundation capable of rationalizing the right of all individuals to exist within a physical reality, whose intention is understood in broad principle by all. The intention of the unified view would be the creation of a universal philosophy. The operative phrases here are *unified view* and *universal*. One of the fundamental principles such a model would need to embrace in order to be unifying and universal is unconditional love, a basic principle of early Christian philosophy.

PHILOSOPHY

*What new insight has **Philosophy**
firmly established within society?*

Renaissance Philosophy: Process of Reason

#0. What does the conceptual framework of Renaissance philosophy have to offer us?

During the Renaissance: ...in the 1400's, 1500's, and early 1600's, philosophers turned their attention to the way things happen on earth, and the way people could seek truth through reason. Scientists of the era were so successful in their methods of investigation that these methods became the criteria for all other fields. Mathematics grew in importance...
–World Book Encyclopedia, p. 349

•

Basically what we are looking at is the development of the field of study called ontology (*see Ontology*). In essence, the realm of faith was not giving way to the realm of reason but rather just making room for reason. 'Renaissance' implies a rebirth, a revival, and there is no denying that applying the concept of reason to our understanding of what the universe is, what we are, and why we exist was a revival of reason from the past period of early Christian philosophy when reason was not the point. Faith was the point. This is not to say that reason was able to answer the questions. Quite the contrary, reason seemed to only add confusion to the debate. Confusion became so prevalent that we began questioning the rationality of our continued search for understanding. We could not prove the validity of our own existence and the existence of our physical reality let alone that of a Causative Force.

•

At this point in time, philosophy became very territorial. Religion was in the process of attempting to keep both science and philosophy out of what they considered to be their turf. Religion was desperately attempting to force scientific thought and pure philosophy back into their shells. Religion was becoming very abusive and the thought of even considering what science and philosophy had to say laid in the realm of heresy unless it totally and unequivocally supported the dogma of religion. But the Pandora box containing pure reason, unshackled by the restraints of faith, had been opened.
   Ontology began the search for the Causative Force and Renaissance philosophy began to search for the reason we exist – the reason 'why,' based entirely upon pure reason and independent of what faith and observation had to tell us. But Renaissance philosophy, ignoring faith and observation, was to find itself incapable of coming to any solid resolution.

#1. What does the conceptual framework of Renaissance philosophy imply about the universe within which we live?

Logic would seem to imply our universe was created. Logic, reason, would now begin its search for the answer to the questions: Why? Why does the universe exist? Why was the universe created? Why are we a part of it?

•

Initially, ontological philosophy, pure reason, may have been biased by faith as it tried to set forth a logical perception regarding what the universe is, why it exists, and why we exist within this reality we call the universe, but there is little denying that our obsession with the questions themselves did not diminish as we entered the Renaissance age of philosophy. In fact, our obsession with the questions may have become even more obsessive, for it not only preoccupied our intuitive thinking, faith, but it also preoccupied our rational thought, reason.

This period of philosophy was a major shift in our philosophical development. Once again, we were to understand that faith alone would not, could not, answer all our questions. This did not imply we were not building unified views regarding basic questions of purpose. Quite the opposite was taking place. Reason and faith were each building their own models of existence separate from the other. The point, however, is a sphere of perception, separate from religion, emerged and began asserting itself. This was the beginning of the process which was to open up the potential for uniting the three spheres of perception into one unified view.

•

To understand why the universe exists, we have to begin from the premise that the universe does exist. In other words, we begin from a point of faith. It is possible we could stumble across the ultimate reason for the existence of a universe, but to prove it is well beyond our ability at this point in time. If we, using pure reason, did accidentally stumble upon the ultimate purpose of existence, we would never know it. The most we can hope for is establishing the reason in terms of what religion/faith and science/observation have to offer us. Building a model explaining why we exist using religion and science is something we can cross check using what we sense and what we observe. Isolated, philosophy was unable to even validate existence. In order to understand existence, to create a unified view, a universal philosophy, we would need more than pure reason.

#2. How does Renaissance philosophy reinforce the concept of panentheism?

It begins to dawn on people that faith, as comforting as it may seem, is not enough. To say something 'is because we say so' does not necessarily make it so.

•

To say that the Causative Force is omnipresent, but the universe is not 'within' Her, does not seem reasonable. To say that we exist for no significant reason does not seem reasonable. To say that we exist 'within' a Causative Force but do not impact Her, we were created by a Creator for no reason, we were created by a Causative Force and placed within Her for no reason, are statements that do not seem reasonable.

Philosophy is the subject of reason intended to provide hypothetical answers based upon what we know at any particular point in time. Philosophy's very purpose is to develop a model, a unified view, capable of providing a reasonable explanation of what it is we see and sense. Philosophy is simply a tool we use to build a picture of what it is science and religion seem to be showing and telling us. Philosophy is a tool we use and reason is the tool philosophy uses.

Science seems to be showing us existence is a continual process of interaction. How can we ignore this? If we cannot ignore this observation, then what makes us think our existence only interacts with what lies within our universe? Reason would seem to imply our universe interacts with whatever it is the universe lies suspended within. As such, we, being a part of the universe, would impact upon what the universe lies within through the process of impacting the universe itself.

Our impact becomes even more significant if our essence moves beyond the physical world science studies and moves directly into the abstract essence of what lies beyond the boundaries of our universe. This is what religion tells us happens to our souls, our essence, our awareness. Science brings us to the boundaries of the universe, our physical reality, and religion carries us from there into the vast expanse of what lies beyond our universe into the Causative Force.

•

Reason would imply, if religions are correct in their presumption of the Causative Force being omnipresent, omniscient and omnipotent, that we actually are already in the Causative Force. Reason would appear to leave no other logical option open to us. Existence is significant not just to us but to the Causative Force Herself.

#3. What does Renaissance philosophy reinforce about the significance of existence, life?

Life has significance. What other reasonable explanation could be given for the effort needed to bring life into existence in the first place?

•

The concept of life having significance does not imply what type of significance. For all we know, we could be the excrement of a greater being having a specific significance. In the process of fulfilling what it is, we could be what was left over. No one can 'prove' or 'disprove' such a statement, but the absurdity of it seems to make it unreasonable. The word *absurdity*, however, is not what it seems to be, for it is no more absurd than the concept, 'You are a figment of my imagination.' The only reason both concepts are 'absurd' is because we do not 'wish' to accept such ideas. The repercussions such ideas would have upon society and ourselves would have what we call a 'negative' impact upon all of us. In other words, such ideas lead to the elimination of hope – hope that standing up to the trials and tribulations of life is meaningful, hope that our seemingly insignificance is not insignificant, hope that things will get better, and hope in an afterlife.

If some perceptions of reality seem to have more validity than others, it is only because we sense and have faith in the concept that there is a reason behind existence. Our faith, in turn, is reinforced by what we see. We do not see the universe as a barren, sterile environment. Rather, we see it as full of potential. We see it as a place filled with beauty and magnificence. We see it as a place teeming with life, breathtakingly colorful, filled with infinite variety. We see the universe as unique both in its entirety and its myriad of components. This endless display of the 'positive' makes it difficult for us to accept ourselves as a pile of waste deposited by some 'superior' being.

If we reject 'negative' perceptions, it is not because we could not rationalize the concepts. We are a most unusual creature. We are capable of rationalizing ourselves as being a pile of excrement if we put our minds to it. But we refuse to do so because of the absurdity of the idea. It would appear to be a waste of time.

•

If we are the ones establishing what we perceive to be the reason for our own existence, then we may as well go all the way and make it as positive, idealistic, and inspiring as is reasonably possible using what we see and the faith we embrace.

#4. How does Renaissance philosophy help us understand what life is?

If religions are correct in their intuitive sense of a Causative Force existing and being all present, then reason would tell us we must be inside Her. We must interact with Her.

•

As we go through life, we experience it as a series of observations and interactions within the physical universe. If the physical has a boundary, the awareness of the physical could conceivably be a part of the nonphysical that may lie beyond the physical. Time, being a function of the physical, implies that eternal existence could be a characteristic of the abstract. And on and on...

The more involved you get in terms of the details, the more intricate the web becomes and the more difficult it is to unravel the strands. The concentration level needed to understand all the ins and outs becomes very intense. So forget the details, ask a few simple questions, and try to give a few simple answers.

Does the universe exist? Yes, it appears to. Do you exist? Yes, you seem to. Do others exist? Yes, they seem to. Does life exist? Yes, it seems to. Are you aware? Yes, you seem to be. Are others aware? Yes, they seem to be. Is awareness physical? No, it does not seem to be. If the physical would be destroyed, would that mean the abstract, awareness, would also be destroyed? It does not seem that this would necessarily be so. Is it possible that your awareness could become a part of total awareness comprised in part of all individual awareness? Possibly.

•

No one is saying this is a fact. No one can 'prove' such concepts. That is why any explanation must be called a model. A model incorporating as many of the observations and faiths we can garner together is called a unified view of what we appear to know. It is called a universal philosophy whose purpose is not to act as a guideline but to act as a foundation for guidelines. It is a model intended to help us understand what it is we think we see. This is the purpose of philosophy. This is what we have been seeking as individuals and as a species but have been avoiding because we don't think it is reasonable to develop a model we cannot 'prove.' What we have forgotten is that we cannot 'prove' anything as being an 'absolute' and, because of this, we have not undertaken the most important task that remains before us. We have shrunk from developing a unified view of what it is we think we are. This reasonable view would elevate or diminish our very behavior as individuals and as a species.

#5. What does Renaissance philosophy have to offer us a:

We can use the process of reason to develop almost any perception we wish to develop regarding the significance of the individual.

•

We have developed perceptions we have of the individual throughout history. To those developing these perceptions, they have all seemed reasonable. We have had many models defining non-believers to be 'heathens' – less than human. These models led to the slaughter of hundreds of millions of individuals. We have had many models defining: 'To the winner go the spoils.' These models led to the slaughter of the 'loser' who numbered in the hundreds of millions. We have had many models defining 'superiority of race.' These models have led to enslavement, inhuman treatment, and death of millions upon millions. We have had models defining the rights of the strong over the weak. These models have led to the abuse, trauma, and death of billions upon billions of people. We could go on with this analysis of models we have built but the result would not change. The point is clear, models built in isolation that attempt to explain the significance of the individual lead to abuse, trauma, and death.

This does not mean we should stop building models that explain our significance for existence. We *should* stop building models in isolation. We must unite what we see with what we believe. We must unite the areas of religion and science. But this can only take place if we use something other than religion or science to do so because religion and science are as much interested in protecting their own turf as individuals are. If this is a reasonable observation, then that leaves only reason as the logical tool to unite the knowledge we have accumulated.

•

What could seem more reasonable than faith and observation, religion and science, united under the umbrella of reason? The very idea fits the defined purpose of philosophy. The very concept leaves science and religion independent of each other, allowing them to further investigate their own realms of perception in order to expand upon the view philosophy is able to assemble in a reasonable manner. And who benefits? You benefit, I benefit, other life forms in the heavens benefit, even the Causative Force benefits if the universal model we build is truly all embracing and universal.

#6. What significance does Renaissance philosophy have to offer us as a species?

It seems only reasonable that the whole is the summation of its parts. But you say, 'If I lose an arm, leg, kidney, I am still who I am.' That is a fair statement. However, there is no denying that you are no longer what you were before; you have changed.

•

Since reason tells us we exist, we have little choice but to assume we are a part of something. We may be part of only the universe and nothing else. But if the universe exists, then it is only reasonable to assume it is a part of something greater. This statement itself is nothing other than a statement confirming what we call a Causative Force. If that is the case, then it would seem reasonable that the Causative Force is a part of something bigger. Again, perhaps this is true. No wonder religion has a difficult time accepting the rationale of pure reason, which Renaissance philosophy opened up. Even Renaissance philosophy has a difficult time understanding itself.

Perhaps it is time we, as a species, divide reason into categories just as we do science and mathematics. Science and mathematics have their practical side and their cutting edge theoretical side. In a sense, this has already been done with philosophy. We have the philosophical study of how our universe interacts with what lies beyond it, cosmology and metaphysics, and how our universe interacts with what lies within it, existentialism, pragmatism, phenomenology. Perhaps if we removed the burden of having to deal with what lay beyond the Causative Force from the realm of cosmology and metaphysics, the two would develop a unified view of a Causative Force and the universe.

•

The process of removing the study of the Causative Force and Her interaction with what lies beyond Her can only take place if we put such a concept into another category. We cannot throw such a concept out and forget about it. There is no denying it exists. Once having created such a category and removing its realm out of the field of cosmology and metaphysics, these two can begin to build a model of a Causative Force, the universe, and ourselves. Cosmology and metaphysics would no longer be distracted by the questions, If the Causative Force created us, who created the Causative Force? If physical matter can be broken down into the abstract, what can the abstract be broken down to? The building of a unified view could then begin and our species could begin to understand why it exists.

#7. What significance does Renaissance philosophy have to offer life forms in the universe?

If we, using reason, can begin to understand the significance for the existence of our species, we would begin to have an understanding of the significance other life forms have for existing.

We have had many experiences with building models and defining significance, and none of them were very beneficial to humanity as a whole. Models based upon religions were very detrimental to the unbelievers. Models based upon what we saw – skin color, physical strength, gender, sexual orientation – proved again to be very detrimental to one group or another within society.

If we build a model of a united view based upon what we as Homo sapiens look like or what we believe, then we will once again have a model that will find itself covered with blood. This time, the blood may not just be human but the blood of other life forms outside our solar system.

The way to avoid this is to fall back upon the concept of Renaissance philosophy and use reason to develop a model broad enough to incorporate what we believe and what we see. But this is not enough. It must be a model so basic it would find itself able to withstand the onslaught of almost any new ideas we encounter. It must be strong enough and basic enough to resist any attempt made to refute it. It cannot be a religion, for religion is only as good as what we believe to be true. It cannot be a science, for science is only as good as what we think we see. It has to be a model based upon what seems reasonable in terms of what we see, believe, and reason.

To be almost irrefutable, the model would have to be based upon something outside the universe. As such, the abstraction would most likely become a model we could carry with us to the very edge of the universe itself. Standing at the very edge of our universe, leaning against the boundary, we would be able to say that the existence of this wall enclosing our very existence is proof of logic upon which our model is built. This wall is the symbol, we, earthlings and otherwise, have to unite in a common reason for existence, a common purpose, for all of us exist within a universe whose very walls we are leaning upon rest within another entity of some form. We, all of us in some manner or other, impact what lies beyond. We all have significance.

#8. What does Renaissance philosophy imply about our significance in eternity?

If there is no eternity, what would exist should the universe dissolve? Why is time a function of mass and energy if time is eternal? Why would the concept of eternal existence be a part of our thought process?

•

Just the fact of an idea existing provides some form of logic to the existence of such an idea. But, some would say, we think of spirits, ghosts, the devil, heaven and hell, and they do not exist. We think of UFO's, traveling to other galaxies, anti-gravity, and death rays, and they do not exist. We think in terms of an outside of the universe, abstract ideas, being pieces of the Causative Force, and purpose, and they do not exist. So what makes us think eternity exists?

First of all, the examples to which we referred are concepts found basically embraced by the fields of religion, science or philosophy. None of these ideas are embraced by all three. Yet most people embrace one or more of these ideas.

Eternity is different from all the concepts mentioned because it is embraced by all three areas. The fields of religion, science, and philosophy may not acknowledge this statement but there is little denying that they are all obsessed with finding eternity in some form or another. Religion holds fast to the concept of eternity out of faith. Science seeks to know what exists beyond time, beyond the universe. Philosophy is obsessed with finding what it calls the essence of life. Not only are all three infatuated with the concept of eternity but all three are infatuated with understanding how we could be connected to it and why. We should all hope eternity has significance, for we are most probably a part of it and, if eternity has no significance, most probably neither do we.

•

We seriously consider an idea to be valid when only one of the three, faith, observation or reason, seriously considers the idea to be reasonable. If such is the case, then why can't we consider an idea to be worthy of serious examination when all three appear to acknowledge the idea as valid? Reason would seem to imply eternity may just as surely exist as a physical world wrapped around time. And if eternity exists, there is no logical reason to think it has any less significance than time, something which most probably is a part – a subset – of eternity.

#9. What does Renaissance philosophy imply about our relationship to the Causative Force?

The idea of our being within a Causative Force leads to the idea of our interacting with a Causative Force. Reason, faith, and observation all seem to point in this direction to some degree or other.

•

Most religions appear to orient around the concept of a Causative Force existing and we being involved with Her. To some religions, we are intended to glorify this Force. To others, we are a means by which She obtains entertainment. Others think we are an object to be fought over by many abstract entities. Whatever the case, interaction takes place. Religions sense it is only reasonable for a Causative Force to exist and to have created this physical universe. Religions feel it is only reasonable to believe the Causative Force is aware of what She created and relates, interacts, in some manner with it.

Science believes we exist and moves on from there. Science does not base its own purpose upon an interaction between the Causative Force of the universe and humankind. Science works in a more aloof manner and begins from the point of our existing and functioning within a universe. But using the concept of our existing as a base is a statement of belief. Science is fairly certain we did not always exist. Science has the concepts of beginning and end, birth and death, expansion and contraction, and cause and effect, impregnated throughout each and every one of its fields of study. The universe is not exempt from this idea, and as such, the concept of a Causative Force is not new to science nor is the idea of our universe somehow interacting with such a Force. It would only seem reasonable, therefore, that we, being a part of the universe, would interact, in some manner or other, with the Causative Force.

•

The Causative Force, the universe, and you and I exist. The Causative Force, the universe, and you and I interact. Reason, supported by religion and science, tells us this is most likely true. Reason begins to offer us options over the religious concept of our being in a subservient state of supplication. Reason begins to offer us options over the scientific concept of our being in a state of existence with no purpose. A relationship between ourselves and a Causative Force begins to emerge as we combine what we know of all three: science, religion, and philosophy.

Conclusion: How do the concepts of Renaissance philosophy reinforce the concept of symbiotic panentheism?

They do not; what is actually taking place is symbiotic panentheism is reinforcing the concepts of the significance of Renaissance philosophy.

•

The process of reason was the major concept established by Renaissance philosophy and reason suggests life is more than life. Science tells us that all things change, change is inevitable, a biome is the sum of its parts, and each biome is a part of a greater biome. Niches fall within niches, all closed systems eventually die, the universe is bounded, and on and on it goes. All of this, all concepts in science, point toward the idea of our universe being a part of something greater than itself, which in turn interacts with its creation and its creation with symbiotic panentheism.

Religion tells us that the Causative Force exists, is located outside as well as inside our universe, is eternal, and is omnipresent. All of these concepts of major modern day religions point toward the idea of our universe being a part of something greater than itself, which in turn interacts with its creation and its creation with it, symbiotic panentheism.

Symbiotic panentheism is a model, only a model. It is a model that supports not only the ideas of science and religion, but the ideas of Renaissance philosophy, ancient philosophy, early Christian philosophy, Confucianism, Taoism, etc. None of these ideas emerged from symbiotic panentheism but, rather, symbiotic panentheism emerged from them. Symbiotic panentheism did not emerge from any *one* of them, but from the sum of them. This is as it should be for any model developed as a unified view, a universal philosophy.

•

But universal philosophies must go further than emerging from what we as humans believe and see. A unified view, a universal philosophy, must reach out to the very edge of the universe and embrace all within the universe or it is not universal. In fact, a universal philosophy must reach even beyond the boundary of the universe and embrace what the universe is a part of. Developing a universal philosophy capable of embracing only what is within the universe limits our existence to the universe, to time, to mortality. A universal philosophy must remain generic and capable of embracing the discovery of a myriad other 'universes,' each working to expand the omniscience of a Causative Force.

Philosophy

*What new insight has **Philosophy**
firmly established within society?*

Appeal to Reason and Experience: Elevating Human Reason and Individual Experience

PHILOSOPHY: MATRIX #370

#0. What does the conceptual framework of reason and experience have to offer us?

Appeal to reason: In the 1600's, human reason was elevated to a position of highest authority. Philosophical interest shifted radically from the supernatural to the natural. Philosophers used deductive reasoning to gain knowledge, with mathematics as their model. They believed that, just as mathematics starts from axioms, philosophic thought could start from axioms that are native to reason and are true independently of experience.

Appeal to experience: During the 1700's, epistemology, rather than metaphysics, became important... the only things we can know are phenomena, experience, all we can reach is probability, not truth. We can have no absolute or certain knowledge.

–World Book Encyclopedia, p. 350

•

There is so much here it is overwhelming. As we move along through the progression of our philosophical development, it becomes apparent we are moving in two directions.

Reason tells us we should be looking outward towards the heavens, towards the outer edge of the universe, to the boundary of the universe itself, and then through the edge into what lies beyond. Metaphysics, with the aid of reason and science, is the means of doing so.

Experience tells us we should be looking inward towards the mind, towards the inner edge of awareness, and then through the edge into what lies beyond. Epistemology, with the aid of experience and faith, is the means of doing so.

•

And just what are reason and epistemology, and how are they different? Reason orients around understanding what we see. In essence, it works outside of faith and within the realm of the concrete, the observable, the sphere of science.

Epistemology orients around understanding what we believe. In essence, it works inside faith and within the realm of the abstract, the conjectural, the sphere of religion.

PHILOSOPHY: MATRIX #371

#1. What does the conceptual framework of reason imply about the universe within which we live?

"...*philosophical thought could start from axioms that are native to reason and are true independently of experience.*"

•

You are number one; you exist. Science then moves to the left on the number line, to the left of the number one, you, and begins the process of dissection. You are made up of organ systems, which are made up of organs, which are made up of cellular tissues, which are made up of cellular particles, which are made up of molecular particles, which are made up of atomic particles, which are made up of subatomic particles, which are made up of... But it all starts with you; science acknowledges existence.

Science then moves to the right on the number line, to the right of the number one, you, and begins the process of building. You are part of an ecosystem, which is part of a planetary system, which is part of a star system, which is part of a galactic system, which is part of a universe, which is part of... But it all starts with you; science acknowledges existence.

There is no denying that science is moving in these directions. Science appears adamant to find what lies beyond our physical universe. Reason gives science the conviction of our being able to continue the progression of increasing size well beyond the universe and into the abstraction that lies beyond. But just as science finds it reasonable to reach beyond the physical boundaries of our universe and into the realm of what religions call a Causative Force, abstraction, it finds it unreasonable to search beyond the physical boundaries of our inner selves and into the realm of what religions call a soul, abstraction.

•

The apparent progression of increasing size would seem to be... The universe is a part of a larger system, abstraction, the Causative Force. The Causative Force, abstraction, is a part of a larger system, the... Reason supports the concept of panentheism, for panentheism simply states that the universe is inside the Causative Force, abstraction. Panentheism goes no further and makes no other claim about the Causative Force. The apparent progression of decreasing size would seem to be... You can be reduced down to the smallest basic part that goes beyond physical smallness and into the soul, abstraction, your awareness. And so it would seem the universe is simply a barrier between the two, intended to keep the two apart in order to provide the soul free will – symbiotic panentheism.

#2. How do the concepts of experience reinforce the concept of panentheism?

"...the only things we can know are phenomena, experience, all we can reach is probability not truth."

•

Experiencing is an abstract concept. We sense what is around ourselves but the experience itself is not concrete. Oh, there is no denying pain appears to be very real but if we had no awareness of pain, we would never feel it. We see the beauty of the sunset and sunrise but if we had no awareness, we would never experience its beauty. Reason tells us all physical events occur regardless of whether we are there to experience them or not. Experience, on the other hand, implies physical events do not occur. If we were not here to experience them, they would not exist for us. 'They would exist to someone else,' you say, but would they? This would only be true if there was other awareness to experience the events. If there was no awareness, would reality exist?

Awareness appears to be the key. If there were no pieces of awareness experiencing, could there be total awareness? And if not, would there be such a concept as 'causation,' a Causative Force? What exists exists even if the Causative Force of what exists has no awareness of existence. If that is the case, another question arises. If a Causative Force has no awareness, is it 'able' to create existence? Could an 'unaware' Causative Force create an abstract concept such as awareness? Such thinking quickly leads to the idea of awareness existing and being composed of pieces of awareness. In short, once again, panentheism jumps into the lead.

•

Put simply, it would appear philosophy is moving into the realm of individual awareness, abstraction, what religions call the soul. But is there such a thing as the soul? Since we can never 'know' 'truth', we must construct 'truths' to the best of our ability based upon the knowledge we have. This knowledge falls into two realms: the concrete and the abstract. The inability to know truth leads us to acknowledge we must accept both faith – what we believe, and observation – what we see. We have only logic – what we reason, to put the two together. We cannot reject either religion or science for observation is the sensing of the concrete which could in fact be the illusionary while faith is the sensing of the abstract which could in fact be the concrete. Since we do not 'know' and most likely never will 'know' which is which we have little choice but to work with both in our effort to create a unified view.

#3. What does reason reinforce about significance of existence, life?

Everything seems to change, but does it? Perhaps the significance of life is what remains constant. Perhaps it is here we will find stability.

•

Things appear complicated. That is because they are complicated. We have moved forward with all our perceptions. Our perception of the universe is based upon what we observe. Our knowledge is advancing so rapidly, we are doubling the total human store of knowledge every seven to ten years. That means seven to ten years from now, we, as a species, will know twice as much as we know now and in an additional seven to ten years, that will double again. This means we will know four times as much as we know now in fourteen to twenty years. This process does not become really understandable until we project this over a life time. Using the conservative figure of doubling our knowledge every ten years, the figures begin to look like the following:

person's age: knowledge since birth	increase in knowledge known	total increase of base knowledge
birth		
ten	2x's	2x's base
twenty	2x's	4x's base
thirty	2x's	8x's base
forty	2x's	16x's base
fifty	2x's	32x's base
sixty	2x's	64x's base
seventy	2x's	128x's base
eighty	2x's	256x's base
ninety	2x's	512x's base

What we reasonably know of our concrete universe will increase by five hundred twelve times from the time of one's birth to the approximate time of one's death. Amazing! Actually, incomprehensible! Yet if we have a significance in life, it is most probably the same now as when life began.

•

All this increase in knowledge implies, change, change, change... There is no comfort there. The only place we may be able to find stability and comfort is in significance. The purpose for life may be the only constant. Is it any wonder a unified view is so important?

#4. How does experience help us understand what life is?

Life exists. Few would refute that statement. However, is life physical existence?

•

There appears to be no end to knowledge. Many times in history, we had the sense we had learned everything. The grass was green and cows ate the grass and that was the end of it. Then we learned plant cells were green and chloroplasts photosynthesized within cells and that was the end of it. Then we learned chlorophyll was the green and the molecules in the chlorophyll absorbed light waves. Then we learned electrons jumped from orbit to orbit and photons of electromagnetic waves were absorbed or produced in the chlorophyll. Each time we were at an end, a new beginning emerged. There appears to be no end to our potential to learn.

Is gaining knowledge about what life 'is' or rather is gaining knowledge just one of many means by which we gain experience? Is life, then, what one has experienced, one's awareness? And if this is true, is this not just a small piece of total awareness? Again and again, we come back to panentheism, we being a part of, being within the total, being a piece of the summation. Again and again, we come back to the idea of 'something' being greater than the universe and we are a part of it located within a universe immersed in this abstract form.

Over and over again, reason appears to lead us to the concept of the concrete not being what life is but rather life is experiences accumulated through the concrete. Over and over again, reason appears to tell us that awareness of experience is the essence of the individual. Without awareness, no amount of interaction with our body would seem to have meaning. Without awareness, any interaction with our body would simply be interaction with a body without awareness. Life appears to be the interaction of the abstract with the concrete.

•

If one assumes awareness begins as a blank slate, one must assume awareness has a beginning and there is a time when one's first experience takes place. If awareness, the abstract, is the ability to experience the concrete, wouldn't it come from something other than the concrete and eventually go somewhere other than into the concrete? This is just what panentheism says. Life is awareness and it exists before life, during life, and after life.

#5. What does reason have to offer us as individuals?

Reason: "...philosophical thought could start from axioms..."
Experience: "...all we can reach is probability not truth."

•

The first axiom: you exist. This may or may not be true. As strange as this may sound, it does not matter which answer is correct. There are only two possibilities we can conceive of at this point. One, you do not exist, or two, you do exist.

Option one: you do not exist. If you do not exist physically, then you are an abstraction. Being an abstraction does not make your existence any less valid. If the universe can be broken down to true nothingness (*see Symmetry*), and if you existed, then you would be a form of abstraction, but you would still exist. Existence is existence. Therefore, if you did not exist physically, you would have to step back further than saying you do not exist physically; you would have to step further back and say your awareness does not exist. But if your awareness does not exist, you would not be in this discussion, for you would have no awareness of it. Descartes was referring to this when he said, "I think therefore I am." It was the abstract form of existence he was implying exists. Descartes was implying this abstraction of awareness would still exist even if the physical universe is found to be nothing but a form of illusion. There is no reasonable way to think of yourself as you, if, after peeling away the physical aspect of yourself, you find no abstract form of yourself. Without your abstract awareness existing, nothing has meaning to you. Without your existing, to you, everything is an illusion. Perhaps a more accurate way of saying this is that you are an illusion to everything if you do not exist.

Option two: you exist. If you exist, you have awareness. If you exist physically, but have no awareness, you do not exist to you. If you exist and have no awareness of your existence, you are simply a part of someone else's existence. For you, it is your awareness that gives your existence validity.

•

This all leads to the first axiom. You exist. The first axiom is not that a Causative Force exists. It is that you exist. Without you, a Causative Force has no significance to you, for you would not exist.

#6. What significance does experience have to offer us as a species?

If your awareness dies, you no longer exist. Your awareness has thus been destroyed. This process would be the beginning of the death of total awareness. No longer existing, for you, removes all significance of your life.

•

'Your existing', being the first axiom, does not diminish the significance of others. To others, the first axiom is the same as yours: they each individually exist. Existing individually does not eliminate the possibility of others existing. It simply allows for the second axiom: others exist. If you do not exist, this axiom is false. 'Others' cannot exist for you without your existing. Thus the axiom, 'Others exist' must be the second axiom after the axiom, 'You exist.'

It could be true that if you exist, 'others' could be figments of your imagination, but whichever the case, 'others' actually existing or 'others' being concepts you developed in your imagination, they still exist. If 'others' are ideas your mind created, they may not exist to themselves but they still exist to you. The second axiom is, 'Others exist.' The axioms are based upon both reason and experience. The order is based upon both reason and experience. The two axioms are not of equal significance. One follows the other and the order is sequential, not random. Without your existence as the base, the existence of others has no significance for you.

•

If you have awareness, are capable of sensing either consciously or subconsciously, and if what gives you awareness exists in others, then total awareness can be no less than the sum of everyone's awareness. As a species, this summation would not only be the sum of the five billion pieces of awareness existing today but the billions upon billions that existed before. This concept would imply awareness may be capable of transcending time, for if it cannot, then the billions upon billions of pieces of awareness that existed in the past would either no longer exist or would no longer exist once the universe died out (*see Entropy*). If these past pieces of awareness did or do die, this would imply they no longer or will no longer exist. The death of your awareness is no longer insignificant, for if your awareness dies, so too may the awareness of billions of pieces of awareness located upon this one tiny planet. Multiply this by trillions upon trillions of other planets and you have huge chunks of awareness dying. Eventually the statement, 'The Causative Force is dead,' could become a reality. Reason and experience lead us to rejecting this scenario.

*#7. What significance do reason and experience ha⸗
forms in the universe?*

A unified view is built upon axioms. The first few axioms are crucial. They not only provide the foundation for the model, they influence its final outcome – appearance.

•

Reason tells us the first axiom should be, 'You exist.' Without this, the Causative Force, the universe, and other life forms have no significance to you. If you are not independent of the Causative Force, you do not exist, rather you are an extension of the Causative Force. But the model of symbiotic panentheism says you are a part of the Causative Force, yet you have your own awareness. Isn't this contradictory? No, because the model says that while you may be a part of the Causative Force, you are independent of the Causative Force while in the state of traveling through, experiencing, this reality. Without this independence, free will, isolation, severance, and amnesia from the Causative Force, total awareness, you would not be you. Without isolation from the Causative Force, total awareness, you would be aware of, privy to, some form of omniscience, omnipresence, omnipotence. In short, you would never be able to be you; you would be a reflection of something else.

This has great significance to you. It has great significance to other Homo sapiens. But just as importantly, it has great significance to all life forms throughout the heavens, our universe, and all universes. This idea of adding to the total sum of awareness, growing total awareness, by independent bits and pieces, is what gives all life forms the 'right' to claim equal status, equal treatment, equal significance – equality. As such, the golden rule becomes a statement of philosophy, not religion.

•

The model of symbiotic panentheism is exemplified by the statement, 'Do unto others as you would have others do unto you,' but this need not be 'the' model. We could decide to consciously develop a model embracing the concept of, 'Do unto others before they can do unto you.' This model, like symbiotic panentheism, is easy to build. It also would act as a guide for general behavior. This alternate model would be based upon two concepts: a Causative Force transcends the universe and Homo sapiens are created to glorify the Causative Force. Under such a model, we would have a responsibility to coerce all awareness to do likewise. In essence, we would be perpetuating our past actions, for these are the two concepts underlying society today.

#8. What does reason and experience imply about our significance in eternity?

Perhaps all life has the same purpose and awareness is the means of preserving it eternally.

•

Is it possible to set up axioms that are native to reason and are truly independent of experience? Without experience, you have no awareness of your own. You could still exist and you could still have awareness, but this existence, awareness, would be premised upon the experience and awareness of some source other than your own. As such, it would not be 'your' awareness of experience. In short, you would not exist as yourself, rather you would exist as someone else.

Philosophy tries to categorize reasoning regarding the physical separately from experience, the abstract. There is nothing wrong with this approach. What becomes a problem is when these areas of philosophy see themselves as independent of each other. One cannot exist without the other. They are an integral part of each other. Therefore, to understand the picture that exists, one must put the pieces of the puzzle together and merge the two into a unified view. That is what brings the picture into better focus. The more integration that takes place, the more detail that is added to the picture, the more detail one obtains of the total picture, the better one understands. Understand what? Understand what life is, why life exists, why we, you and I, exist. With understanding comes behavioral changes. But can we ever truly understand? It doesn't matter because if we truly understood, we wouldn't 'know' this to be 'truth' anyway. Therefore, we may as well attempt to understand as best we can. We may as well develop an understanding that we are proud of having created. We may as well develop a model capable of sustaining the rigorous tests of the physical universe and a hypothetical abstract eternity.

•

Philosophy may find itself to be more productive if it would begin a practical development of a unified view. To do this, it would need to place the less practical matter of understanding the Causative Force into a separate category from the building of a unified view or universal philosophy. The mystery of understanding the creator of the Causative Force has been sidetracking philosophy for too long. The only way to get philosophy back on track in building a unified view is to place this theoretical concept of a creator of the creator into its own category.

#9. What does reason and experience imply about our relationship to the Causative Force?

Without you, nothing exists for you. Without you, everything reduces to zero. Zero may still exist but it has no significance for you.

•

Science to the right of me, religion to the left. The concrete to the right of me, abstract to the left. Reason to the right of me, experience to the left... However you wish to express the concept, essentially you are saying the same thing. You basically are saying you exist, you have awareness, and all else is derived from using your awareness as 'the' reference point. Without you, there is no awareness of which you are aware. Without you, nothing exists as far as you are concerned. In mathematics 'a' unit is measured by the number one. There are many number one's. Using a number line, we can see there are two number one's, the positive number one to the right of zero and the negative number one to the left of zero. There are also two number two's, etc. Graphing on an x, y axis, you will find four number one's, a positive number one on the x axis and a positive number one on the y axis. Then there are the two mirror images, a negative number one on the x axis and a negative number one on the y axis. In three dimensional space, there are a total of six number one's on the x, y, and z axis.

You can then move from three dimensions to four dimensions, x, y, z, and t (for time). The only number that has total uniqueness is zero. Be it 'coincidence' or 'significance,' the number zero is called, 'the origin.' But we are not talking about the origin here, we are talking about you. You are number one for without you, nothing exists for you. From this point of number one, we have the concrete on your right and the abstract on your left. All things are measured, all things move outward from, all significance, all concepts, all reason, all experience for you, orients outward from you. Without you, everything loses meaning, for things can only have meaning to you if you exist.

•

All relationships begin with you. The relationship between yourself and the Causative Force has to begin with you, with your awareness, for without you, there can be no relationship between you and the Causative Force. Perhaps the purpose of life is to provide total awareness – new and unique awareness of experiences. Your unique awareness of experiences could potentially grow what normally couldn't grow without you.

Conclusion: How do the concepts reason and experience reinforce the concept of symbiotic panentheism?

They do not; what is actually taking place is symbiotic panentheism is reinforcing the concept of the significance of reason and experience.

•

There is only one number zero. The number zero is the sum of all the positive and negative numbers. In a sense, you are one of these numbers. You are not zero. But being one of many is nothing to be disappointed about. The elimination of any number from the set of all numbers makes the set incomplete. If the number eight is removed from the set of numbers, a huge number of addition problems becomes impossible. Multiplication, division, subtraction, exponential operations, absolute values, summations, statistics, geometry, physics, astronomy, biology, chemistry, government, society, religion, philosophy, all collapse when the number eight disappears. The number eight is so important, if it were rejected from the set of numbers, all of reality would change, the Causative Force Herself, the origin, would be something different than what She is today.

You may wish to be the number zero, you may wish to be the origin, but this makes no sense. You did not, in your present state of existence, create the universe or other universes. Without you, things may be different; without you the Causative Force may be different, but they would still exist. Without you, you would not know existence existed but it would exist nonetheless. Because of this, it is not reasonable to think your experience is all there is. On the other hand, without all the pieces, without all the numbers, it is apparent that the number zero would have much less significance, much less potential for expression. Without all the other numbers, zero would be just that, zero, nothing, no awareness. Zero would disappear. The Causative Force would no longer exist. You are important to the Causative Force, which symbiotic panentheism verifies.

•

You exist, others exist, the summation of the elements, pieces, makes up the total. The total exists separate from, but at the same time as, a summation of its parts. The third axiom emerges, totality of awareness exists, a Causative Force exists. You exist, others exist, a Causative Force exists. All three are dependent upon the interaction of the others. Symbiotic panentheism emerges.

PHILOSOPHY

*What new insight has **Philosophy**
firmly established within society?*

Appeal to Humanism and Adjustment: The Human Being and Individual Adjustment

#0. What does the conceptual framework of humanism and adjustment have to offer us?

Appeal to humanism: Philosophers of the 1800's turned their attention to various aspects of human experience. The human being became the center of philosophic attention.

The Appeal to Adjustment: In the 1900's, philosophy has taken two major directions.
1. tried to build a systematic picture of physical reality based upon scientific development.
2. the other, on an increasing concern about humanity... They are concerned with how we can survive in, and adjust to, our changing world.
–World Book Encyclopedia, p. 351

•

The 1800s and 1900s brought the emphasis of the individual. It was the individual that experienced life, not the species as a whole. It was the individual that had to endure trauma and pain, not the species. It was the individual that loved and sang, not the species.

Sure it was the species that created the choir, but without the uniqueness of each individual voice, the whole meant nothing. As such, it was the individual upon whom we centered our attention as we addressed the issues of racism, genderism, sexualism, genocide, capital punishment, assisted suicide, cloning... Our efforts were being focused into what we had been drifting towards for thousands of years – the individual matters most.

•

Our attention encompassed more than the physical individual, however. Our attention focused in upon the essence of the individual. Religion seemed to be far ahead of science and philosophy in this regard. For thousands of years, religion held to the concept of the essence being nonphysical. Science, after centuries of searching, appears to be heading in this direction (*see Set Theory*), and philosophy seems to be on the verge of accepting this idea.

#1. What does the conceptual framework of humanism and adjustment imply about the universe within which we live?

We have no idea what we will find within the far distant locations of space. But we can be fairly sure that we will not find total compatibility and agreement awaiting us.

•

We have no reason to believe the universe will be awaiting us with open arms, acceptance, and utopian existence. If nothing else, we should have learned from religion, science, and philosophy that life runs rampant with change. Life is not an existence of pure pleasure. Life does not and has never exposed humanity to an existence of pure joy, happiness, and leisure. We have had to expend sweat, tears, blood, and life itself to get to a time in history where it appears we are solidifying the importance of the individual. This is not to imply the rights and significance of the individual have been established as an absolute. It simply appears to be where we are headed.

If this is where we are headed, history shows us we will be challenged over and over again regarding this perception. We have spilled our blood repeatedly in our refusal to let go of this idea. Blood has been sacrificed so often and in such great quantities that had the soil and water retained the blood, the surface of our planet would no longer be blue and brown as seen from space. Instead, the soil would be crimson and the waters would be bright red. In order to keep the appearance of the planet as it is rather than shades of red, we must remember.

•

We must never forget. We must never pass off our unselfish sacrificing as an exercise in futility. We will again have the choice of being dominated or face conflict and violence. Will we give up what we worked to accomplish, thinking that we are accepting something better? Will we attempt to hide the ugliness of our past in shame?

We must never forget. We must never hide from our past. We must stand up and be proud of what we have overcome. Our past has made us what we are and it is what we are that we will take with us into the far reaches of the universe. Our belief in the significance of the individual will be taken into space. The last step is to solidify this concept by raising the level of the individual to the level of the Causative Force Herself – a level so idealistic and untouchable that no physical or abstract concept we encounter will shake it.

#2. How do the concepts of humanism and adjustment reinforce the concept of panentheism?

Both humanism – the person being the center of philosophic attention, and adjustment – an increasing concern about humanity, did not develop as a trend. They evolved as offshoots of the direction we were historically taking as a species.

•

Philosophy is built upon reason and reason is not the primary element individuals within our species use as a base for their behavior. We are a visual creature, we react to what we see. 'Look out! Watch this! Let's see what happens if... It doesn't look right. Look what's happened. Seeing is believing.' We are also an intuitive creature; we react according to what we sense. 'That seems ludicrous! It doesn't feel right. It ought to be... I don't think so. I believe so. Have some faith in yourself.' These two areas, seeing and believing, are simply science and religion. Reason and philosophy do not have the ability to replace or dominate what we see or what we believe. It may never reach the point of doing so due to the type of creature we are and it is not being implied that it ever should.

But reason can reinforce the two. If the fundamental principles religion and science have in common are placed upon the table of reason, then a solid model, a unified view, of what it is we think we are and why we exist, can be built. This model could act as a beacon, a directional guide, a reference point, a stabilizing factor, a homing device for us as we travel throughout the far reaches of space.

And what is it that religion, science, and philosophy seem to either agree upon or are close to agreeing upon? Religion and science seem to agree we exist and philosophy seems to agree this is a reasonable idea. Religion and science seem to agree others exist and philosophy seems to agree this is a reasonable idea. Religion and science are close to agreeing the universe exists, is limited, is less than something beyond it and philosophy seems to agree this also is a reasonable idea. The word that describes this flow is *panentheism.*

•

We are on the verge of being able to establish a unified view. Creation of such a view would represent the first primitive model philosophy intends to build. And it is the philosophy of humanism and adjustment that are continuing the process of pointing us in the direction of the significance of the individual as the basic principle of this model.

#3. What do humanism and adjustment reinforce about the significance of existence, life?

Individual awareness becomes the basic building block of total awareness. Total awareness may be evolving from an infinite number of points within our universe as well as other universes.

•

We may be only one of many locations for individual pieces of awareness, but nevertheless we are one such location. With this in mind, we must then examine what it is we have to offer reality and a greater Reality should it exist.

If humanism and adjustment are correct in pointing towards the significance of the individual, then perhaps what we have to offer reality, our universe, is just such a perception. This may or may not be the case; there is, however, no denying the effort, sweat, and struggles we have persevered in order to establish just such a concept within our society. In fact, this struggle has permeated every inch of our historical timeline to the point of being one of the most universal principles we, as individuals, have attempted to establish globally. The struggle to establish the essence of the individual as being the basic building block of existence and establish the right of the individual to fulfill their own purpose in life unimpeded, are the number one and two fundamental principles for which we have consistently sacrificed our very lives, our very existence throughout history.

It is not our lives we said were important but rather the right to travel, journey through life unimpeded, free of the dominance of others, free to develop as we each individually saw fit to do. This drive through history was predicated upon the significance of life (which we had not defined) extending into eternity. Since we could not compare the impact different life journeys had upon the abstract concept of eternity, we accepted the concept of elevating all life onto a plane of equality.

•

The evolution of the concept of equality is a natural outcome from an understanding of the impact we have upon eternity should eternity exist. The further our perception of impacting existence reached, the greater our resolve became to establish the value of the individual and with it, the expectation we had regarding how the individual should be treated. We are now capable of making another leap regarding our potential impact upon eternity. We are now capable of making the leap of understanding how life could be a form of abstraction interacting with a Causative Force.

#4. How do humanism and adjustment help us understand what life is?

Humanism and adjustment focus on the individual. They imply that the individual is the basic component of life.

•

The individual is the basic component of life, not the hand, foot, arm, leg, heart or brain. Religion says the soul is the basic component of life. Science says awareness is the basic component of life. And what of philosophy? Philosophy says they are both correct. The philosophy of humanism centers around the individual and the philosophy of adjustment concerns itself with the well-being of the individual and helping it to adjust to change.

All three emphasize the individual. All three emphasize the essence of the individual. All three emphasize pieces of awareness, components of total awareness.

But it is not just religion, science, and philosophy that emphasize the essence, the awareness of the individual, as the basic building block of total awareness, which may well extend far beyond the confines of our physical universe. The totality of our historical past from beginning to end has been one struggle after another to establish the right of the individual to be who they are, to travel unimpeded, to be free from the domination, intimidation, abuse, and control others attempt to force upon them.

Religion, science, philosophy, and human history point towards our obsession with, our tenacity to establish, our willingness to sacrifice our very lives for the rights of the individual. And what do we see as the individual? We see it as life. We see it as an essence. We see it as awareness. We see it as part of a whole. In short, as a species, we see it as panentheism, symbiotic panentheism. We may not 'want' to call it that and we may not be 'willing' to call it that, but that is what it is. We may be able to deny the words but we cannot deny the actions, for after all, actions speak louder than words.

•

We understand what life is, we just haven't put it into words. We haven't put it into words because science, religion, and philosophy haven't agreed upon a vocabulary. One of them must step forward and mediate the process. This is the function of philosophy. It is time for philosophy to act.

#5. What do humanism and adjustment have to offer us as individuals?

We have developed an understanding of the importance of the individual. Any model we build must either accept this concept or deny the cause for which our blood has flowed throughout history.

•

If one steps back and looks at our history from a distance, an interesting picture appears to unfold. Our existence appears to be built upon alternating layers of behavior. One layer is composed of violence, abuse, intimidation, intolerance, jealousy, hate, vengeance, and self-serving actions reinforcing themselves to the point of generating a feeding frenzy of 'negative' human behavior. This behavior accelerates until it culminates with the development of such atrocious human behavior that it becomes unbearable to the mass of individual essences traveling through society. When this occurs, the individual essences, which have been independently journeying and experiencing life, unite to overcome the force emerging as a potential threat to the survival of the rights of the individual to travel life independently and unhindered by others. This pulling together begins the closure of the layer of negativism and begins a layer of positivism reinforcing the right of the individual to be unique and journey life in their own fashion.

These layers appear to build upon each other but are not totally isolated from each other. The 'good' is filled with the 'bad.' As the 'good' continues its progression through time, the 'bad' grows and accelerates until it eventually dominates, at which point it becomes the layer of the 'bad.' The 'bad' then continues its progression through time. During this segment of time, the 'good' grows and accelerates until it eventually overcomes the 'bad.' It then becomes the layer of the 'good' and as the 'good' continues its progression through time, the 'bad' grows and accelerates until it eventually overcomes the 'good.' At this point, it becomes the layer of the 'bad' and as the 'bad' continues its progression through time...

But it is not the 'good' and the 'bad' that are at the heart of these cycles. It is the individual responsible for individual behavior.

•

'Good' and 'bad' are not entities in and of themselves. They are terms we use to judge specific behavior. In essence, humanism and adjustment offer us, the individual, the burden of being responsible for our own individual actions.

#6. What significance do humanism and adjustment have to offer us as a species?

We have given blood, suffered trauma, lived through despair, and endured pain in order to establish the significance of the individual over the species.

•

We have come too far, suffered too much to abandon what we have established, what we believe as a species. And what is it we believe as a species? We believe the species is not an entity; we believe the species is simply a summation of its individuals. We believe it is the individuals who possess the soul. We believe the species is derived from the summation of its individual parts.

This is why philosophy in the 1800s and 1900s turned its attention to humanism and adjustment. In the 1800s, "The human being became the center of philosophic attention," and in the 1900s, philosophy became "concerned with how we can survive in, and adjust to, our changing world."

There is no denying the species is important. Most of us do not want to see the extinction of our species. But is it because we do not want to see the extinction of our species or is it because we know, once the species is extinct, there will be no humans left. Perhaps it is not even the elimination of the last human that concerns us as much as the thought that all of what we have achieved through human suffering and effort will have been endured for no apparent reason.

We are a species whose individual members, for the most part, have a strong sense of purpose. We clutch to it, we pray for it, we endure for it, we die for it. If one were to step back to overlook earth from a distance and focus in upon the individual struggles to maintain and perpetuate this sense of purpose and significance, one would undoubtedly feel great pride in the tenacity we display.

•

While pride would swell up in one's heart, so would humor and laughter. This would not be laughter at the pain. This would be a laughter of pride, for these individual humans would be seen for what they are. These individual humans are running around clutching a sense of significance and purpose they are so sure they have, but which they have not even defined for themselves because they don't realize this is what they must do as a species – define their own purpose, their own significance.

#7. What significance do humanism and adjustment have to offer other life forms in the universe?

We develop philosophy. Philosophy does not develop on its own. We believe we are discovering truths, but truths are what we develop them to be. Truths are fundamental perceptions we develop through the process of religion, science, and reason.

•

Humanism concentrated upon the individual. Adjustment concentrated upon finding understanding to help the individual survive and adjust to the changing world (*see Appeal to Reason and Experience*). Both orient around the individual.

It appears our orientation is leaning towards the individual. This will be very significant to other life forms that may exist in the universe. This direction logically leads to the recognition of all individuals as being significant, not just the human individual. Whether we consciously or subconsciously understood the process of developing the significance of the individual over the species is not what is important, nor what is being addressed within this trilogy. What is being addressed is the concept. If we continue our present direction and reinforce this infant concept, we will be developing an expanded form of the Magna Carta. We will be establishing the recognition of the significance of the individual as a universal concept, not a human concept.

It may well be that we find this concept to be unique to ourselves but that in no way makes it less valid. In fact, that should actually reinforce the belief we have in our having a purpose, a significance for existing. If we should turn out to be the only known life form capable of, willing to, establish the concept of all individuals, human or otherwise, having a higher order of purpose for existing, then we are unique amongst the life forms of the galaxy.

•

We appear to have been working towards the establishment of the rights of the individual ever since we have existed as a species. This is a universal goal. It is not universal in the sense that it is being courted by all life forms, rather it is a universal goal to establish a generic idea intended for all life forms. Attempting to establish the significance of the individual reaches beyond our species and embraces all species, all life forms throughout our universe. In fact, it reaches beyond our universe and into the infinite other universes that may exist. We, as a species, have much to offer other life forms in our universe or otherwise. We have hope to offer all life as we step into the heavens.

#8. What do humanism and adjustment imply about our significance in eternity?

If we are an immortal abstract being traveling within a mortal physical body, then we may actually impact eternity through the experiences we acquire. We may actually create newness.

•

We cannot ignore this possibility; it is too important. If we do not impact eternity, then so be it. But nothing is lost if we raise our goals to such an idealistic state. If we do impact eternity, then what better way to orient one's existence than attempting to improve eternity itself?

If we should define the purpose for ourselves as being an attempt to improve eternity, it not only could improve eternity, should eternity exist, but it would establish a priority for us to significantly improve upon the environment through which we travel as individuals. This would not only improve the quality of existence for ourselves but for other life forms throughout the universe and maybe even other life forms in other universes.

How does such an idealistic behavioral direction come about? It comes about through examination of what religion senses, science sees, and philosophy reasons. Philosophy is rapidly moving towards the significance of the individual and how to help individuals adjust to change. Science has shown us a system is a summation of the whole. No system is the same when a piece of it is permanently removed *(see Ecological Niche)*. Once the termination of a part of the system occurs, the system is changed. Religion has shown us that the individual being is so significant that whole faiths have grown up around concepts of 'an' eternal soul *(see Hinduism and Judaism)*, elimination of the suffering of the individual *(see Buddhism)*, unconditional love of the individual *(see Christianity)*, and justice for the individual *(see Islam)*.

We should never be ashamed of idealism. It is the means by which we set the high and lofty goals that move us forward, provide us with purpose, and give us hope. Working to improve eternity may be a goal higher than any we have yet established, but this should only reinforce its significance and potential for benefiting us all.

•

As a species, we have always established goals that were lofty and idealistic. Why would we quit now? Part of our problem appears to be the lack of such a lofty goal. It is time to establish a philosophical unified view to act as our foundation for the future.

#9. What do humanism and adjustment imply about our relationship to the Causative Force?

A Causative Force? We don't even know one exists! But we don't know one doesn't exist either.

•

Setting a universal goal based upon a model fusing religion, science, and philosophy develops a much stronger model than any formulated in isolation. It is more probable we will need, rather than not need, a strong model to support our resolve and sense of purpose as we travel the universe. Without our own sense of unique purpose defined, we would be all too vulnerable to losing our own identity as a species.

This may sound like a bunch of gibberish but all we have to do is examine our past history to find hundreds of examples where whole cultures literally or figuratively died out because they did not conform to their conquerors' beliefs and traditions.

If we have nothing to offer the universe as a summation of what individuals have worked to establish, then should we die out, our death would be no loss to either the universe or eternity. But if, on the other hand, we have something to offer our universe, offer eternity, then we have a better chance of making that offer and establishing it universally if we know what it is. The parts of such a concept would seem to need to include a minimum of three things: your awareness, the awareness of others, and total awareness.

Your awareness existing, the awareness of others existing, and total awareness existing as a sum of its parts, seem to be acceptable to the fields of religion, science, and philosophy. The degree of acceptance, the agreement regarding the meaning behind the three concepts, the uniformity of perception for each of these concepts is, however, not a given. There is no doubt there is a lot of work to do to establish a model acceptable to religion, science, and philosophy at the same time, but the effort needed to establish such a basic philosophical model could have a monumental positive impact upon not only ourselves as individuals but to all life and possibly upon the Causative Force Herself.

•

Such a possibility is so far reaching, to turn our back upon it would seem ludicrous. To turn our back upon it would in fact be turning our back upon what it is we appear to have been pursuing our entire existence.

Conclusion: How do the concepts of humanism and adjustment reinforce the concept of symbiotic panentheism?

It does not; what is actually taking place is symbiotic panentheism is reinforcing the concept of the significance of humanism and adjustment.

•

Panentheism simply states that the all is in the Causative Force. This is not a statement of religion, of faith. It simply states the universe is in something. This is not a guideline for behavior. It is a support of behavior we have been professing to be appropriate for ourselves as individuals. It is a logical statement capable of supporting all fundamental religious beliefs. It doesn't destroy the fundamentals. It provides a means by which we can rationalize them. It is simply a statement, but it is a statement that becomes the headwaters from which religions can claim origination. It is a fundamental upon which religion can fuse with science and philosophy.

Stating that the all is in the Causative Force is not a statement of science, of observation. It simply says the universe is in 'something.' It is a statement capable of explaining what we see. It supports what we see, what we have been observing all along. It is a logical statement capable of explaining the 'why' for entropy, the Big Bang, symmetry, larger sets, emptiness, niches, Homo sapiens, ... supporting all fundamental observations of what we have seen. It doesn't destroy the fundamentals. It provides a means by which we can rationalize them. It is just a statement, but it is a statement that becomes the headwaters from which science can claim origination. It is a fundamental upon which science can fuse with religion and philosophy.

And regarding philosophy? Panentheism is a philosophical statement of size upon which religion and science can rest.

•

But what of symbiosis? Symbiosis is the interaction between the parts, the parts and the whole, and the whole and its parts. Symbiosis is simply a word. Panentheism is a religious word, symbiosis is a scientific word and it is philosophy that brings them together. Philosophy remains neutral by not introducing its own terminology into the model of a unified view. Through the use of logic to fuse a religious concept science might accept with a scientific concept religion might accept, philosophy may find itself able to accomplish its task of building a unified view stronger than any one of the three could have built on their own. And who would benefit? All would benefit, from the smallest part to the largest whole.

Philosophy

*What new insight has **Philosophy**
firmly established within society?*

Symbiotic Panentheism: Understanding the Puzzle

#0. What does the conceptual framework of symbiotic panentheism have to offer us?

Symbiotic panentheism: a unified view. Panentheism is a concept of size. The Causative Force is omnipresent, all present. As such the universe is immersed within Her. Symbiosis is the concept of an interactive relationship. If we exist within something and it has an effect upon us, that is one thing. If we exist within something and it has an effect upon us but we also have an effect upon it, that is quite another.
  −You and I Together, In the Image of God, Stepping Up to the Creator

•

Symbiotic panentheism is a model of a unified view and what a unified view is capable of doing for us as individuals. Its purpose is to provide an example of how a unified view might be constructed. The model is not being put forward as the 'correct' model. It is simply constructed as 'a' model, a place from which philosophers, scientists, religious leaders, and the layman can begin the construction of what they believe the model should be. It is a model presenting a challenge: Here I am, now see if you can do better.

The process of developing a unified view is divided into six segments:
1. constructing the model
2. examining the impact the model would have upon the past, present, and future
3. examining the capability of the model to resolve present day social issues
4. examining the capability of the model to resolve future social issues
5. validating the model using religious, scientific, and philosophical concepts society has established
6. testing the model's capability to reduce trauma generated by hypothetical cataclysmic events.

•

This challenge is not just a figurative challenge; it is literal. You can find more regarding this challenge at the internet address: www.wehope.com.

#1. What does the conceptual framework of symbiotic panentheism imply about the universe within which we live?

Our universe is a big place. It is not going to reveal its secrets easily.

•

To go from Europe to the Americas was not easy in the beginning. To go from earth to the moon, to go from our solar system to another star, to go from this galaxy to another galaxy, to go from our universe to another universe... all these accomplishments will not be easy. But as difficult as the process of expanding our presence has been, it has always intrigued us. We have constantly sought to explore the frontiers we saw before us. As we gained more and more knowledge, we found more and more frontiers. New frontiers seem neverending. They now reach into the far expanse of the heavens, the inner sanctum of subatomic particles, the blackest depths of the oceans, the mysterious realm of the chromosomes, the silent complexity of the brain, the curious abstraction of existence, and the perplexing riddle of life.

Still we search even as the endless parade of new frontiers expose themselves to our insatiable curiosity. Each revelation opens new perceptions which we eagerly examine as we search for the understanding of the most elusive questions we ask: What is life? Why does it exist? What is our purpose for existing? What is the universe? Where is the universe? The questions are metaphysical and the answers we obtain from science and religion are the means by which we gain knowledge that allows us to develop hypothetical answers. The universe offers us the understanding of its immense size and with this understanding comes the realization that we must use reason to incorporate what the universe has to show us with what we believe, in order to understand ourselves, in order to understand the universe, in order to understand what lies beyond the universe.

•

We cannot understand the total picture unless we understand its parts and we cannot understand the parts unless we understand the total picture. The universe is part of the picture. You are a part of the picture. I am a part of the picture. Whether or not the Causative Force is just a part of the total picture or is viewed 'as' the total picture is unimportant. What is important is that the concepts of the universe, you, I, and the Causative Force appear to exist and in order to understand one or the other, we have no choice but to understand them all. They all appear to be interconnected. Science and religion appear to be the means of studying them and philosophy, reason, appears to be the glue to hold the pieces together.

#2. How do the concepts of symbiotic panentheism reinforce the concept of panentheism?

We exist within the universe. The universe is a place within which we can experience, create, produce ripples, speculate, and form perceptions.

•

Some would say all this experiencing does not come from the framework of free will. If this is true, then it is not creative, it is simply a rehash of what has taken place before. The implication is that life is a series of reruns taking place here on earth. Further, this would imply the reruns are repeated over and over and over throughout our universe. As if this wasn't enough, the events are then repeated in the same manner an infinite number of times throughout time. Can we stop there? No, for we may very well find the concept of parallel universes and multiple universes to be a fact. In such an event, the reruns would be constantly showing at all theaters throughout the greater Reality within which all these universes lie.

Our universe lying within a greater Reality and other universes lying within this same Reality is simply panentheism. The concept of predetermined action makes no sense. The monotony of an infinite number of reruns would be enough to drive an intelligent being insane. Some would argue such is the case, but this trilogy begins with the assumption that the Causative Force is sane.

As such, one would have little choice but to reject the concept of determinism along with all the paradoxes it generates, in favor of free will. Accepting free will does not place one in isolation. Free will is reinforced by religion, by science, and by philosophy – you are responsible for your actions.

•

Without free will, there would be no accountability for the individual, the universe would have no meaning, and the Causative Force would have no way of changing, growing, using its omnipresence, omniscience, and omnipotence to Her fullest potential. Without free will, action has no meaning. Without free will, the individual, the universe, and the Causative Force Herself become meaningless. Panentheism provides the understanding regarding why the individual is so important and why free will, freedom, is the key.

#3. What does symbiotic panentheism reinforce about the significance of existence, life?

Life has no apparent significance to itself if life's experiences are predetermined.

•

We exist. We exist within the universe. As such, the universe offers us a place to travel and experience. Free will provides us with the ability to travel as we determine, not as has been determined for us. As such, our new experiences become unique to us and form our awareness. If we are our awareness, then we are a form of abstraction. If total awareness is total, it would imply our awareness must be a part of it.

Free will gives us the potential to develop as a unique piece of awareness with unique experiences. The same process would seem to apply to total awareness or what we call the Causative Force, for total awareness would appear to be a summation of its unique pieces just as we are a summation of our total experiences.

The process is reinforced by the concept of panentheism, the concept of being immersed within total awareness. Under symbiotic panentheism, life becomes significant for two reasons. Not only is it a piece of the Causative Force, but it actually is a process by which the Causative Force grows. Free will provides the process by which it can grow and the universe becomes the means by which a piece of the Causative Force can isolate itself from itself in order to gain unique awareness uninfluenced by its power, knowledge, and presence. Panentheism provides the location, the place, for the universe. The universe provides the location, the place, for pieces of individual awareness. Individual awareness provides the location, the place, for experiencing. Experiencing provides the location, the place, for free will to operate. Individual life forms have no meaning to themselves within the confines of predestination. Free will, on the other hand, provides a significance for life to both a Causative Force and to all individual life forms.

•

Freedom and free will are, in essence, the same thing. Freedom implies the right of self determination without being dominated, abused or manipulated by other physical life forms, terrestrial or otherwise. Free will implies the right of self determination without being dominated, abused or manipulated by a Causative Force. To have one without the other is the same as having no freedom at all.

#4. How does symbiotic panentheism help us understand what life is?

Life exists but what is life? It is one thing to quarrel within the family; it is quite another to quarrel within the company of others.

•

We have been arguing and bickering over the definition of life ever since we came up with the term. We cannot say 'ever since we came up with the concept' because, after all these thousands of years, we don't even understand what the concept is. We haven't defined the concept. Without defining what life is, how are we to know when we are protecting life, respecting life or providing life freedom?

Religion, not science, goes the furthest towards defining what life is. Religion describes three levels of existence.

Level one: existence – atom, rock, river, planet, star...

Level two: existence with awareness of physical surroundings – bacteria, worm, bird, deer...

Level three: existence with awareness of physical surroundings and awareness of abstraction – humans...

Science has accepted levels one and two but is still wrestling with level three. Philosophy has accepted level one but is still wrestling with levels two and three.

As Homo sapiens, we quarrel over the idea of what life is and, as such, we have our family feuds: abortion, assisted suicide, genocide, infanticide, capital punishment, artificial insemination, fetal tissue research... The quarrels go on and on with no apparent end because we haven't defined one four letter word: life. All this quarreling takes place because the three, religion, science, and philosophy, have not come to a consensus as to what life is. In addition, the quarreling will continue to go on until they do come to some form of consensus.

It is one thing to stay confined on our own planet and quarrel; it is quite another to continue sniping at each other across the vastness of space. It is time we define life.

•

Defining life is the function of philosophy. Do not misunderstand. It is not the function of philosophy to define life while disregarding science – what we see, and religion – what we believe. It is the function of philosophy to define life through the process of mediation. Establishing a unified view, building a universal philosophy regarding life, is just such a process and like all things in the universe, it changes with time and understanding.

#5. What does symbiotic panentheism have to offer us as individuals?

Symbiotic panentheism offers us freedom. It offers us not only freedom from the oppressive hand of our fellow humans, nor from the potentially oppressive hand of other life forms, but freedom from the potentially oppressive hand of the Causative Force Herself.

•

The idea of our living in a state of free will goes to the heart of what we as individuals, comprising the species Homo sapiens, have been striving to establish throughout our history. Responsibility for one's actions depends upon the acceptance of just such a concept. Hope depends upon the concept. Significance for life, willingness to struggle with adversities, idealism, sacrifice, compassion, and tolerance all depend upon the concept that we, you and I, have the free will to act as we so determine. Without free will, we do not have the obligation to shoulder the responsibility for any of these behaviors.

Without free will, awareness, each of us loses our independence and simply becomes awareness. Without free will, the ability to influence total awareness loses its potential. Without free will, awareness becomes simply a means by which experience flows into total awareness rather than an independent entity capable of creating the awareness it takes back to total awareness. The difference is what separates an entity from being an entity itself or just an extension of a greater being. In short, without free will, you do not exist as yourself.

•

Free will begins with the word *free* and it is freedom for the individual to travel and experience that we have been attempting to establish throughout our history. Why would we spill human blood throughout history in order to establish the concept of freedom and then turn around and give up freedom by accepting a philosophical concept known as determinism, predestination?

It is not just religion, science, and philosophy that give free will validity. The voluntary sacrifice of the rivers of blood throughout our history also adds validity to the concept of free will. We have earned the right, the freedom, to choose how we define our own destiny, our purpose for existence. Having earned the right, we must now choose to do so and then proceed to do so. If we do not, some other life form may choose to define our purpose in life for us and we may find our freedom gone forever.

#6. What significance does symbiotic panentheism have to offer us as a species?

We as a species must have faith in what it is we have been doing in the past, are doing in the present, and appear to be headed towards in the future.

•

We cannot stop what we are doing and change directions just because what we are doing may be perceived to be ludicrous to another life form. We cannot give up in despair and declare all of what we see, believe, and reason to be invalid just because it could be perceived differently by another life form with a different interpretation. We cannot second guess ourselves and become mired in conflict, disagreements, self doubt, and inferiority regarding our ability to interpret what it is we see, believe, and reason when we come into contact with what we may believe to be 'more intelligent' life forms that we admire.

We must remain strong. We must remain sure of ourselves and what it is our whole history of suffering and pain has directed us towards. We are so naive as a species. We are so young as a species. We are so impressionable as a species. We are almost sure to buckle, fold, compromise our significance, compromise our purpose for existing when being exposed to perceptions of other life forms, unless we define the purpose and significance before such a contact.

This examination is a process of understanding. It is a process of developing a mission statement for our species that represents what it is we as individuals throughout history have been attempting to protect. It is a process of building a model of what it is we represent, believe, and wish to establish globally, galacticly, universally. This understanding is nothing less than the establishment of a unified view that is truly universal.

•

We have so much to be proud of as a species. The summation of our behavior has been valiant, filled with hope, compassionate, tenacious... Many would say, 'No, our behavior has been shameful, despicable, inhumane, lustful, greedy, self serving...' There is no denying these perceptions. But there is no denying that for every negative act, people have come forth and worked to overcome these indecencies. Not only have they come forward to do so, they have given their very lives to do so. The glass is not half empty; the glass is half full and rising.

#7. What significance does symbiotic panentheism have to offer other life forms in the universe?

We have worked as individuals and as a species to develop the concept of equality. Will we insist equality is a right of all life or will we insist equality belongs only to our genus and species, to Homo sapiens?

•

Universal truths are universal truths. This is an important concept because it applies directly to this particular situation. Either freedom to travel reality is a basic fundamental of the universe or it is not. If it is, we have no choice but to accept the concept as belonging to all beings in the universe. If we do not accept the concept of freedom being a universal truth, we open up the prospect of being isolated from the rest of the universe in an attempt to keep this idealistic concept as our own.

Idealism is only the correct word if we share the idea with others. If we selfishly keep the idea as our own, the word remains idealistic only within our own ranks but loses it sense of idealism outside of humanity.

And who is to be granted this concept of freedom, freedom from each other and freedom from the Causative Force? We exist. We exist and are aware of our physical surroundings. We exist, are aware of our physical surroundings, and are aware of our abstract surroundings. We not only love but we are aware we love. This appears to be a level above most other life forms on earth. We not only are sad; we are aware of what this means. We are capable of understanding the abstraction. A dog may love its master but it does not appear capable of going to the next level of understanding that it loves. Can other life forms such as dolphins do so? It is difficult to say. We have much to learn. But until we know, we have an obligation under the model of symbiotic panentheism to treat them as if they do have this capacity.

•

Under symbiotic panentheism, simple existence deserves respect for what it is, existence within the Causative Force. As such, it is a piece of the Causative Force and, if for no other reason, deserves respect. But existence, any existence, terrestrial or otherwise, with awareness of the abstract raises one to the level of being made in the image of the Causative Force, earning one not only the right to respect but the right to freedom.

#8. What does symbiotic panentheism imply about our significance in eternity?

Symbiotic panentheism offers hope when it appears there is no hope.
•
Science may be on the verge of telling us the universe will someday die. We are in the universe. It appears there is no hope. But symbiotic panentheism says there is more to life than the physical. Symbiotic panentheism says there is awareness. Science says awareness is an abstraction. This puts science in the position of having to modify what it says. Now science must say, 'The physical universe will someday die.' Science does not know enough about abstraction or awareness – awareness of love, awareness of hate, awareness of jealousy, awareness of hope, awareness of despair – to know if awareness can be destroyed or if it exists forever in some form or other. The point is, symbiotic panentheism forces science into modifying its statements of gloom and doom with the qualifier its statements apply to physical existence. Hope is maintained.

Religion is on the verge of telling us we have no moral right to 'create life.' The implication is that life can be created. If we, mere mortals, can create life, then life may not be as significant as we had presumed. But symbiotic panentheism says the physical body is not what life is. Symbiotic panentheism says life is a piece of the Causative Force placed by the Causative Force into a vehicle capable of perceiving its surroundings on various levels of consciousness. To be more specific, symbiotic panentheism says life is a piece of the Causative Force operating within a temporary physical universe, amnesiac of Herself, existing as an individual, in order to travel and experience uninfluenced by Her own greatness. This purity of travel allows true free will to operate. The concept of creating life no longer becomes creation of life but rather creation of a vehicle capable of hosting a piece of the Causative Force. The vehicle is not made in the image of the Causative Force but rather a piece of the Causative Force may be placed by Her within a creation of humankind. What an honor, and again despair turns to hope.
•
And what of philosophy? Philosophy is the only branch of the three purely abstract enough to bring science and religion together within a model, a unified view capable of explaining such concepts. Philosophy is the uniting force – the mediator for physical reality and abstract eternity.

#9. What does symbiotic panentheism imply about our relationship to the Causative Force?

Be proud of what we have accomplished. There may be more to do but we have already accomplished much. We have not completed our growth and we are still moving forward.

•

We have two choices, we can hang our heads in shame over our past or we can hold our heads high, proud of our past. But why should we be ashamed? Every attempt upon the part of a few individuals to dominate, abuse, intimidate, and subjugate others within our society has been met with resistance and, in the end, has been repelled. Our concept of having the right to be free has never left us. Thousands of years ago, it was only a small seed waiting to germinate. Today, it has grown tall, proud, and healthy. It has grown so tall and spread so far, it has gotten to the point where one man, unarmed and standing his ground against a forty ton roaring steel monster, can bring that monster to a grinding halt. This action at Tiananmen Square in China in 1989 was very symbolic of just how far the rights of the individual have come. The concept of one individual being able to bring a government of two billion people to a halt by standing his ground would have been unfathomable in 1500 BC, the point at which this book began.

Symbiotic panentheism is just one more step in the direction of freedom. Symbiotic panentheism is a model establishing the concept of our having free will. Under such an idea, freedom becomes a concept connected directly to eternity and establishes a new relationship between ourselves and the Causative Force. Now existence and our actions while existing become a serious responsibility. Under symbiotic panentheism, not only do we exist 'within' the Causative Force and not only does the Causative Force affect us, but we actually impact and affect the Causative Force. Just as importantly, so do others, and with this established, we have no option but to provide the respect to others due the Causative Force Herself.

•

Symbiotic panentheism establishes a new interactive relationship between ourselves and a Causative Force. As such, it elevates the concept of responsibility for yourself, others, and the environment. Behavior is based upon the perceptions we have regarding what we are, symbiotic panentheism elevates what we are to the level of the Causative Force, and with this elevation of perception would come an elevation of behavior.

Conclusion: How do the concepts of symbiotic panentheism reinforce the concept of understanding?

It does not; what is actually taking place is understanding is reinforcing the concept of symbiotic panentheism.

•

At this point in time, we have an intuitive sense of what symbiotic panentheism is, but we have not verbalized it, formally formulated it, built a model of it or unilaterally acknowledged it. This process of formulating symbiotic panentheism is simply a process of developing a unified view, a universal model of what we stand for.

But is symbiotic panentheism 'the' model, the 'correct' model? In our present state of existence, we most probably will never 'know.' But that is not the point. In our present state of existence, we most probably will never 'know' anything for sure. We don't even 'know' if we exist. All we can do is make assumptions and create perceptions based upon what we see, what we believe, and what we are capable of reasoning.

Science, religion, and philosophy have been fretting over life and what it is for thousands of years. Until they take on the responsibility of helping the rest of us understand what it is we are and why we exist, we are going to continue to remain in a state of confusion and conflict. Abortion will continue to pit one against the other, racism, genderism, sexism, elitism, … all the …isms will continue to divide us as individuals and as a species.

Our world is a beautiful blue and white sphere floating within a void of black velvet sparkling with specks of the rainbow. And as we watch in awe, the blood of the oppressed and subjugated drips from our home, our planet into the void of darkness. The blood can be seen to come from two sources: the blood of the victims and the blood of the valiant warriors who have willingly sacrificed their own blood to change the future. It is time to build a model, a unified view, founded upon the blood of our past and entrenched in idealism.

•

Are we going to share the results of this bloodletting with others throughout the universe or are we going to stop the abuse by sharing our new found freedom with all life forms throughout the heavens? Will the Magna Carta become simply a human document or will it become a universal proclamation of freedom?

Philosophy – Conclusion

Panentheism says you do not have to worry about eternity. You are a part of eternity. You are already within eternity. You are the abstract. You are a piece of awareness and the Causative Force is total awareness. If you have awareness, there is no apparent alternative but to accept the idea that you are a part of total awareness or total awareness is not total. In other words, if your awareness is not a part of total awareness, then the Causative Force is not all knowing, omniscient. This then, by definition, implies the Causative Force is not the Causative Force.

If the Causative Force is not the Causative Force, we would have to look further out or in to find the attention of our affection. But no matter how far we look, we would have little option but to recognize we are a part of whatever we find, for the source defined by the definition of omniscience, omnipotence, and omnipresence must contain you, for you have awareness and your awareness must be part of the whole. The whole is equal to the sum of its parts. The whole cannot be 'the' whole without the small piece you represent being included, for without your inclusion, the whole is not whole. This is panentheism.

And what of your significance to the whole? Who would question the idea that while you travel through life, you grow? Who would question that the experience of life is a means of expanding your knowledge, your awareness? And if you are a part of the whole, then your growth is a part of the Causative Force. If such is the case, how could your growth in life not cause the Causative Force to grow? Thus it is you appear to affect the Causative Force directly. You appear to be the means by which the Causative Force grows and learns. You appear to impact the Causative Force. You appear to have the free will to impact the Causative Force in either a positive or negative manner. It is your choice. It is your responsibility. You are in a symbiotic relationship with the Causative Force.

What is so significant about any unified view philosophy creates? Any model of a universal philosophy builds a perspective regarding what we are, what the universe is, what the Causative Force is, and how the three interact. Symbiotic panentheism is a philosophical model of a unified view. As a universal philosophy model, it builds a perspective capable of providing answers to these questions. It is not the model that is important; it is the answers to our fundamental questions that are important. As such, the model is only as good as the answers it provides.

Let's take only one of thousands of questions a unified view should be able to address. How does one 'get into heaven'?

Eastern religions say they are the keepers of the keys. The East says they know how to provide you with the keys. They say you must obtain them yourself with their guidance. You are the only one that can get them. It is a long and arduous task. They will show you how to get the keys. Eastern religions say it is their job to teach you. They have the knowledge. Follow their teachings and, after years of reincarnation, you will get there. Eastern religions say they hold the power. The power is knowledge.

Western religions, on the other hand, say they know how to provide you with the keys. They say you may obtain the keys from them. Western religions say that if you say the magic words, you will be given the keys. If you 'believe,' you will obtain the keys. If you prove you believe through the ultimate test, giving of what you have – money, time, power – to 'the cause,' you will get there. Western religions say they hold the power. The power is knowledge.

Symbiotic panentheism says that no one holds the key but you. Religions may be able to guide you but they cannot keep you out of eternity, out of the arms of the Causative Force, because the Causative Force is omnipresent. As such, you are already in the arms of the Causative Force; there is nowhere else to be.

There you have it: panentheism – you are already inside the Causative Force. Symbiosis – you have a direct impact upon the Causative Force. Meditation is needed. The best place to meditate is nature. It is the purest form of the creation of the Causative Force; it has much to teach us. Nature is the home of the Causative Force and it is your home. Your body is a vessel carrying a piece of the Causative Force – you. Eastern religions can teach us how to connect inwardly to the Causative Force, how to accept ourselves and our plight through being in touch with ourselves, and how to bring ourselves as close as possible to the whole of the Causative Force through internal meditation. Western religions can teach us how to connect outwardly to the Causative Force through outward meditation, sending your spirit out of your body and accepting the world outside yourself.

Eastern and western religions are doing the same thing only in different manners. Each is attempting to help the individual 'touch' the Causative Force, come into contact with the Causative Force. The East looks inward; the West looks outward. 'East is east and West is west and never the twain shall meet,' now becomes East is east and West is west and both end up together. Go to the temples; they are a place of concentrated thought. The thoughts of others will help whisk your thoughts toward the Causative Force. Go to your mosques, they are a place capable of setting a mood that will inspire you and give your sense of connection a jump start as you begin your meditations. Go to your synagogues, they are a place capable of sparking your sense of commonality; you are all brothers and sisters through the soul. Go to your Hindu temples, Buddhist temples, they are all places for your essence to come into contact with a greater form of abstraction.

Go out and meditate in nature. It is a place of cleansing and communion. Just as the temples must be built by us, maintained by us, preserved by us for the present and future generations, so too must nature be protected, maintained, and preserved by us for the present and future generations. Nature is the temple we all have in common. We, Homo sapiens, built the mosques, churches, and synagogues. Nature is the temple built by the Causative Force. Nature is the common temple shared by all of us.

Antiquity, culture, history, the sense of past souls having walked the interior of the temples can only come through time and the entrance of millions of souls. We must maintain the temples of our past. They must be preserved for the future generations for they are the temples built by us. Nothing can replace the unique contributions they have to offer in terms of a place for meditation. The old buildings of worship all over the world must not be forgotten. The ones standing alone in the prairies, alone in the deserts, alone in the mountains, alone in the inner cities, must be preserved and respected for what they are – places for the soul to rest. They are important. They are the source of hope. They stand as lighthouses in the midst of the fog. They must be prepared for the entrance of the lone traveler, whoever they are. They must be repaired, maintained, and made to represent our belief in idealism. The Hindu must repair the Christian temple, the Christian must repair the Buddhist temple, the Muslim must repair the Jewish temple. They must become sacred places for us all for they represent our sense of oneness with each other. They are the symbol. The priest must be there for the Hindu, and the Rabbi must be there for the atheist, not as a source of conversion but as a source of refuge. We must open the doors of religions for the Hindu, the Buddhist, the Christian...

This is the time for a new enlightenment. This is the beginning of the third millennium. This is a unique time when we may very well be able to fuse our religious faiths with our scientific observations using the logic of philosophy as the means of putting the puzzle together before we disperse throughout the heavens. This may be the time we finally come to terms with ourselves as a unique species. Maybe we will finally be able to feel proud of who we are, proud of our past, proud of our present, and proud of the future we have to offer ourselves and others.

Not I, but the whole world says it:
All is one.

–Heraklictos Diogenes
Heraclitus

PROPHECY
What We've Been Told

It is said that the truth will set you free. The question is, however, just what is truth? Are we, are you, ready for truth?

This is an unusual juncture in time. It is the point in time when prophecies stretching back as far as ten thousand years have been predicting a major setback, a major trauma for humankind. Prophecies that are written on the walls of the Egyptian pyramids, into the Mayan calendars of central America, upon the sacred rocks of the North American Hopi Indians, within the visions of Europe's Nostradamus, in the prophecies within the Vatican Papal libraries, and even within the igneous rock itself.

But do the prophecies say absolutely that trauma and catastrophes will occur? Actually, no. They say catastrophes will occur unless… Unless what? Unless we change significantly.

Do they tell us how to change? No. Do they tell us what to change? No. Do they tell us we will change? No. Do they tell us we are capable, have the knowledge, and have the free will to change significantly? Yes. They tell us we are capable, do have the knowledge, and do have the power to change significantly. They also tell us that whether we do so is up to us. They tell us we, you and I, can change if we wish to change. The decision is ours.

Our journey appears to have purpose. We sense it. We search for it. But we have not found it. We have not reasoned it out. The journey appears to be a search for significance, purpose, and understanding. And what is it that we need to understand? We, you and I, yearn to understand:

1. what lies beyond our universe
2. what our universe is
3. what the significance of our universe is
4. what we, you and I, are
5. what your, my, our significance and purpose is for existing.

If we ever are able to put this understanding into words everyone can understand, we will have a universal philosophy. Does such a model exist? Yes, it is called symbiotic panentheism. Keep in mind it is only a model. It is not "the" answer but rather the beginning to the answers to the five questions we have been seeking for a long time.

We have never understood the answers to these questions. Why is it so important to understand the answers after all these years? We must understand who we are, what we are, and why we are, before we step into the vastness of space. We must define our significance ourselves rather than let others we may encounter in space define it for us. We must take charge of our significance rather than let it be done by others. If we do not define it ourselves, others may do so for us and they may not define it with our best interests in mind, but rather with their interests in mind.

We have been told over and over to take charge. Change things. You are responsible. If you don't take charge, history will repeat itself with the same results. You have the free will, use it. Nostradamus has said, 'Listen, I have told you, unless...' The Mayan calendar has said, 'Look, time is running out, unless...' The Buddhists say the 2,500 year spin of the Wheel of Dharma is about to come to a standstill, unless... Unless what? Unless we change. Unless we give the Wheel of Dharma a new spin. Who is responsible for creating this change? The prophecies all imply no one has to take responsibility to initiate change. The prophecies all imply it is okay to turn away from change because if we cannot muster the courage to create the change necessary, then change will come of its own accord.

What kind of change could we, you and I, initiate which would have a significant impact upon our future? There are probably many possibilities. Looking at the past, many significant changes that took place within our history dealt with perceptions we had of ourselves and others. Many major turning points in our history dealt with the manner in which we defined individual significance.

As we elevated individual worth, we radically modified our behavior towards ourselves, others, and our environment. Our perception of our potential significance appears to be limited by the size we place upon the Causative Force. As such, it appears we might be able to radically alter our perception of ourselves through the process of expanding the size of the Causative Force. This process is what is addressed within the matrix. This process would make room for our efforts to expand our significance, our purpose for existing, and thus initiate a modification of our behavior.

The process of defining ourselves through the development of a unified view set forth by philosophy is nothing other than model building. It is a process of building a model of our significance using our faith – religion, observations – science, and reason – philosophy. We cannot use just one of the three to build the model. Such a model would not be able to sustain the continual challenge presented by the other two over the period of the next millennium. We need to define our significance in such an impeccably logical and lofty manner that it will serve us unfailingly as we disperse throughout the vastness of space. This next millennium will confront us with many perplexing observations and potentially ego shattering experiences and we will be in need of a strong foundation to support what we believe and represent. Today, we have no unified view of who we are. This, in fact, is the very purpose of this trilogy, to begin focusing upon the development of just such an understanding.

The third millennium will be as humbling a millennium as the second millennium was ego-building. We, as individuals, as a species, will need every ounce of conviction we can muster to overcome the dilemmas and ego shattering experiences that we will encounter as we step deep into the wonders of the heavens.

How can we muster any ounce of conviction regarding our significance when we have never defined our significance? We have never defined what we are let alone the reason for our existence. If we cannot define what we are, if we cannot define the reason for our existence, then maybe we are not ready to step into the heavens.

The concept that we are not ready to step into the heavens is not a new one. The prophets have been saying this for over ten thousand years. They have all said that our stepping into the heavens will not occur during the early part of the third millennium. They all tell us we will experience trauma of unknown proportions unless we change.

But how can we change if we do not know what to change or how to change? That is what the journey through this trilogy is about. It is up to you to decide whether or not to take this journey. And then it will be up to you to decide what to do with what you learn.

Our religions, sciences, and philosophies have brought us to the edge of this new era. And where is this edge, this new era? The edge is the time in history when humanity will emerge from the earth and step into space itself. The new era is where science has advanced us. The new era is the beginning of humankind accomplishing the dream it has had since the beginning of recorded time. The new era is the time in history when humanity will disperse throughout the universe itself and mingle as an equal with whatever it is we find out there. We will mingle as equals if we build a universal philosophy regarding the significance of life based upon a fusion of what we believe, see, and reason. We must build a model that can sustain us as we separate from each other and travel in isolation of our home base, the earth.

Mexico
65,000,000 BC: It's Happened Before

Sixty five million years ago, dinosaurs dominated the earth's biosphere. Evidence has been accumulating that indicates their sudden extinction was caused by a large meteor striking the earth.

Mammals existed but only as small critters barely able to avoid the ravenous appetites of the reptilian world. Suddenly, the world shook, tidal waves swept across the lands, fires ignited, and the sky grew dark. The dust kicked up by a meteor impact of phenomenal proportions began to cloud the skies. Smoke and ash from the ensuing fires and volcanic eruptions added to a blanket of dust clouds that became so thick, it blocked the sun's light for months. The day gave way to darkness. Plants, the source of food for herbivores, began to die out from the lack of sunlight that they needed to survive. As the plants died, the herbivores died, followed by the carnivores, omnivores, and eventually the scavengers.

The smaller animals, mammals included, were able to survive by eating the deposits of seeds and roots left by the dead and decaying plants. As the dust began to settle out of the blackened skies, the sun began once again to shine upon the earth. The water and sunlight stimulated life within seeds, spores, tubers, and buds, and they began to germinate and sprout. With the return of sunlight, plant life began to thrive and, with it, what remained of animal life regained its grip upon the land and within the sea, but the reign of the dinosaurs was over. A reign of dominance lasting over 200,000,000 years was over in less than a blink of an eye. What was left was a huge number of biological niches void of life. These niches proved to be the breeding grounds for the development of a new group of animals that would evolve to dominate the earth. Mammals were about to reign supreme.

Change lies at the heart of our universe and we are a part of it. Will it happen again? It is not a case of will it but rather when will it and how we will handle it. History tells us how we will handle it unless we change.

The Great Pyramid
4,500 BC: Whispers from the Far Past

It is estimated that the Great Pyramid was constructed approximately 6,500 years ago. What can be found within this pyramid is what may be of great significance.

The behemoth stone structure of the Great Pyramid appears to have been constructed to withstand time itself. Within this amazing structure of stone lies a passageway leading upward to a large empty chamber. The passageway marks what some believe to be a walk through time. Interesting impressions are made along the path of this timeline. The parting of the Red Sea, the birth of Christ, World War I and World War II do not go unnoticed. The final culmination of this passageway opens itself up to a large room with an empty sarcophagus. The coffin is empty and it is theorized by some that the coffin represents choice.

The choice: to change voluntarily or be forced to change. The passageway is believed by some archeologists to symbolize our passage through history culminating in the King's Chamber. The passage appears to clearly and accurately mark many important events in history. The final date of entry into the King's Chamber is the year 2000 AD. Up to this point, the initial timeline moved from one year per inch to one month per inch. Within the King's Chamber, however, time accelerates as the inch gives way to a day. The date represented by the solid block wall at the end of the King's Chamber: September 2001 AD.

Humans have tinkered with the calendar many times throughout history. The accuracy of our present calendar is debatable. One thing we do know for certain is that it is not an accurate depiction of time when cross referenced as far back as the building of the Great Pyramid. The date of September 2001 AD is believed to be as accurate as a decade and as inaccurate as many decades. We also know trauma can happen as the events in Mexico indicated. Many believe the large King's Chamber at the end of the passageway represents a window of opportunity for our species to change or be changed. This small group of archaeologists believe we must either reach a new stage of consciousness or else face global trauma the likes of which the earth has not seen for over 65,000,000 years.

Mayan Calendar
3000 BC: The Keepers of Time

The Mayan calendar is one of the most complex calendars in the world. Its present cycle of 5125.40 years will come to an end by December 21, 2012 AD.

Once again, synchronizing dates becomes a problem. Our present Gregorian calendar has been modified for convenience rather than scientific accuracy. As such, the date established regarding the end of this Mayan age is a date generally agreed upon by scholars. This date represents the culmination of the present 5,125 year cycle.

To the Mayans, the calendar represents their understanding of order and chaos within the universe. Their prophecies oriented around five ages of equal length. Since each age ended in a cataclysm, the accuracy of their calendar was crucial in order to warn people of coming events. Each age ended abruptly. But just as each age culminated with a global cataclysm, each ending initiated a new beginning.

Global trauma generated by a meteor is not the only catastrophe we could face. Pole shifts, ozone depletion, global warming, and global cooling are just a few other examples. But the event can be far less traumatic than the repercussions. The only way we can reduce human-generated trauma after the occurrence of a natural cataclysm is to begin looking at ourselves differently, gaining a new perspective regarding who and what we are. We may well face a major global trauma of our own making, following a naturally occurring cataclysm, unless we change. We can be a ruthless creature when we feel we need to be and shortages of food, water, and shelter in the past have taken their toll.

The Mayan calendar is the most accurate calendar on earth. Its prophecy of an end to an age encompassing over five millenniums happening at the same approximate time as the ending of the Great Pyramid timeline seems more than coincidental. The Great Pyramids were in Egypt and the Mayans in central America. An ocean of water separated the two as well as over 1,000 years of time, but both offer a ray of hope through the concept of change.

Prophecy Rock
2000 BC: Keepers of the Message

The time has come: two brothers, one white and one red, each took a stone with the sign of a circle. The white brother left for another land to learn to create and invent. The red brother stayed behind to develop his spiritual powers. They were to meet once again and combine their specialties to build a paradise. The sign of a peaceful union would be each meeting once again, carrying the sign of the circle. But if the white brother should return with the sign of a circle replaced by a cross, the red brother would know the white brother had succumbed to materialism and forgotten the ways of brotherhood, and conflict would ensue.

The Europeans brought with them the symbol of the cross as they stepped upon the shores of North America in the late 1400s. Their first actions involved piercing the ground with the cross and claiming the land for God and King. The union was not to be. The white brother had embraced materialism over brotherhood and so the warnings of the Hopi legends were about to become truth.

The prophecies of the Hopi would remain secretly guarded until the 1900s. Then the prophecy legends of the Lost White Brother, the metal roads for iron horses (trains), cobwebs filling the sky (telephone lines), and men leaving their footprints upon the moon, would be told. The final prophesied danger sign: men building a great house in the sky (Mir, skylab?).

The last danger sign before what? The Hopi elders say they have preserved the message from generation to generation that we must seek to change inwardly if we are to avoid a great cataclysm. The Hopi Prophecy Rock indicates we have one last opportunity to choose between materialism or living in peace and harmony with nature and humanity.

Materialism and global cataclysms or peace and harmony are the two choices. The Hopi Prophecy Rock indicates the road we have taken – materialism. But the drawing upon the rock offers hope. The drawing shows we are at a point in time where we have the ability to once again choose between the two. If we continue with materialism, the prophecy predicts major trauma. But if we choose harmony with nature and others, the prophecy predicts peace and bounty. Change is our choice.

Wheel of Dharma
500 BC: Moving On

Buddhism initiated the spin of the wheel of enlightenment. Buddhism prophesied the wheel would spin 2,500 years with the aid of an infusion of new energy at 500 year intervals. The prophecy, however, predicted the infusion of new energy would not be enough to keep the wheel from slowing down and eventually stopping by the year 2000 AD.

Buddhists believe enlightenment is generated by a form of momentum. They relate it to a spinning wheel. The wheel must be assisted in its spin or eventually it will stop spinning. Their prophecy established in 500 BC says Buddhism began the spin of the wheel at which point the 500 year cycles began. Christ in 0 AD, Islam in 500 AD. Beyond that, it becomes debatable what 500 year factors contributed energy to the spin. It could be argued the development of religious philosophy, ontology in 1000 AD, was the next factor, followed by the development of modern science in 1500 AD. What one wishes to conjecture as to what were the causes of the 500 year energy bursts is not of importance. What is of interest is the idea that, like the Great Pyramid time line, the Hopi Indian's prophecy Rock, the Mayan calendar, as well as so many other ancient prophecies developed worldwide, Buddhists also predict a very significant juncture in time will occur at the end of this millennium.

Buddhists believe the wheel will stop spinning at the end of the 2,500 year cycle. They do not forecast only gloom and destruction. They leave a message of hope. They imply, we, you and I, can spin the wheel ourselves if we wish to do so. We can give the wheel a fresh spin that will last another 2,500 years. But just looking at the wheel is not enough. We can only spin the wheel if we reach out, take hold of it, and intentionally spin it. What can we do to create a spin capable of enduring 2,500 years? Whatever it is, it will have to be something very basic to endure the onslaught of time. The initial spin of the wheel oriented around a change in perception – the elimination of suffering. Each additional energy infusion also oriented around a change in perception. Perhaps the initiation of the next spin must do the same.

Revelations
0 AD: The Thunder of Horses' Hooves

We hear it from the pulpits – the time is at hand: a rider on each of four horses, one white, one red, one black, one pale. The four riders and their horses accompanied by four hell riders. The eight will come thundering down the plain of time, one after the other. And as we watch, we will stand in awe and fear doing nothing.

Revelations, like all the other prophecies, does not predict what will be. Revelations prophecies what will be if... If what? If we do not change, if we continue on the path we are currently on, if we continue to ignore the big picture.

The prophecies do not come right out and tell us what we must do to change. If they had, they would have shorted out the process of growth that had to take place for our species. There was so much for us to learn in order to understand. A child of nine or ten may be able to survive without assistance, but what about one, two or three years old? Growth must take place. A time for learning must be allowed. A species is no different. The species may be composed of individuals, but the individuals can only absorb so much. How could caveman ever understand the concept of the need to eliminate suffering? How could the first Roman emperor ever understand the Christian concept of unconditional love or the Muslim concept of justice for all? Ontology, the concept of understanding a Causative Force without religion getting in the way, or the evolutionary development of humans being understood by the first few popes? Hardly! Time was needed for growth. Revelations had nothing new to offer us. This is not belittling the need for Revelations. We had been told before but the message had to be made clear, told over and over, by many cultures – not just by one!

Before, we could not understand; we were still learning. We learned through great teachers, some would say by the intervention of the Causative Force Herself. This is not the point of debate being addressed in this trilogy. The point being addressed is change. What do we have to change in order to significantly reduce trauma? This trilogy does more than say we have to change; it suggests a means to do so.

Papal Prophecies
1100 AD: Two to Go

In 1139 AD, St. Malachy left Ireland and began a pilgrimage to Rome. On his way, he fell into a trance and began reciting in Latin. His servant recorded his phrases, all 111 of them. Time proved to be the element needed to tie the phrases to the succession of popes, each phrase describing the next succeeding pope. 109 of the 111 phrases have been descriptive of the last 109 popes. There are two prophetic phrases left and then a prediction: destruction and judgment.

What does it mean? What kind of destruction and judgment will follow the next two popes? And is this destruction and judgment a certainty? Again, as so often put forward within this trilogy, there are two possibilities. Either the destruction and judgment is a certainty or it is not. If it is a certainty, then we have no free will.

If the future is predetermined, then there is nothing to worry about, for whatever will be will be. However, if we have free will, then we have the ability to act. Free will gives us the ability to change things. If we cannot change the future, we do not have free will and we are back to determinism, predestination. Without free will, it would make no difference what we did; the future would remain the same. Without free will, should eternity exist, we could not be held responsible for neglecting all the warning signs of prophecy.

If, however, the future is not predetermined, if we have free will, then we are responsible for the future. If free will exists, we will be held responsible for not having listened to the prophecies. There is no denying the vast number of prophecies that exist. There is no denying the notoriety that they all have worldwide. There is no denying the fundamental message they all give us: change or else trauma of unbelievable proportions will occur. And there is no denying they all tell us that we can change and that the future is not an absolute.

St. Malachy's message is no different just because it resides in the papal library of the Vatican. Where it resides is important for it places responsibility for change upon the Catholic leadership where it belongs.

Nostradamus
1500 AD: Gloom and Destruction, and Hope

The prophecies of Nostradamus are so well known and respected that they were used by both the allies and the axis powers in their attempt to apply psychological warfare against each other during World War II.

Nostradamus is not just another voice in the sea of human utterances warning of the end of times to come. Nostradamus lived from 1503 to 1566 and his prophetic predictions have done nothing but gain respect and status over the last 400 years.

Nostradamus did not predict only destruction. Nostradamus gave us hope. His prophecies not only strongly implied change of phenomenal proportions would occur at the turn of the millennium, but they implied it could occur in one of two manners. Nostradamus said the change would occur either through our historical process of just letting change occur randomly or we could do the changing ourselves, intentionally. The results would be entirely different in each case. If we just let change happen of its own accord, it would be violent, global, and on a scale the likes of which we had never seen. If, on the other hand, we took charge and guided the change intentionally, it would be much less traumatic and humane. Whatever the case, Nostradamus has prophesied that cataclysmic change will occur by the end of this millennium. The only choice we have is how change will occur. We have free will to choose.

This sounds a lot like determinism but, in actuality, it is not. Change is a natural part of our universe. How we deal with the change is not. The Earth's orbit of the sun may be predetermined, but how we deal with the seasons created by revolving around the sun is not.

Nostradamus is a seer as was St. Malachy. The Mayan calendar, the Great Pyramid timeline, and the Hopi Prophecy Rock are physical objects. The Wheel of Dharma and Revelations are religious warnings. All of these prophecies are scattered throughout history. They cannot all be found originating during one particular point in time. They all have been trying to tell us something: change, change, change… or else.

Edgar Cayce
1900 AD: Natural Cataclysms

Edgar Cayce was a simple man with simple wants and needs, yet he was a seer with a special gift. Some would say such 'gifts' were delusions and fantasies. Perhaps, but it's interesting that they are universal not only globally, but in terms of time.

Cayce was not chosen as one of the prophets because he is the best known but rather because he is one of the better known in our more recent history. We have been told. We have been shown. Some would say that prophecies are pure primitive fantasies we create out of fear of the future. But are they? Hasn't history shown us change is not a unique event? Hasn't change been with us throughout our entire existence as a species? What is so primitive about believing change will occur again in the future?

Mexico provides us with fairly solid evidence that global eradication of an entire class of animals can occur in a few short months. The dinosaurs grip our interest not just because they were big but because they don't exist anymore. The dinosaurs are gone. They may have existed all over the world and in all the seas, but, poof, they are gone. The lesson we can learn from this is that it could happen again.

Prophecy of future cataclysms is not gloom and doom; it is a voice of hope. It is a voice saying that we do not need to be like the dinosaurs, we are intelligent enough to survive, and we are intelligent enough to reduce the aftereffects of global cataclysms if we think ahead and plan.

Planning ahead involves preparing for the possibilities of global cataclysms. These are not foolhardy actions. These are realistic, practical actions based upon what has happened in the past and based upon the understanding that we live in a universe filled with change – dramatic change.

But how does one prepare? Society must prepare and that includes sciences, religions, and philosophies. Each must do their jobs. Each must prepare society for the worst as best they can. And what is society? Society is the individual, which is where the significance of our species lies.

Others:
Unless We Change…

They span time. They span cultures. They span the globe. Some even come from we know not where. They lie as grains of sand upon the beach, too numerous to count and too intriguing to ignore. The nine prophecies listed were only nine of thousands. The internet is a wonderful source for exploring the universal characteristics of these messages of hope. Yes, hope, because they all imply the message they have to offer us is not a message of the end of times but the beginning of a new time. They all say the transition from our present emphasis upon the material will change to the social, to concern over the individual, to concern over the rights of the individual to travel because the individual is more than an individual. They all imply we will break through to a new level of consciousness.

What could that new level of consciousness be? That new level of consciousness is supposedly a new form of understanding what it is we are and why we exist, a new sense of connection. Whatever the case, the implication is that we will continue to grow as individuals and as a summation of individuals, as a species. None of the prophecies imply the end of the world has come but rather the end of an age. They say the transition will be turbulent, but we will get through it. They also say we have the ability, the free will, to reduce the turbulence if we choose to do so.

PROPHECY

This trilogy was not written as doom or gloom, nor to attempt to give validity to prophecy. Rather it was written based upon the concept that criticism is worthless as pure criticism and thus the only way criticism can be of value is if it is constructive. Constructive criticism is an action that suggests a flaw and then suggests a reasonable solution. The trilogy may appear to be centered around the concept of suggesting that the model of symbiotic panentheism should be adapted by society. This appearance, however, is what comes from examining the surface instead of exploring the message. The message is that it is time to build a model of what we think we are by using what we believe, what we see, and what we reason. It is time to build a unified view, a universal philosophy, because it could help us make our next great leap as a species. It could help prepare us for our next step forward, to step into the heavens themselves.

The Pyramids, the Hopi, the Mayan calendar, Revelations, the Wheel of Dharma, Papal Prophecies, Edgar Cayce, Nostradamus, and palaeomagnetism have told us the same thing: change will occur and with the change will come major trauma, unless... unless we change. These prophecies have not left us a message of despair. They have left a message of hope. They have told us we can reduce the trauma if we wish to do so and if we are willing to make the effort.

The question is: are we willing to do so?

Conclusion

This trilogy has taken what we believe – religion, what we see – science, what we reason – philosophy, and what we've been told – prophecy, and used them to build a universal philosophy capable of uniting religion, philosophy, and science. This trilogy represents an example of the type of change we are capable of generating. Symbiotic panentheism may be a leap great enough to be the central theme for our next 500 years, but that is not the point. The point is we need to begin to look for a means by which we are able to make the next leap of enlightenment without having it forced upon us. The process involves building a model we can accept as a species of individuals. The model cannot be 'the' answer, but needs to be a working model that undergoes constant change to fit our changing perceptions and understandings as they develop.

Symbiotic panentheism is a unifying, peace generating, tolerance oriented, justice provoking, significance inducing, loving rationality. It creates a logically oriented, observation supported foundation incapable of destroying anything we hold dear and capable of reinforcing our significance in the universe. Significance is something we need to understand before we encounter the mysterious events that will present themselves as we emerge into space itself.

If the concept of symbiotic panentheism leads people to become Christian, it will have failed in its purpose. If symbiotic panentheism leads the Christian to be come Hindu, it has failed. If it leads the atheist to become a theist, or a Jew to become Muslim or a Muslim to become Buddhist, it has failed. Conversion is the sign of failure of the model for conversion proves the model is not a universal model, a 'unified view,' but rather conversion shows the model is slanted toward one side or the other. Conversion shows the model is a statement of faith rather than a statement of the uniqueness of all three: faith, observation, and reason.

The only way the model could be considered successful is with its establishment of a desire to change who we are in order to prevent major catastrophe predicted by prophecies. The model of symbiotic panentheism cannot prevent a meteor from striking the earth, but the model could change our perception of what life is and thereby change this most traumatic se-

CONCLUSION

quence of events. Trauma may be initiated by a meteor strike, terrorist detonation of a hydrogen bomb over New York or anthrax being introduced into the water supply of Tel Aviv, but these episodes themselves are not where the major trauma will lie. The major trauma will lie in how we will react to these events both individually and as a species. As a species, global war, global economic collapse, and global retaliation will generate the most trauma. As individuals, small bands of humans attempting to profit from the cataclysm by establishing their own turf, their own dominance of individuals, their own definition of inclusion into their group, could create trauma worldwide on a level the likes of which we have never before seen.

Change in perception could circumvent both the species and individual regression into our past actions of domination, power struggles, self righteousness, abuse, and self-serving actions. Only a change in perception uniting the logic of reason, the strength of faith, and the 'absolute' of observation can form a model of perception capable of overriding our historical behavior of building great civilizations only to have them destroyed in order to make room for new ideas. Only by changing ourselves voluntarily, intentionally, can we possibly prevent the traumatic prophecies that have stood before our species since time began.

Change will occur whether we like it or not. It is the way of the universe. It is the way of reality. It may well be the way of the larger Reality, the Causative Force Herself. This time, however, we can control the change by changing ourselves. This cannot take place on a basis of triviality nor on a basis of governmental decree. It has to take place on a basis of global individual consensus. The only manner to obtain such an independent consensus is through a construction of a 'unified view' uniting religion, science, and philosophy by fusing faith, observation, and reason.

The construction of such a model would not convert a Hindu to a Christian nor a Muslim to a Jew. Rather it would change them all by broadening the idea of inclusiveness. The Hindu would now become a Hindu Christian and the Christian a Christian Hindu. The Muslim would become a Muslim Jew and the Jew a Jewish Muslim. One could even become a Hindu Jewish, Buddhist, Christian, Muslim.

All would worship in each other's houses of worship. All would respect the uniqueness of the other. All would take pride in knowing the others existed as monuments of our historical struggles to establish the uniqueness of the individual. The Jew would feel at ease and at peace celebrating as a Jew within the church of Christianity and the Christians would take the Jew under their wing. The Christian would feel at ease worshipping within the mosque of the Muslim as the Muslim took the Christian under their wing. And so it would go...

You believe it cannot happen, and you are right. It cannot happen presently because we do not have a unified view in place and so things remain as they are. Things will continue as they are until we change. With a major cataclysmic tragedy, we will once again, as individuals and as a species, amplify the trauma of the tragedy through repeating the tragedies of our past. As much as we may not want it to occur, change will take place whether we like it or not.

This time, something will be different. This time, we will undergo the trauma of change knowing that we had a choice. We will undergo the trauma knowing we understood the process but chose to do nothing about it. In the past, history looked back upon such collapses of civilizations and understood why we did not prevent the tragedies. Our predecessors did not and could not understand how to circumvent the historical cycle of collapse and tragedy. This time, however, history will look back upon our actions differently. This time, history will look back and sadly shake its head, for history will see that we *did* have the understanding available to us to change in a less traumatic manner, but consciously chose not to do so. It's our choice.

Bibliography

Concise Science Dictionary, Third Edition. Oxford: Oxford University Press, 1996.

Reese, William L. *Dictionary of Philosophy and Religion: Eastern and Western Thought.* NJ: Humanities Press, 1996.

World Book Encyclopedia. IL: World Book, Inc., 1985.

About the Author

Daniel J. Shepard, author of *You & I Together* and *In the Image of God*, earned a B.S. Degree from the University of Michigan and a Master's Degree in Physical Science from Eastern Michigan University. He is currently a teacher in Livonia, Michigan. *Stepping Up to the Creator* is his third book within a trilogy exploring symbiotic panentheism. Also available is the *Trilogy Cross Reference and Index*.

To correspond with Daniel J. Shepard, write to:
W.E. Hope, Inc.
118 Main Center, Suite 226
Northville, Michigan 48167
(810) 349–1317

www.wehope.com
www.panentheism.com